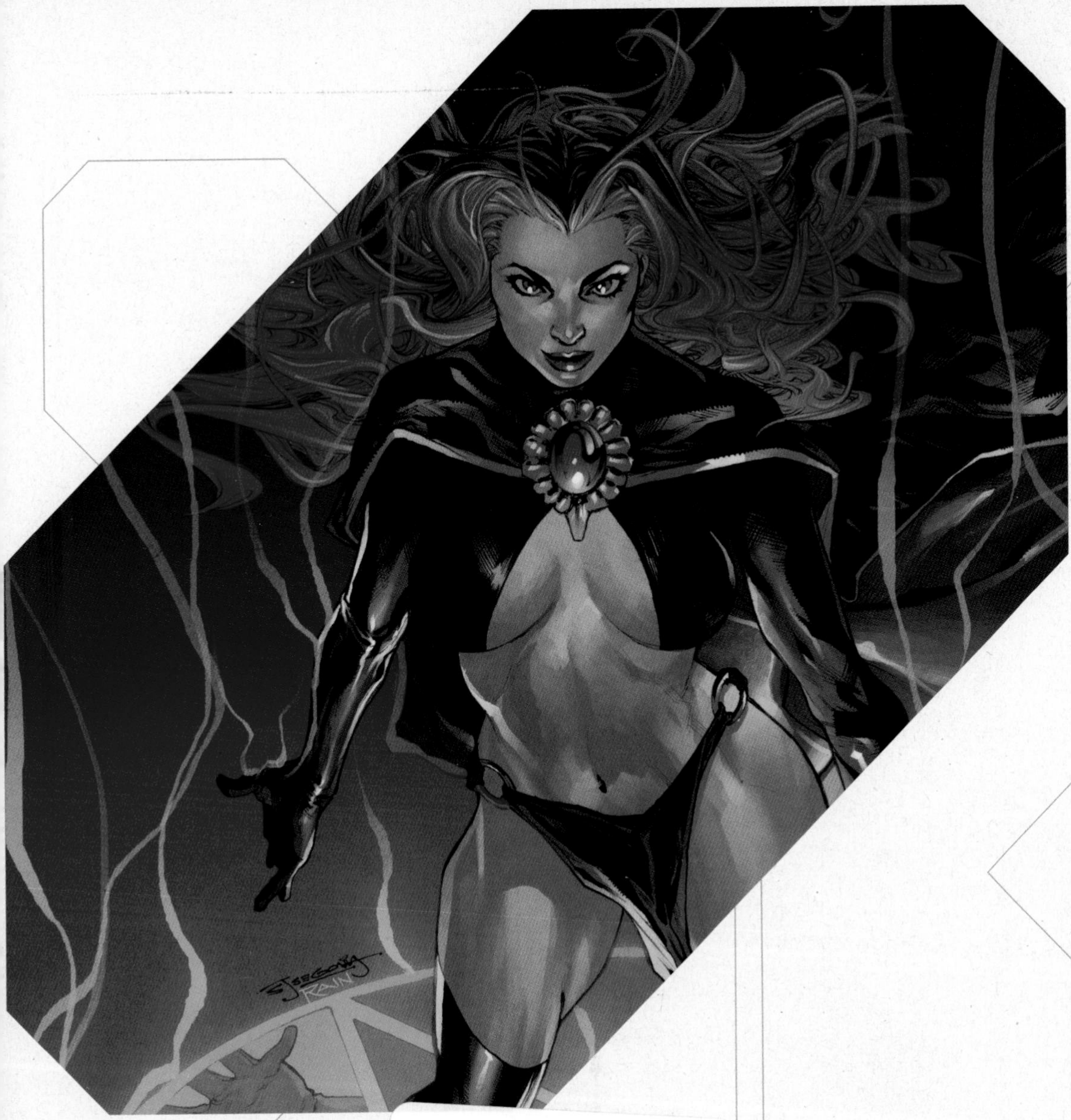

DAWN OF X VOL. 11. Contains material originally published in magazine form as NEW MUTANTS (2019) #10-11, WOLVERINE (2020) #1, EXCALIBUR (2019) #10 and HELLIONS (2020) #2-3. Second printing 2021. ISBN 978-1-302-92768-4. Published by MARVEL WORLDWIDE, INC., a subsidiary of MARVEL ENTERTAINMENT, LLC. OFFICE OF PUBLICATION: 1290 Avenue of the Americas, New York, NY 10104. © 2020 MARVEL No similarity between any of the names, characters, persons, and/or institutions in this magazine with those of any living or dead person or institution is intended, and any such similarity which may exist is purely coincidental. **Printed in the U.S.A.** KEVIN FEIGE, Chief Creative Officer; DAN BUCKLEY, President, Marvel Entertainment; JOE QUESADA, EVP & Creative Director; DAVID BOGART, Associate Publisher & SVP of Talent Affairs; TOM BREVOORT, VP, Executive Editor; NICK LOWE, Executive Editor, VP of Content, Digital Publishing; DAVID GABRIEL, VP of Print & Digital Publishing; JEFF YOUNGQUIST, VP of Production & Special Projects; ALEX MORALES, Director of Publishing Operations; DAN EDINGTON, Managing Editor; RICKEY PURDIN, Director of Talent Relations; JENNIFER GRÜNWALD, Senior Editor, Special Projects; SUSAN CRESPI, Production Manager; STAN LEE, Chairman Emeritus. For information regarding advertising in Marvel Comics or on Marvel.com, please contact Vit DeBellis, Custom Solutions & Integrated Advertising Manager, at vdebellis@marvel.com. For Marvel subscription inquiries, please call 888-511-5480. **Manufactured between 5/14/2021 and 6/15/2021 by FRY COMMUNICATIONS, MECHANICSBURG, PA, USA.**

10 9 8 7 6 5 4 3 2

DAWN OF X

●

Volume
11

X-Men created by Stan Lee & Jack Kirby

Writers:	**Ed Brisson, Benjamin Percy, Tini Howard & Zeb Wells**
Artists:	**Flaviano, Viktor Bogdanovic, Marcus To & Stephen Segovia**
Color Artists:	**Carlos Lopez, Matthew Wilson, Erick Arciniega & David Curiel**
Letterers:	**VC's Travis Lanham, Cory Petit & Ariana Maher**
Cover Art:	**Rod Reis; Mike del Mundo; Adam Kubert & Frank Martin; Mahmud Asrar & Matthew Wilson; and Stephen Segovia & Rain Beredo**
Head of X:	**Jonathan Hickman**
Design:	**Tom Muller**
Assistant Editors:	**Annalise Bissa & Lauren Amaro**
Editors:	**Jordan D. White & Mark Basso**
Collection Cover Art:	**Stephen Segovia & Rain Beredo**
Collection Editor:	**Jennifer Grünwald**
Assistant Managing Editor:	**Maia Loy**
Assistant Managing Editor:	**Lisa Montalbano**
VP Production & Special Projects:	**Jeff Youngquist**
SVP Print, Sales & Marketing:	**David Gabriel**
Editor in Chief:	**C.B. Cebulski**

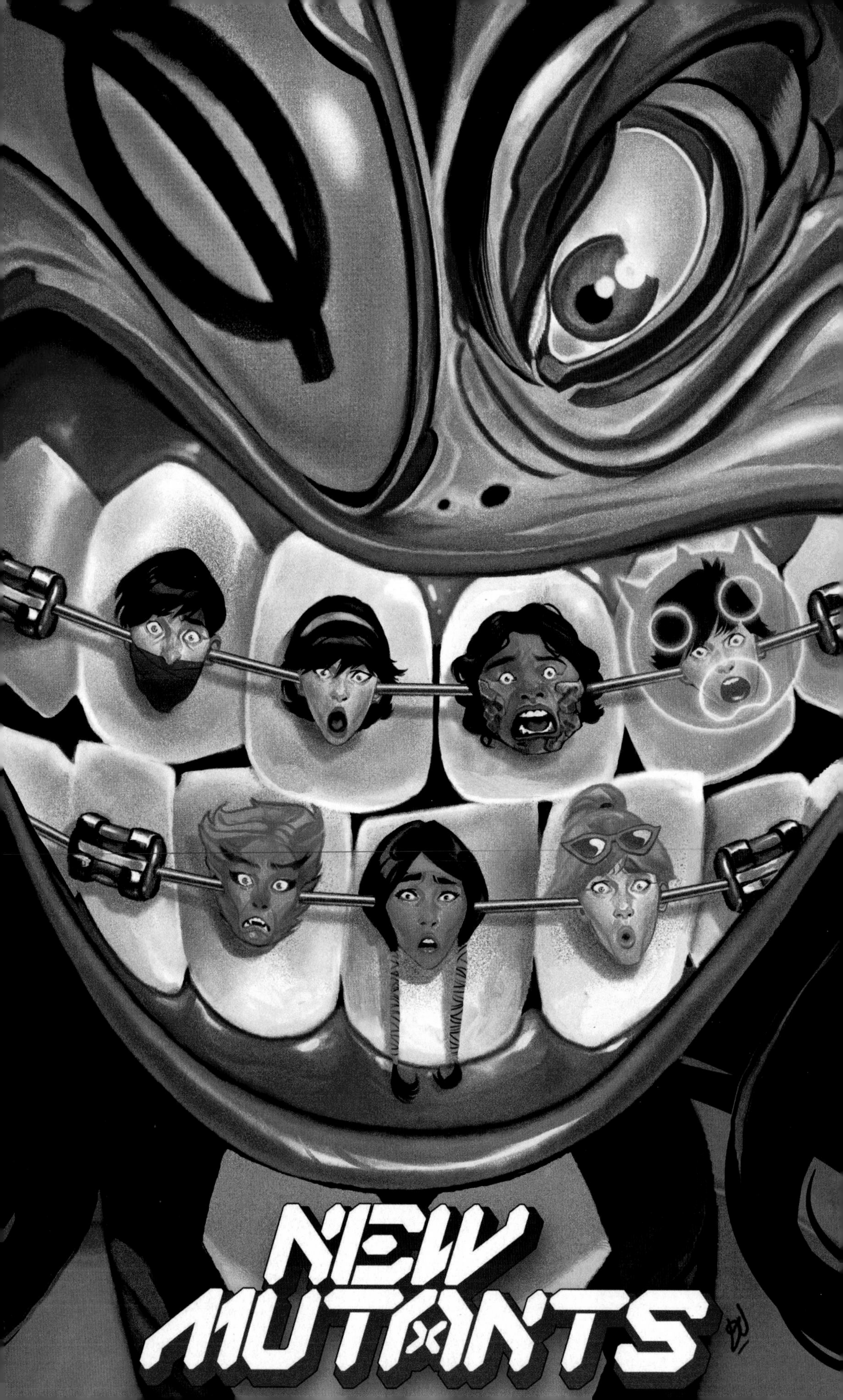
NEW
MUTANTS

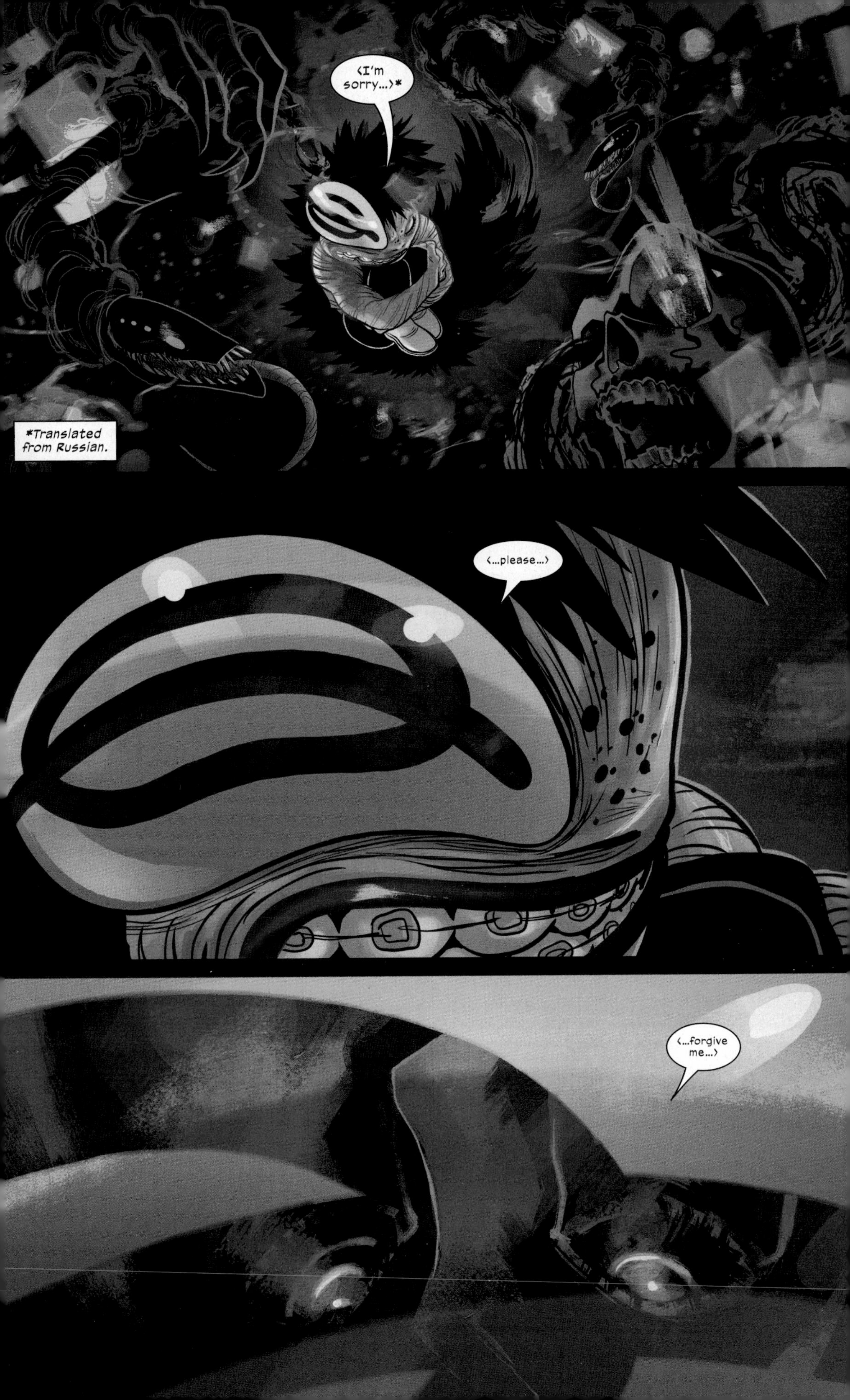

‹I'm sorry...›*
*Translated from Russian.
‹...please...›
‹...forgive me...›

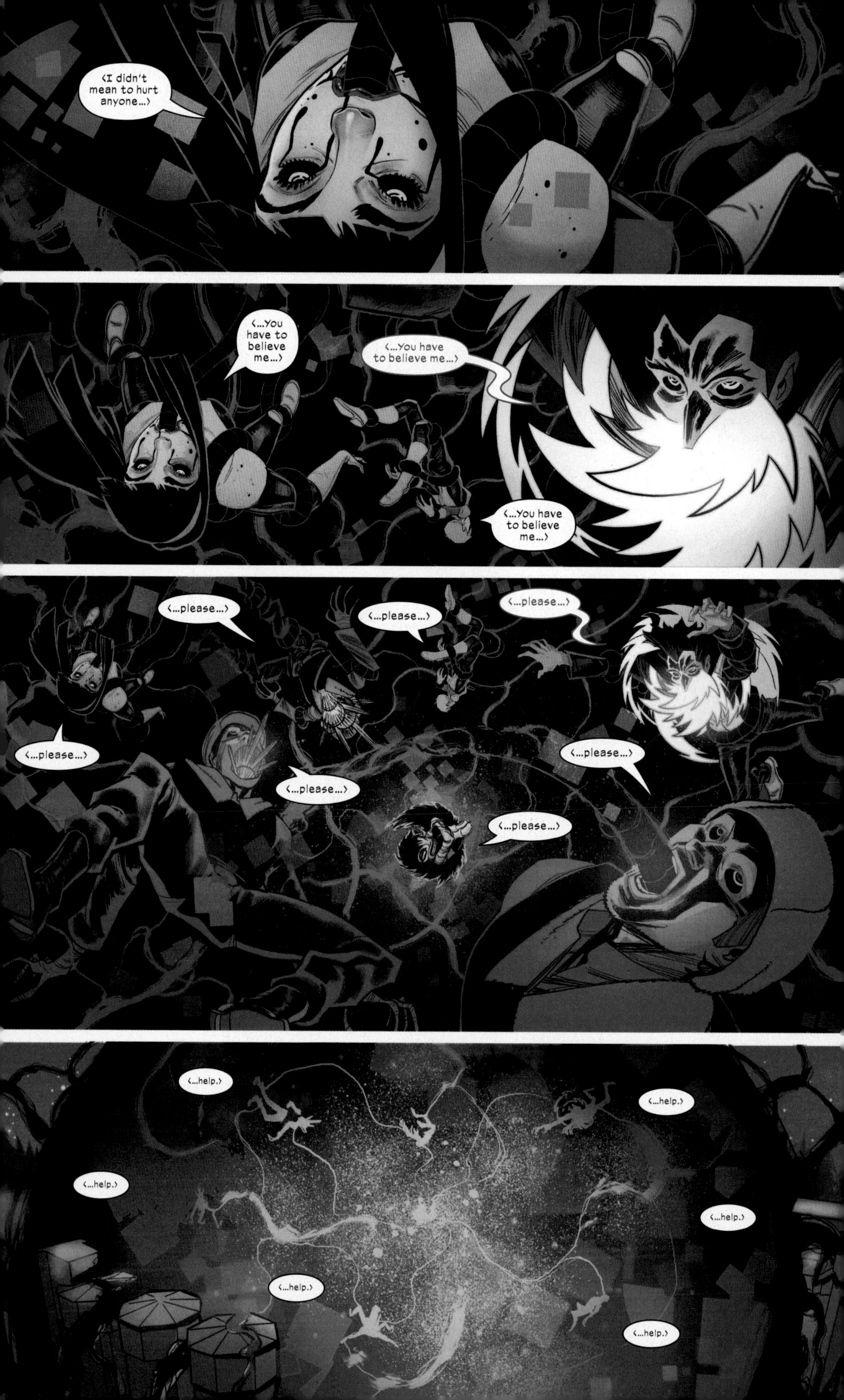

‹I didn't mean to hurt anyone...›
‹...You have to believe me...›
‹...You have to believe me...›
‹...You have to believe me...›
‹...please...›
‹...please...›
‹...please...›
‹...please...›
‹...please...›
‹...please...›
‹...please...›
‹...help.›
‹...help.›
‹...help.›
‹...help.›
‹...help.›
‹...help.›

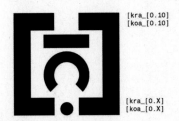

[kra_[0.10]
[koa_[0.10]

[kra_[0.X]
[koa_[0.X]

SPHERE OF INFLUENCE

A teenager in Carnelia has begun to manifest mutantpowers in the form of a fast-growing orb of nightmares -- a dangerous situation in a country which has rejected Krakoan sovereignty and is openly hostile to mutants. The NEW MUTANTS arrived to help, but Karma's attempt at psychic intervention resulted in her and her teammates being overtaken. Now backup is on its way...for better or for worse.

Boom-Boom

Chamber

Magma

Mirage

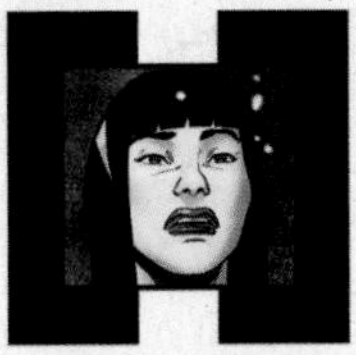

Karma

Cypher

Mondo

Armor

Wolfsbane

Wildside

Glob

Magik

[kra_[0.10]..]
[koa_[0.10]..]

[night...MARE]

[00_night____X]
[00_mare_____X]

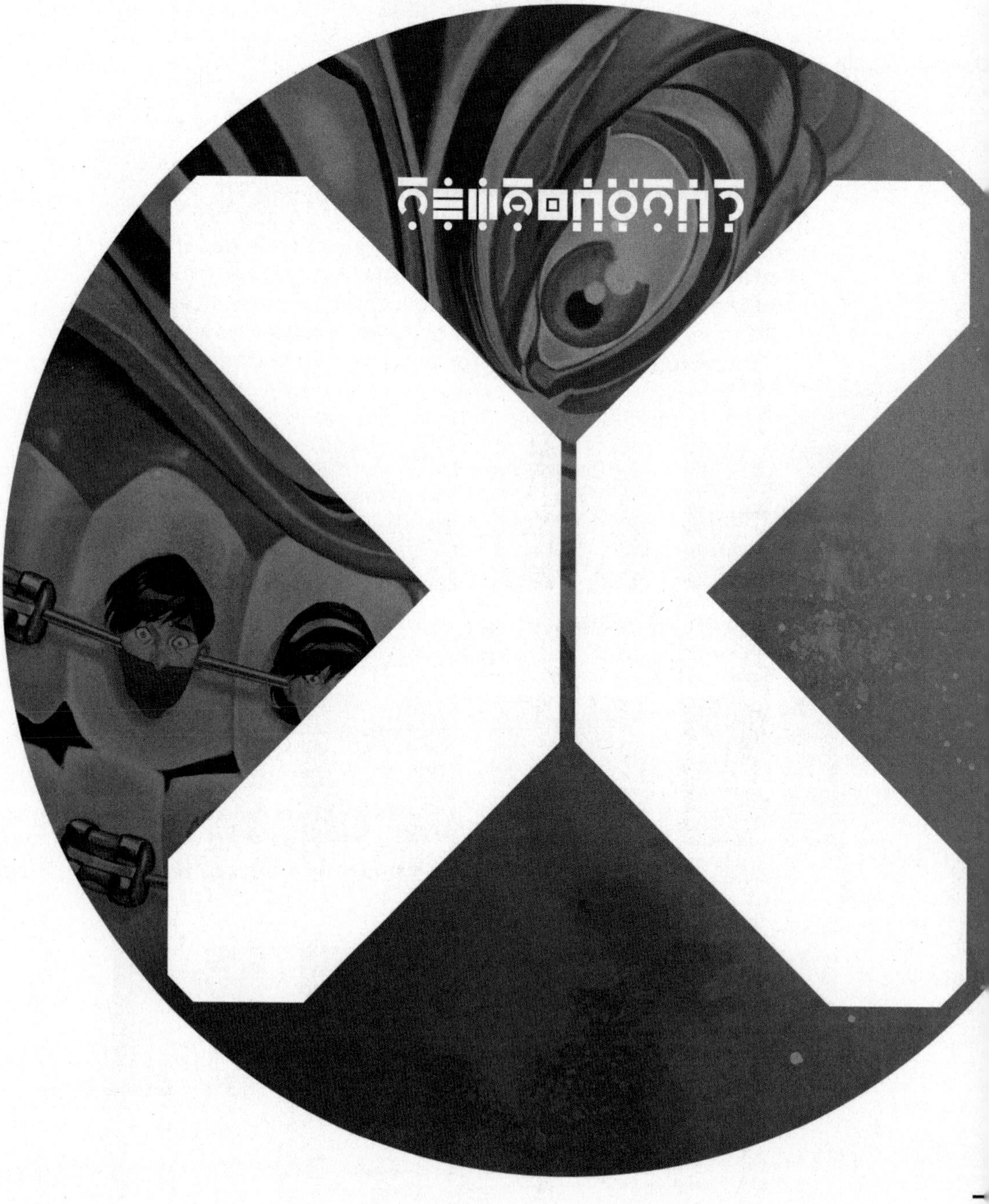

ED BRISSON...................................[WRITER]
FLAVIANO.....................................[ARTIST]
CARLOS LOPEZ............................[COLOR ARTIST]
VC's TRAVIS LANHAM........................[LETTERER]
TOM MULLER...................................[DESIGN]

ROD REIS................................[COVER ARTIST]

NICK RUSSELL.............................[PRODUCTION]

JONATHAN HICKMAN..........................[HEAD OF X]
ANNALISE BISSA...............................[EDITOR]
JORDAN D. WHITE.......................[SENIOR EDITOR]
C.B. CEBULSKI.......................[EDITOR IN CHIEF]

[10] NEW MUTANTS

[ISSUE TEN]....................PARASOMNIA

[00_night____X]
[00_mare_____X]

[00_00.....0]
[00_00....10]

[00_for_____]
[00____give_]

[00_____]

[00_ness____]

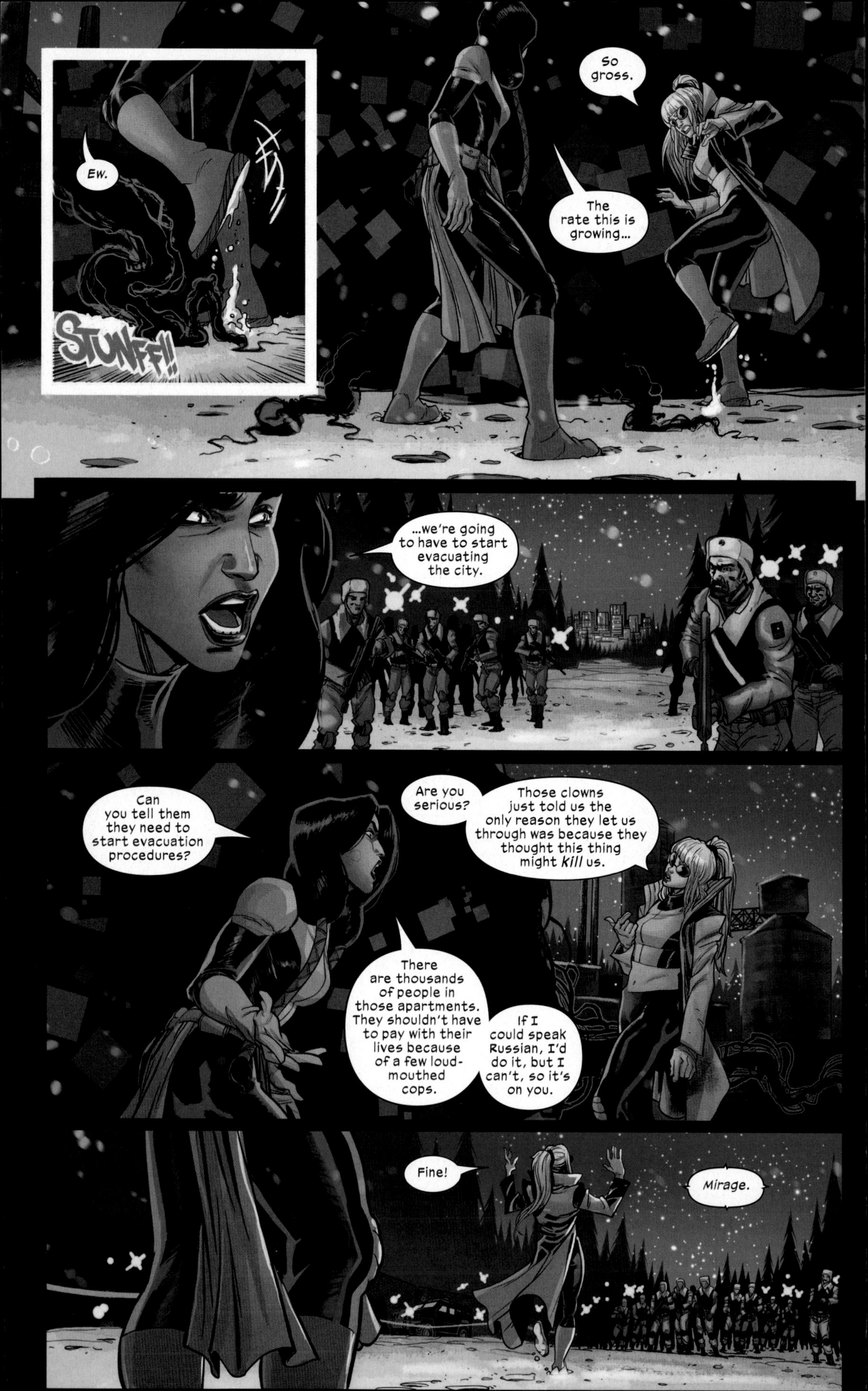
Ew.
STUNFF!!
So gross.
The rate this is growing...
...we're going to have to start evacuating the city.
Can you tell them they need to start evacuation procedures?
Are you serious?
Those clowns just told us the only reason they let us through was because they thought this thing might *kill* us.
There are thousands of people in those apartments. They shouldn't have to pay with their lives because of a few loud-mouthed cops.
If I could speak Russian, I'd do it, but I can't, so it's on you.
Fine!
Mirage.

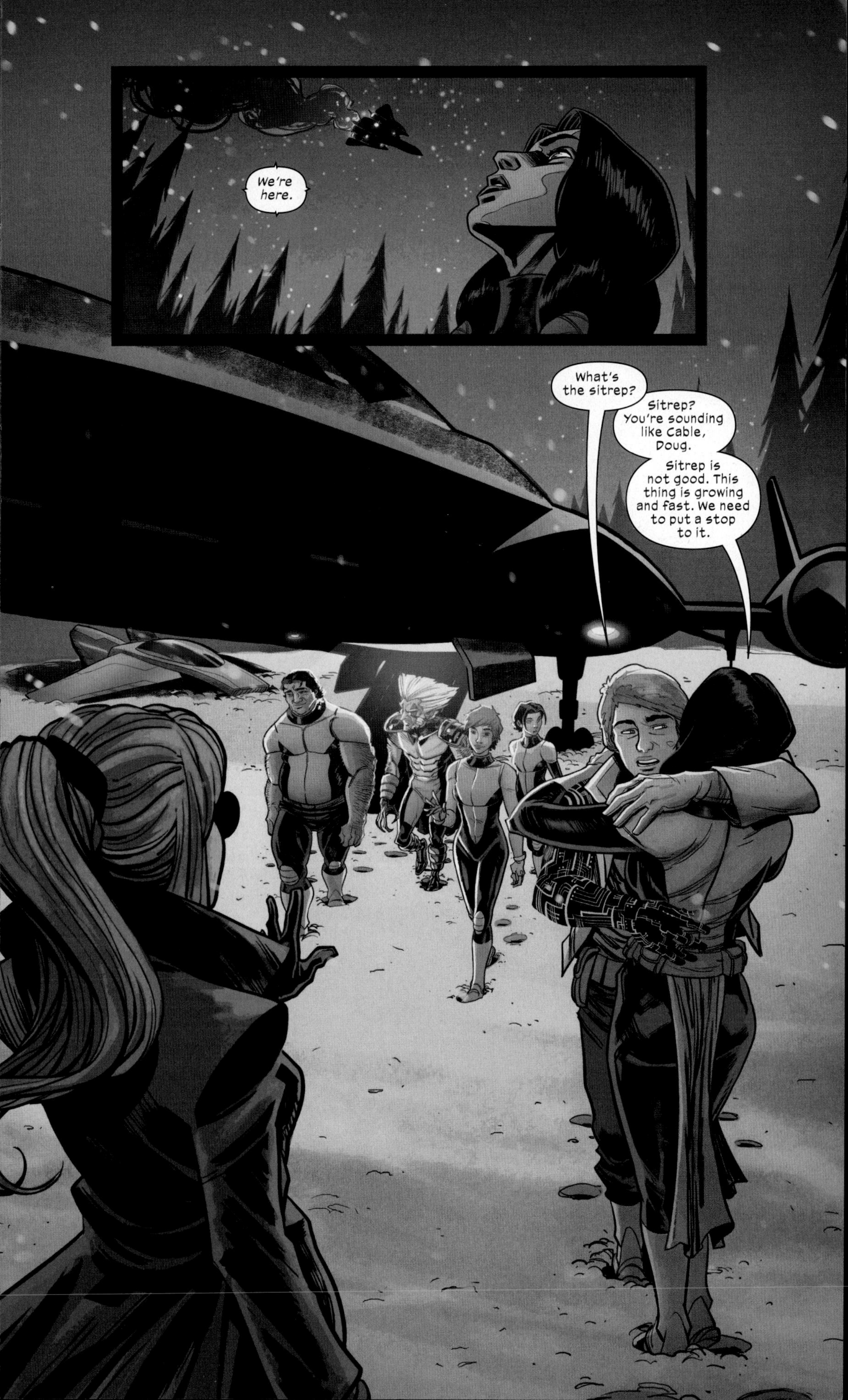
We're here.
What's the sitrep?
Sitrep? You're sounding like Cable, Doug.
Sitrep is not good. This thing is growing and fast. We need to put a stop to it.

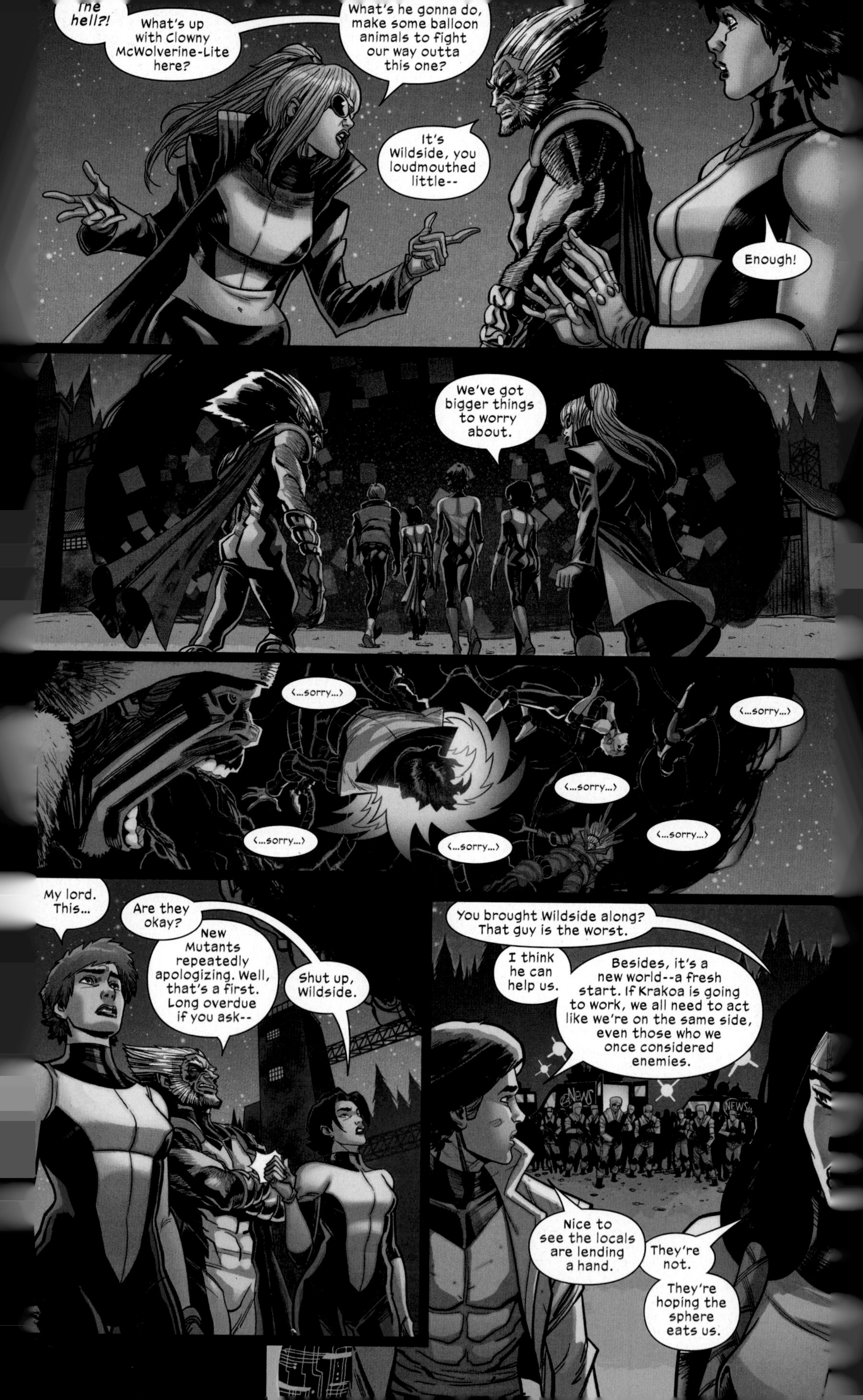
The hell?!
What's up with Clowny McWolverine-Lite here?
What's he gonna do, make some balloon animals to fight our way outta this one?
It's Wildside, you loudmouthed little--
Enough!
We've got bigger things to worry about.
‹...sorry...›
‹...sorry...›
‹...sorry...›
‹...sorry...›
‹...sorry...›
‹...sorry...›
My lord. This...
Are they okay?
New Mutants repeatedly apologizing. Well, that's a first. Long overdue if you ask--
Shut up, Wildside.
You brought Wildside along? That guy is the worst.
I think he can help us.
Besides, it's a new world--a fresh start. If Krakoa is going to work, we all need to act like we're on the same side, even those who we once considered enemies.
Nice to see the locals are lending a hand.
They're not.
They're hoping the sphere eats us.

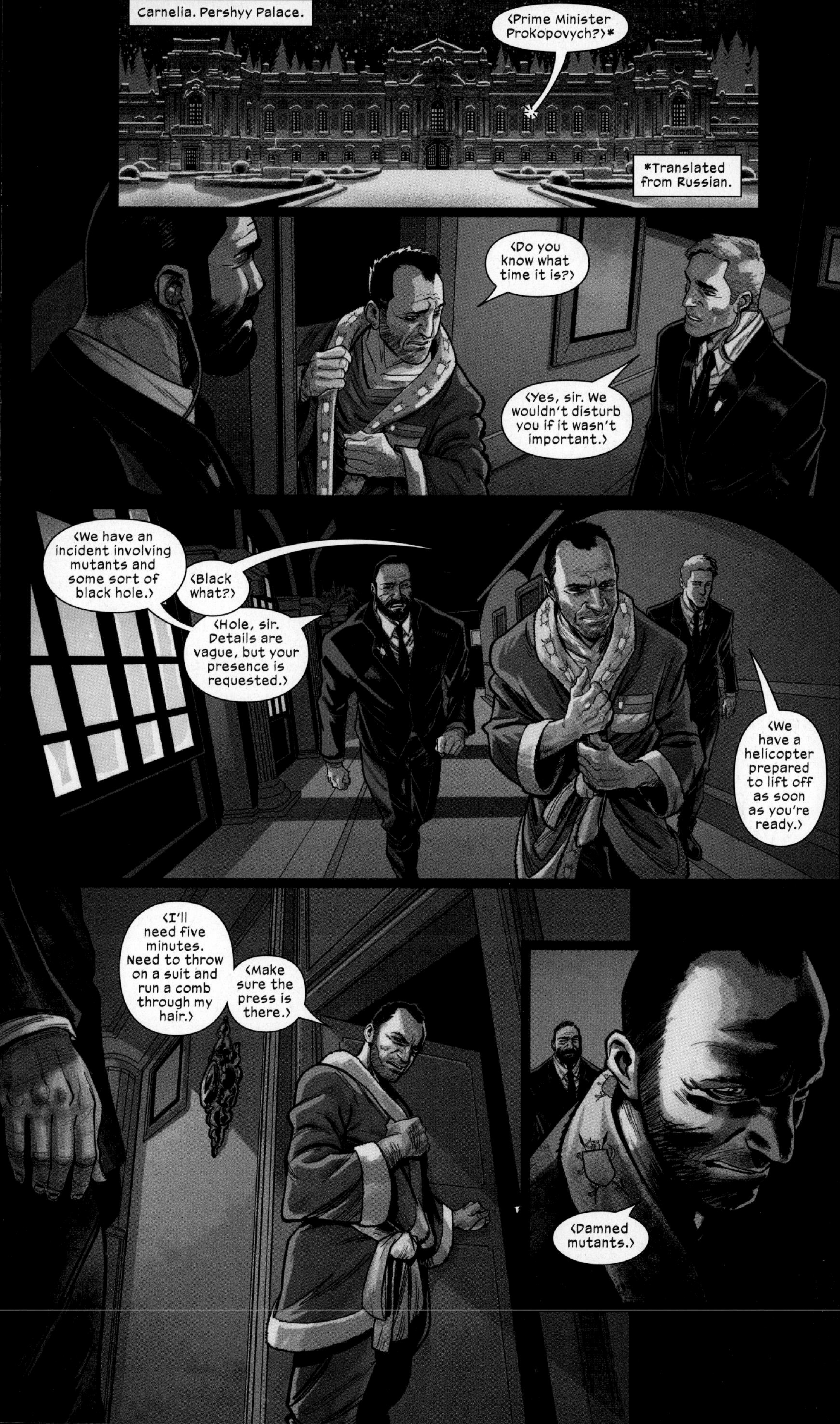
Carnelia. Pershyy Palace.
<Prime Minister Prokopovych?>*
*Translated from Russian.
<Do you know what time it is?>
<Yes, sir. We wouldn't disturb you if it wasn't important.>
<We have an incident involving mutants and some sort of black hole.>
<Black what?>
<Hole, sir. Details are vague, but your presence is requested.>
<We have a helicopter prepared to lift off as soon as you're ready.>
<I'll need five minutes. Need to throw on a suit and run a comb through my hair.>
<Make sure the press is there.>
<Damned mutants.>

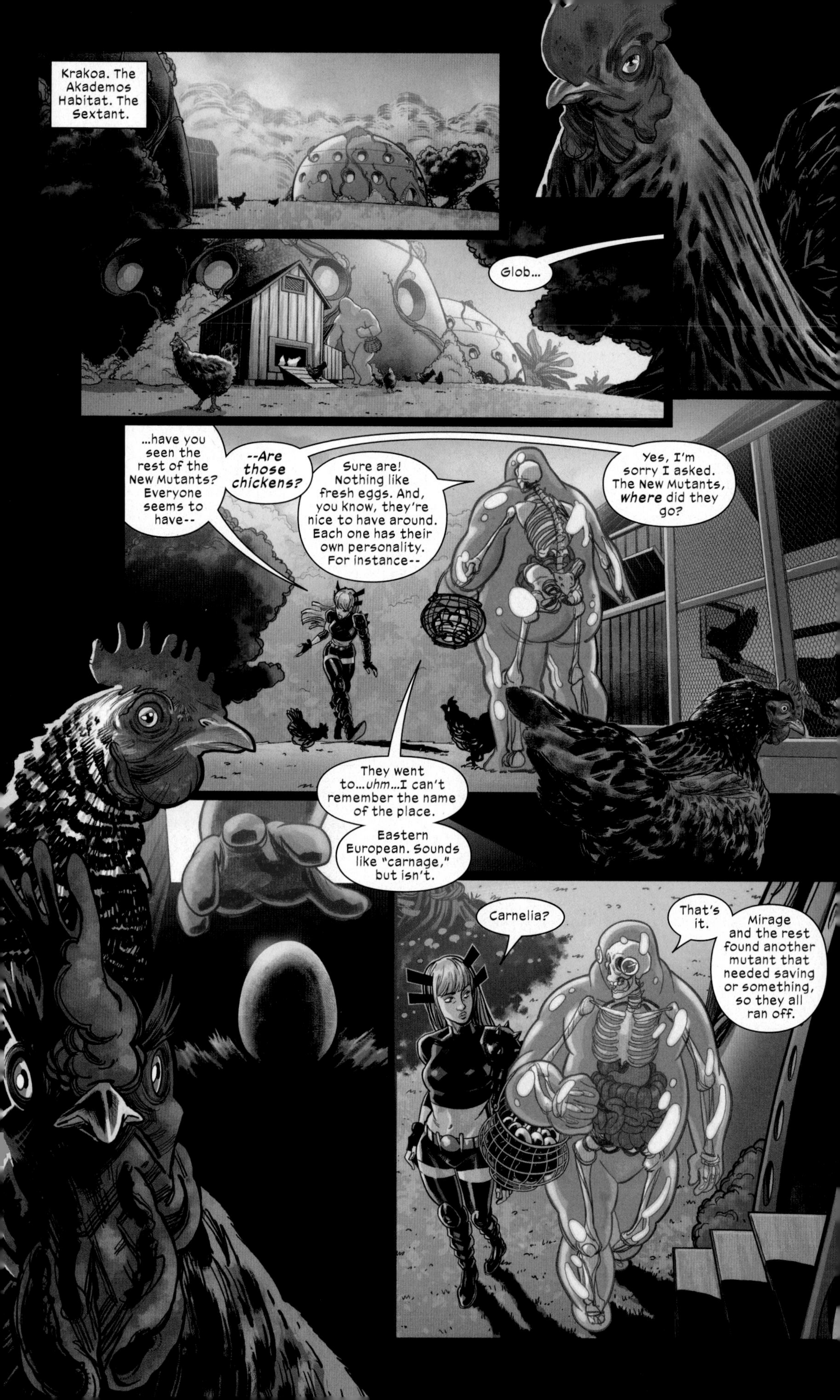

Krakoa. The Akademos Habitat. The Sextant.
Glob...
...have you seen the rest of the New Mutants? Everyone seems to have--
--Are those chickens?
Sure are! Nothing like fresh eggs. And, you know, they're nice to have around. Each one has their own personality. For instance--
Yes, I'm sorry I asked. The New Mutants, where did they go?
They went to...uhm...I can't remember the name of the place.
Eastern European. Sounds like "carnage," but isn't.
Carnelia?
That's it.
Mirage and the rest found another mutant that needed saving or something, so they all ran off.

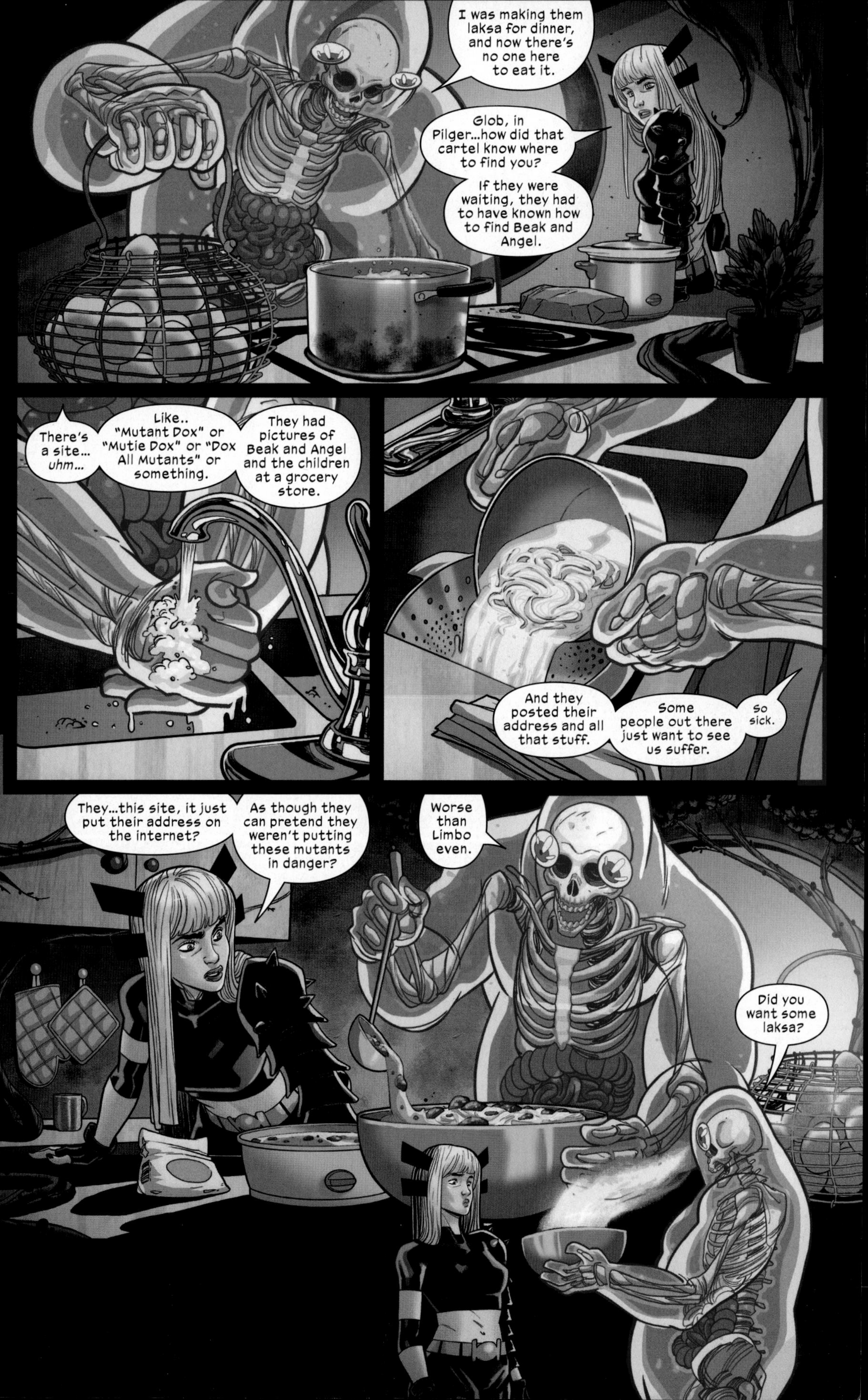
I was making them laksa for dinner, and now there's no one here to eat it.
Glob, in Pilger...how did that cartel know where to find you?
If they were waiting, they had to have known how to find Beak and Angel.
There's a site... *uhm*...
Like.. "Mutant Dox" or "Mutie Dox" or "Dox All Mutants" or something.
They had pictures of Beak and Angel and the children at a grocery store.
And they posted their address and all that stuff.
Some people out there just want to see us suffer.
So sick.
They...this site, it just put their address on the internet?
As though they can pretend they weren't putting these mutants in danger?
Worse than Limbo even.
Did you want some laksa?

GLOB'S VEGETARIAN LAKSA RECIPE

INGREDIENTS:

SOUP BASE

- 3 14oz cans coconut milk
- 4 cups vegetable broth
- 1 lb tofu (freeze the night before, remove, allow to thaw and cut into ¼ inch cubes)
- 1 tbsp lemongrass paste
- 2 tbsp ginger (freshly grated)
- 3 tbsp fresh lime juice
- 3 tbsp soy sauce
- 2 tbsp yellow curry paste
- 3 tbsp brown sugar

OTHER INGREDIENTS:

- 2 cups sliced cremini mushrooms
- Handful fresh cilantro, chopped
- 1 cup bean sprouts
- Hardboiled eggs, peeled and sliced lengthwise -- enough for one egg per bowl
- 100 grams ramen noodles per person (or use whatever type of noodles you want)
- Spicy chili crisp sauce (homemade or store bought)
- Lime, cut into wedges

INSTRUCTIONS

Prepare eggs the night before! Or that afternoon, though I find the night before easier. One less thing to worry about.

Place all soup base ingredients into a slow cooker and cook on high for 3-4 hours. Fifteen minutes before it's done, add mushrooms (and any other veggies you may want to mix in). About 5 minutes before the slow cooker is done, cook noodles according to instructions, slice hardboiled eggs and chop up your cilantro.

Fill bowl about 1/3-1/2 full of noodles, add laksa soup base, top with sliced egg, cilantro, slice of lime and bean sprouts, and serve.

Serve with spicy chili crisp on the side for those who like to spice it up a little.

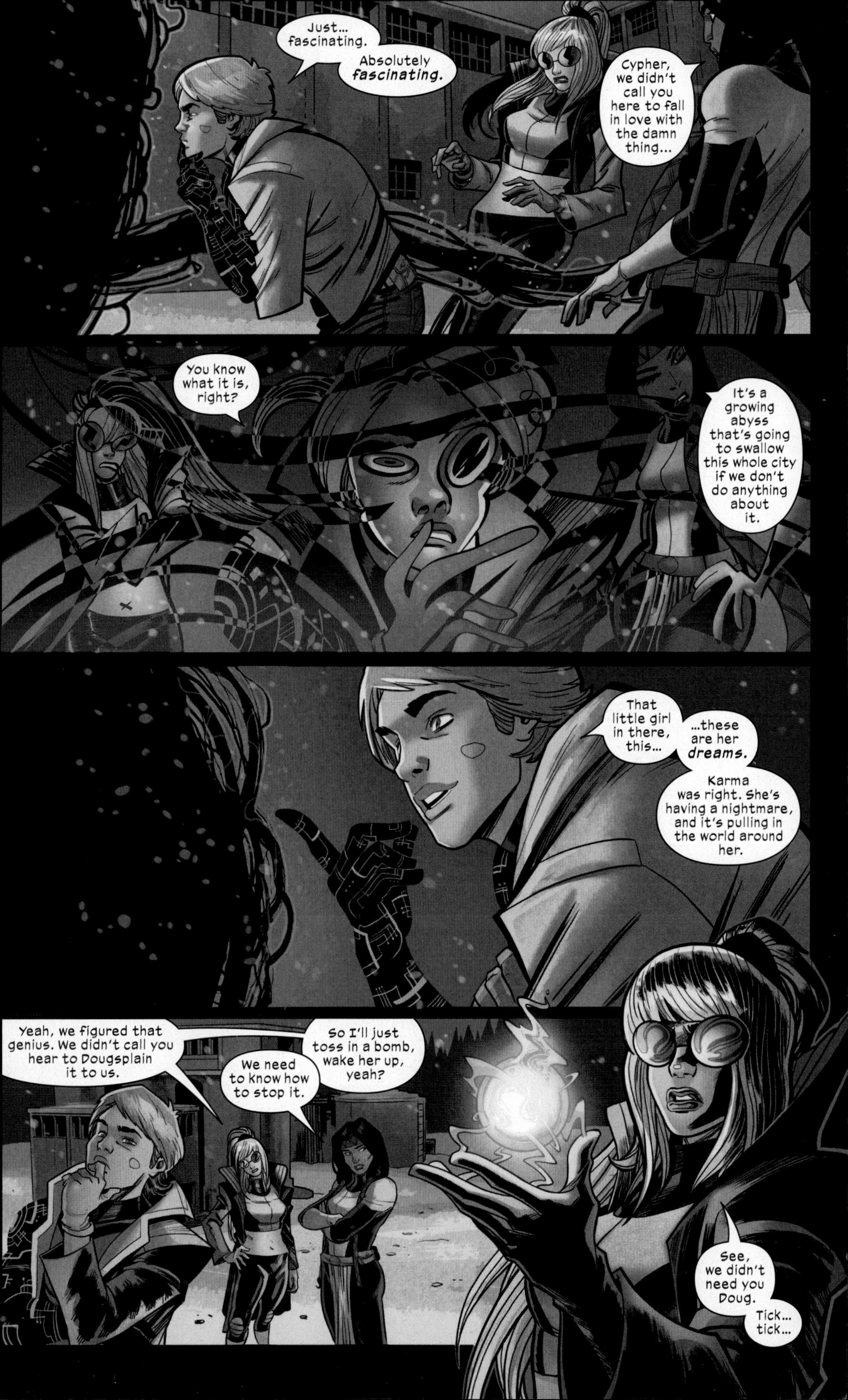

Just... fascinating.
Absolutely *fascinating.*
Cypher, we didn't call you here to fall in love with the damn thing...
You know what it is, right?
It's a growing abyss that's going to swallow this whole city if we don't do anything about it.
That little girl in there, this...
...these are her *dreams.*
Karma was right. She's having a nightmare, and it's pulling in the world around her.
Yeah, we figured that genius. We didn't call you hear to Dougsplain it to us.
We need to know how to stop it.
So I'll just toss in a bomb, wake her up, yeah?
See, we didn't need you Doug.
Tick... tick...

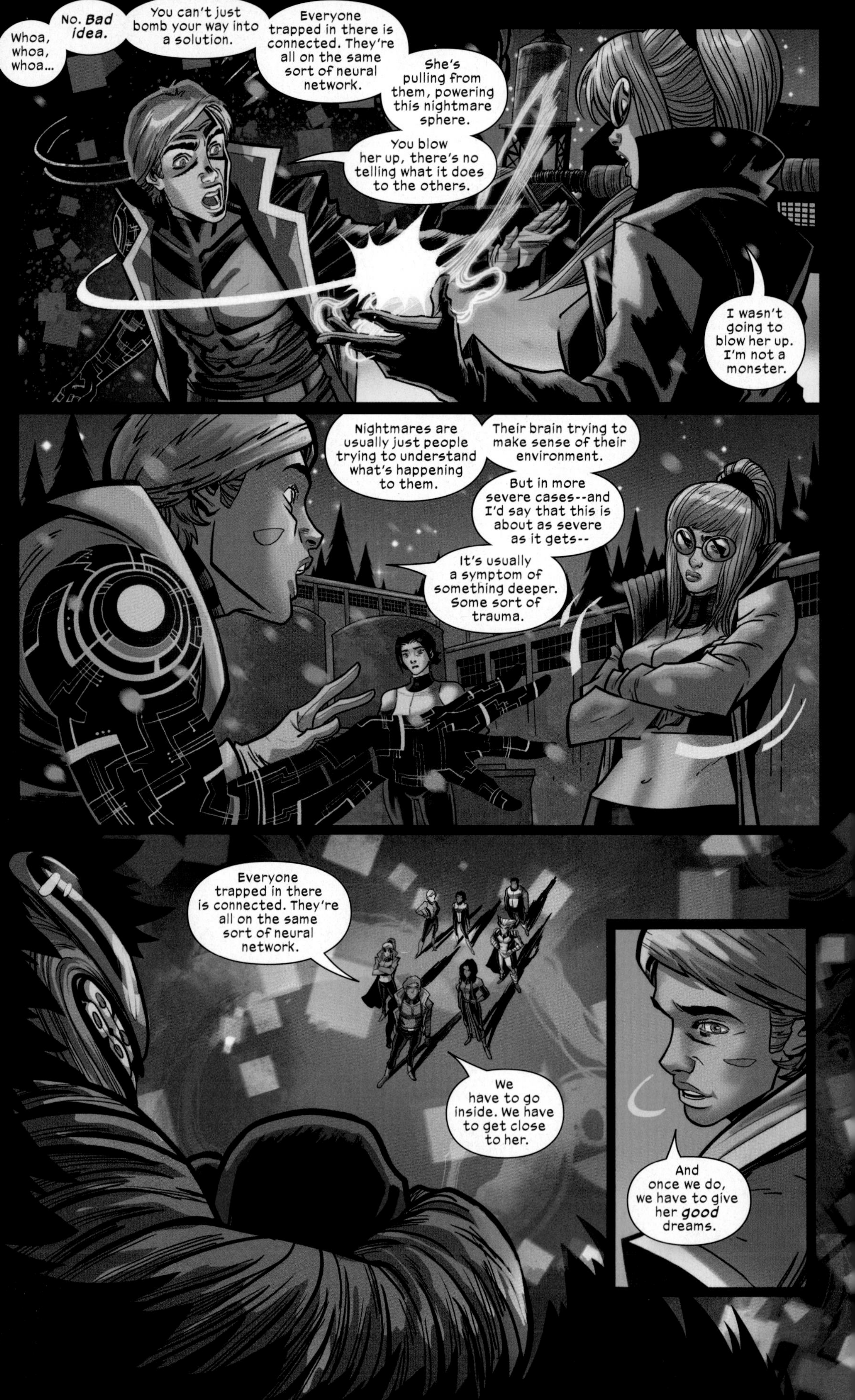

Whoa, whoa, whoa...
No. *Bad idea.*
You can't just bomb your way into a solution.
Everyone trapped in there is connected. They're all on the same sort of neural network.
She's pulling from them, powering this nightmare sphere.
You blow her up, there's no telling what it does to the others.
I wasn't going to blow her up. I'm not a monster.
Nightmares are usually just people trying to understand what's happening to them.
Their brain trying to make sense of their environment.
But in more severe cases--and I'd say that this is about as severe as it gets--
It's usually a symptom of something deeper. Some sort of trauma.
Everyone trapped in there is connected. They're all on the same sort of neural network.
We have to go inside. We have to get close to her.
And once we do, we have to give her *good* dreams.

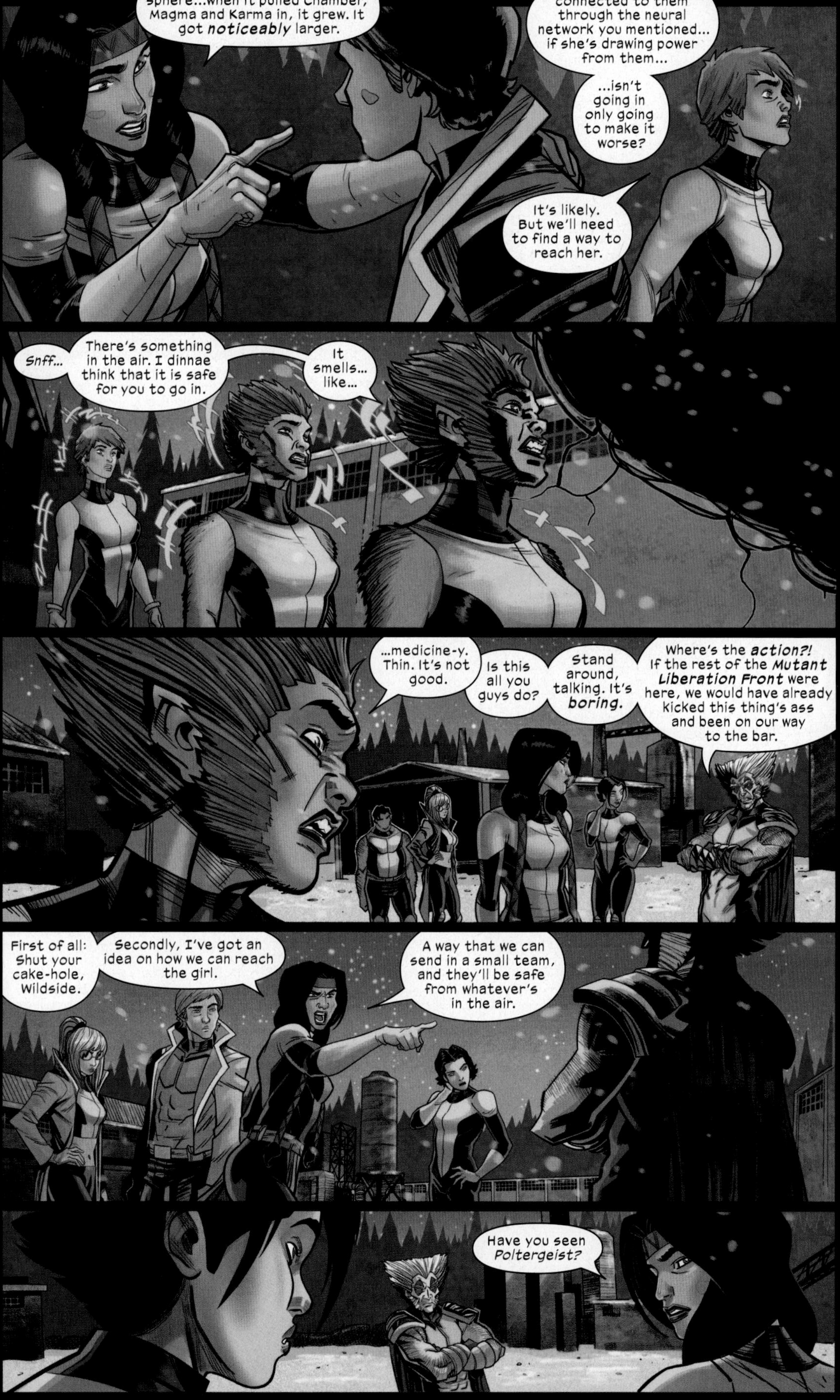
That...the nightmare sphere...when it pulled Chamber, Magma and Karma in, it grew. It got *noticeably* larger.
If that girl is connected to them through the neural network you mentioned... if she's drawing power from them...
...isn't going in only going to make it worse?
It's likely. But we'll need to find a way to reach her.
Snff...
There's something in the air. I dinnae think that it is safe for you to go in.
It smells... like...
...medicine-y. Thin. It's not good.
Is this all you guys do?
Stand around, talking. It's *boring.*
Where's the *action?!* If the rest of the *Mutant Liberation Front* were here, we would have already kicked this thing's ass and been on our way to the bar.
First of all: Shut your cake-hole, Wildside.
Secondly, I've got an idea on how we can reach the girl.
A way that we can send in a small team, and they'll be safe from whatever's in the air.
Have you seen *Poltergeist?*

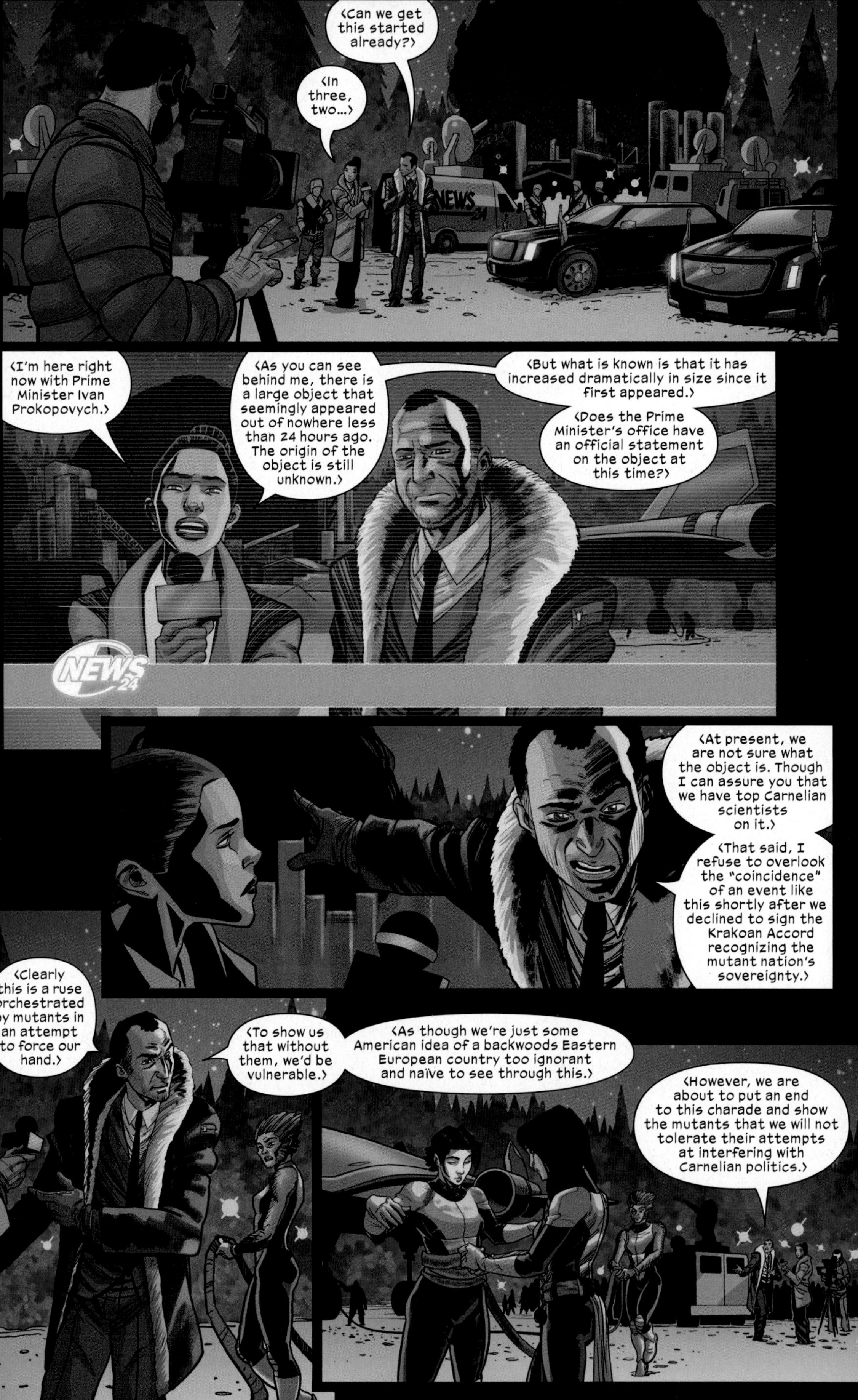

‹Can we get this started already?›
‹In three, two...›
NEWS 24
‹I'm here right now with Prime Minister Ivan Prokopovych.›
‹As you can see behind me, there is a large object that seemingly appeared out of nowhere less than 24 hours ago. The origin of the object is still unknown.›
‹But what is known is that it has increased dramatically in size since it first appeared.›
‹Does the Prime Minister's office have an official statement on the object at this time?›
NEWS 24
‹At present, we are not sure what the object is. Though I can assure you that we have top Carnelian scientists on it.›
‹That said, I refuse to overlook the "coincidence" of an event like this shortly after we declined to sign the Krakoan Accord recognizing the mutant nation's sovereignty.›
‹Clearly this is a ruse orchestrated by mutants in an attempt to force our hand.›
‹To show us that without them, we'd be vulnerable.›
‹As though we're just some American idea of a backwoods Eastern European country too ignorant and naïve to see through this.›
‹However, we are about to put an end to this charade and show the mutants that we will not tolerate their attempts at interfering with Carnelian politics.›

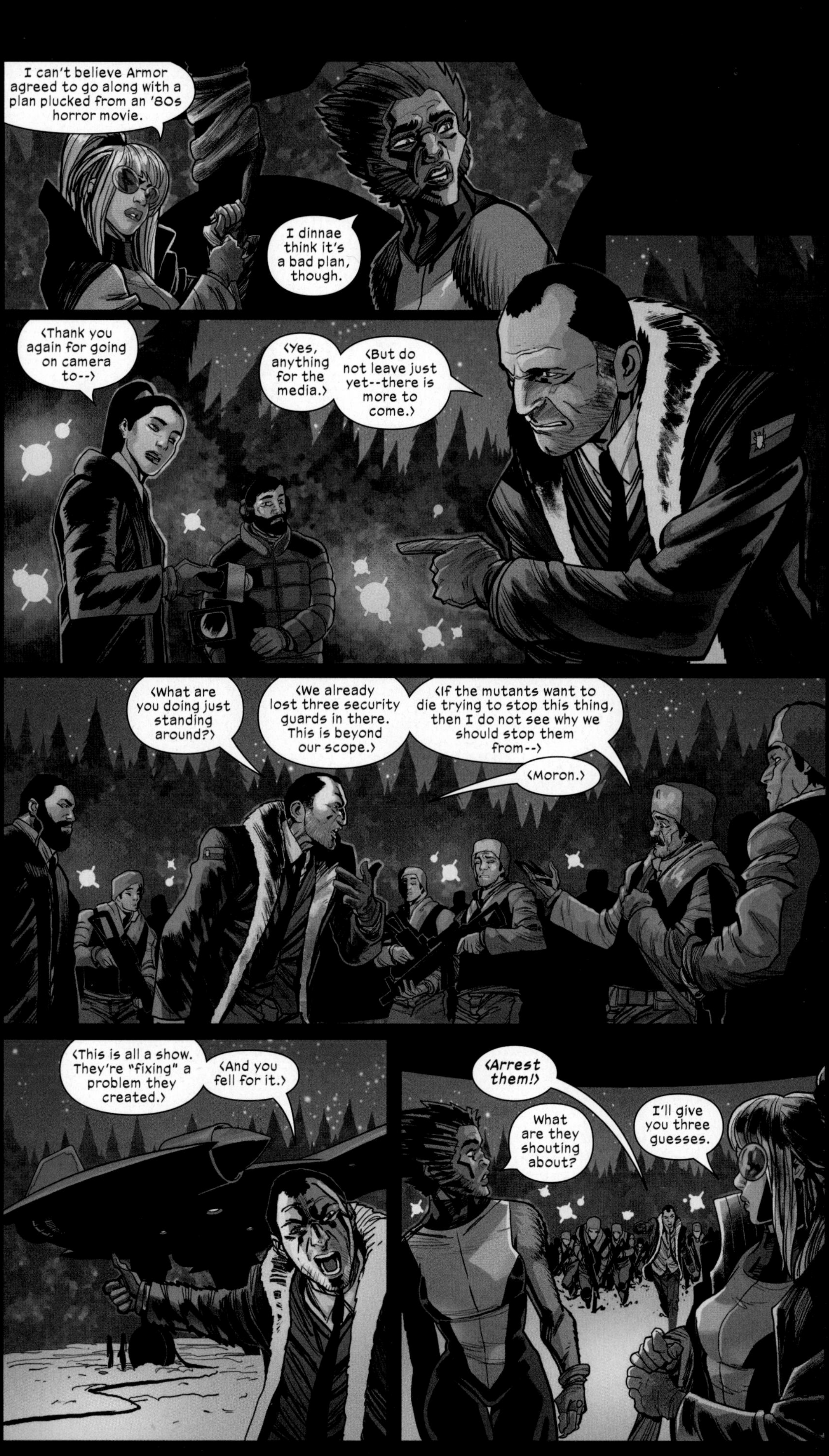
I can't believe Armor agreed to go along with a plan plucked from an '80s horror movie.
I dinnae think it's a bad plan, though.
<Thank you again for going on camera to-->
<Yes, anything for the media.>
<But do not leave just yet--there is more to come.>
<What are you doing just standing around?>
<We already lost three security guards in there. This is beyond our scope.>
<If the mutants want to die trying to stop this thing, then I do not see why we should stop them from-->
<Moron.>
<This is all a show. They're "fixing" a problem they created.>
<And you fell for it.>
<Arrest them!>
What are they shouting about?
I'll give you three guesses.

DOX
MUTANTS IN CARNELIA!

Well, it looks like the mutants are at it again. This time, they've taken their dog and pony show abroad.

As reported widely on all major networks, a group of mutants -- a few of which appear to be the same involved in the Pilger Incident (link) -- have popped up in Carnelia, and they've brought what many are describing as a "black hole" with them.

According to Ivan Prokopovych, prime minister of Carnelia, the mutants brought the black hole to his country in an attempt to stage (and we mean STAGE as in FAKE) a rescue in a bizarre attempt to convince the Carnelian Government to recognize Krakoa as a sovereign nation.

Thankfully for Carnelia (and us), Ivan Prokopovych was able to see through their ruse and has issued a warrant for the arrest of the trespassing mutants.

DOX would like to encourage all of our readers in Carnelia to forward us footage and reports from the ground so that we can keep all of our readers updated on this latest attack to global freedoms.

Okay, the moment it seems you're in trouble, I'll pull you out.

With all this extra cargo, I'm not sure how long I'll be able to keep my armor up.

We won't need that long. If we can reach the little girl, hopefully Wildside can disrupt her nightmare and induce more pleasant dreams, and we'll be out before we know it.

Hopefully?

It's what I do, Cypher. Done it a million times.

If you guys are gonna do this, you might wanna do it now.

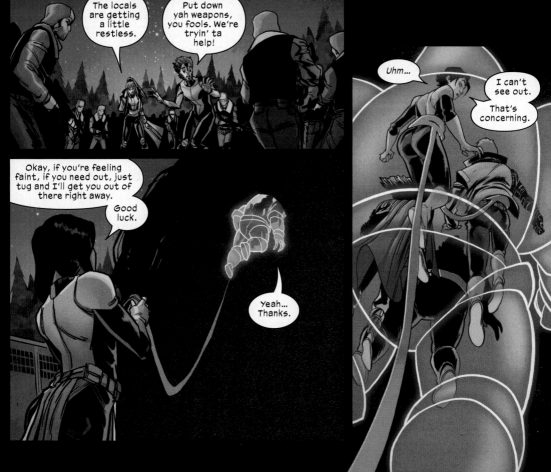

The locals are getting a little restless.

Put down yah weapons, you fools. We're tryin' ta help!

Uhm...

I can't see out. That's concerning.

Okay, if you're feeling faint, if you need out, just tug and I'll get you out of there right away.

Good luck.

Yeah... Thanks.

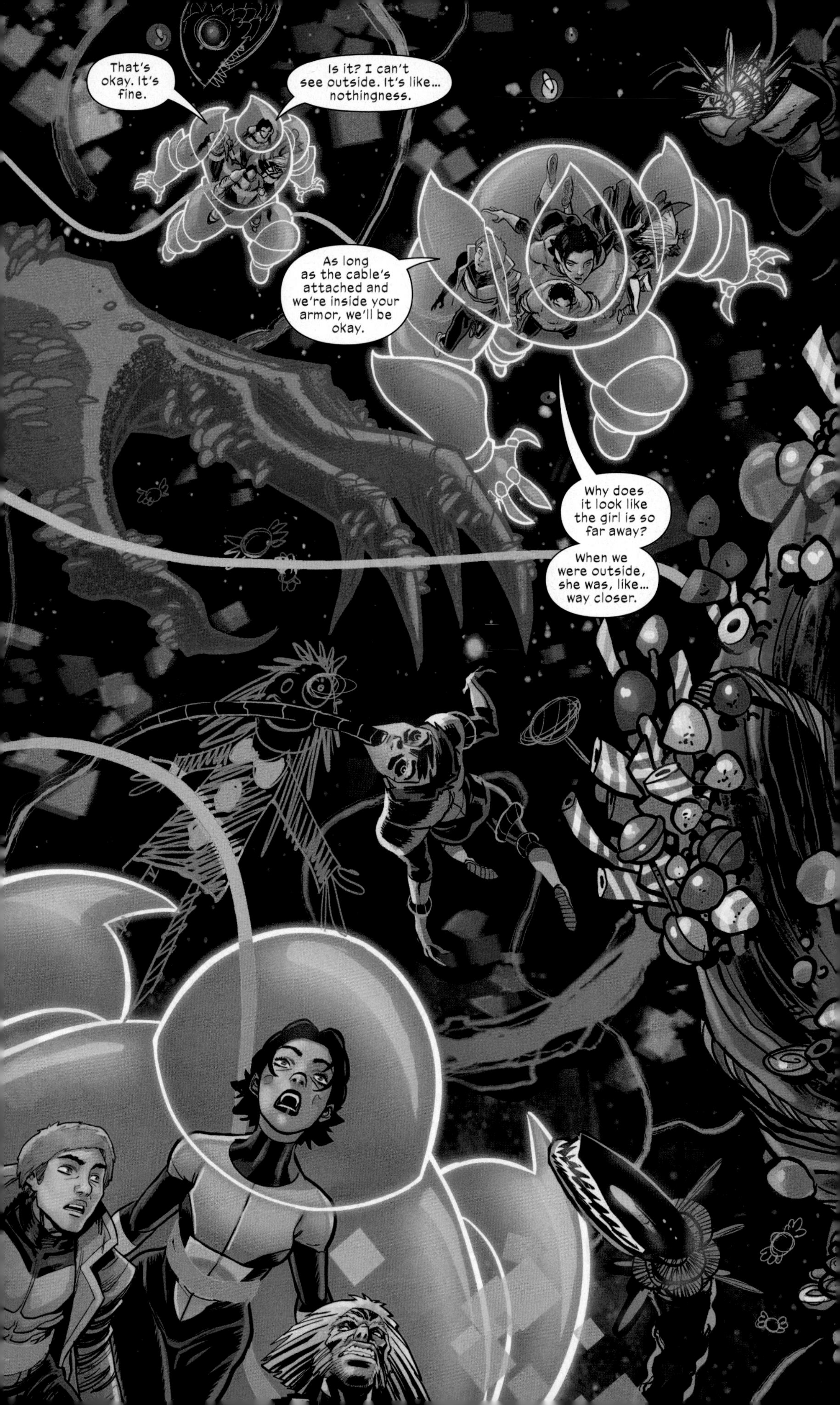
That's okay. It's fine.
Is it? I can't see outside. It's like... nothingness.
As long as the cable's attached and we're inside your armor, we'll be okay.
Why does it look like the girl is so far away?
When we were outside, she was, like... way closer.

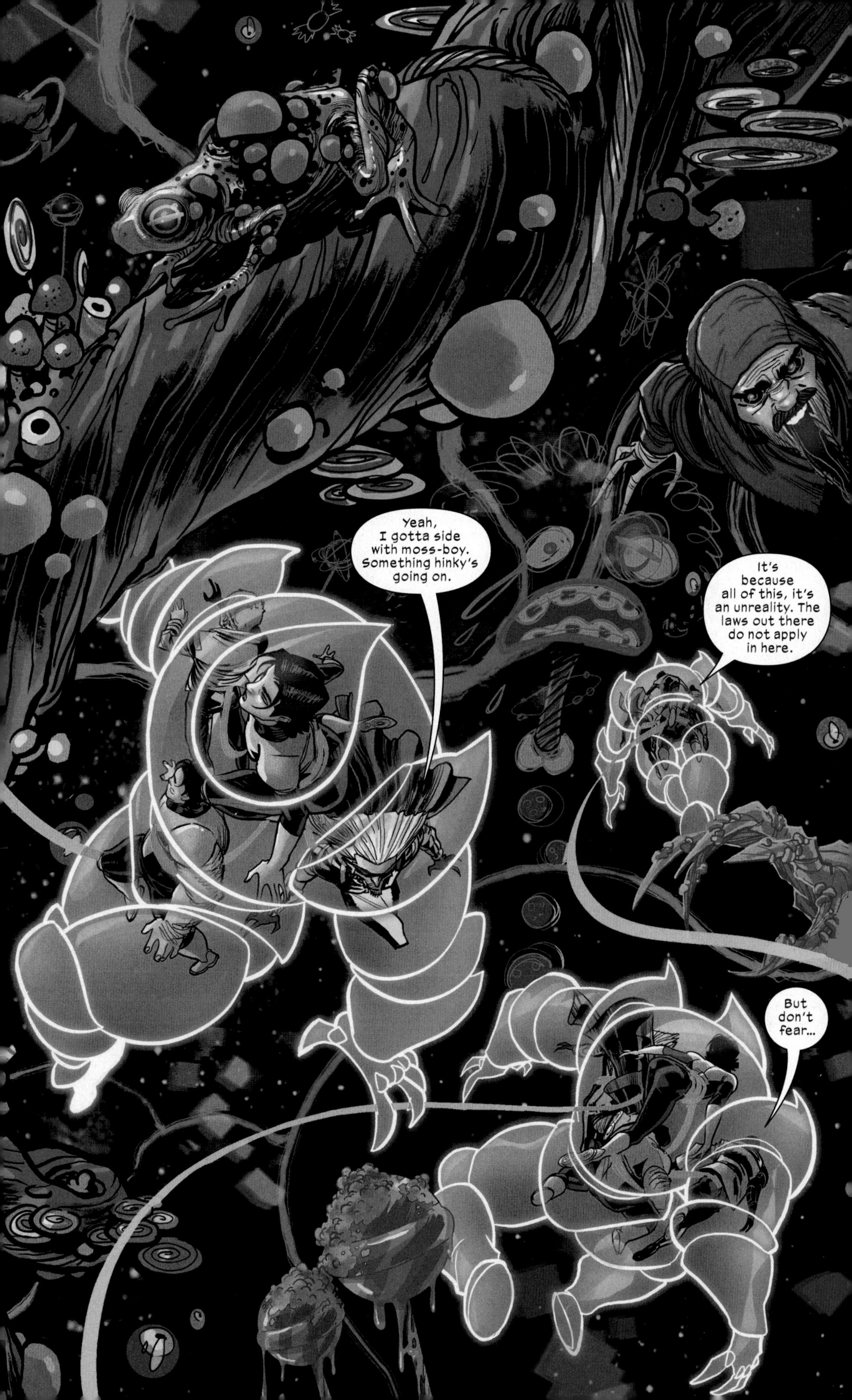

Yeah, I gotta side with moss-boy. Something hinky's going on.
It's because all of this, it's an unreality. The laws out there do not apply in here.
But don't fear...

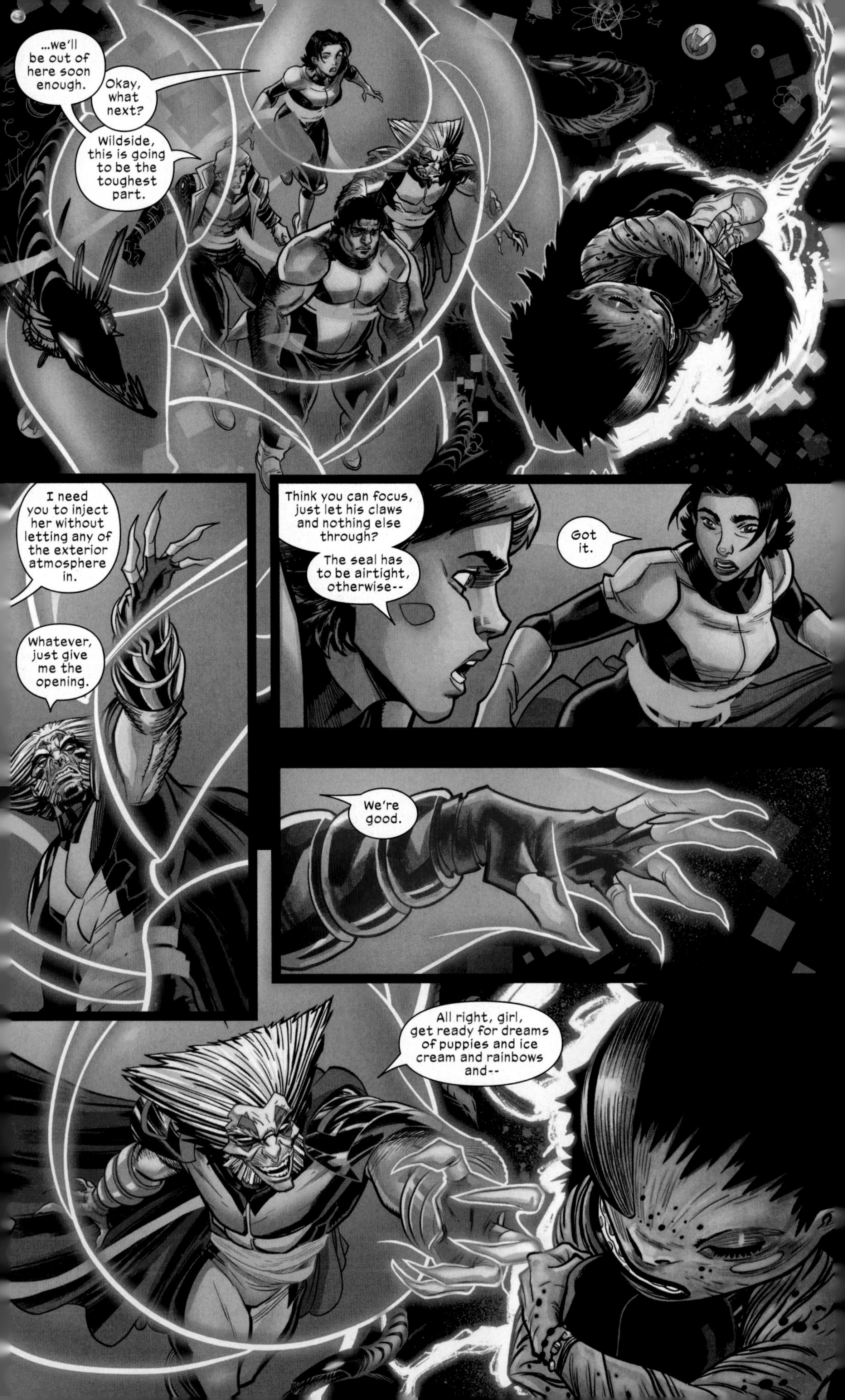
...we'll be out of here soon enough.
Okay, what next?
Wildside, this is going to be the toughest part.
I need you to inject her without letting any of the exterior atmosphere in.
Whatever, just give me the opening.
Think you can focus, just let his claws and nothing else through?
The seal has to be airtight, otherwise--
Got it.
We're good.
All right, girl, get ready for dreams of puppies and ice cream and rainbows and--

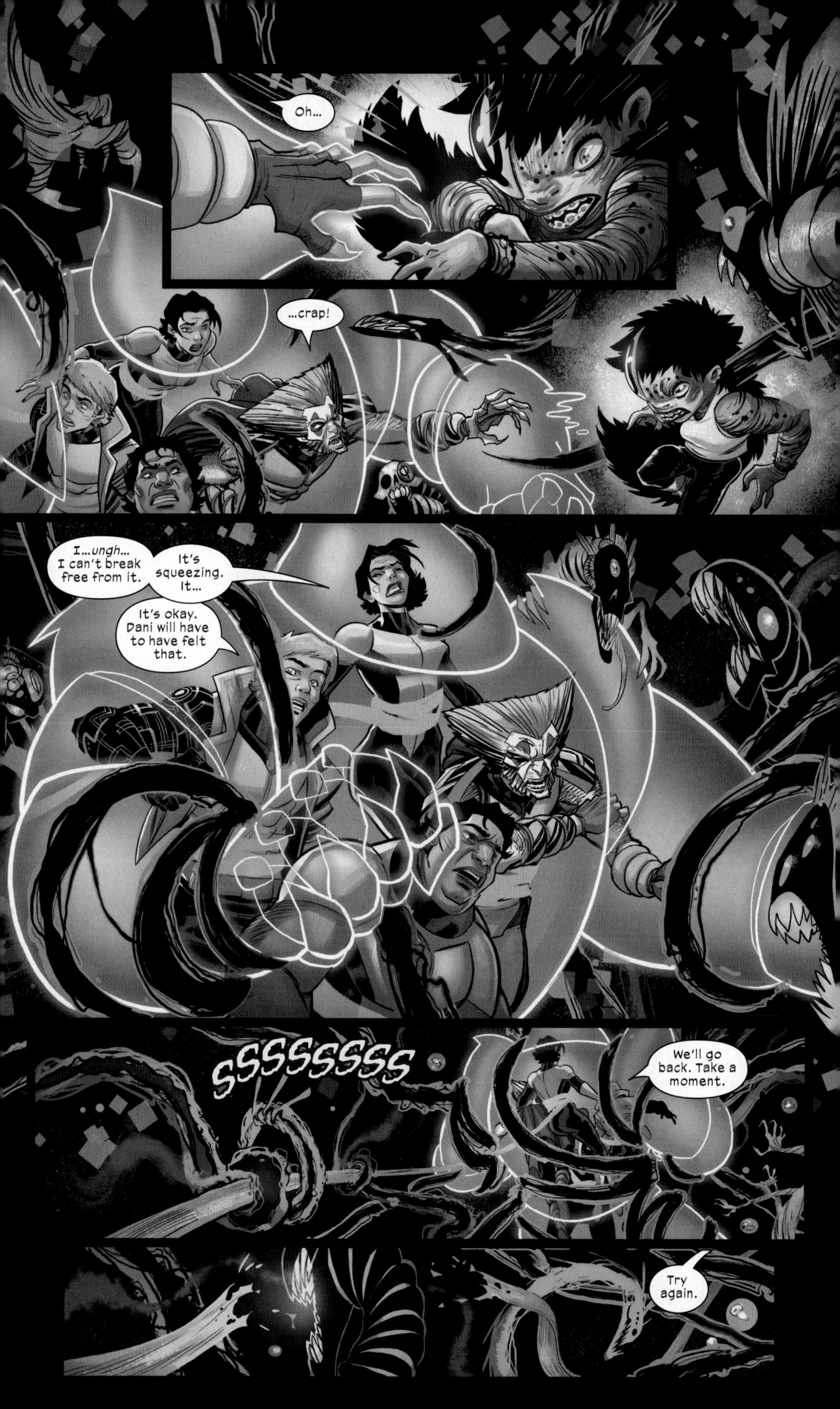
Oh...
...crap!
I...ungh... I can't break free from it.
It's squeezing. It...
It's okay. Dani will have to have felt that.
SSSSSSSS
We'll go back. Take a moment.
Try again.

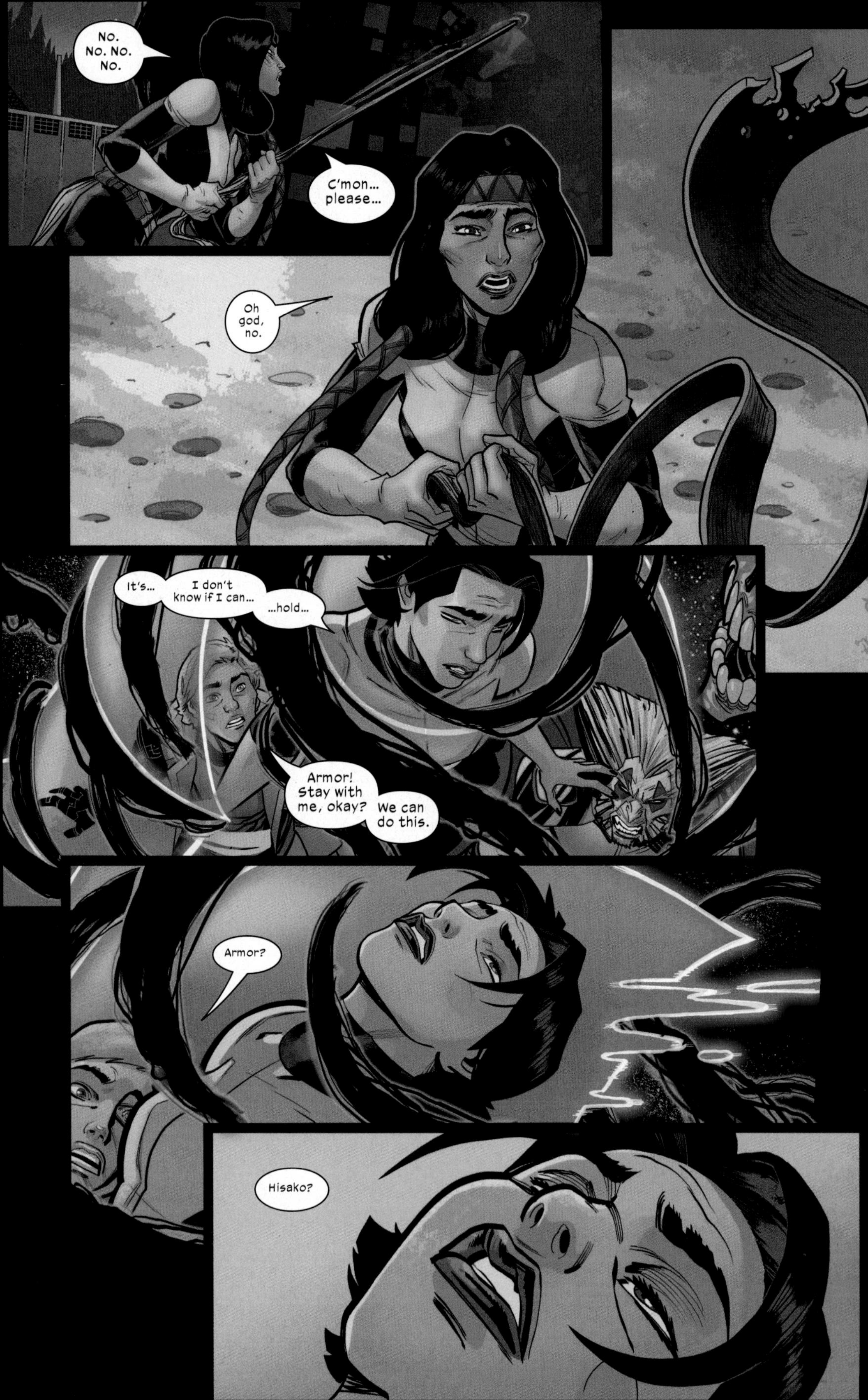
No. No. No. No.
C'mon... please...
Oh god, no.
It's...
I don't know if I can...
...hold...
Armor! Stay with me, okay?
We can do this.
Armor?
Hisako?

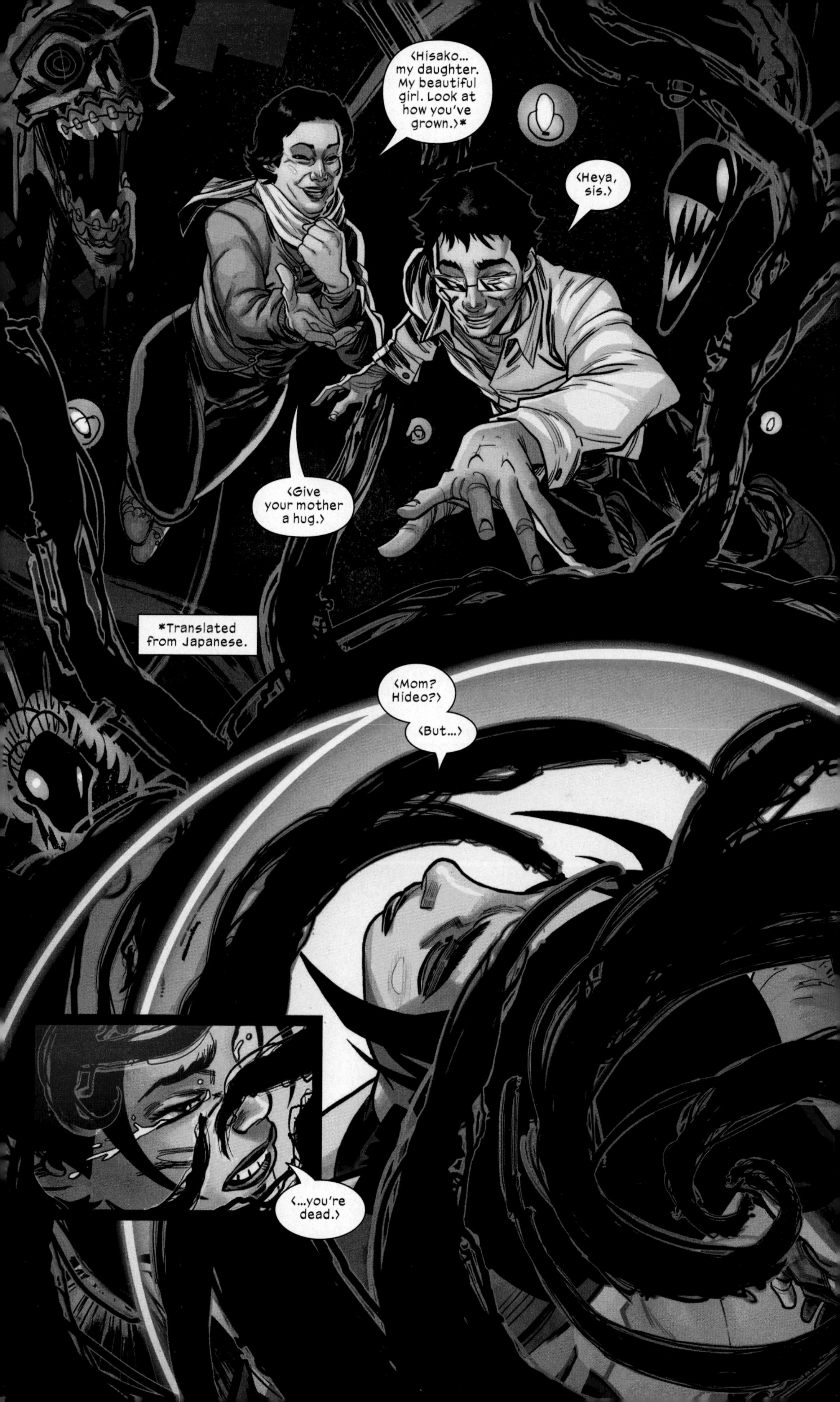
‹Hisako... my daughter. My beautiful girl. Look at how you've grown.›*
‹Heya, sis.›
‹Give your mother a hug.›
*Translated from Japanese.
‹Mom? Hideo?›
‹But...›
‹...you're dead.›

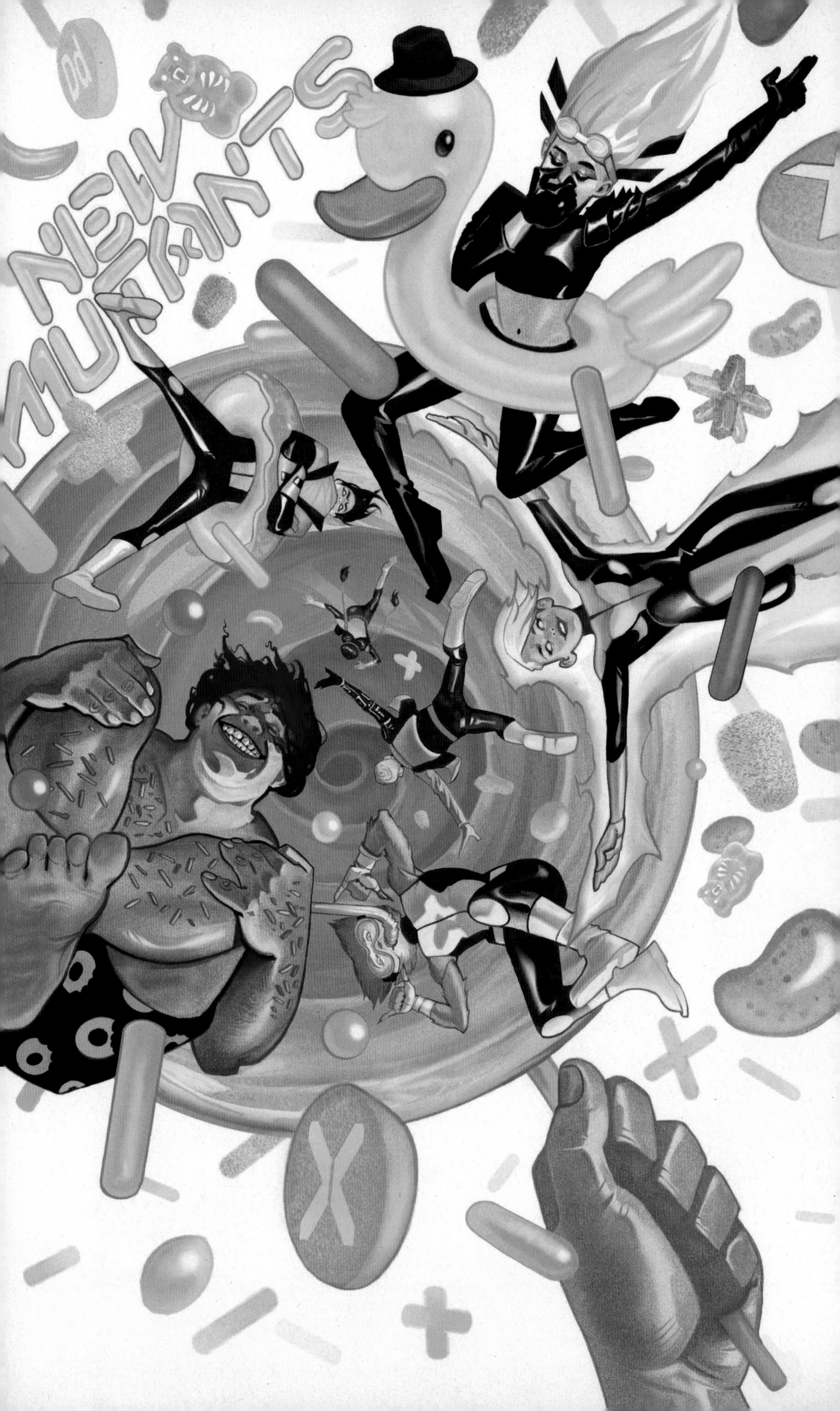
NEW MUTANTS

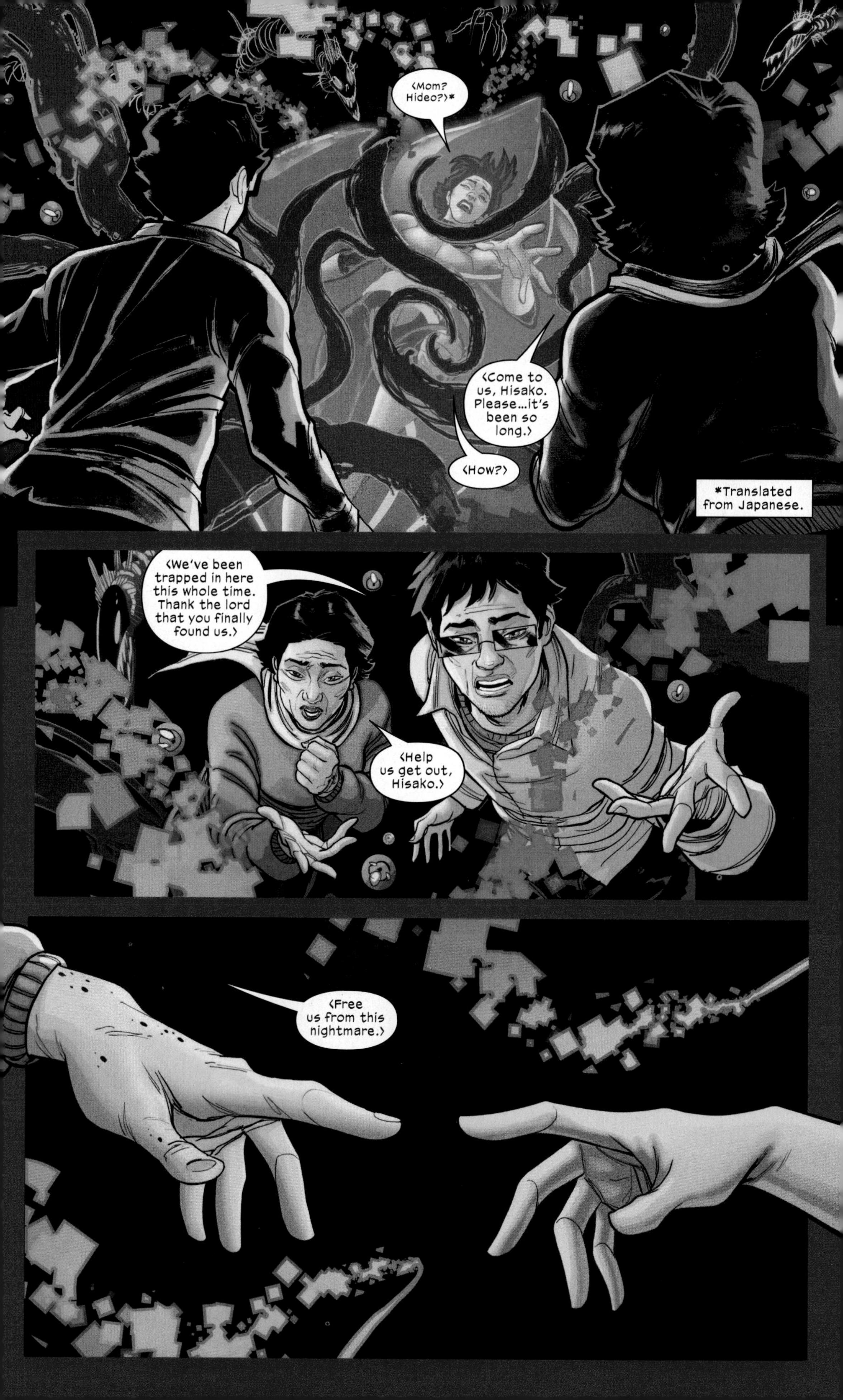
‹Mom? Hideo?›*
‹Come to us, Hisako. Please...it's been so long.›
‹How?›
*Translated from Japanese.
‹We've been trapped in here this whole time. Thank the lord that you finally found us.›
‹Help us get out, Hisako.›
‹Free us from this nightmare.›

[00_night____X]
[00_mare_____X]

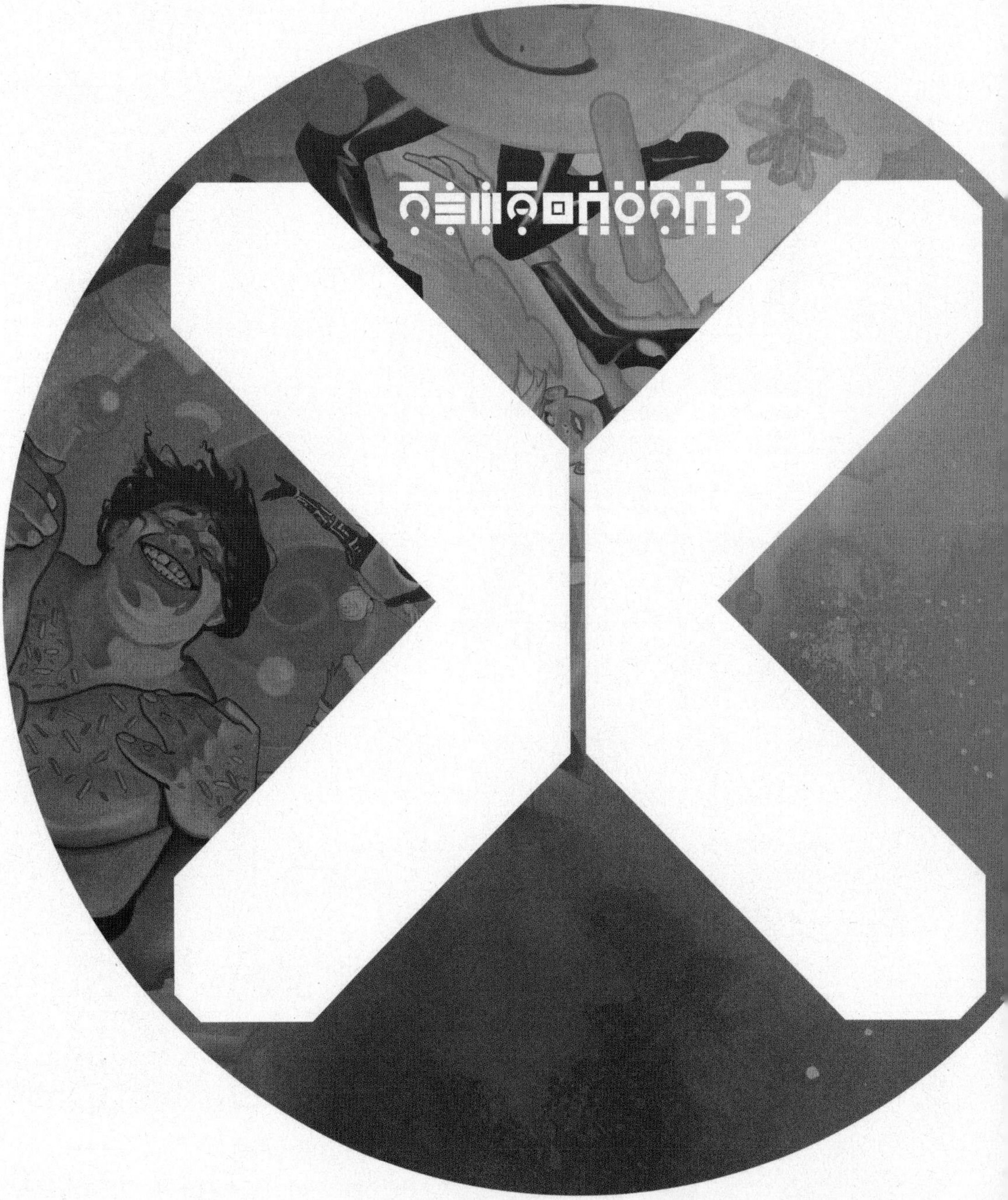

ED BRISSON.......................................[WRITER]
FLAVIANO...[ARTIST]
CARLOS LOPEZ...............................[COLOR ARTIST]
VC's TRAVIS LANHAM............................[LETTERER]
TOM MULLER.......................................[DESIGN]

MIKE DEL MUNDO...........................[COVER ARTIST]

NICK RUSSELL.............................[PRODUCTION]

JONATHAN HICKMAN...........................[HEAD OF X]
ANNALISE BISSA...................................[EDITOR]
JORDAN D. WHITE........................[SENIOR EDITOR]
C.B. CEBULSKI........................[EDITOR IN CHIEF]

[11] NEW MUTANTS

[ISSUE ELEVEN]...........ICE CREAM DREAMS

[00_night____X]
[00_mare_____X]

[00_00.....0]
[00_00....10]

[00_for_____]
[00____give_]

[00_____]

[00_ness____]

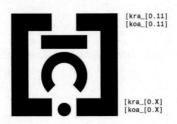

[kra_[0.11]
[koa_[0.11]

[kra_[0.X]
[koa_[0.X]

ADRIFT

When a teenager in the mutant-hostile nation of Carnelia
began to manifest an enormous sphere full of nightmare
creatures, the NEW MUTANTS were eager to help.
Unfortunately, as more of the team was subsumed by the
orb's psychic control, the Carnelian army arrived, escalating
the situation considerably. Now, within the sphere but
untethered from the outside world, Armor's protective
shielding has fallen...

Boom-Boom

Chamber

Magma

Mirage

Karma

Cypher

Mondo

Armor

Wolfsbane

Wildside

Glob

Magik

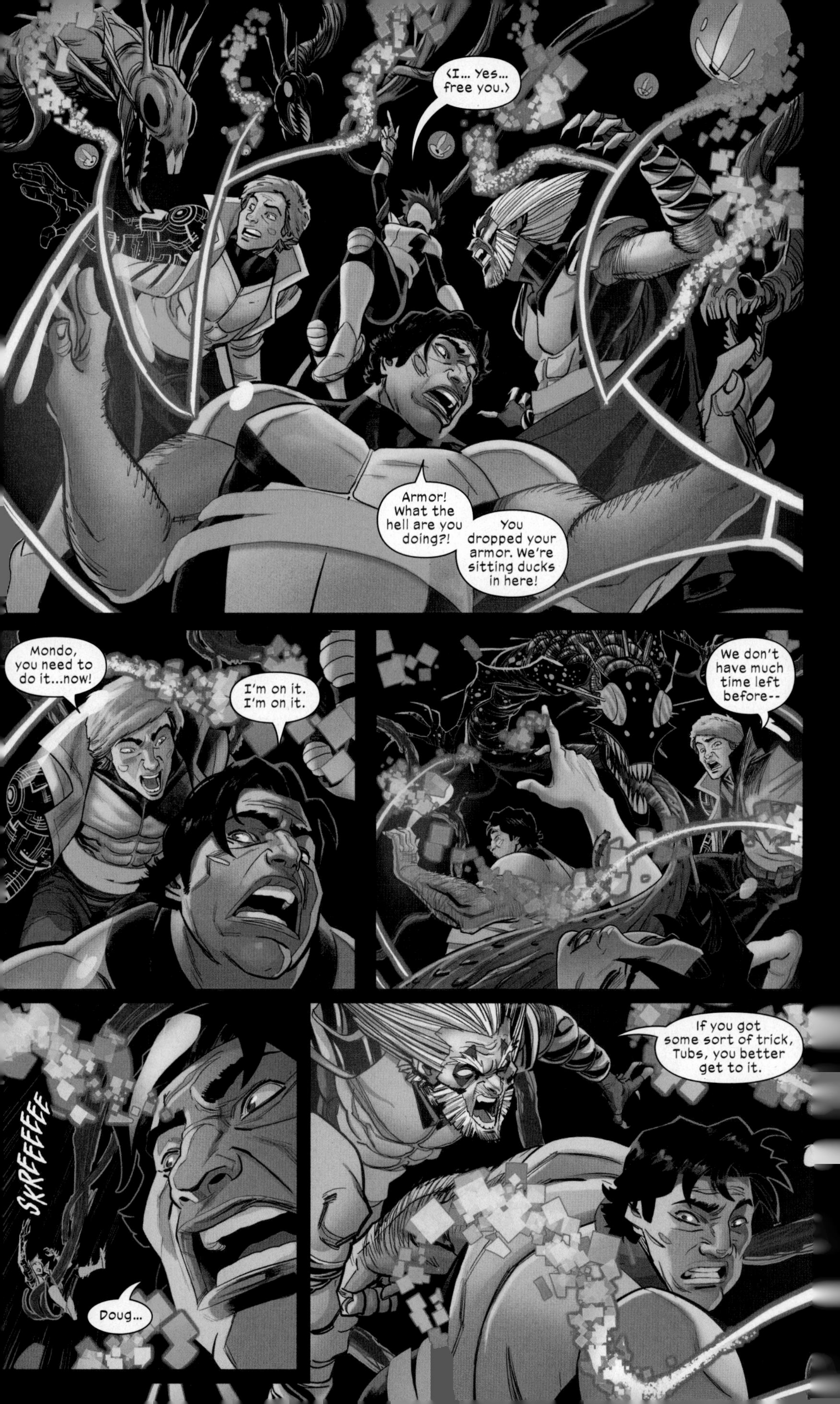

‹I... Yes... free you.›
Armor! What the hell are you doing?!
You dropped your armor. We're sitting ducks in here!
Mondo, you need to do it...now!
I'm on it. I'm on it.
We don't have much time left before--
SKREEEEEE
Doug...
If you got some sort of trick, Tubs, you better get to it.

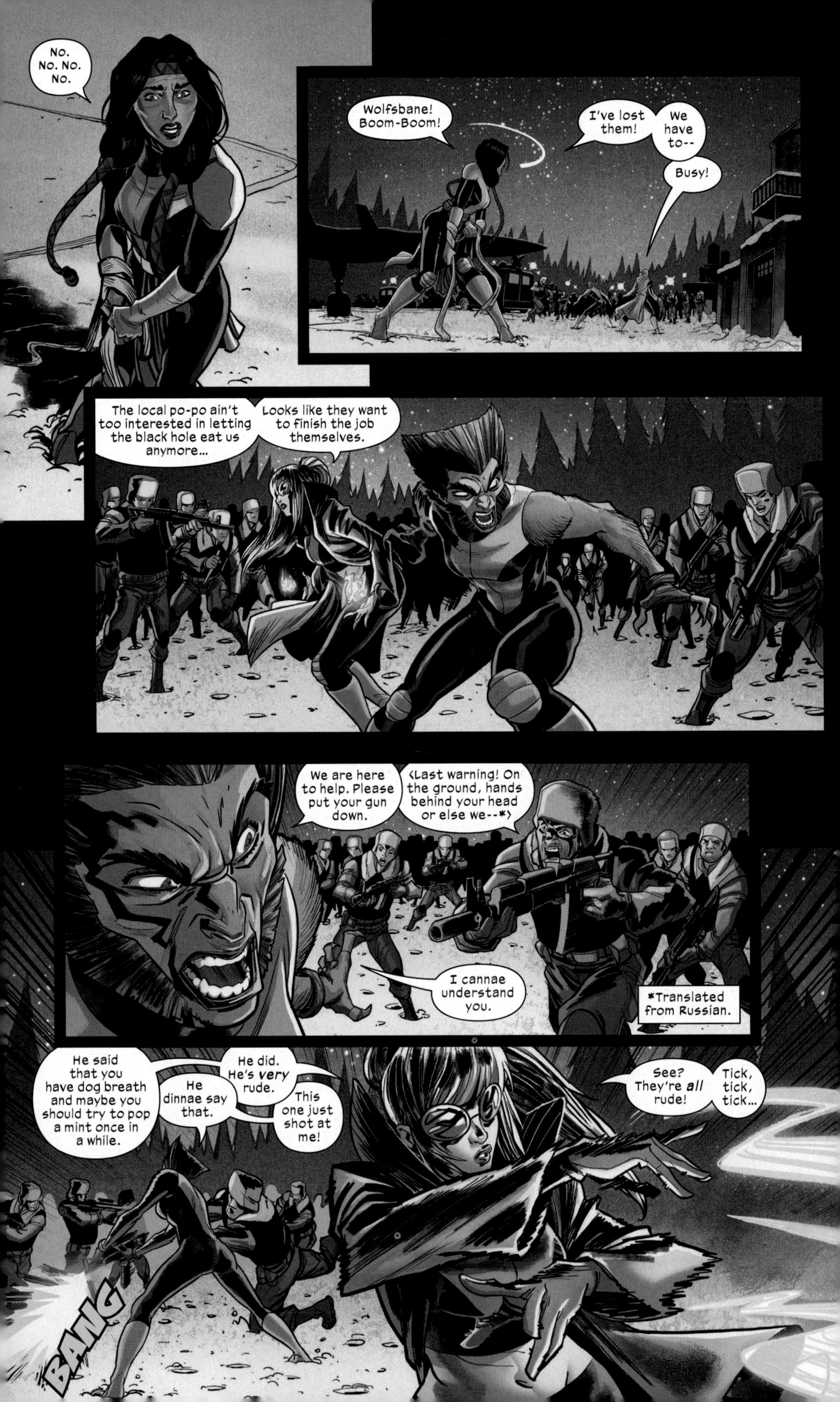

No. No. No. No.
Wolfsbane! Boom-Boom!
I've lost them!
We have to--
Busy!
The local po-po ain't too interested in letting the black hole eat us anymore...
Looks like they want to finish the job themselves.
We are here to help. Please put your gun down.
‹Last warning! On the ground, hands behind your head or else we--*›
I cannae understand you.
*Translated from Russian.
He said that you have dog breath and maybe you should try to pop a mint once in a while.
He dinnae say that.
He did. He's *very* rude.
This one just shot at me!
See? They're *all* rude!
Tick, tick, tick...
BANG

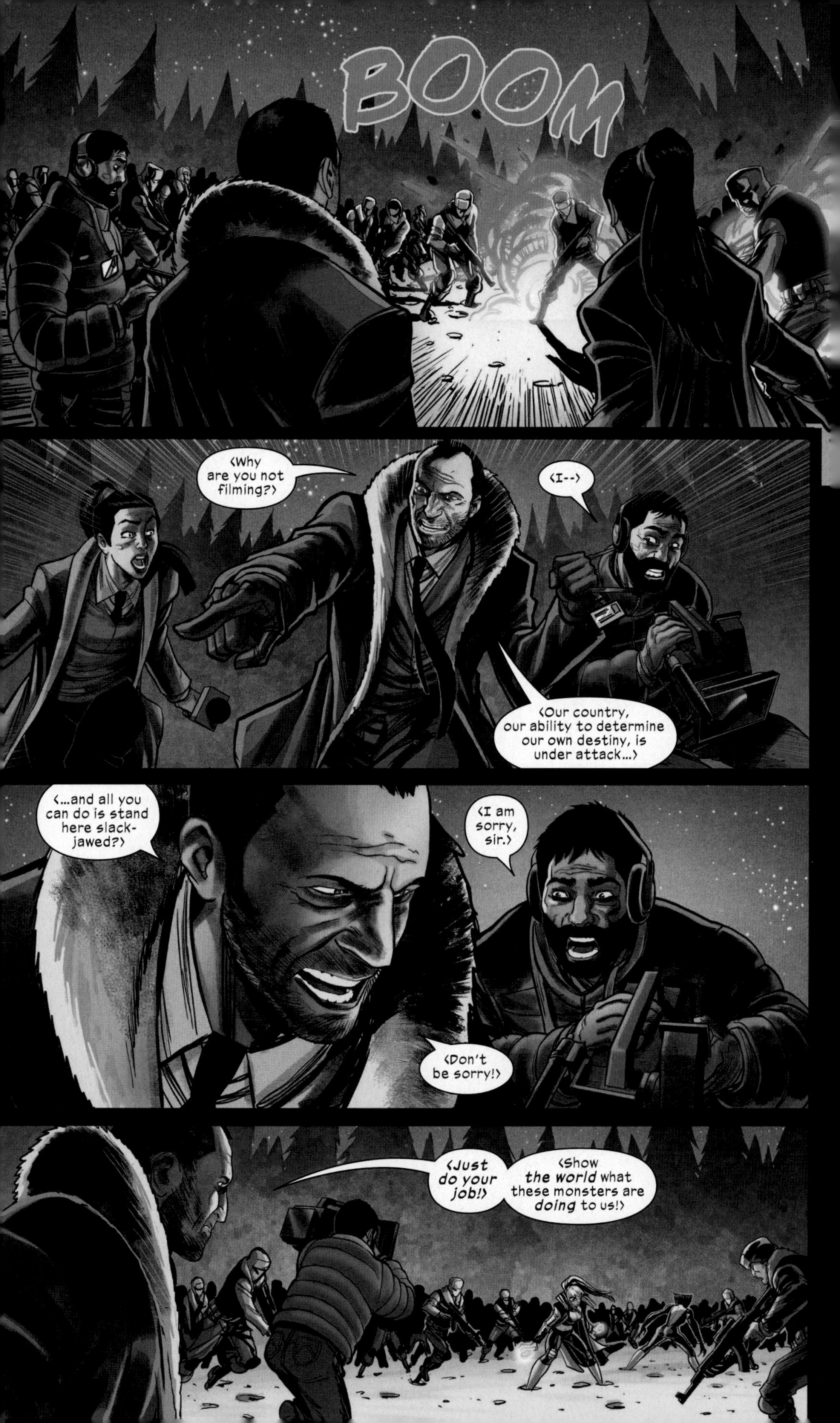
BOOM
‹Why are you not filming?›
‹I--›
‹Our country, our ability to determine our own destiny, is under attack...›
‹...and all you can do is stand here slack-jawed?›
‹I am sorry, sir.›
‹Don't be sorry!›
‹Just do your job!›
‹Show *the world* what these monsters are *doing* to us!›

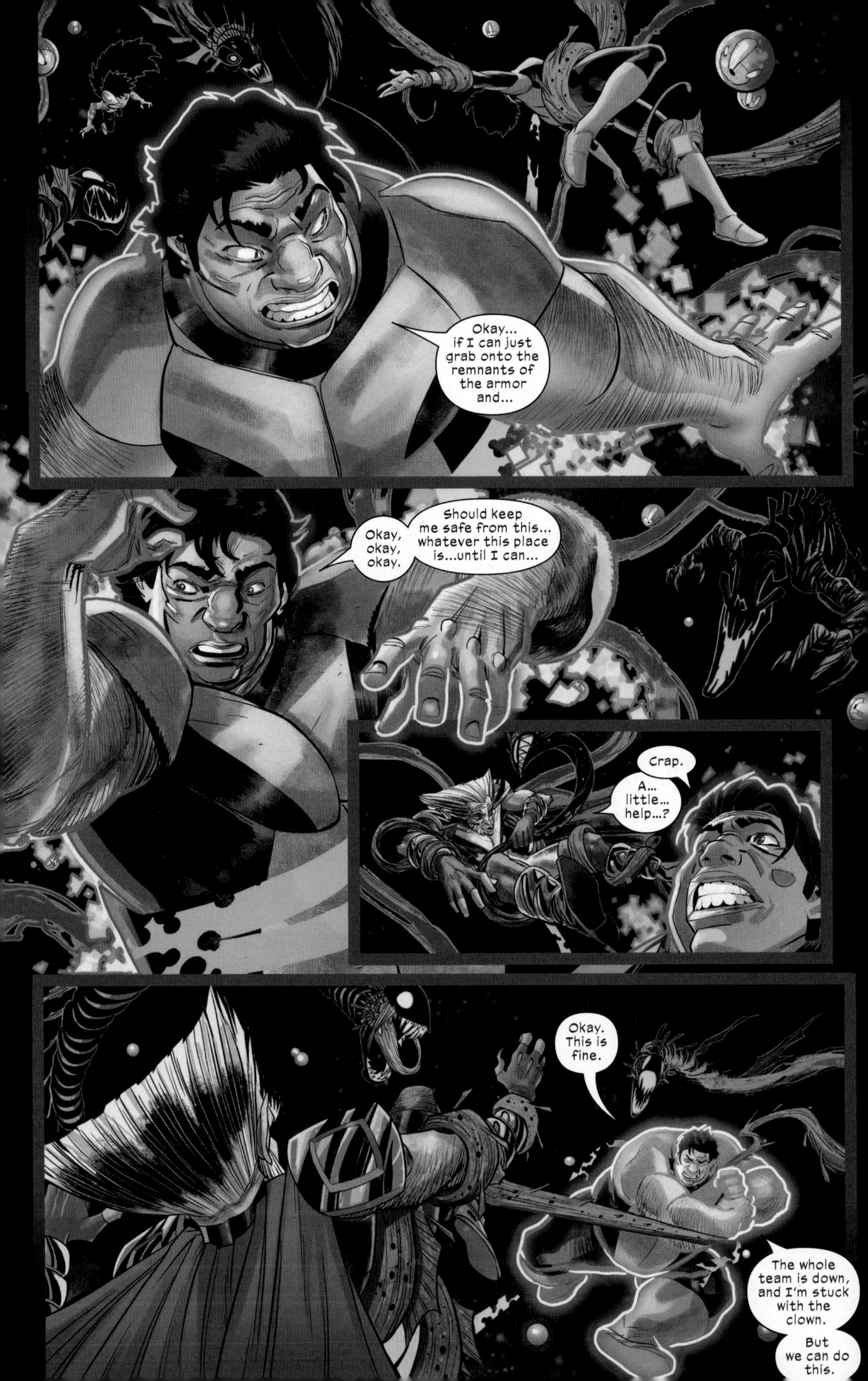
Okay... if I can just grab onto the remnants of the armor and...
Okay, okay, okay.
Should keep me safe from this... whatever this place is...until I can...
Crap.
A... little... help...?
Okay. This is fine.
The whole team is down, and I'm stuck with the clown.
But we can do this.

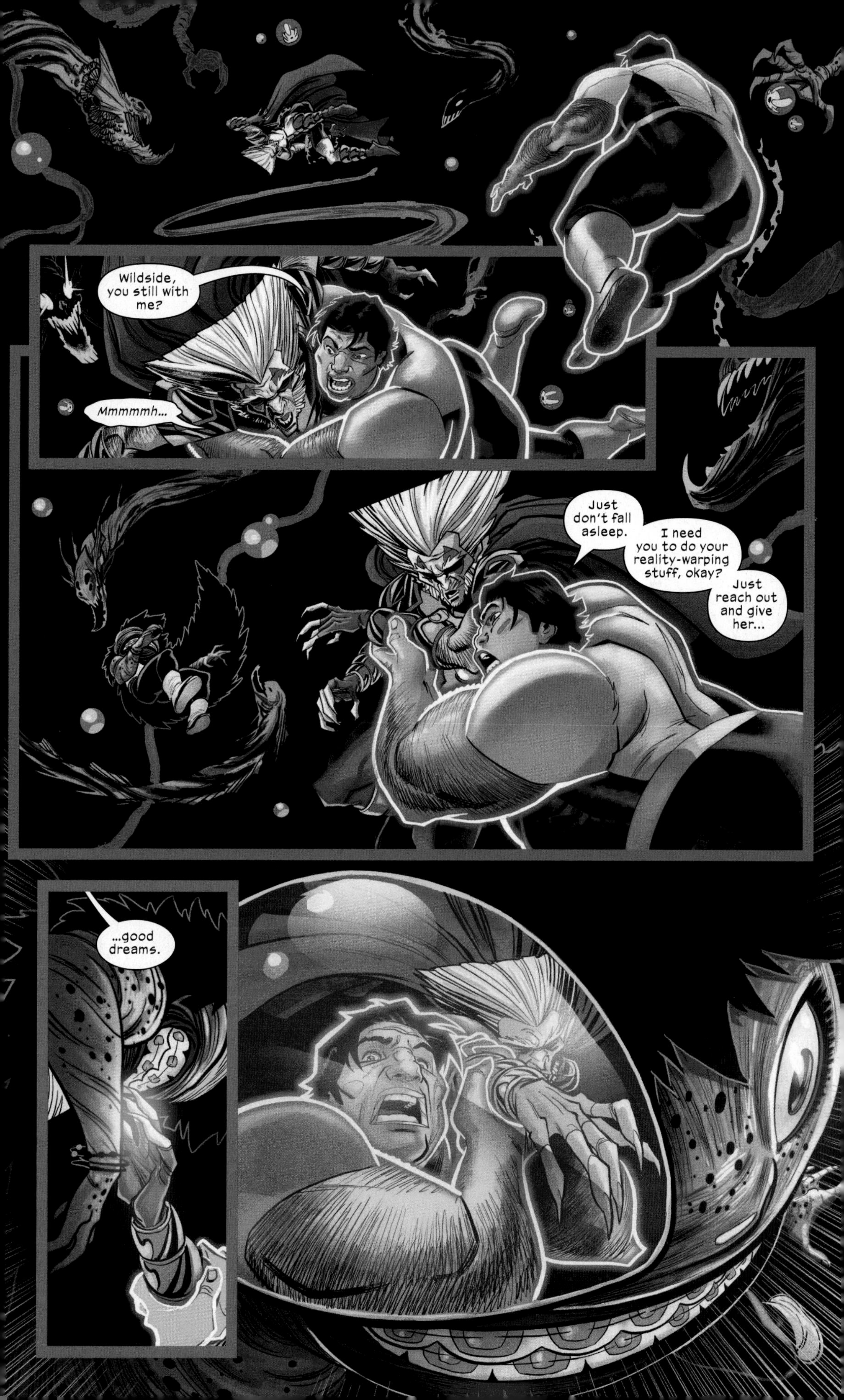
Wildside, you still with me?
Mmmmmh...
Just don't fall asleep.
I need you to do your reality-warping stuff, okay?
Just reach out and give her...
...good dreams.

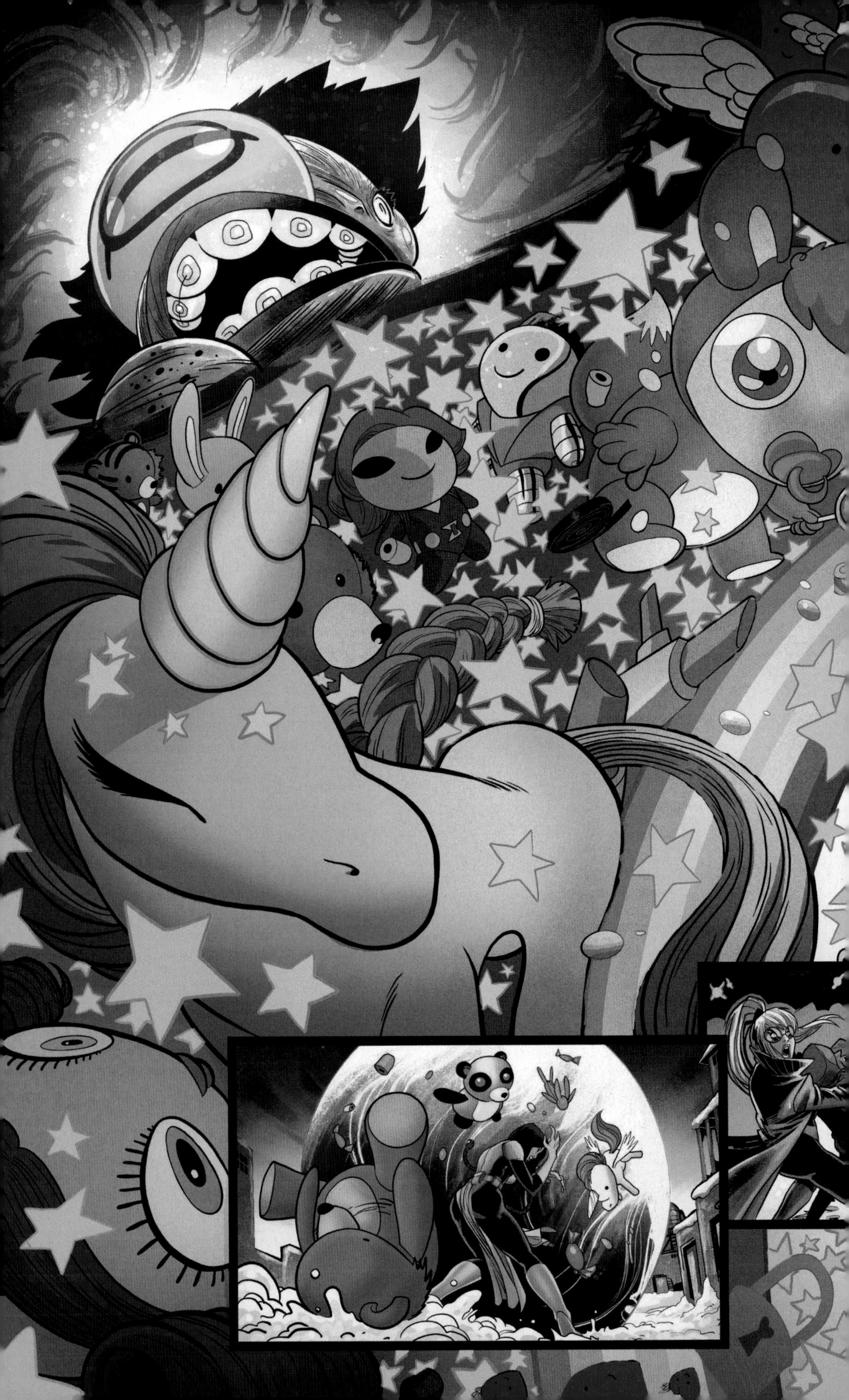

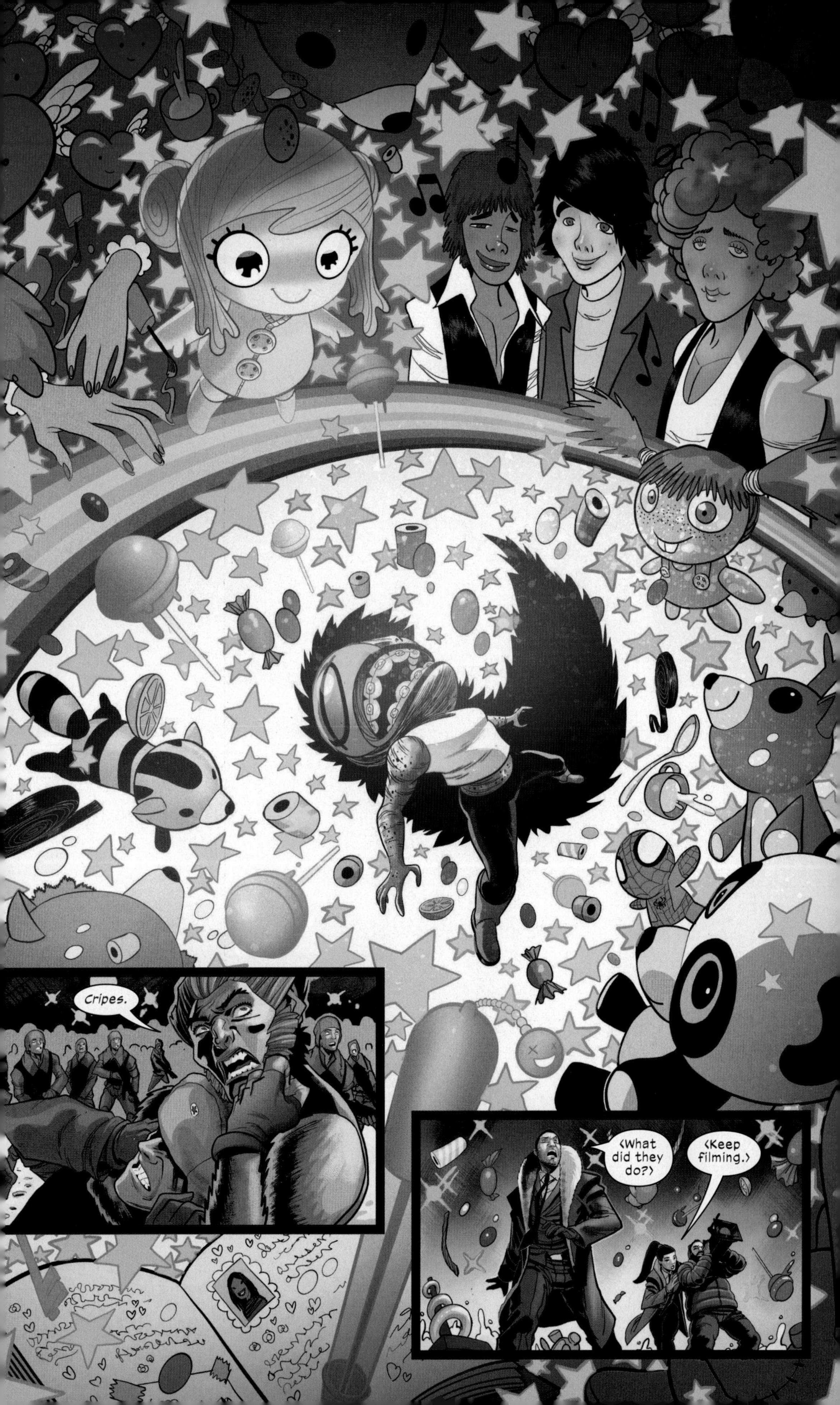

Cripes.
‹What did they do?›
‹Keep filming.›

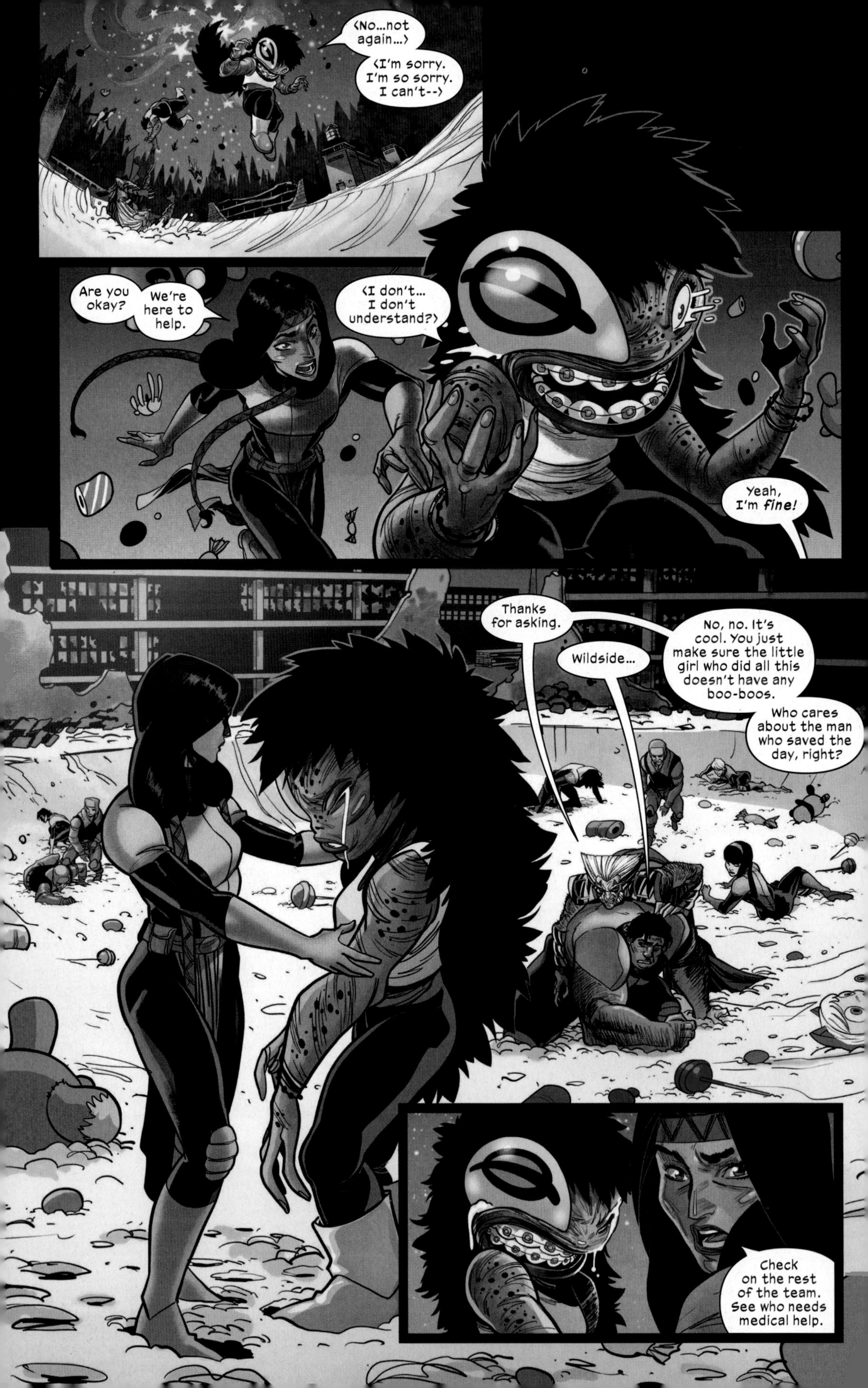

‹No...not again...›
‹I'm sorry. I'm so sorry. I can't--›
Are you okay?
We're here to help.
‹I don't... I don't understand?›
Yeah, I'm *fine!*
Thanks for asking.
Wildside...
No, no. It's cool. You just make sure the little girl who did all this doesn't have any boo-boos.
Who cares about the man who saved the day, right?
Check on the rest of the team. See who needs medical help.

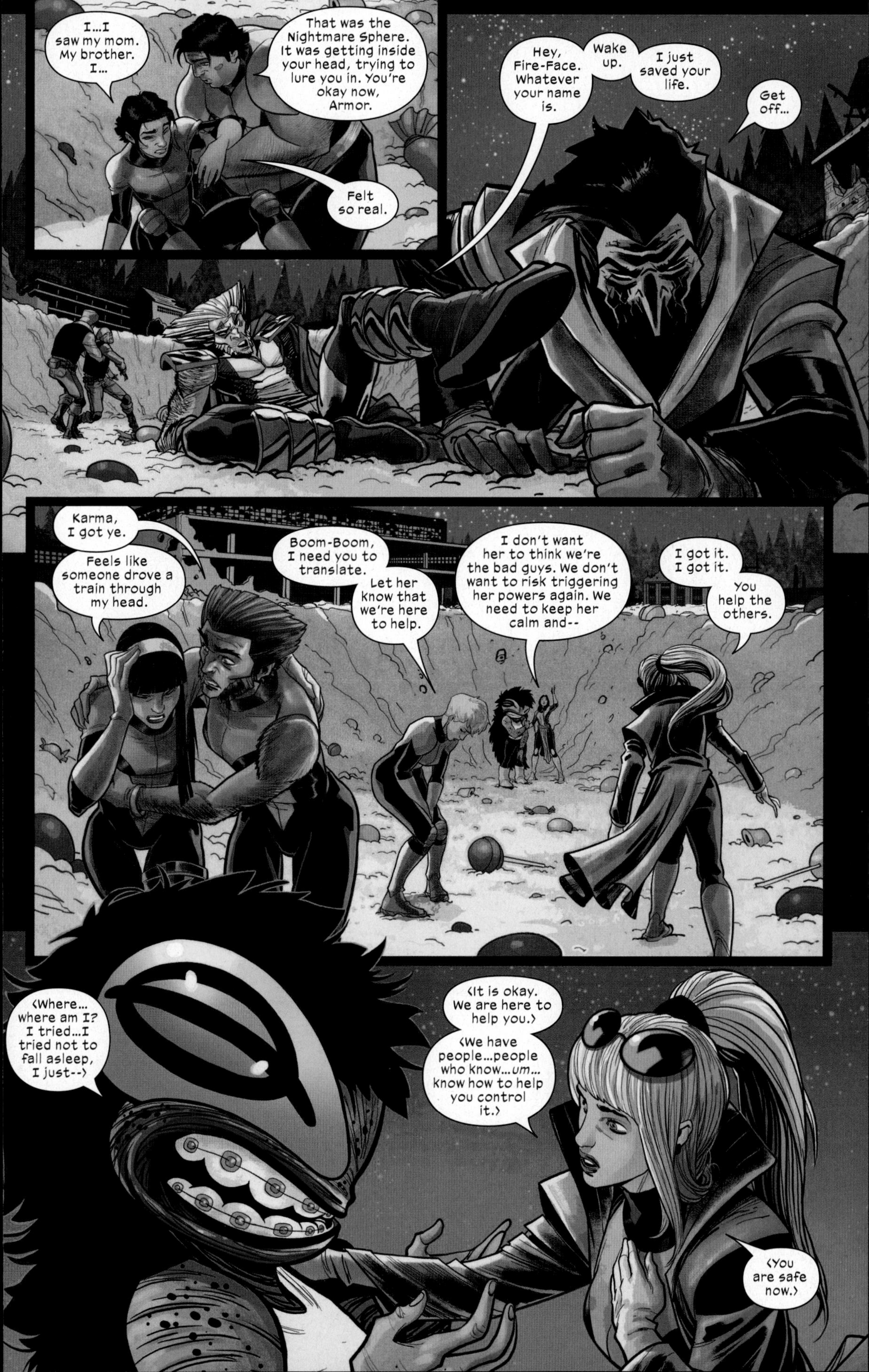
I...I saw my mom. My brother. I...
That was the Nightmare Sphere. It was getting inside your head, trying to lure you in. You're okay now, Armor.
Felt so real.
Hey, Fire-Face. Whatever your name is.
Wake up.
I just saved your life.
Get off...
Karma, I got ye.
Feels like someone drove a train through my head.
Boom-Boom, I need you to translate.
Let her know that we're here to help.
I don't want her to think we're the bad guys. We don't want to risk triggering her powers again. We need to keep her calm and--
I got it. I got it.
You help the others.
‹Where... where am I? I tried...I tried not to fall asleep, I just--›
‹It is okay. We are here to help you.›
‹We have people...people who know...*um*... know how to help you control it.›
‹You are safe now.›

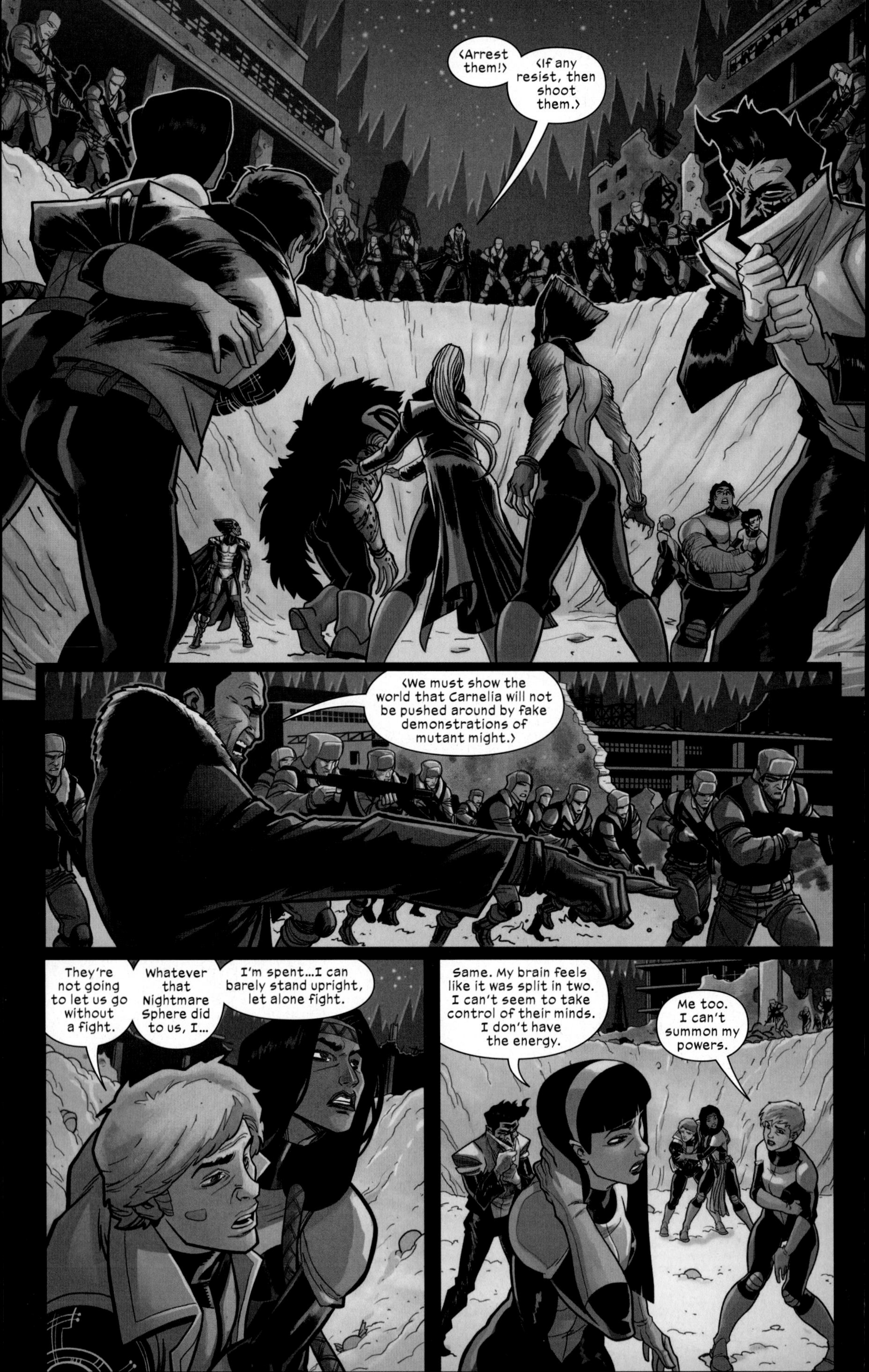
‹Arrest them!›
‹If any resist, then shoot them.›
‹We must show the world that Carnelia will not be pushed around by fake demonstrations of mutant might.›
They're not going to let us go without a fight.
Whatever that Nightmare Sphere did to us, I...
I'm spent...I can barely stand upright, let alone fight.
Same. My brain feels like it was split in two. I can't seem to take control of their minds. I don't have the energy.
Me too. I can't summon my powers.

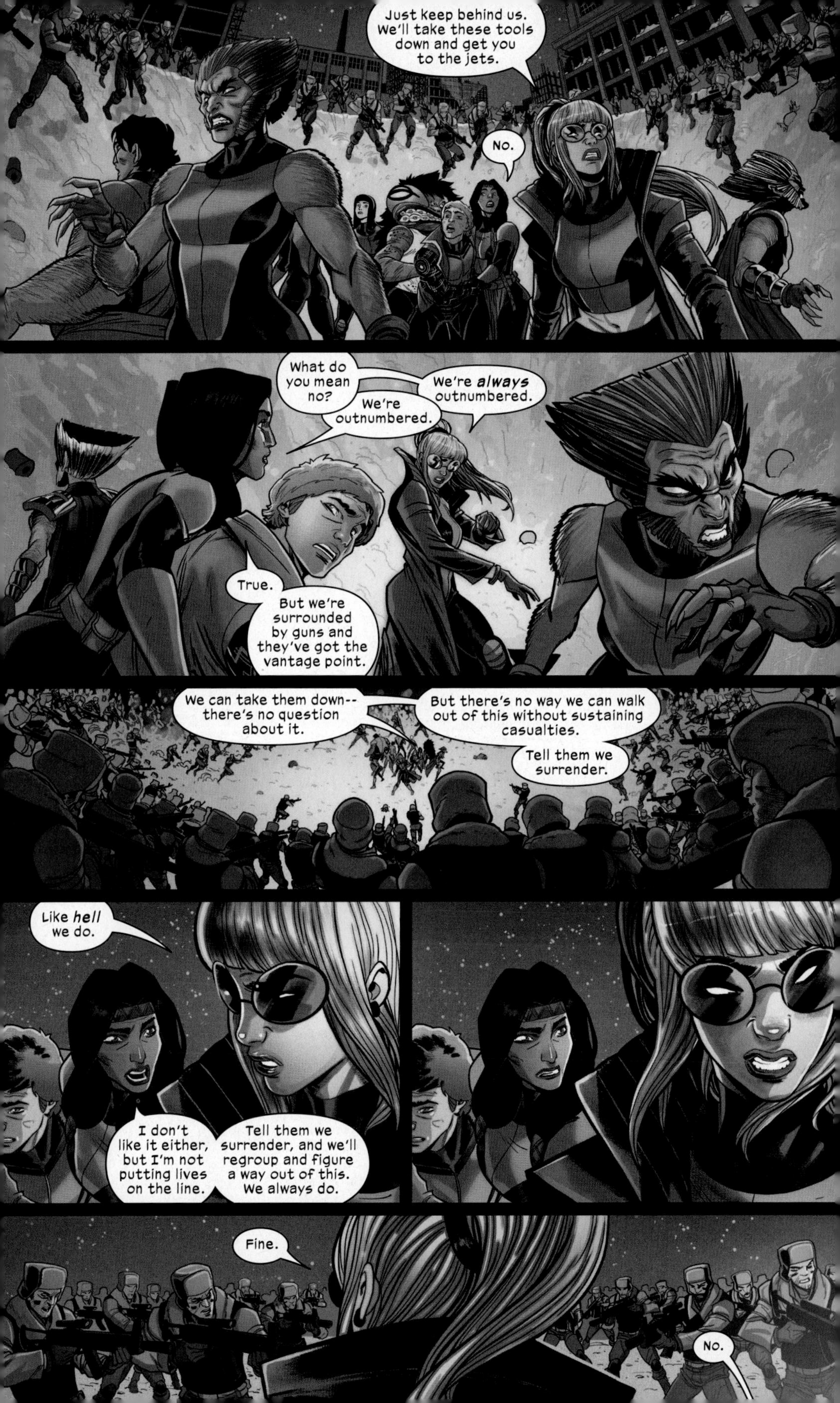

Just keep behind us. We'll take these tools down and get you to the jets.
No.
What do you mean no?
We're outnumbered.
We're *always* outnumbered.
True.
But we're surrounded by guns and they've got the vantage point.
We can take them down-- there's no question about it.
But there's no way we can walk out of this without sustaining casualties.
Tell them we surrender.
Like *hell* we do.
I don't like it either, but I'm not putting lives on the line.
Tell them we surrender, and we'll regroup and figure a way out of this. We always do.
Fine.
No.

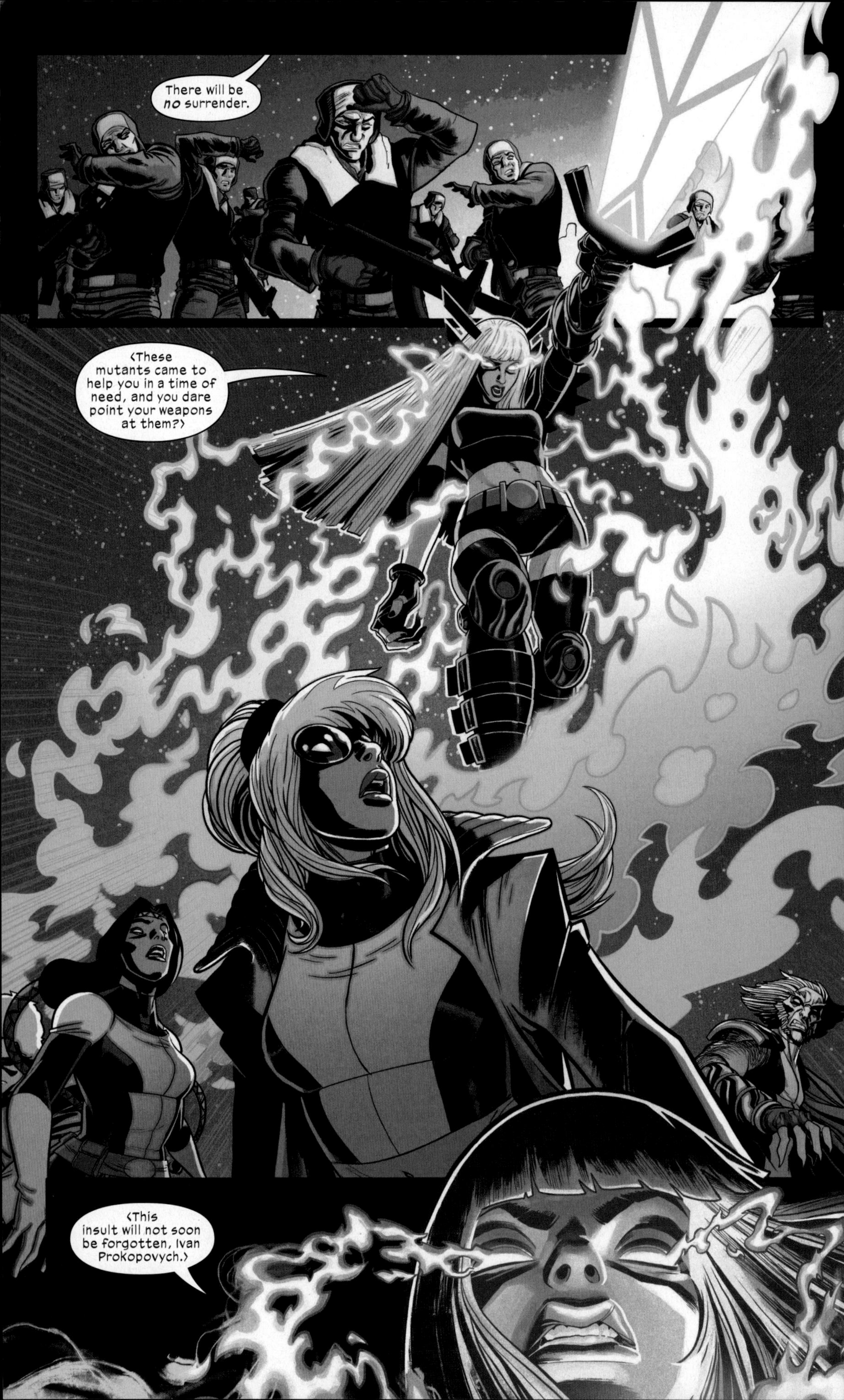
There will be no surrender.
<These mutants came to help you in a time of need, and you dare point your weapons at them?>
<This insult will not soon be forgotten, Ivan Prokopovych.>

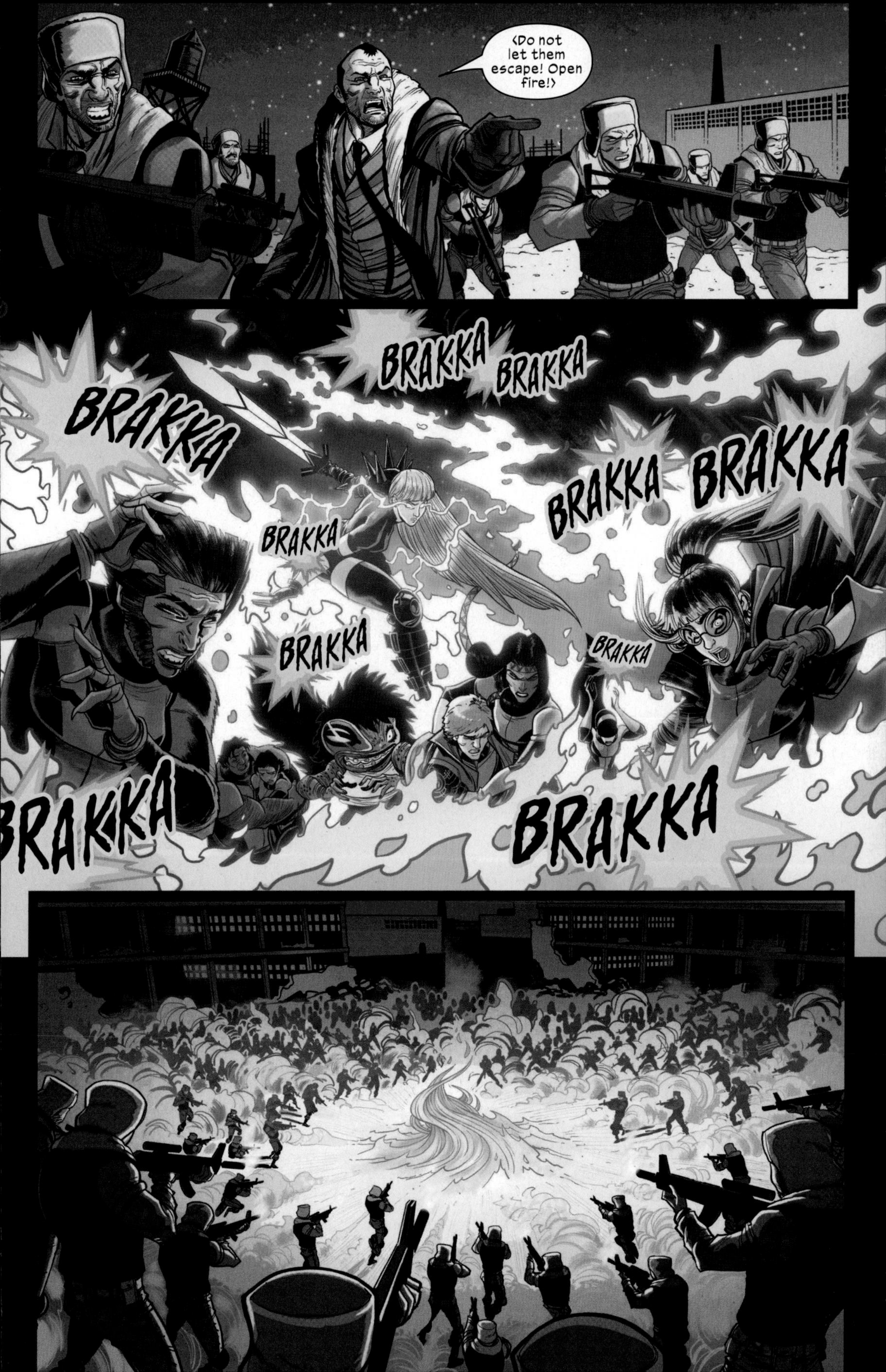
‹Do not let them escape! Open fire!›
BRAKKA
BRAKKA
BRAKKA
BRAKKA
BRAKKA
BRAKKA
BRAKKA
BRAKKA
BRAKKA
BRAKKA

DOX

CARNELIAN CARNAGE

CONTINUES

As first reported by DOX earlier today, a group of mutants have invaded Carnelia to perpetrate their mutant hoax of trying to help.

Through our message boards, we've been able to identify the mutants as: Mirage (A.K.A. Psyche), Karma, Boom-Boom (A.K.A. Boomer, Time Bomb, Meltdown, Firecracker), Wolfsbane, Cypher, Karma, Magma and Chamber.

Ivan Prokopovych, Prime Minister of Carnelia, has issued a warrant for the arrest of the trespassing mutants, but as of yet, they have not complied. No surprise there, given the illegal nature of their activity.

Stay tuned for updates.

COMMENTS:

MR. R1GHT NOW: Why are we puting up with this @#$%$#&%. The presidant needs to shut down Krakoa and put these monsters in jail.

FLYTRAP87: How many names has Boomer had? Why she keep changing it? What she tryin to hide?

DAVE405: Where the hell is Carnelia? Never heard of it. Smells like HOAX.

DNKMEMES9875: Follow me for the dankest memes.

K-ROCK452675: Don't arrest them! Shoot them!

DUBZILLA: This is boring. Who cares abt these nobodys. Where's Wolverine?

TRASKWUZRIGHT: This is desgusting. They say they r hear to help but this proves that they are all liars. They shold have been in jail already. We need a president who will stand up to these thugs.

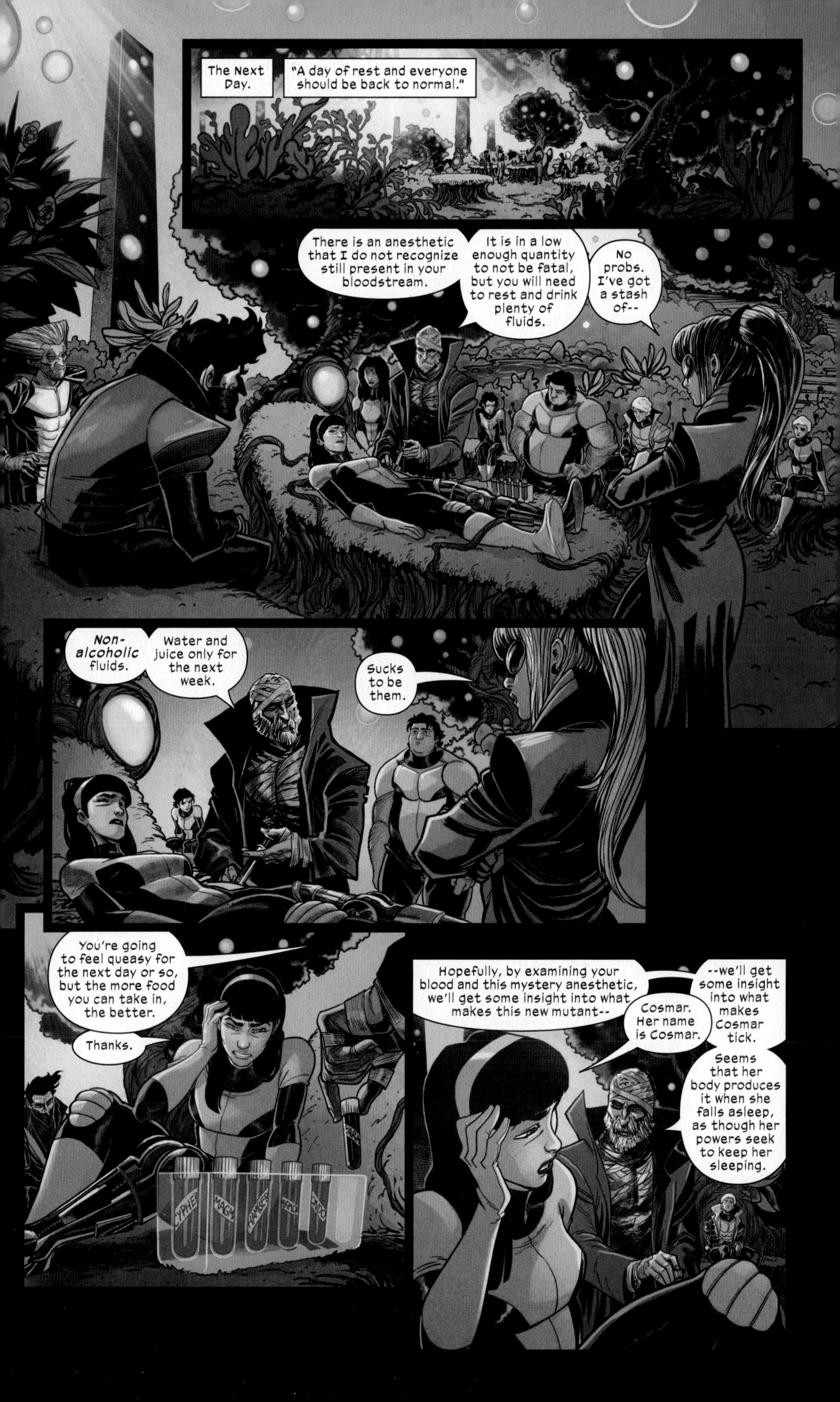
The Next Day.
"A day of rest and everyone should be back to normal."
There is an anesthetic that I do not recognize still present in your bloodstream.
It is in a low enough quantity to not be fatal, but you will need to rest and drink plenty of fluids.
No probs. I've got a stash of--
Non-alcoholic fluids.
Water and juice only for the next week.
Sucks to be them.
You're going to feel queasy for the next day or so, but the more food you can take in, the better.
Thanks.
Hopefully, by examining your blood and this mystery anesthetic, we'll get some insight into what makes this new mutant--
Cosmar. Her name is Cosmar.
--we'll get some insight into what makes Cosmar tick.
Seems that her body produces it when she falls asleep, as though her powers seek to keep her sleeping.
CYPHER
MAGM
HAMBER
DUDO

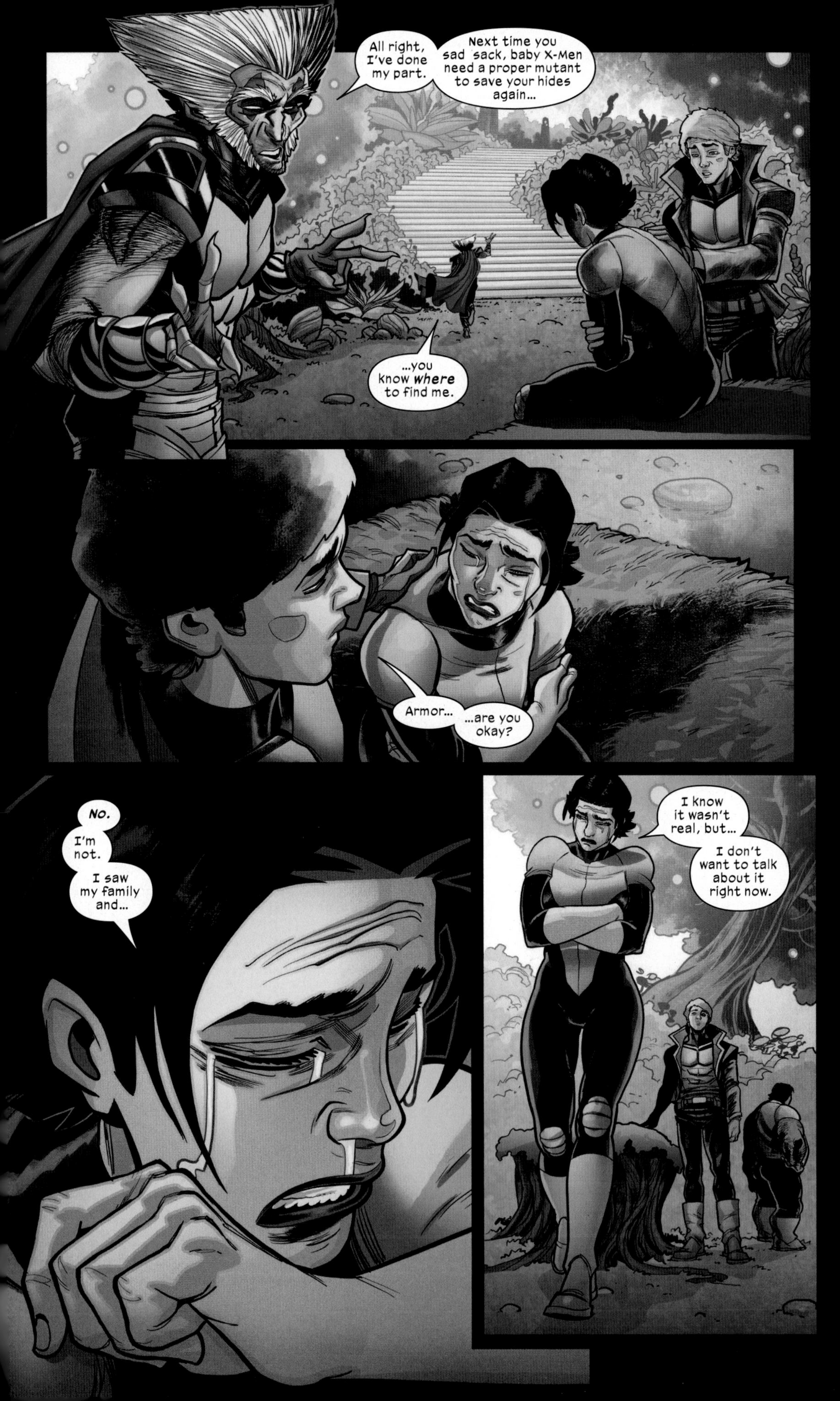

All right, I've done my part.
Next time you sad sack, baby X-Men need a proper mutant to save your hides again...
...you know *where* to find me.
Armor...
...are you okay?
NO.
I'm not.
I saw my family and...
I know it wasn't real, but...
I don't want to talk about it right now.

EXCERPT FROM THE DIARY OF TABITHA SMITH

Okay, so I guess I'm still doing this stupid thing. I swear, if you find this and I've started crimping pages or adding stamps or devoting a page to my vision board...please find me and put me out of my misery. Deal? (Also, if you are reading this and I'm still alive, know that I will find out and I'll come end you).

This welcome wagon for new mutants (actual new mutants, not caps New Mutants, like our team) is not going as well as everyone hoped. So far, we have welcomed a brand-new mutant to Krakoa -- her name is Cosmar and she's basically like Freddy Krueger as a satellite. Her dreams kind of eat the world around her and drag people in. So, yeah...I'm sure that'll come in useful in a pinch, right? Everyone knows that every good team has a leader, a powerhouse, a flyer, a psychic and a nightmare machine, right?

Where was I?

Right, so we brought in Cosmar. We brought in all those kids from Nova Roma (too many kids, no way I can remember their names). We brought in Beak, Angel and their kids. But...we lost Beak's parents. All those cartel members died (even if they had it coming). The security guards in Carnelia. Our average is not great. We need to figure a way to be better about it. Stealthier. I dunno.

Anyhow, this whole thing has got me bummed out. Thinking about going back down to Brazil, seeing if there are more of those mutant-hunting monsters that need blowing up. Boom-Boom needs to blow off a little steam.

Later,
Boom-Boom

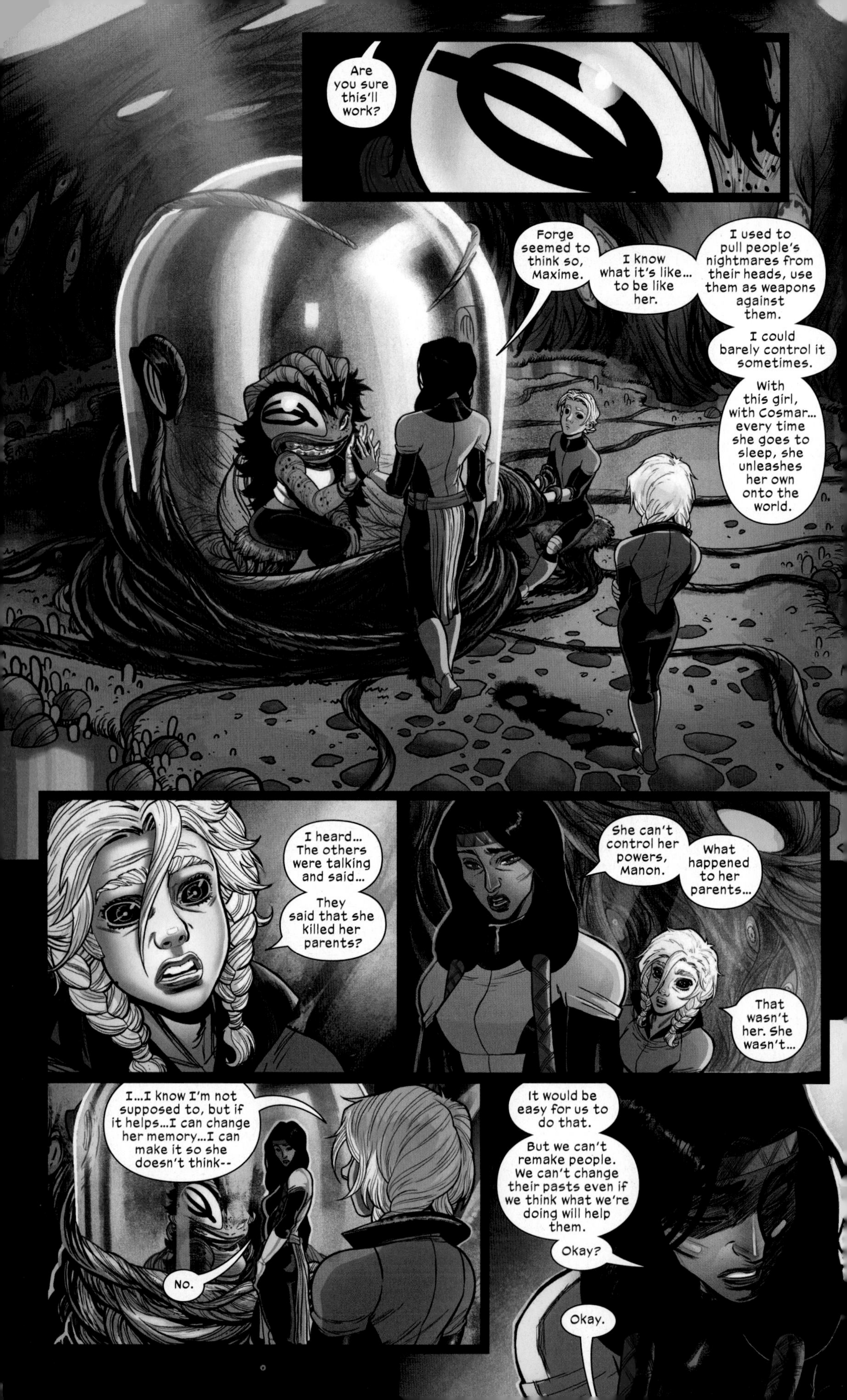
Are you sure this'll work?
Forge seemed to think so, Maxime.
I know what it's like... to be like her.
I used to pull people's nightmares from their heads, use them as weapons against them.
I could barely control it sometimes.
With this girl, with Cosmar... every time she goes to sleep, she unleashes her own onto the world.
I heard... The others were talking and said...
They said that she killed her parents?
She can't control her powers, Manon.
What happened to her parents...
That wasn't her. She wasn't...
I...I know I'm not supposed to, but if it helps...I can change her memory...I can make it so she doesn't think--
No.
It would be easy for us to do that.
But we can't remake people. We can't change their pasts even if we think what we're doing will help them.
Okay?
Okay.

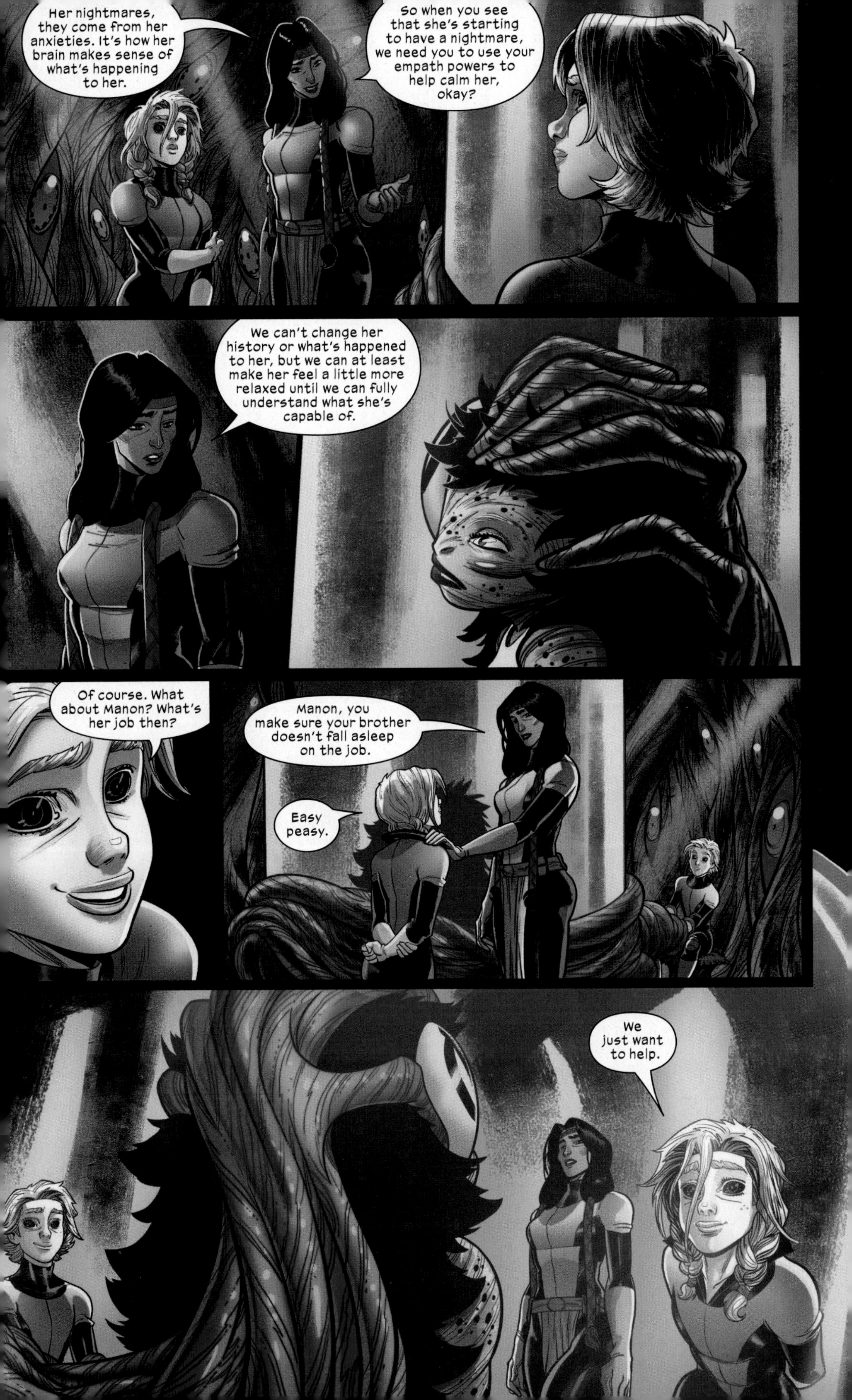

Her nightmares, they come from her anxieties. It's how her brain makes sense of what's happening to her.
So when you see that she's starting to have a nightmare, we need you to use your empath powers to help calm her, okay?
We can't change her history or what's happened to her, but we can at least make her feel a little more relaxed until we can fully understand what she's capable of.
Of course. What about Manon? What's her job then?
Manon, you make sure your brother doesn't fall asleep on the job.
Easy peasy.
We just want to help.

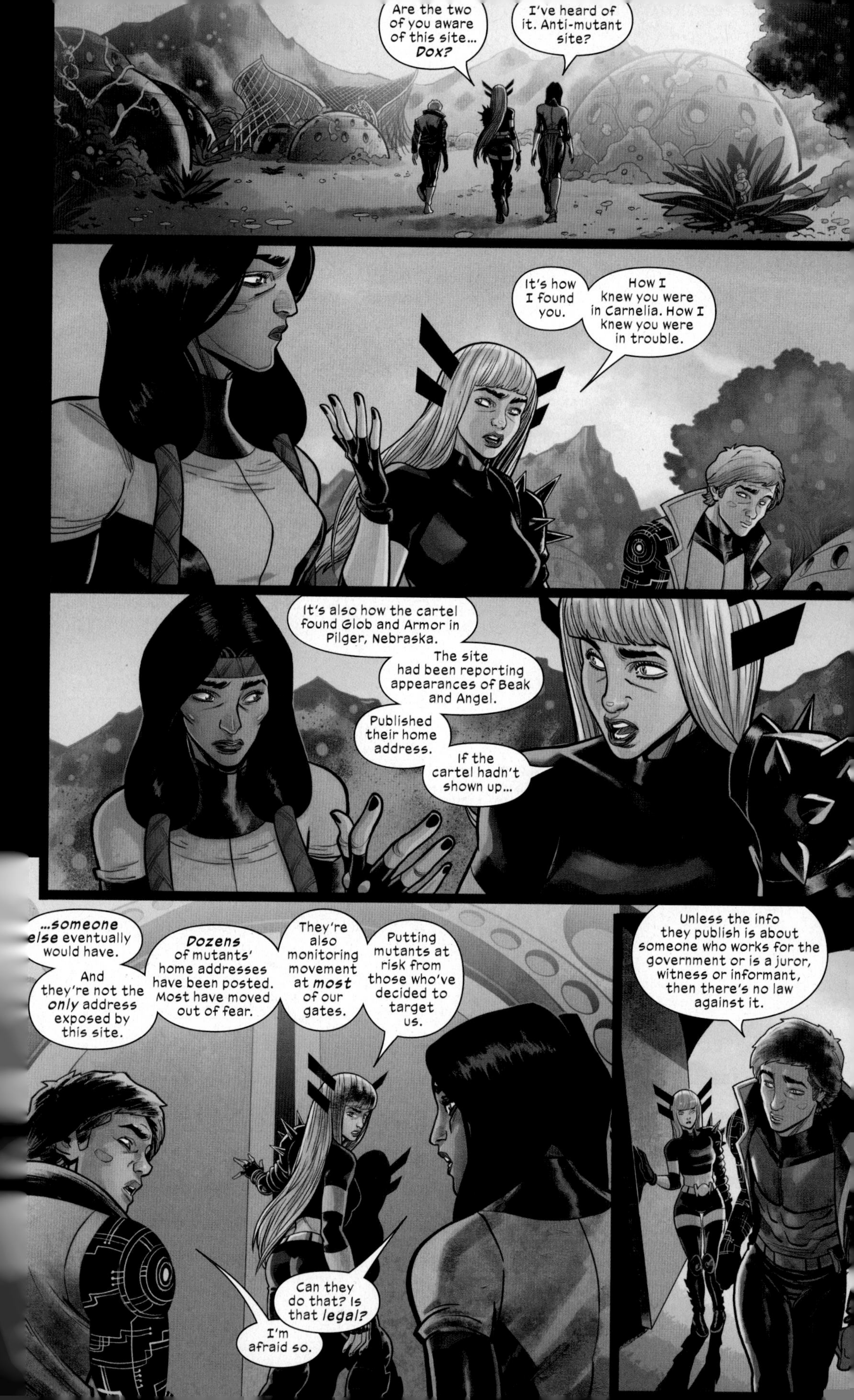
Are the two of you aware of this site... Dox?
I've heard of it. Anti-mutant site?
It's how I found you.
How I knew you were in Carnelia. How I knew you were in trouble.
It's also how the cartel found Glob and Armor in Pilger, Nebraska.
The site had been reporting appearances of Beak and Angel.
Published their home address.
If the cartel hadn't shown up...
...someone else eventually would have.
And they're not the only address exposed by this site.
Dozens of mutants' home addresses have been posted. Most have moved out of fear.
They're also monitoring movement at most of our gates.
Putting mutants at risk from those who've decided to target us.
Can they do that? Is that legal?
I'm afraid so.
Unless the info they publish is about someone who works for the government or is a juror, witness or informant, then there's no law against it.

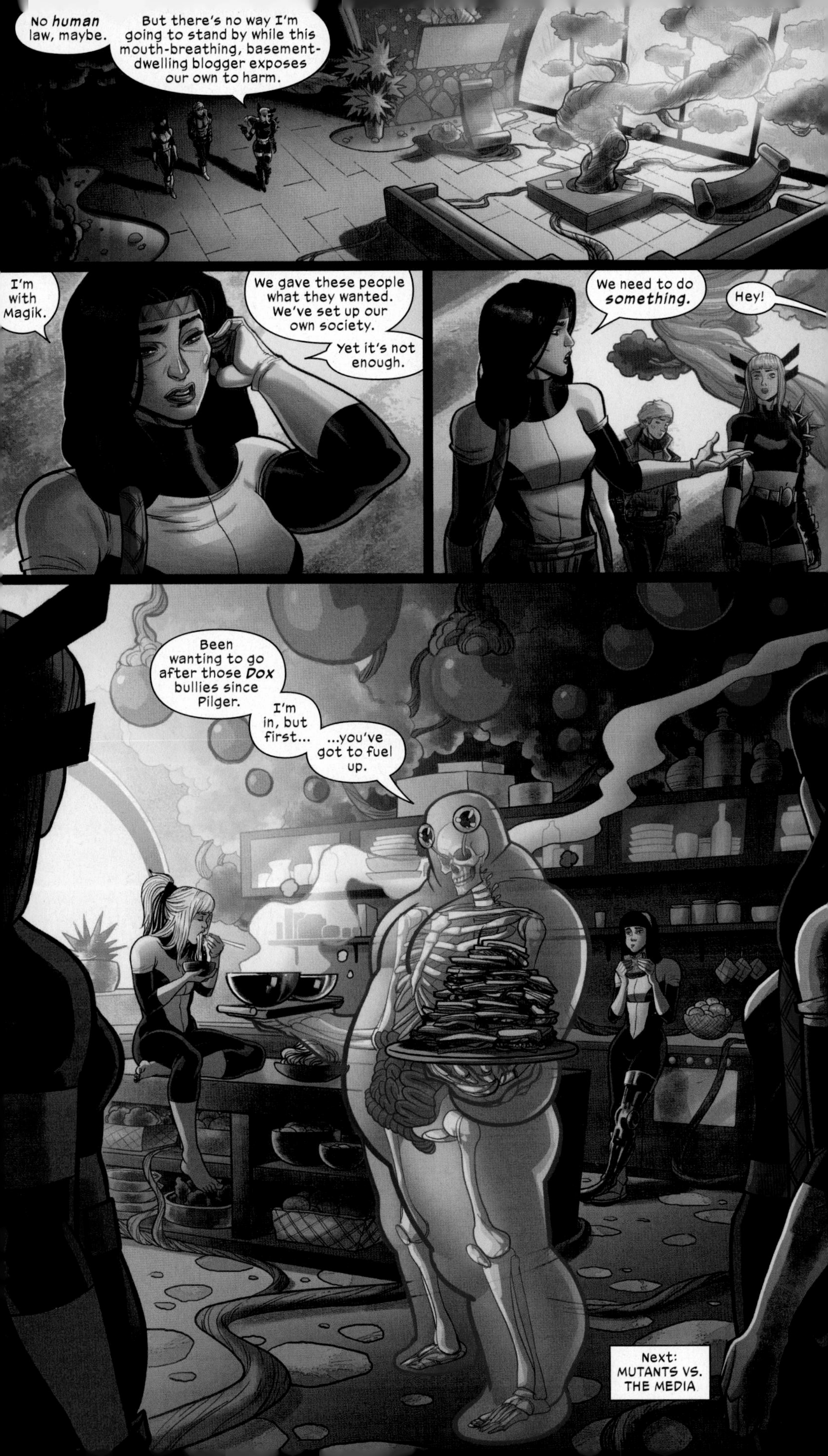

No *human* law, maybe.
But there's no way I'm going to stand by while this mouth-breathing, basement-dwelling blogger exposes our own to harm.
I'm with Magik.
We gave these people what they wanted. We've set up our own society.
Yet it's not enough.
We need to do *something.*
Hey!
Been wanting to go after those *Dox* bullies since Pilger.
I'm in, but first...
...you've got to fuel up.
Next: MUTANTS VS. THE MEDIA

[dawn_of_x]

[kra_]
[koa_]

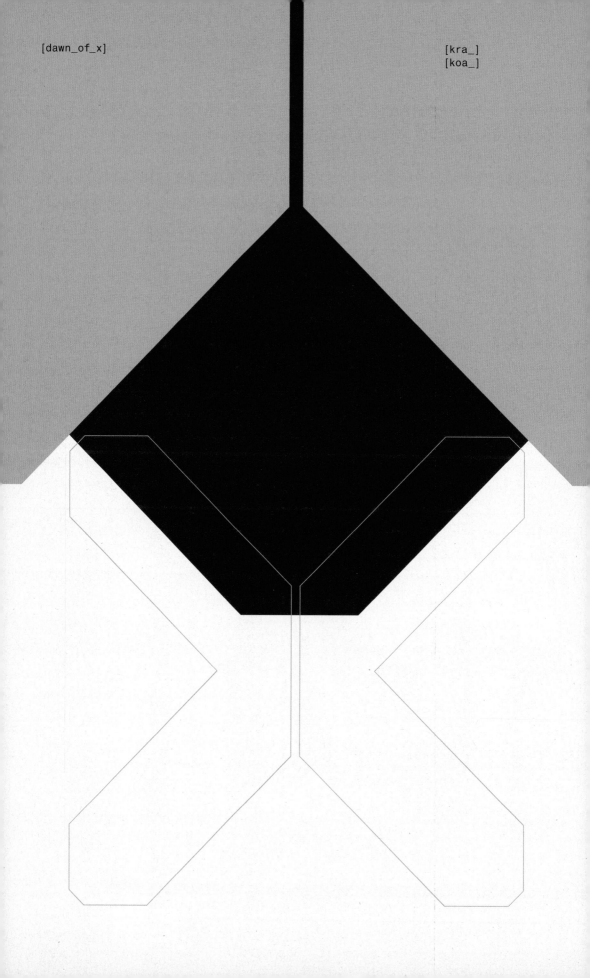

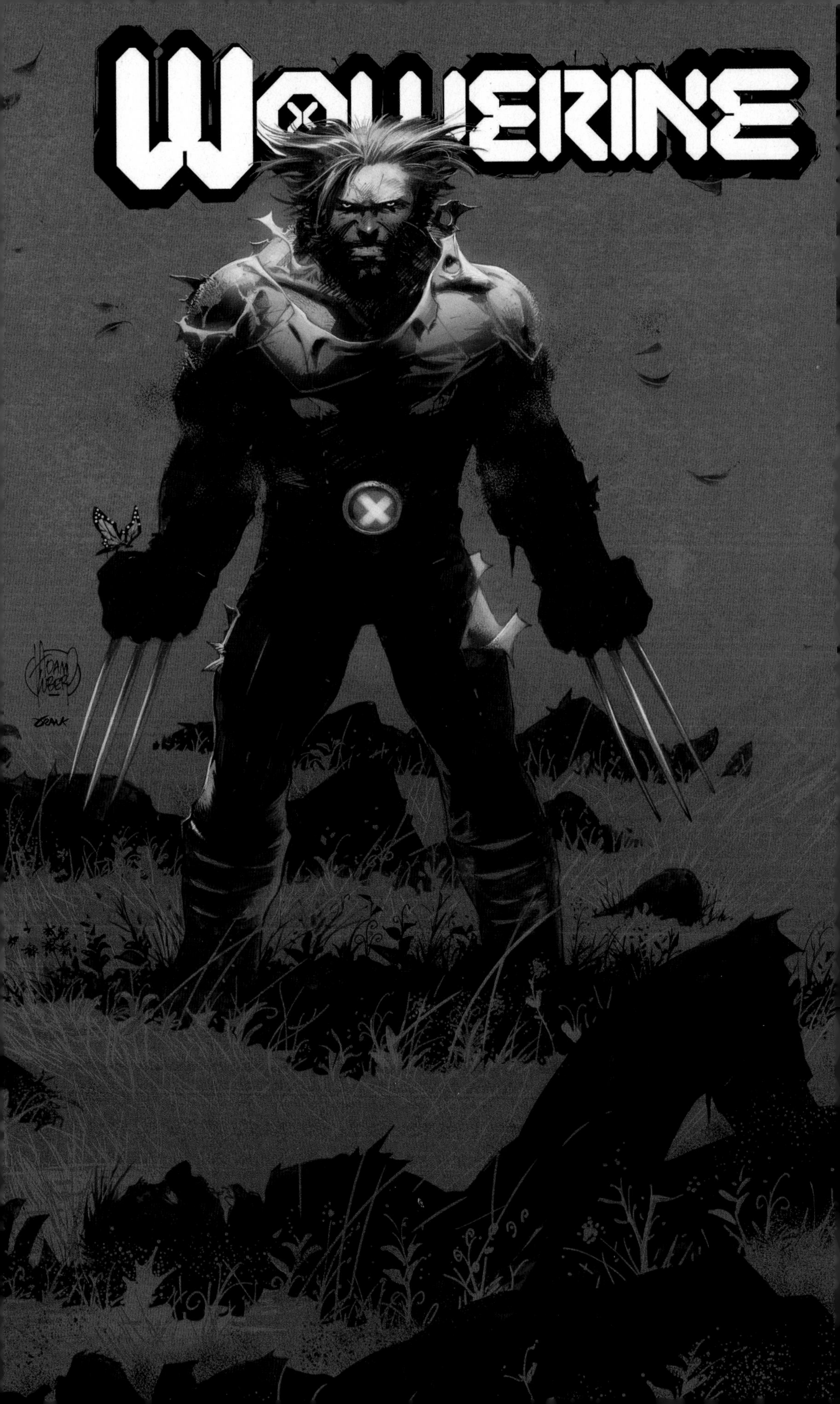
WOLVERINE

[00_best_]
[00_there]

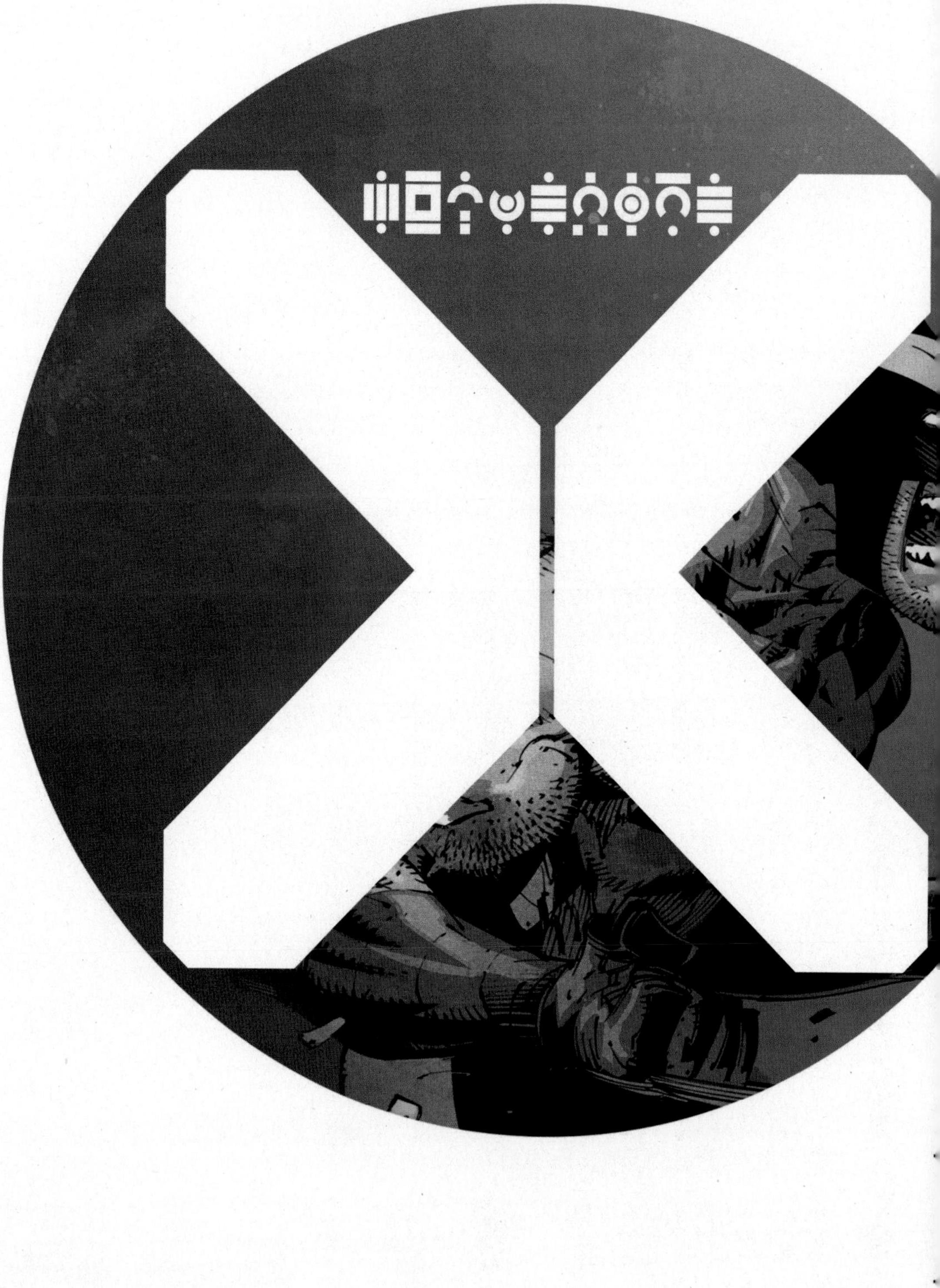

[00_best_]
[00_there]

BENJAMIN PERCY..............................[WRITER]
VIKTOR BOGDANOVIC...........................[ARTIST]
MATTHEW WILSON........................[COLOR ARTIST]
VC's CORY PETIT.........................[LETTERER]
TOM MULLER..................................[DESIGN]

WOLVERINE

[ISSUE ONE]....................CATACOMBS

[00_best_]
[00_there]

[00_00...0]
[00_00...1]

[00_is____]
[00_______]

[00_bub___]

[00______X]

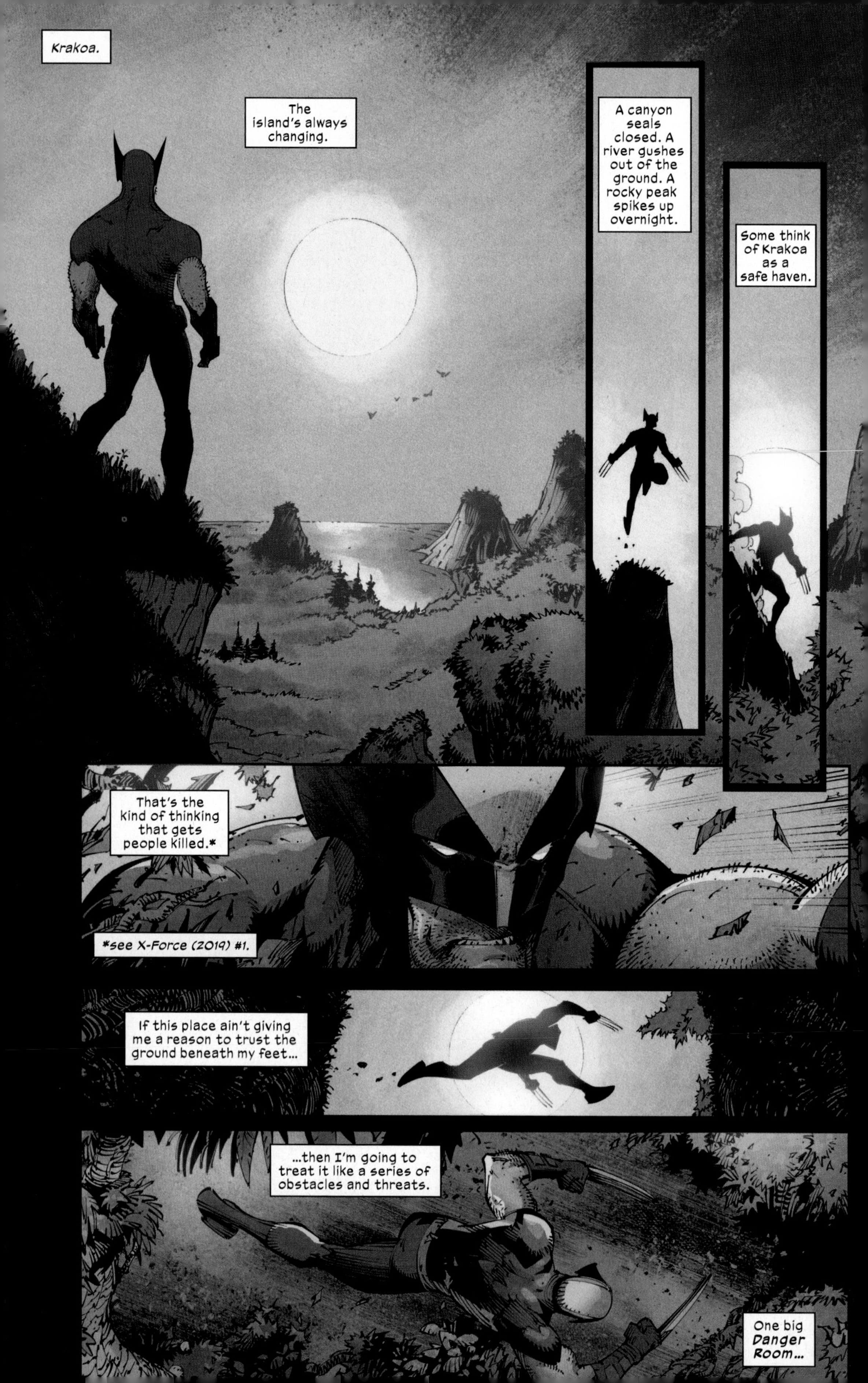
Krakoa.
The island's always changing.
A canyon seals closed. A river gushes out of the ground. A rocky peak spikes up overnight.
Some think of Krakoa as a safe haven.
That's the kind of thinking that gets people killed.*
*see X-Force (2019) #1.
If this place ain't giving me a reason to trust the ground beneath my feet...
...then I'm going to treat it like a series of obstacles and threats.
One big Danger Room...

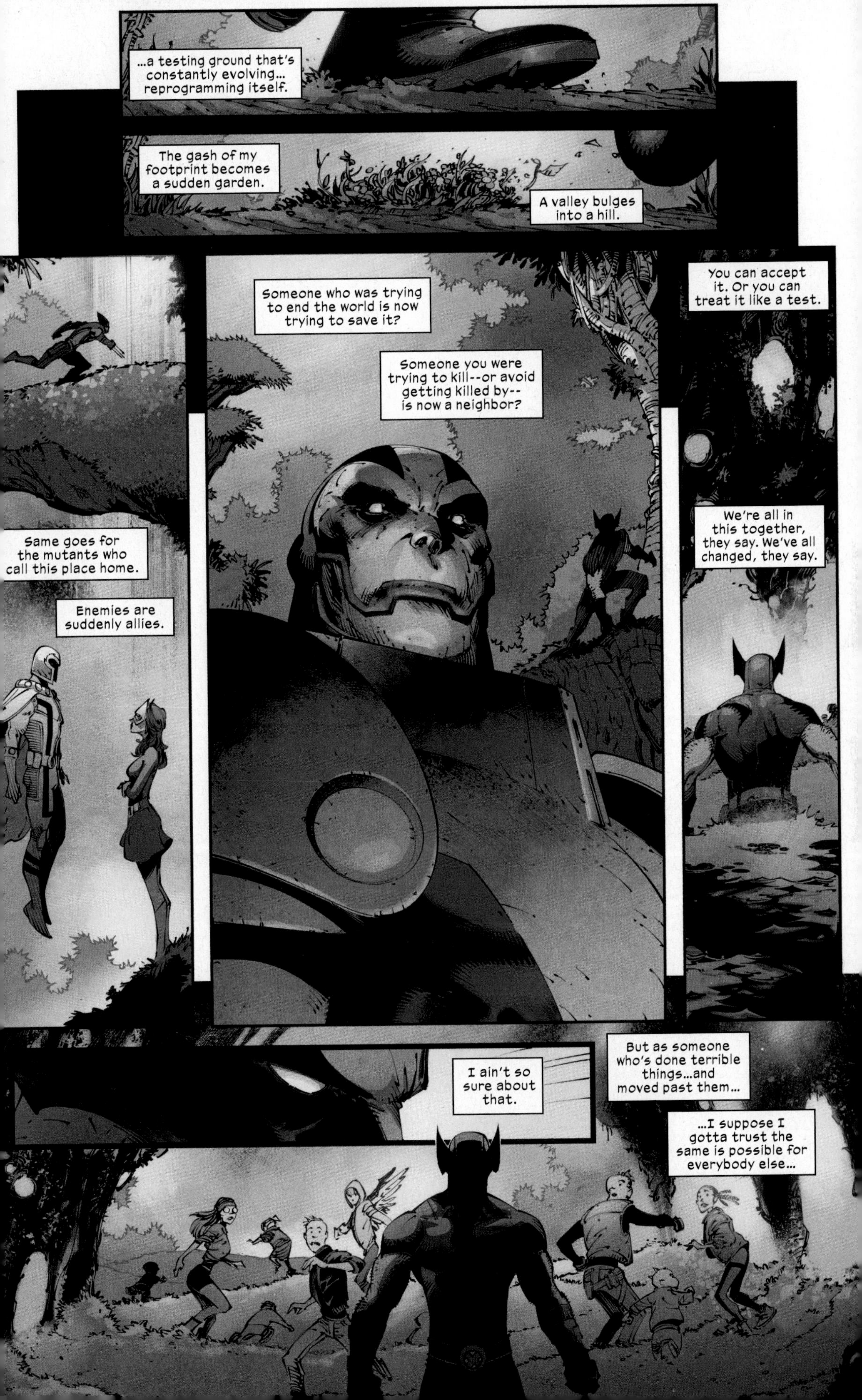
...a testing ground that's constantly evolving... reprogramming itself.
The gash of my footprint becomes a sudden garden.
A valley bulges into a hill.
Same goes for the mutants who call this place home.
Enemies are suddenly allies.
Someone who was trying to end the world is now trying to save it?
Someone you were trying to kill--or avoid getting killed by--is now a neighbor?
You can accept it. Or you can treat it like a test.
We're all in this together, they say. We've all changed, they say.
I ain't so sure about that.
But as someone who's done terrible things...and moved past them...
...I suppose I gotta trust the same is possible for everybody else...

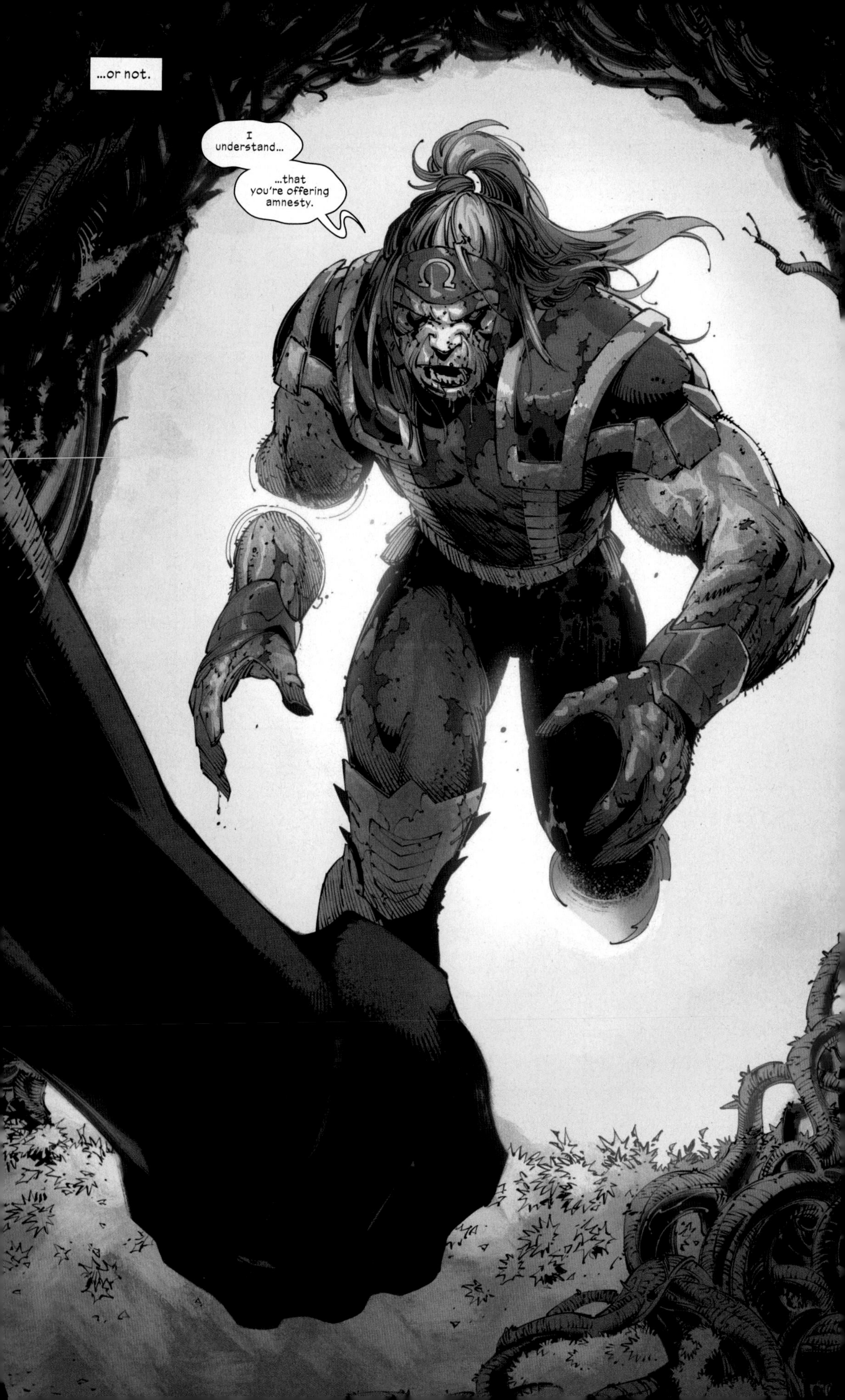
...or not.
I understand...
...that you're offering amnesty.

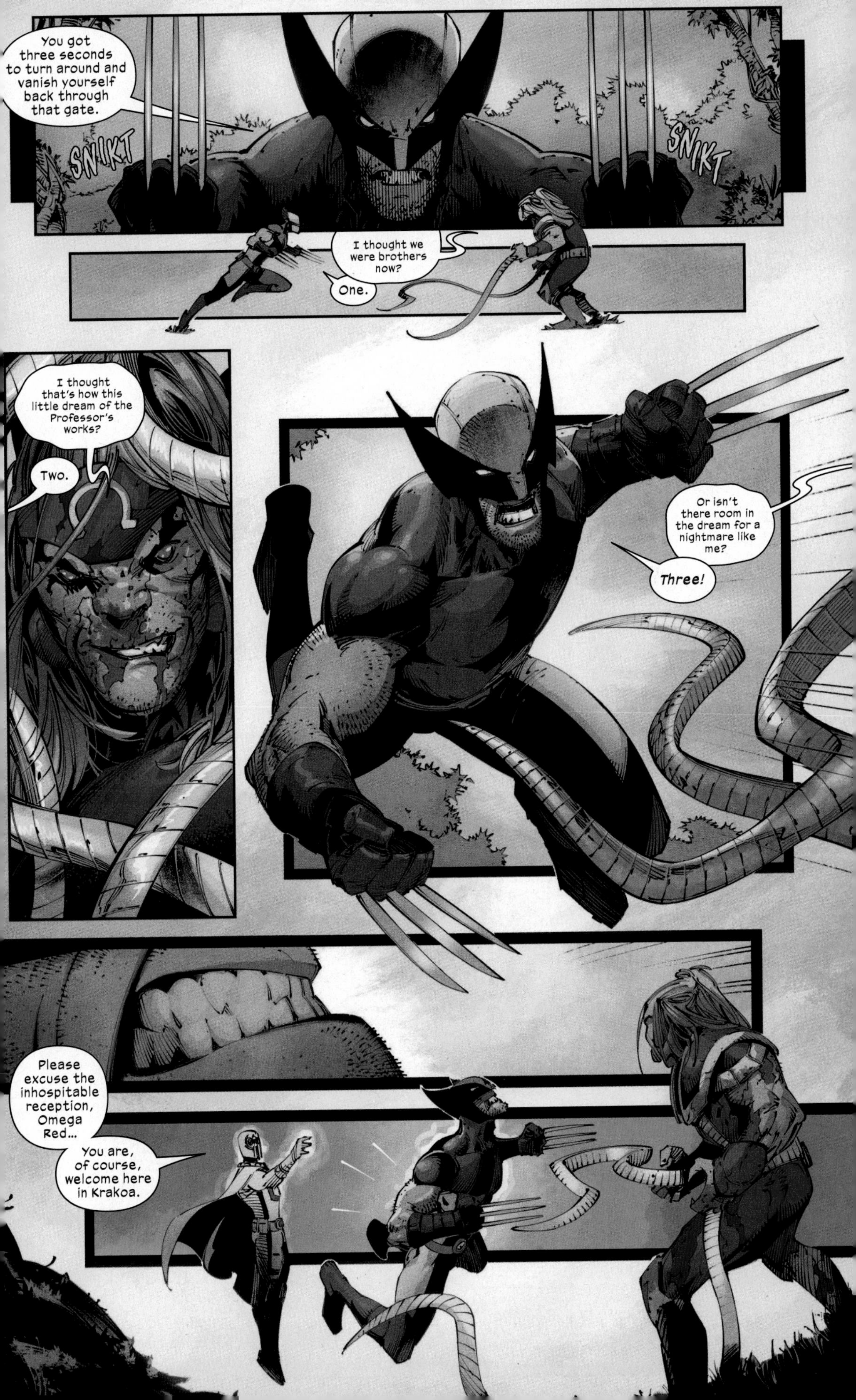
You got three seconds to turn around and vanish yourself back through that gate.
SNIKT
SNIKT
I thought we were brothers now?
One.
I thought that's how this little dream of the Professor's works?
Two.
Or isn't there room in the dream for a nightmare like me?
Three!
Please excuse the inhospitable reception, Omega Red...
You are, of course, welcome here in Krakoa.

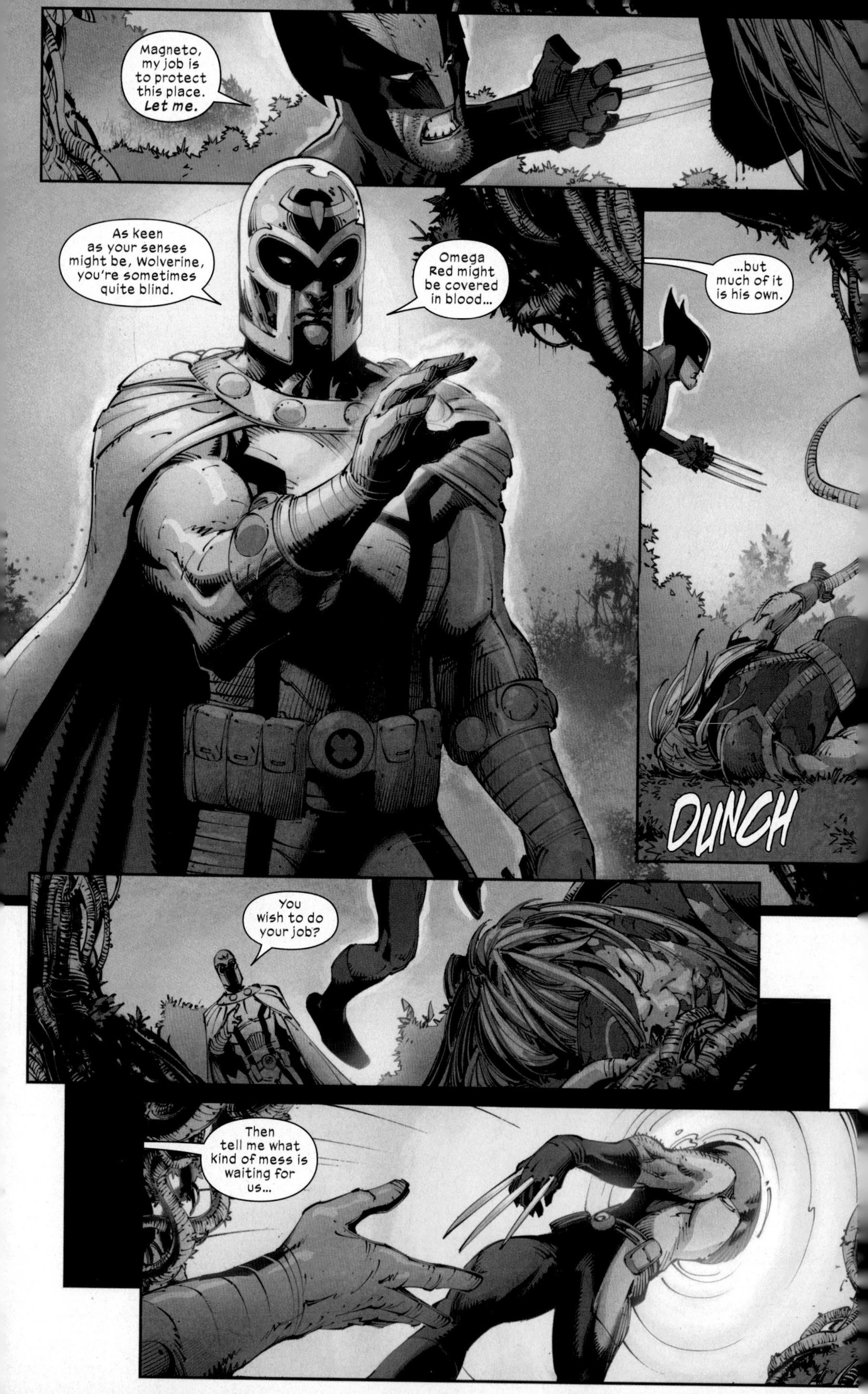
Magneto, my job is to protect this place. **Let me.**
As keen as your senses might be, Wolverine, you're sometimes quite blind.
Omega Red might be covered in blood...
...but much of it is his own.
DUNCH
You wish to do your job?
Then tell me what kind of mess is waiting for us...

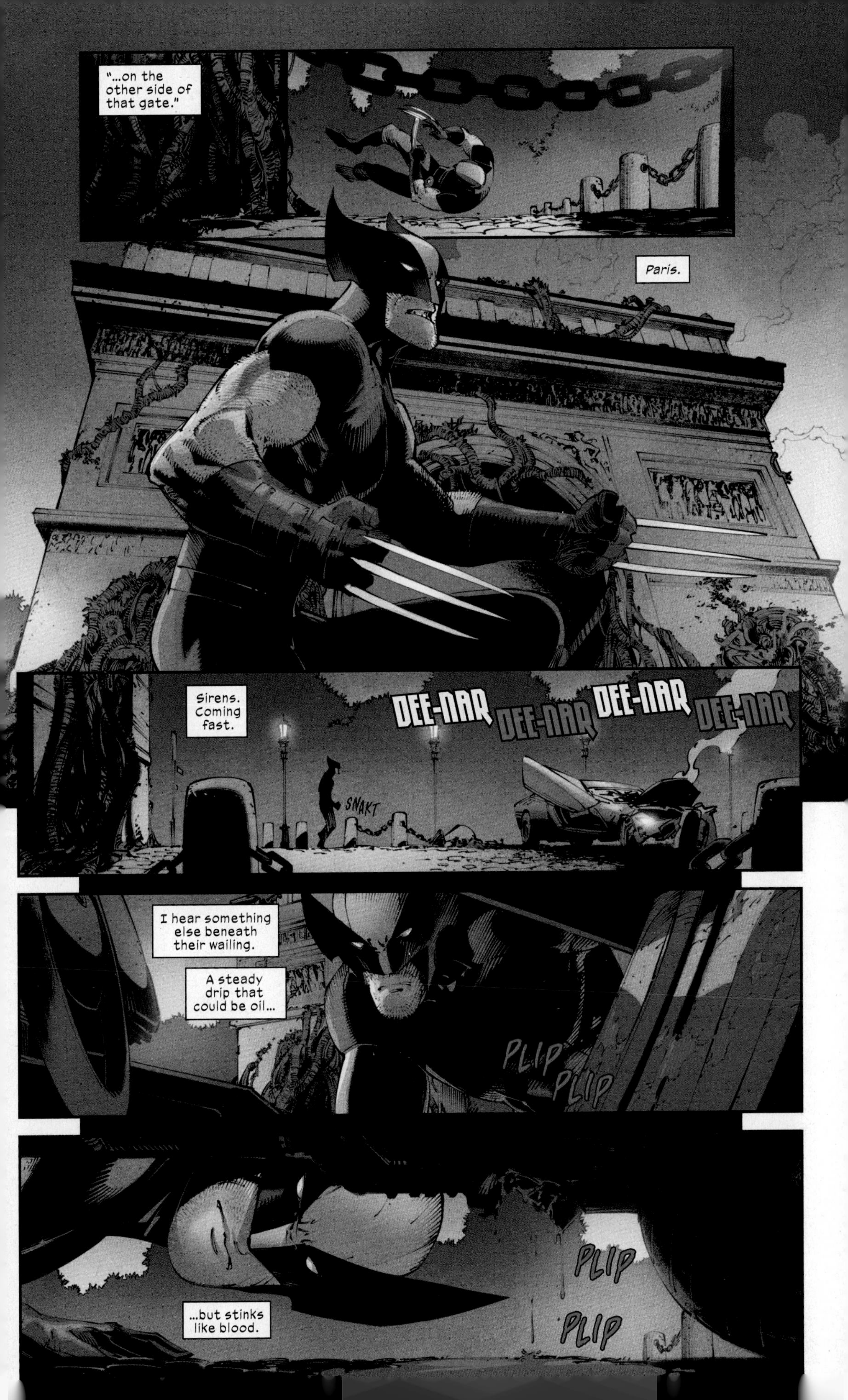
"...on the other side of that gate."
Paris.
Sirens. Coming fast.
DEE-NAR DEE-NAR DEE-NAR DEE-NAR
SNAKT
I hear something else beneath their wailing.
A steady drip that could be oil...
PLIP PLIP
PLIP
...but stinks like blood.
PLIP

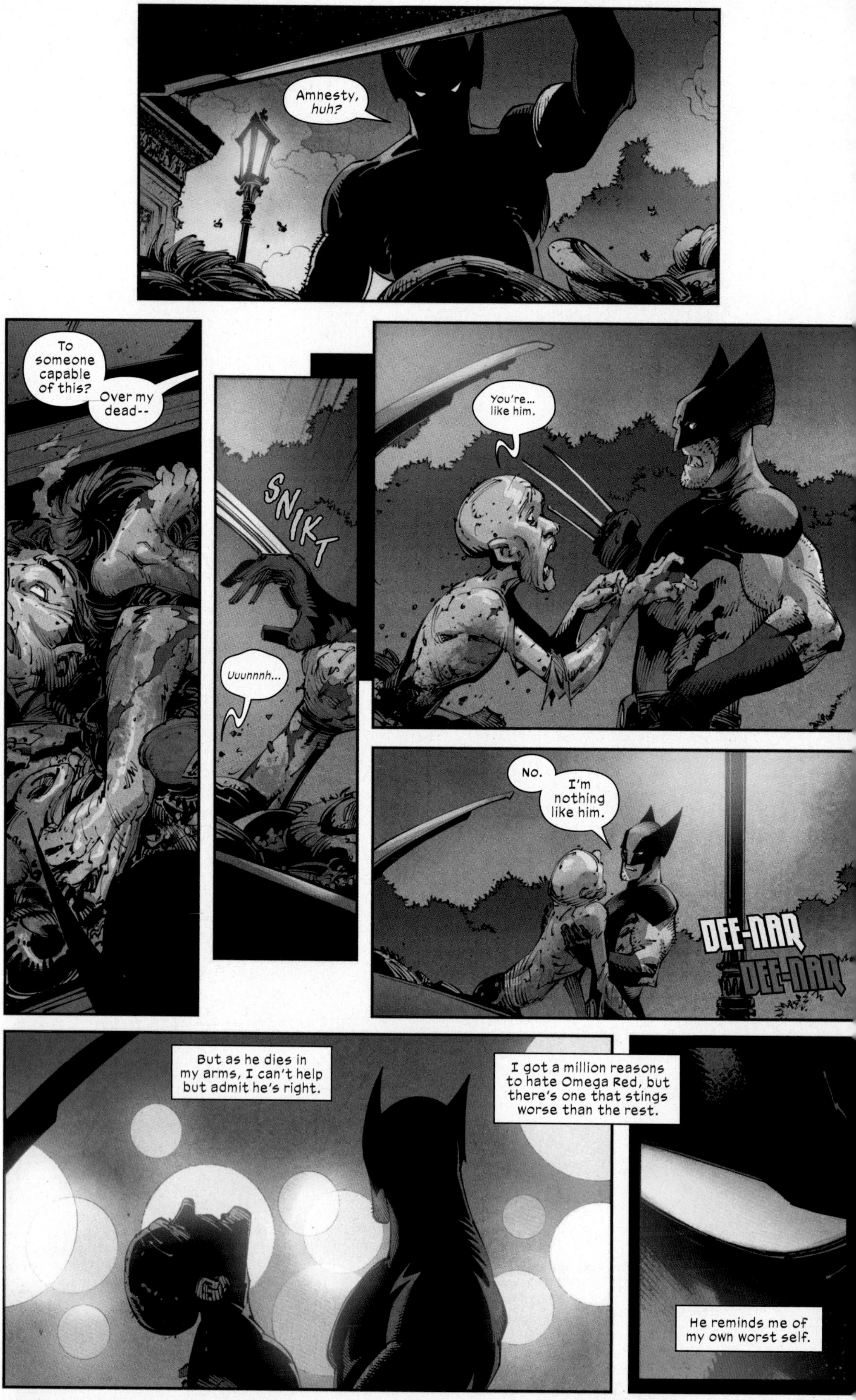

Amnesty, *huh?*
To someone capable of this?
Over my dead--
SNIKT
Uuunnnh...
You're... like him.
No.
I'm nothing like him.
DEE-NAR
DEE-NAR
But as he dies in my arms, I can't help but admit he's right.
I got a million reasons to hate Omega Red, but there's one that stings worse than the rest.
He reminds me of my own worst self.

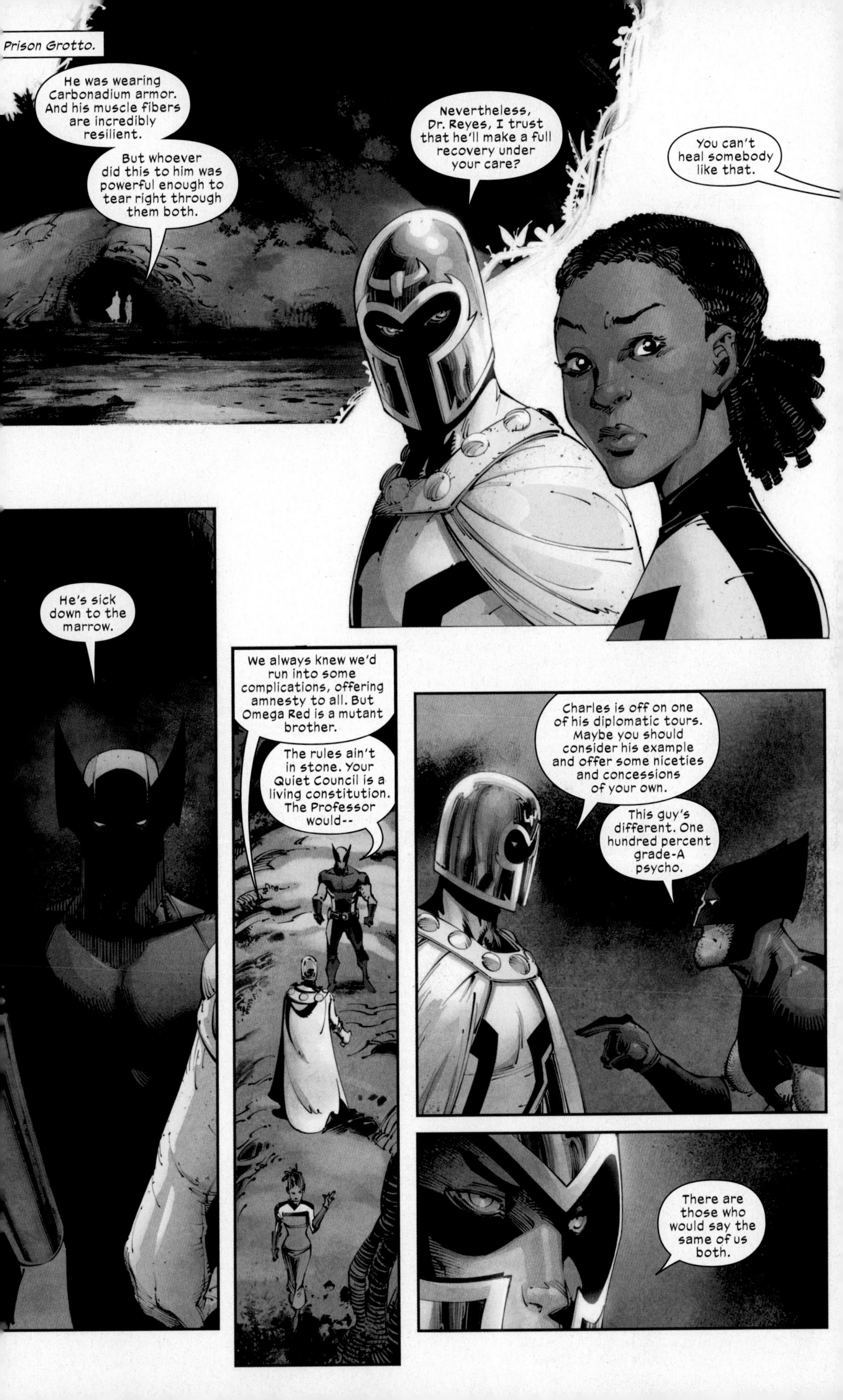

Prison Grotto.
He was wearing Carbonadium armor. And his muscle fibers are incredibly resilient.
But whoever did this to him was powerful enough to tear right through them both.
Nevertheless, Dr. Reyes, I trust that he'll make a full recovery under your care?
You can't heal somebody like that.
He's sick down to the marrow.
We always knew we'd run into some complications, offering amnesty to all. But Omega Red is a mutant brother.
The rules ain't in stone. Your Quiet Council is a living constitution. The Professor would--
Charles is off on one of his diplomatic tours. Maybe you should consider his example and offer some niceties and concessions of your own.
This guy's different. One hundred percent grade-A psycho.
There are those who would say the same of us both.

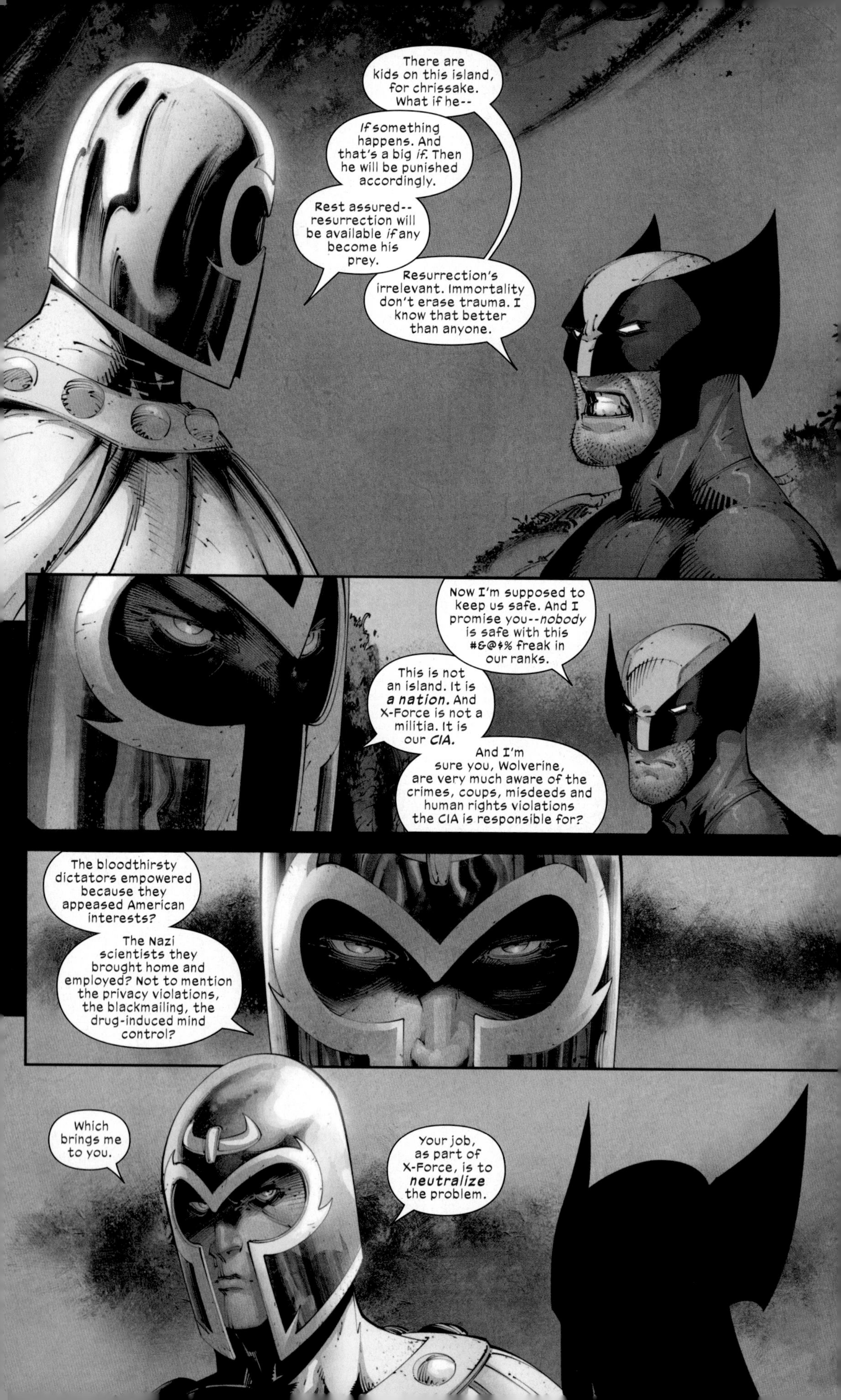

There are kids on this island, for chrissake. What if he--
If something happens. And that's a big *if*. Then he will be punished accordingly.
Rest assured-- resurrection will be available *if* any become his prey.
Resurrection's irrelevant. Immortality don't erase trauma. I know that better than anyone.
Now I'm supposed to keep us safe. And I promise you--*nobody* is safe with this #&@$% freak in our ranks.
This is not an island. It is ***a nation.*** And X-Force is not a militia. It is our ***CIA.***
And I'm sure you, Wolverine, are very much aware of the crimes, coups, misdeeds and human rights violations the CIA is responsible for?
The bloodthirsty dictators empowered because they appeased American interests?
The Nazi scientists they brought home and employed? Not to mention the privacy violations, the blackmailing, the drug-induced mind control?
Which brings me to you.
Your job, as part of X-Force, is to ***neutralize*** the problem.

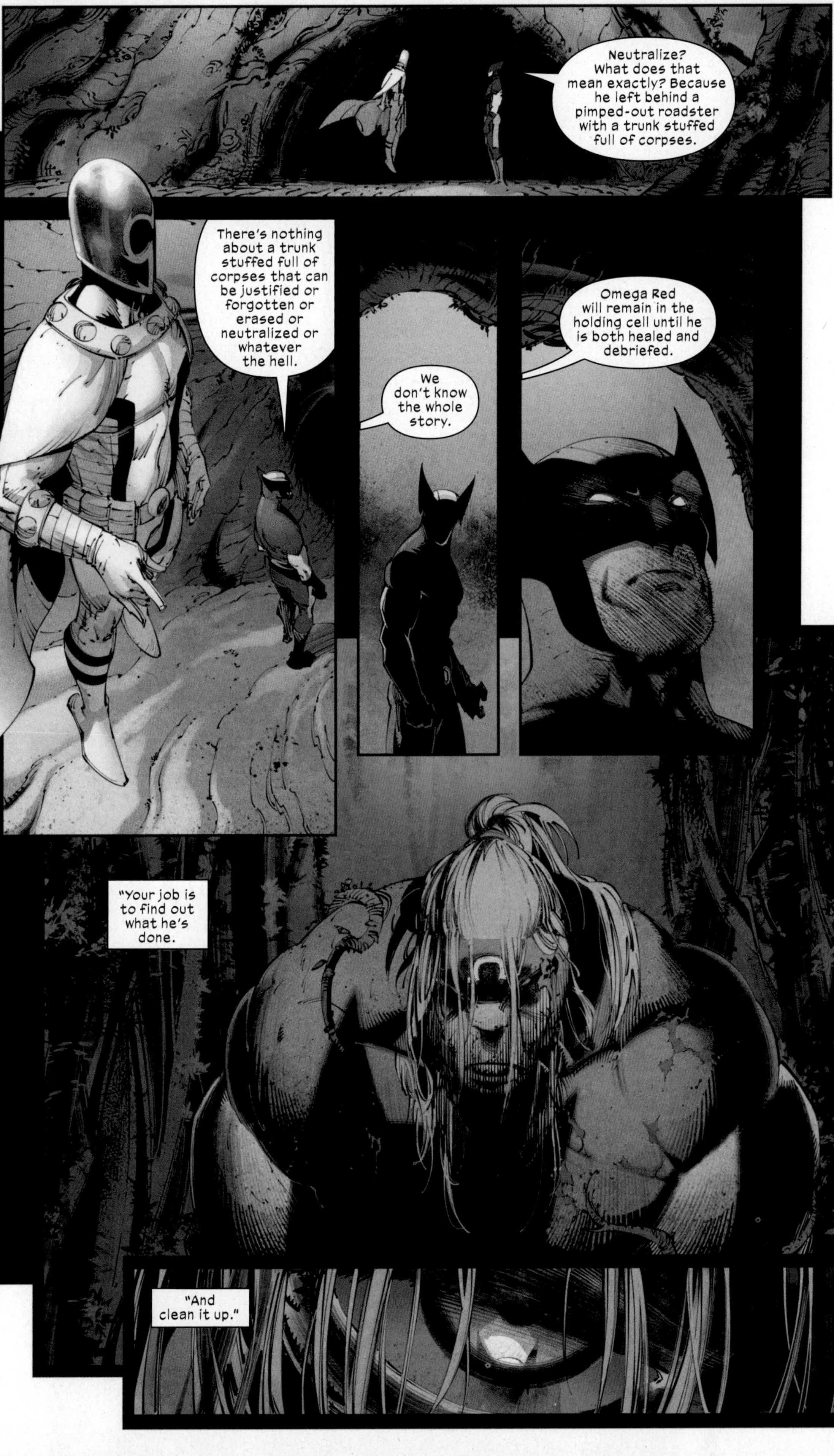

Neutralize? What does that mean exactly? Because he left behind a pimped-out roadster with a trunk stuffed full of corpses.
There's nothing about a trunk stuffed full of corpses that can be justified or forgotten or erased or neutralized or whatever the hell.
We don't know the whole story.
Omega Red will remain in the holding cell until he is both healed and debriefed.
"Your job is to find out what he's done.
"And clean it up."

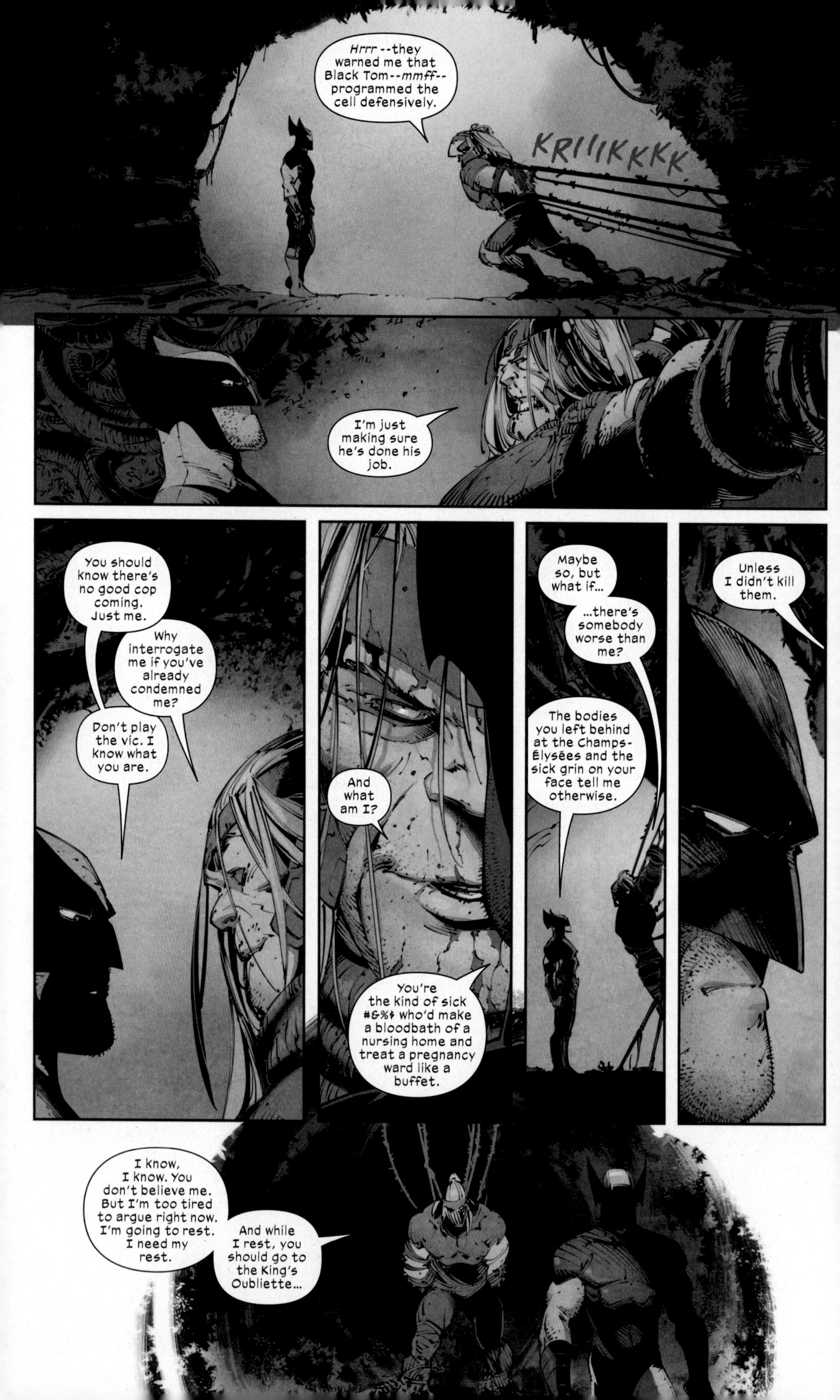
Hrrr --they warned me that Black Tom--mmff-- programmed the cell defensively.
KRIIIKKKK
I'm just making sure he's done his job.
You should know there's no good cop coming. Just me.
Why interrogate me if you've already condemned me?
Don't play the vic. I know what you are.
And what am I?
You're the kind of sick #&%$ who'd make a bloodbath of a nursing home and treat a pregnancy ward like a buffet.
Maybe so, but what if...
...there's somebody worse than me?
The bodies you left behind at the Champs-Élysées and the sick grin on your face tell me otherwise.
Unless I didn't kill them.
I know, I know. You don't believe me. But I'm too tired to argue right now. I'm going to rest. I need my rest.
And while I rest, you should go to the King's Oubliette...

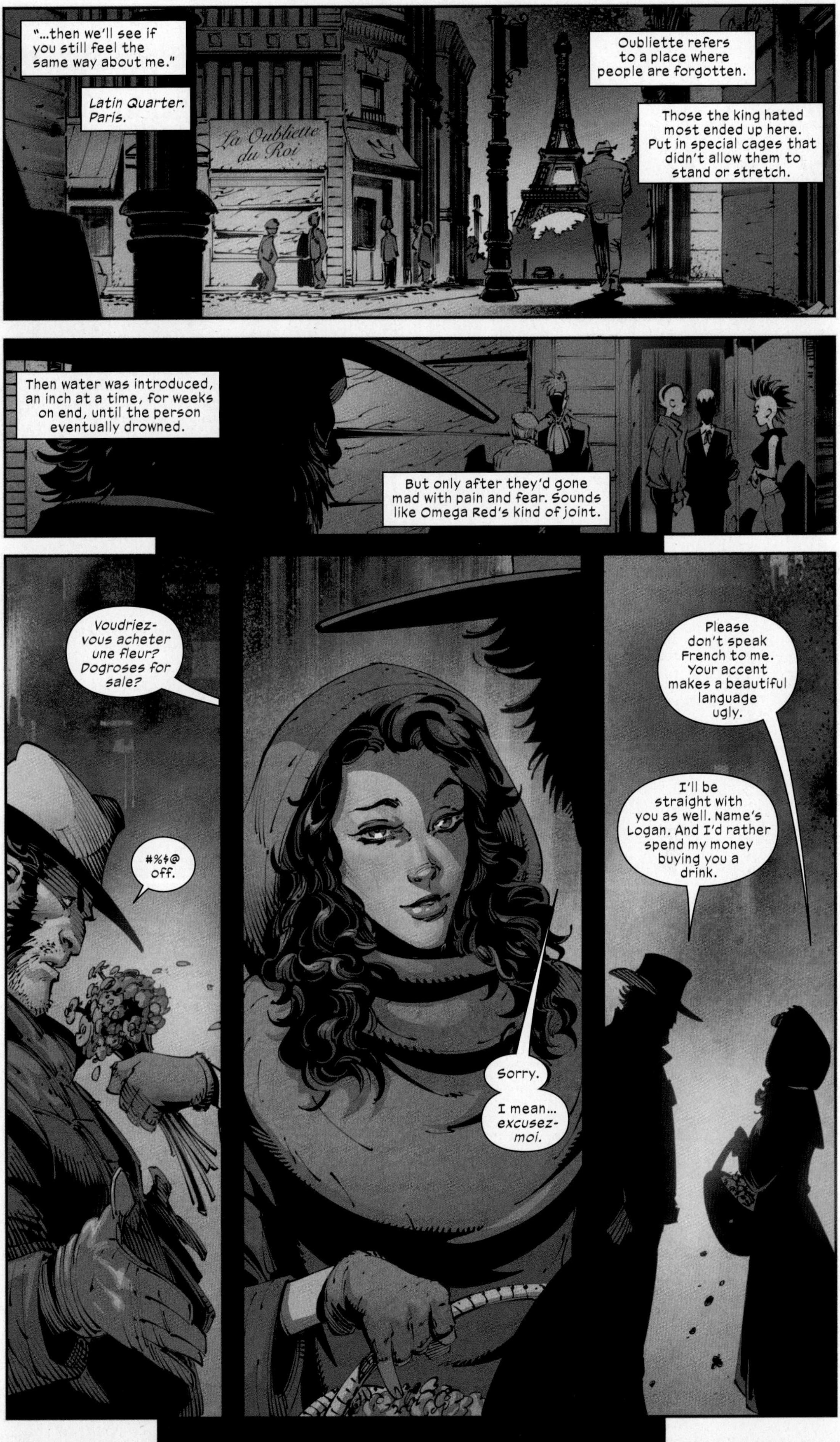
"...then we'll see if you still feel the same way about me."
Latin Quarter. Paris.
La Oubliette du Roi
Oubliette refers to a place where people are forgotten.
Those the king hated most ended up here. Put in special cages that didn't allow them to stand or stretch.
Then water was introduced, an inch at a time, for weeks on end, until the person eventually drowned.
But only after they'd gone mad with pain and fear. Sounds like Omega Red's kind of joint.
Voudriez-vous acheter une fleur? Dogroses for sale?
#%$@ off.
Sorry.
I mean... excusez-moi.
Please don't speak French to me. Your accent makes a beautiful language ugly.
I'll be straight with you as well. Name's Logan. And I'd rather spend my money buying you a drink.

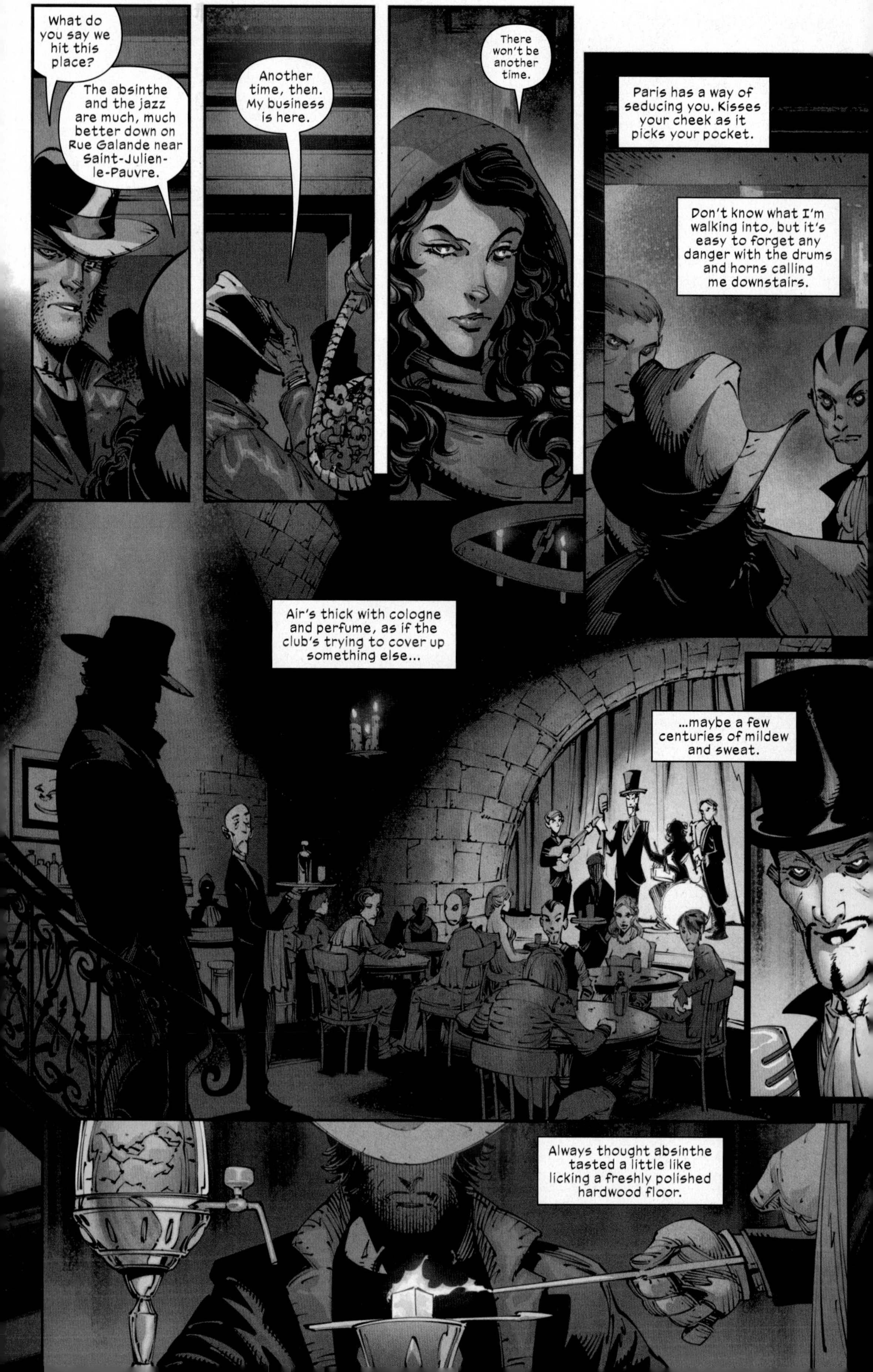
What do you say we hit this place?
The absinthe and the jazz are much, much better down on Rue Galande near Saint-Julien-le-Pauvre.
Another time, then. My business is here.
There won't be another time.
Paris has a way of seducing you. Kisses your cheek as it picks your pocket.
Don't know what I'm walking into, but it's easy to forget any danger with the drums and horns calling me downstairs.
Air's thick with cologne and perfume, as if the club's trying to cover up something else...
...maybe a few centuries of mildew and sweat.
Always thought absinthe tasted a little like licking a freshly polished hardwood floor.

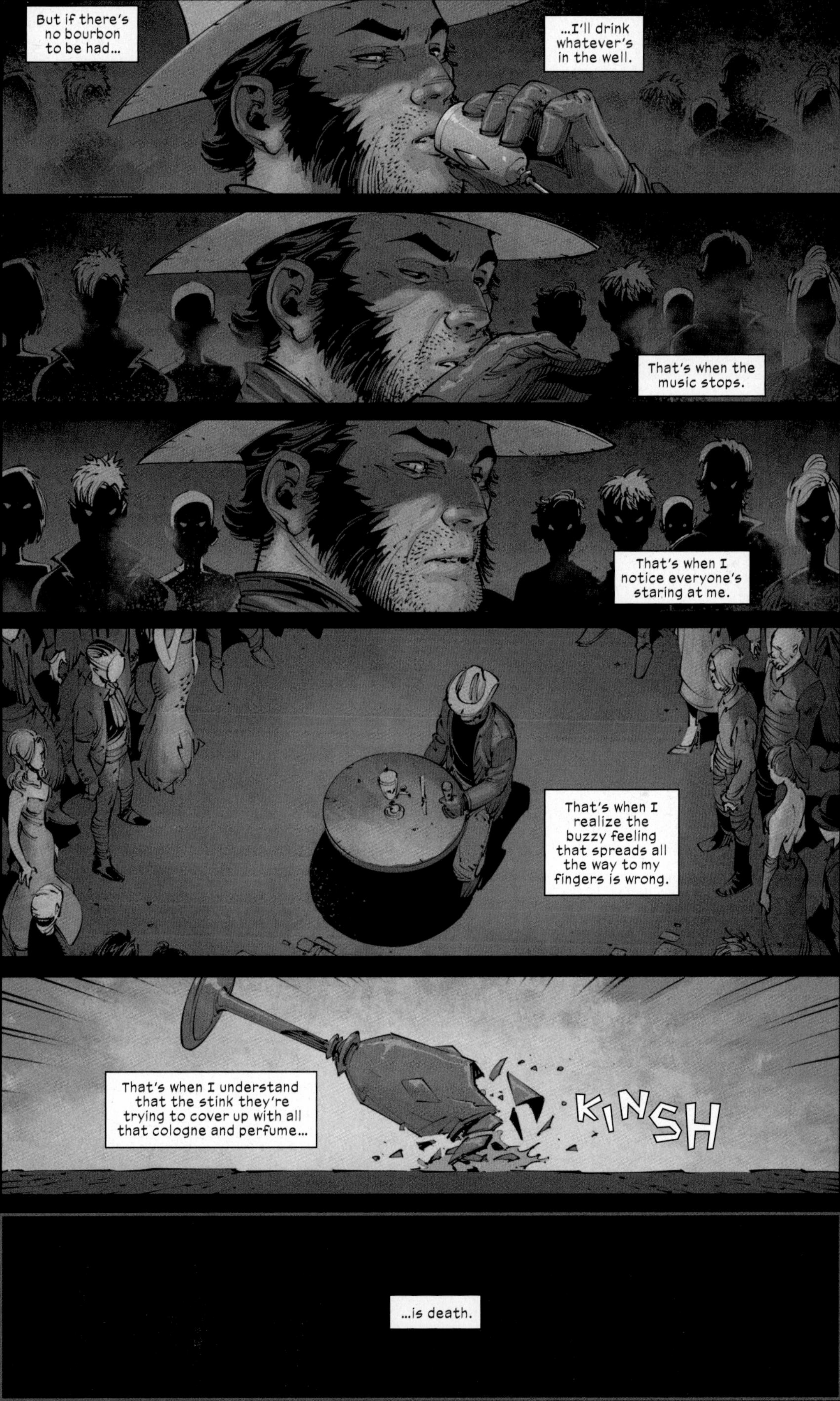
But if there's no bourbon to be had...
...I'll drink whatever's in the well.
That's when the music stops.
That's when I notice everyone's staring at me.
That's when I realize the buzzy feeling that spreads all the way to my fingers is wrong.
That's when I understand that the stink they're trying to cover up with all that cologne and perfume...
KINSH
...is death.

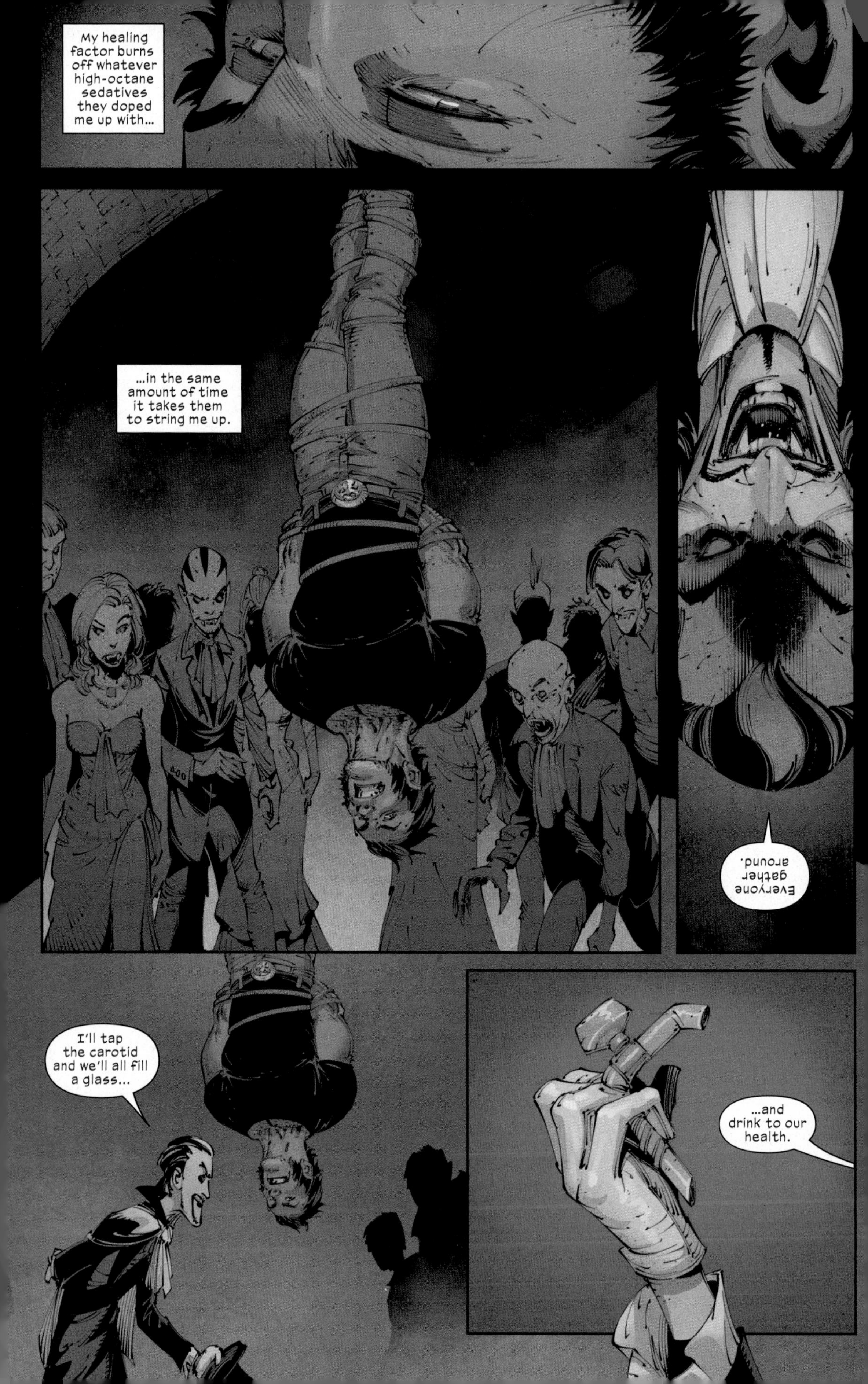
My healing factor burns off whatever high-octane sedatives they doped me up with...
...in the same amount of time it takes them to string me up.
Everyone gather around.
I'll tap the carotid and we'll all fill a glass...
...and drink to our health.

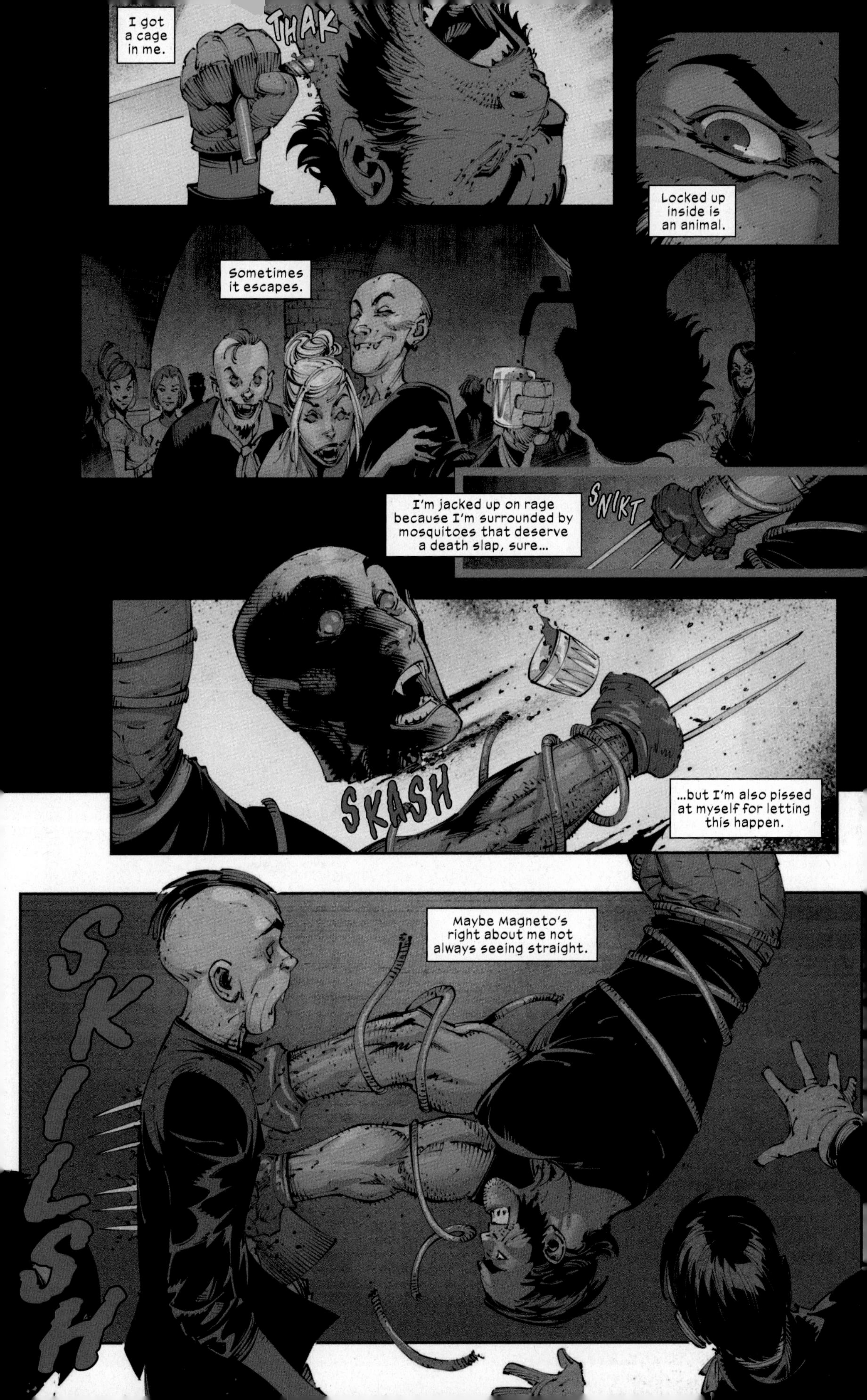
I got a cage in me.
THAK
Locked up inside is an animal.
Sometimes it escapes.
I'm jacked up on rage because I'm surrounded by mosquitoes that deserve a death slap, sure...
SNIKT
SKASH
...but I'm also pissed at myself for letting this happen.
Maybe Magneto's right about me not always seeing straight.
SKLLSH

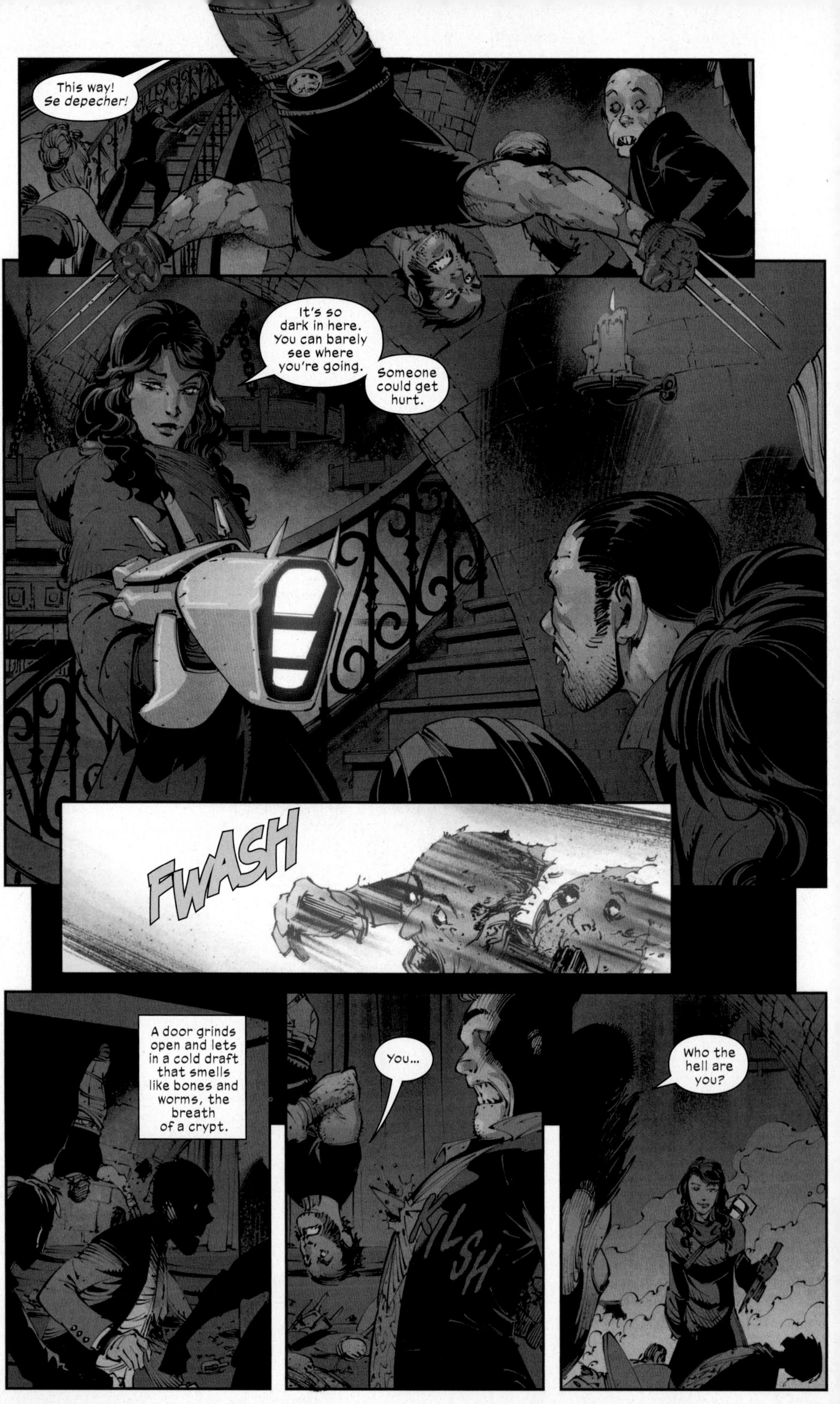
This way! Se depecher!
It's so dark in here. You can barely see where you're going.
Someone could get hurt.
FWASH
A door grinds open and lets in a cold draft that smells like bones and worms, the breath of a crypt.
You...
KLSH
Who the hell are you?

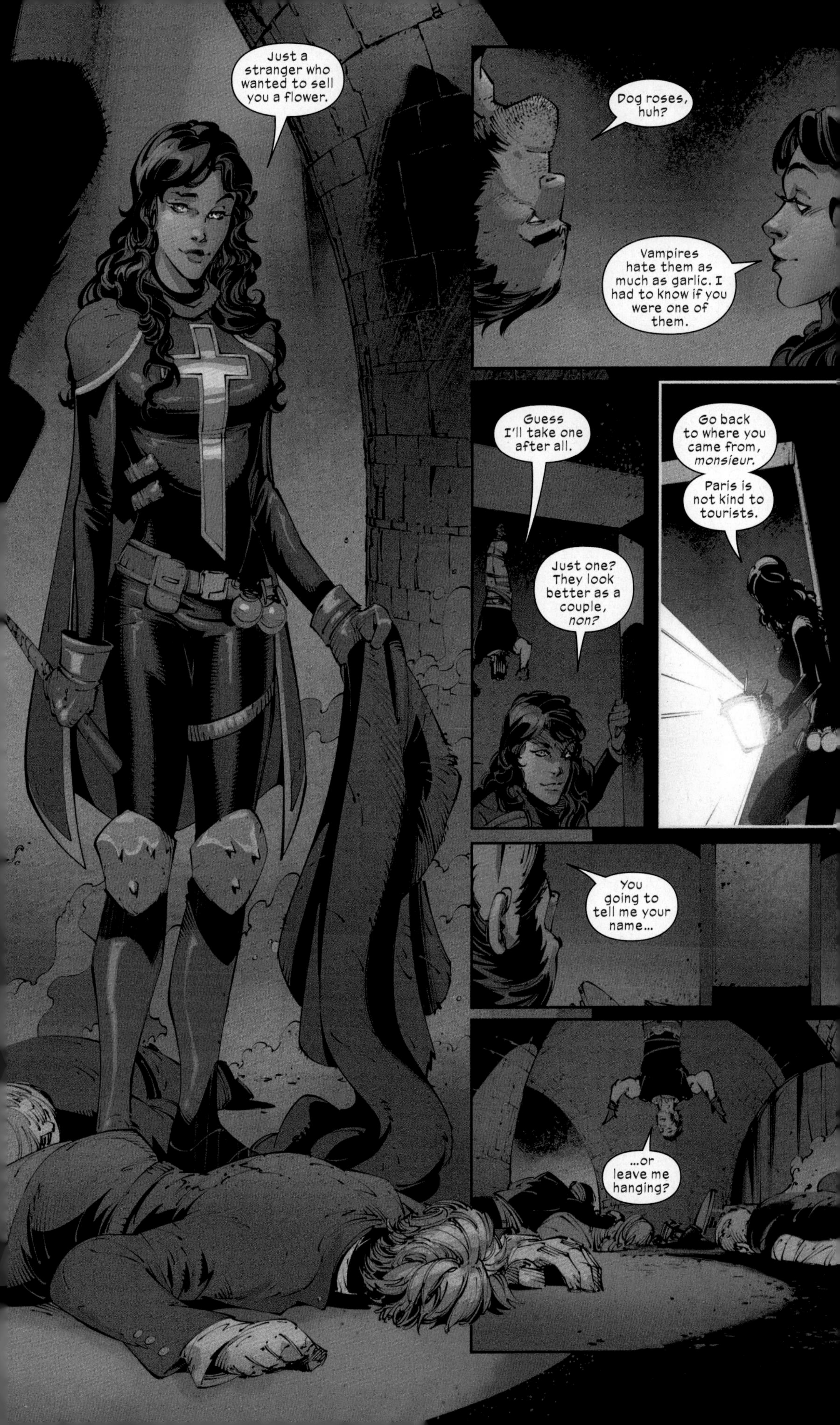
Just a stranger who wanted to sell you a flower.
Dog roses, huh?
Vampires hate them as much as garlic. I had to know if you were one of them.
Guess I'll take one after all.
Just one? They look better as a couple, *non?*
Go back to where you came from, *monsieur.*
Paris is not kind to tourists.
You going to tell me your name...
...or leave me hanging?

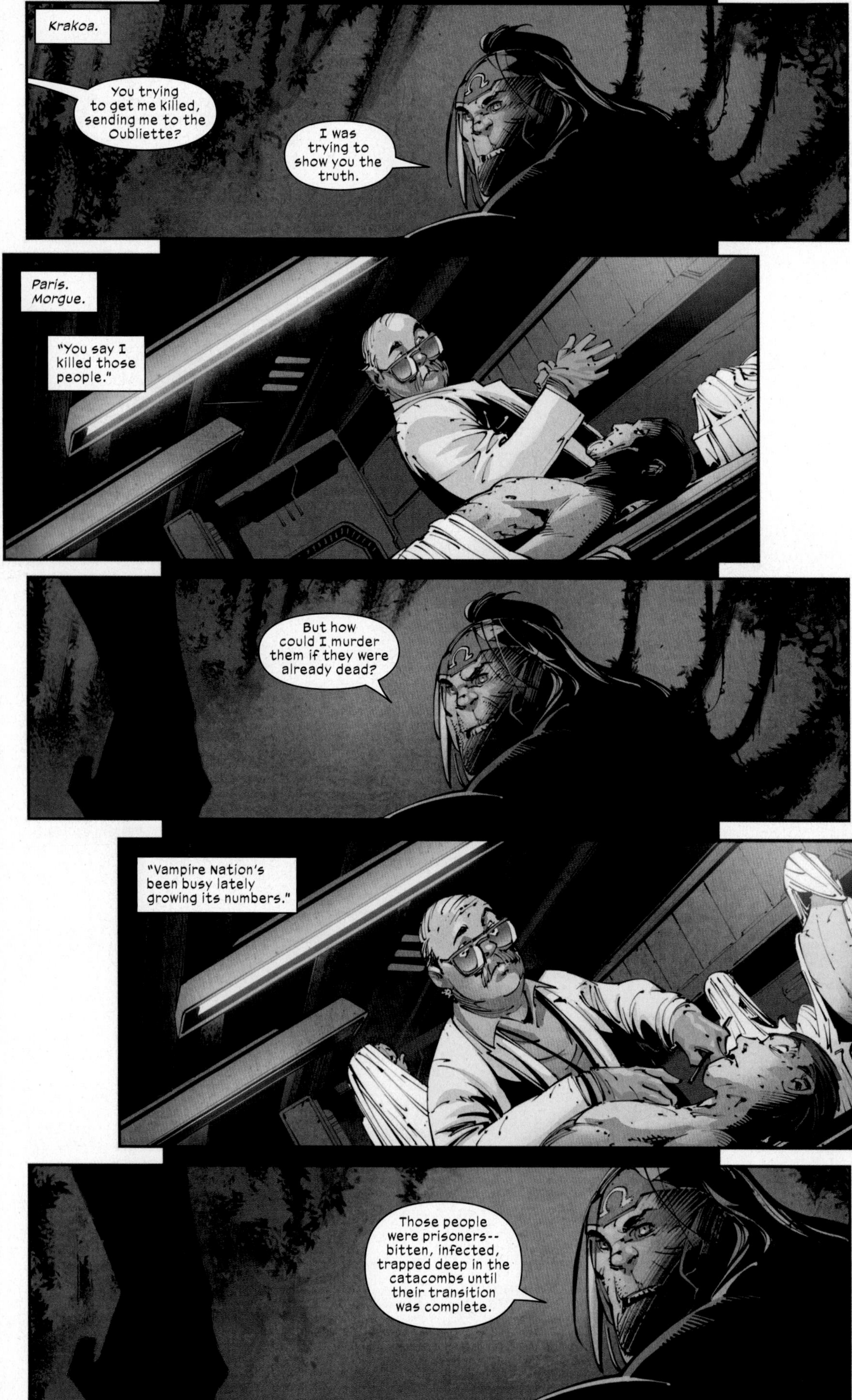

Krakoa.
You trying to get me killed, sending me to the Oubliette?
I was trying to show you the truth.
Paris. Morgue.
"You say I killed those people."
But how could I murder them if they were already dead?
"Vampire Nation's been busy lately growing its numbers."
Those people were prisoners-- bitten, infected, trapped deep in the catacombs until their transition was complete.

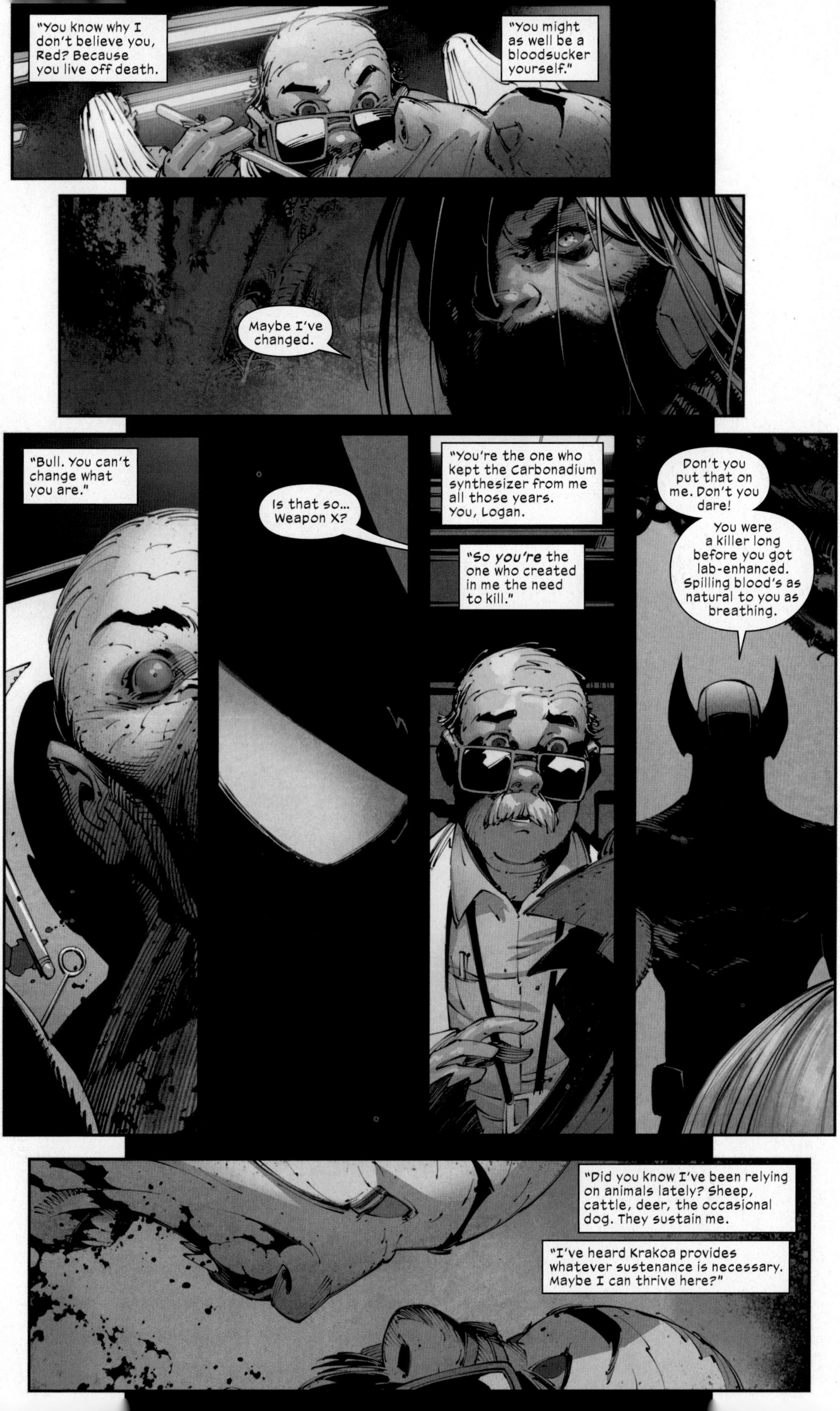
"You know why I don't believe you, Red? Because you live off death.
"You might as well be a bloodsucker yourself."
Maybe I've changed.
"Bull. You can't change what you are."
Is that so... Weapon X?
"You're the one who kept the Carbonadium synthesizer from me all those years. You, Logan.
"So *you're* the one who created in me the need to kill."
Don't you put that on me. Don't you dare!
You were a killer long before you got lab-enhanced. Spilling blood's as natural to you as breathing.
"Did you know I've been relying on animals lately? Sheep, cattle, deer, the occasional dog. They sustain me.
"I've heard Krakoa provides whatever sustenance is necessary. Maybe I can thrive here?"

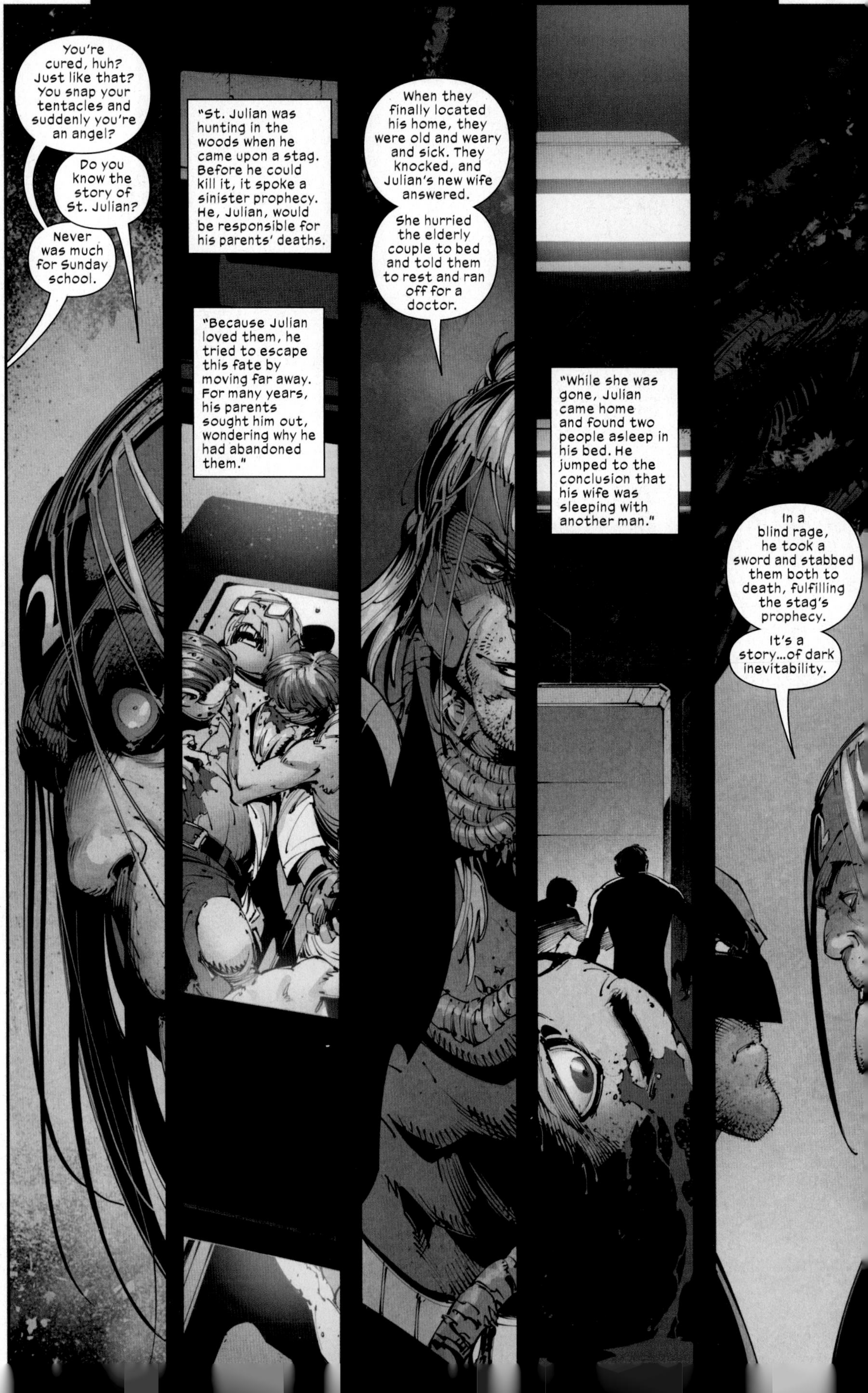
You're cured, huh? Just like that? You snap your tentacles and suddenly you're an angel?
Do you know the story of St. Julian?
Never was much for Sunday school.
"St. Julian was hunting in the woods when he came upon a stag. Before he could kill it, it spoke a sinister prophecy. He, Julian, would be responsible for his parents' deaths.
"Because Julian loved them, he tried to escape this fate by moving far away. For many years, his parents sought him out, wondering why he had abandoned them."
When they finally located his home, they were old and weary and sick. They knocked, and Julian's new wife answered.
She hurried the elderly couple to bed and told them to rest and ran off for a doctor.
"While she was gone, Julian came home and found two people asleep in his bed. He jumped to the conclusion that his wife was sleeping with another man."
In a blind rage, he took a sword and stabbed them both to death, fulfilling the stag's prophecy.
It's a story...of dark inevitability.

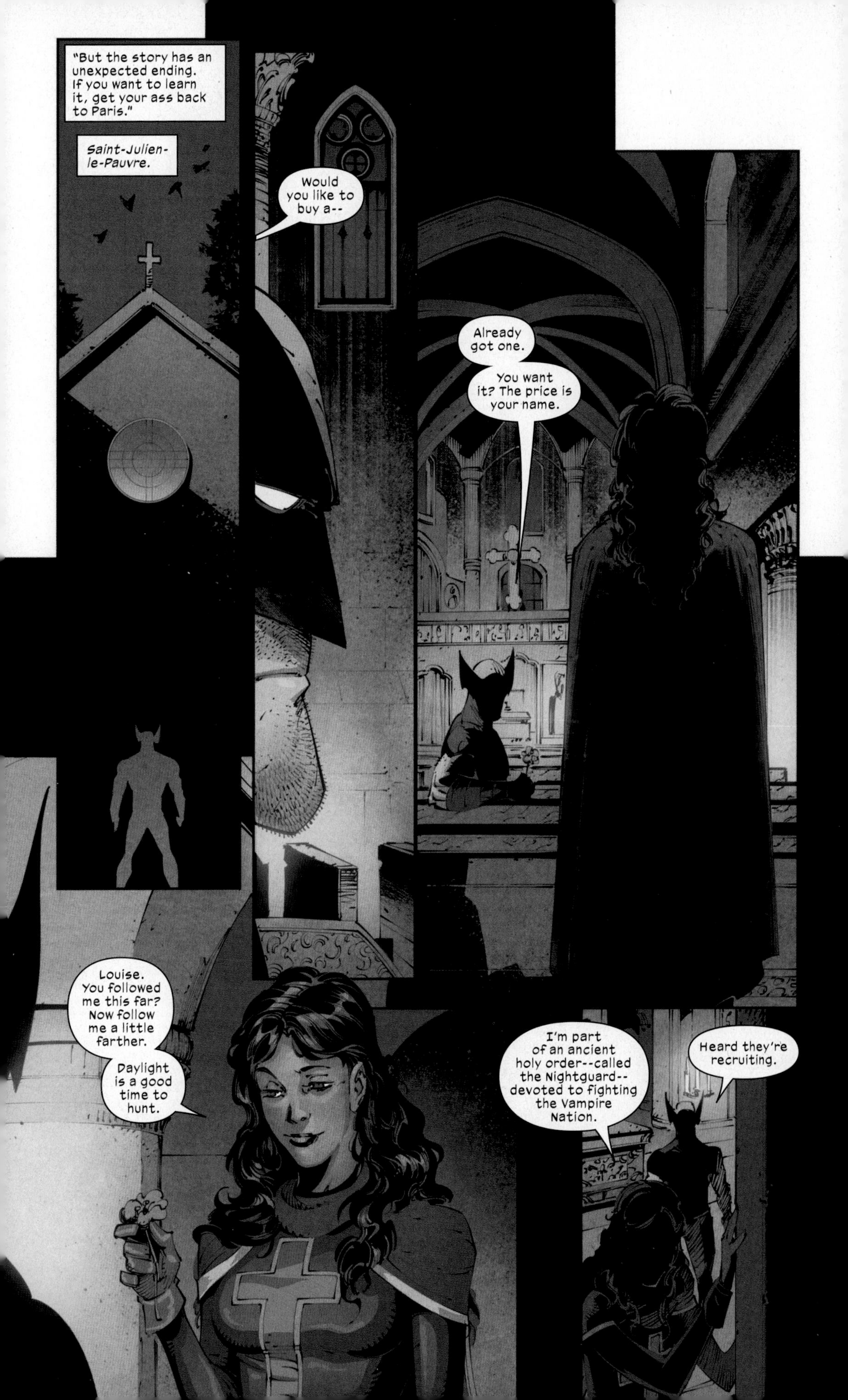
"But the story has an unexpected ending. If you want to learn it, get your ass back to Paris."
Saint-Julien-le-Pauvre.
Would you like to buy a--
Already got one.
You want it? The price is your name.
Louise. You followed me this far? Now follow me a little farther.
Daylight is a good time to hunt.
I'm part of an ancient holy order--called the Nightguard--devoted to fighting the Vampire Nation.
Heard they're recruiting.

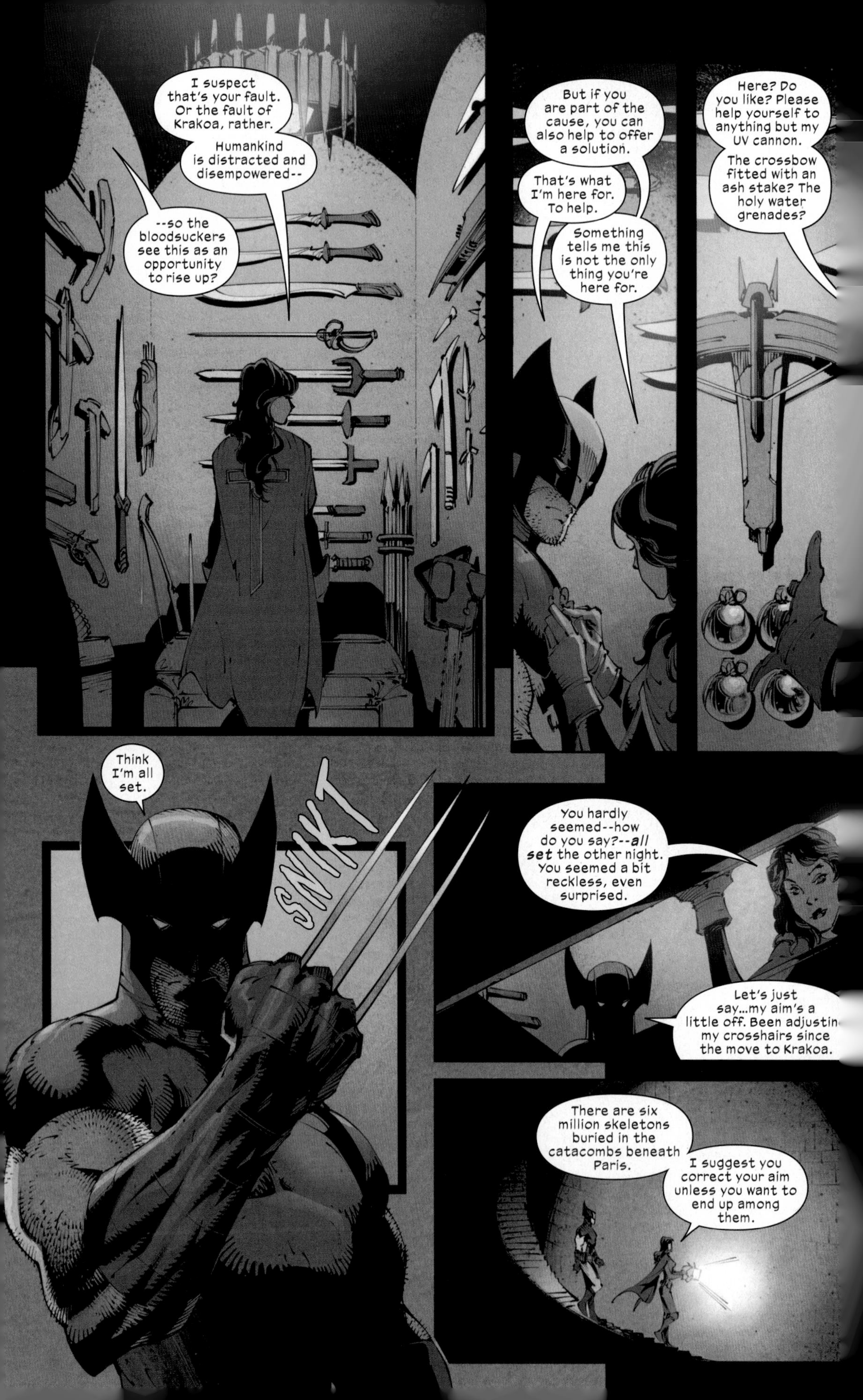
I suspect that's your fault. Or the fault of Krakoa, rather.
Humankind is distracted and disempowered--
--so the bloodsuckers see this as an opportunity to rise up?
But if you are part of the cause, you can also help to offer a solution.
That's what I'm here for. To help.
Something tells me this is not the only thing you're here for.
Here? Do you like? Please help yourself to anything but my UV cannon.
The crossbow fitted with an ash stake? The holy water grenades?
Think I'm all set.
SNIKT
You hardly seemed--how do you say?--*all set* the other night. You seemed a bit reckless, even surprised.
Let's just say...my aim's a little off. Been adjustin' my crosshairs since the move to Krakoa.
There are six million skeletons buried in the catacombs beneath Paris.
I suggest you correct your aim unless you want to end up among them.

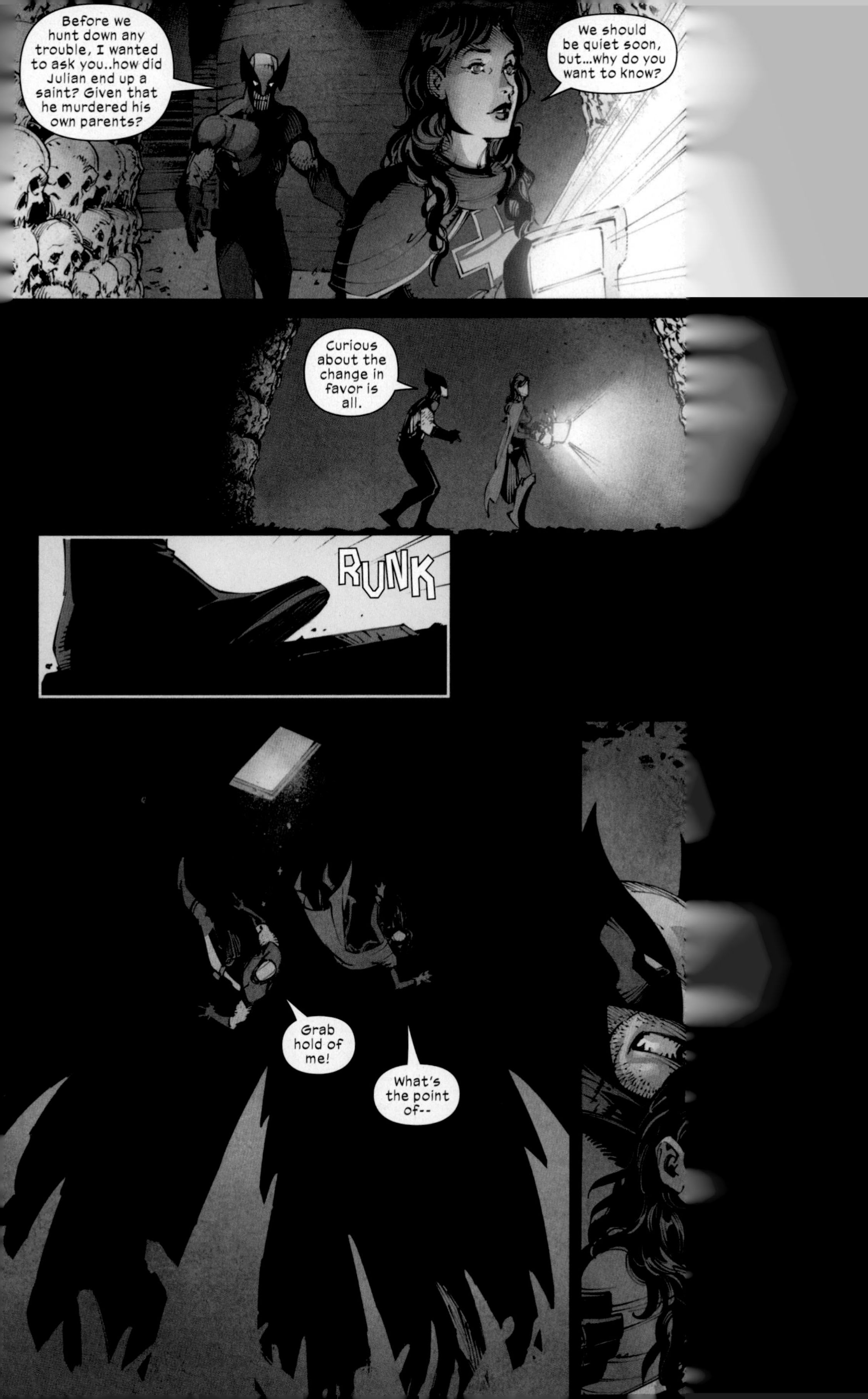
Before we hunt down any trouble, I wanted to ask you..how did Julian end up a saint? Given that he murdered his own parents?
We should be quiet soon, but...why do you want to know?
Curious about the change in favor is all.
RUNK
Grab hold of me!
What's the point of--

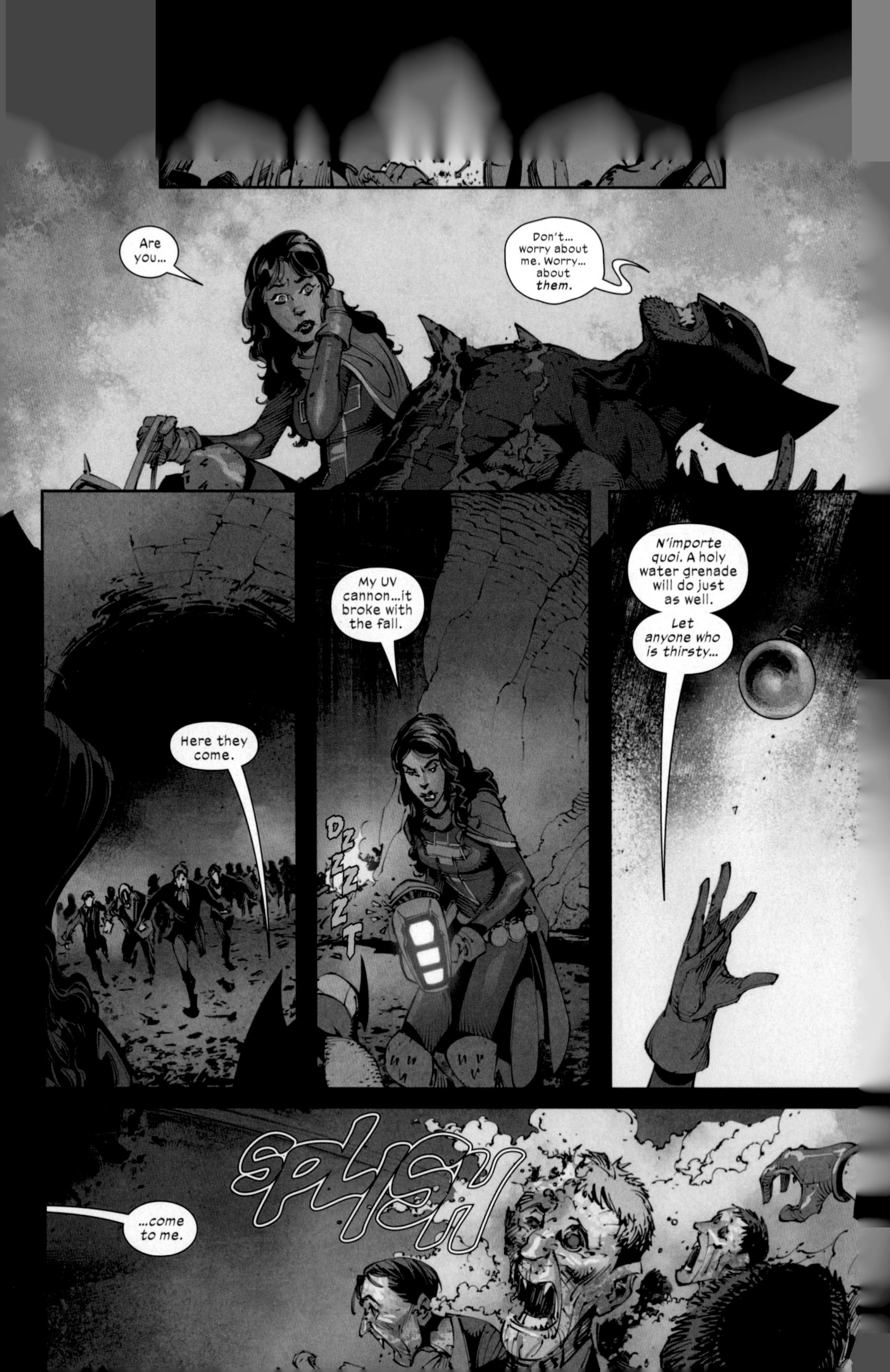
Are you...
Don't... worry about me. Worry... about *them.*
Here they come.
My UV cannon...it broke with the fall.
DZZZZT
N'importe quoi. A holy water grenade will do just as well.
Let anyone who is thirsty...
SPLISH
...come to me.

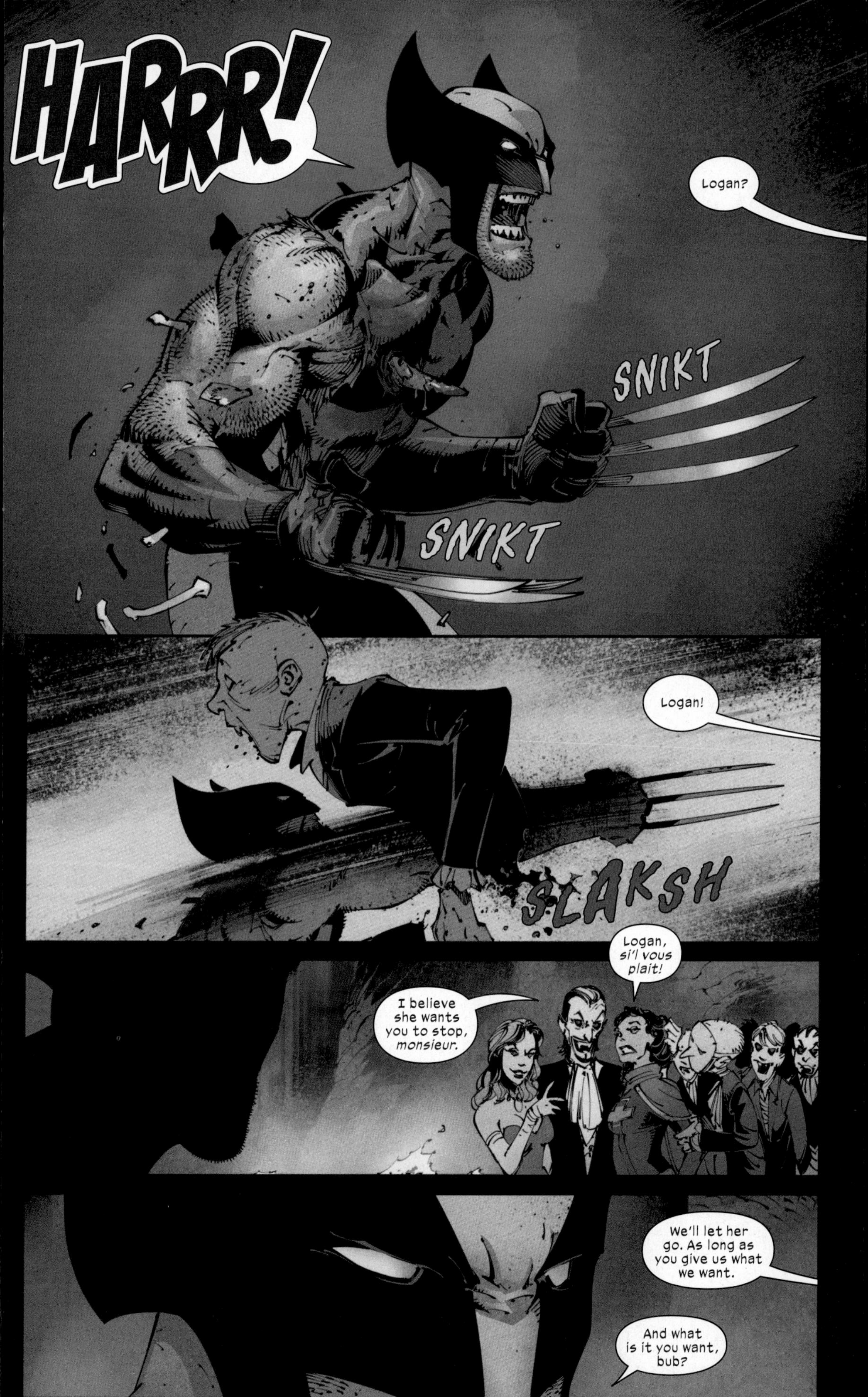
HARRR!
Logan?
SNIKT
SNIKT
Logan!
SLAKSH
Logan, si'l vous plait!
I believe she wants you to stop, monsieur.
We'll let her go. As long as you give us what we want.
And what is it you want, bub?

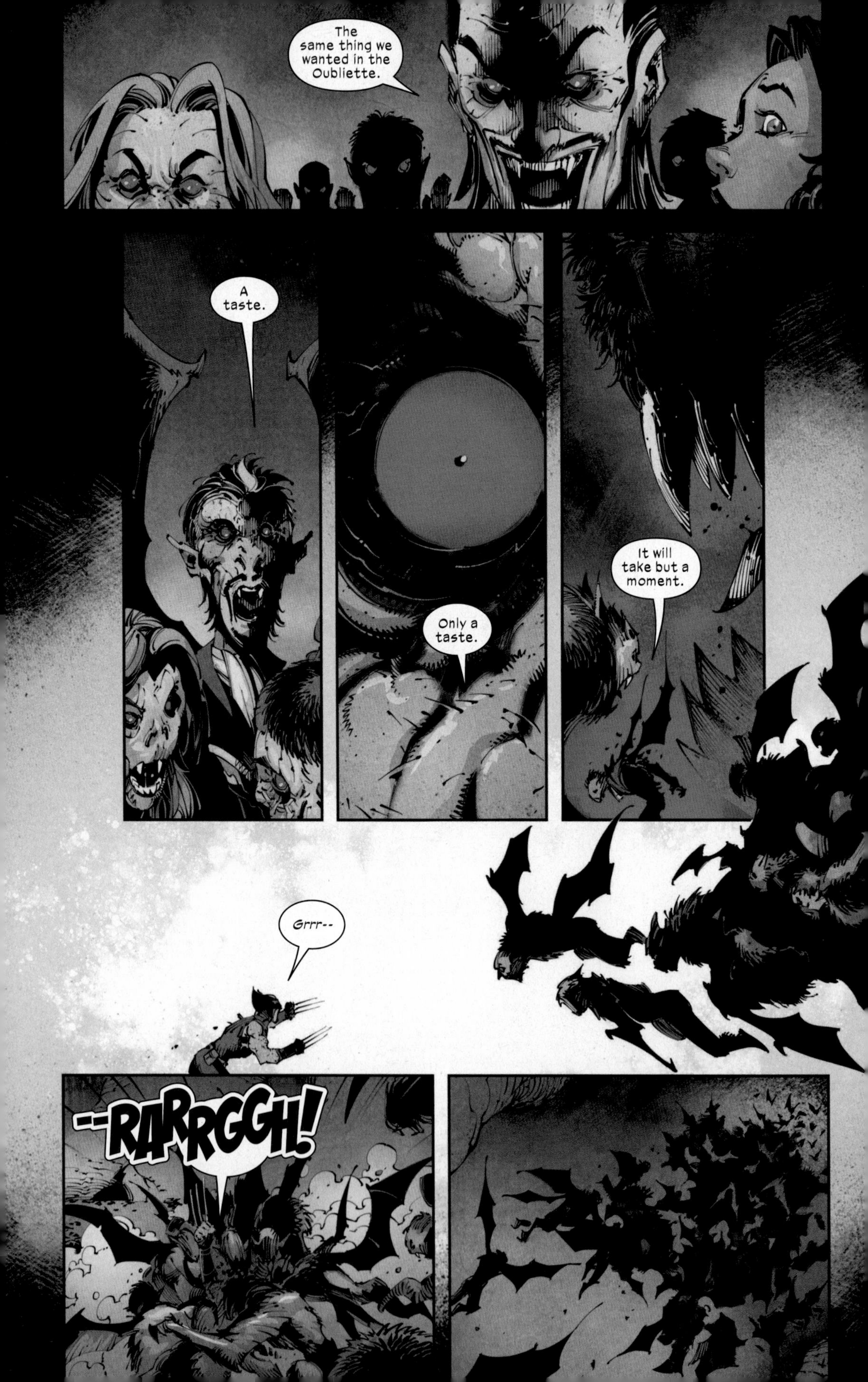
The same thing we wanted in the Oubliette.
A taste.
Only a taste.
It will take but a moment.
Grrr--
--RARRGGH!

You said not to worry about you, but...

That's because you don't need to worry about me.

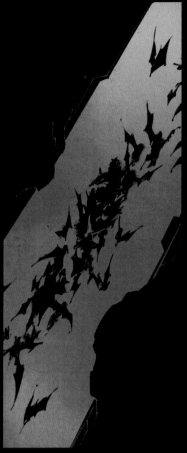

I won't turn, if that's what they were hoping for.

"My healing factor kills off the enzyme."

Anyway... one down.

And thousands to go.

"Logan...they shouldn't have left us like that..."

"Sure, they should've. I killed their leader. The rest ran off. That's good news."

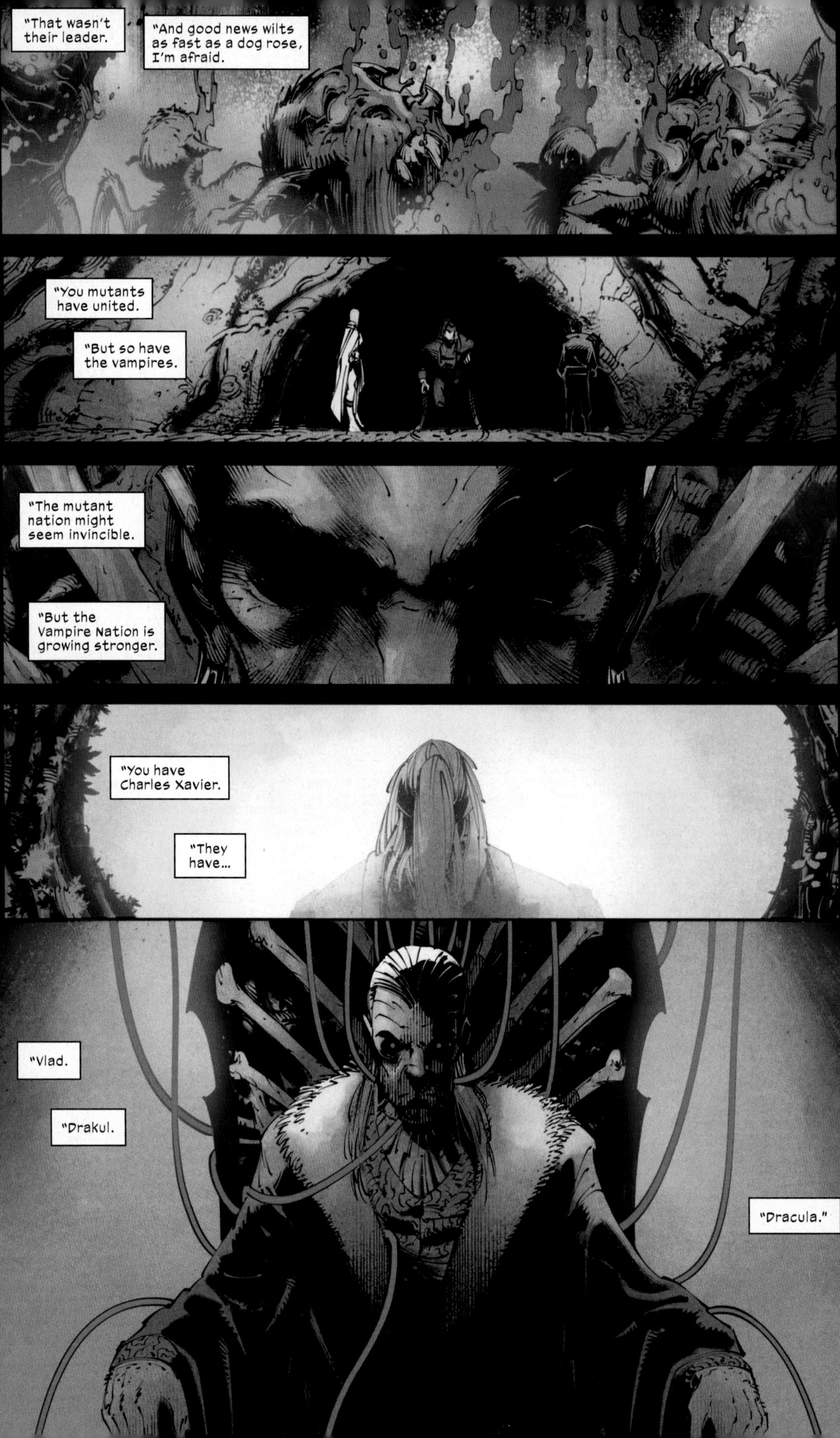
"That wasn't their leader.
"And good news wilts as fast as a dog rose, I'm afraid.
"You mutants have united.
"But so have the vampires.
"The mutant nation might seem invincible.
"But the Vampire Nation is growing stronger.
"You have Charles Xavier.
"They have...
"Vlad.
"Drakul.
"Dracula."

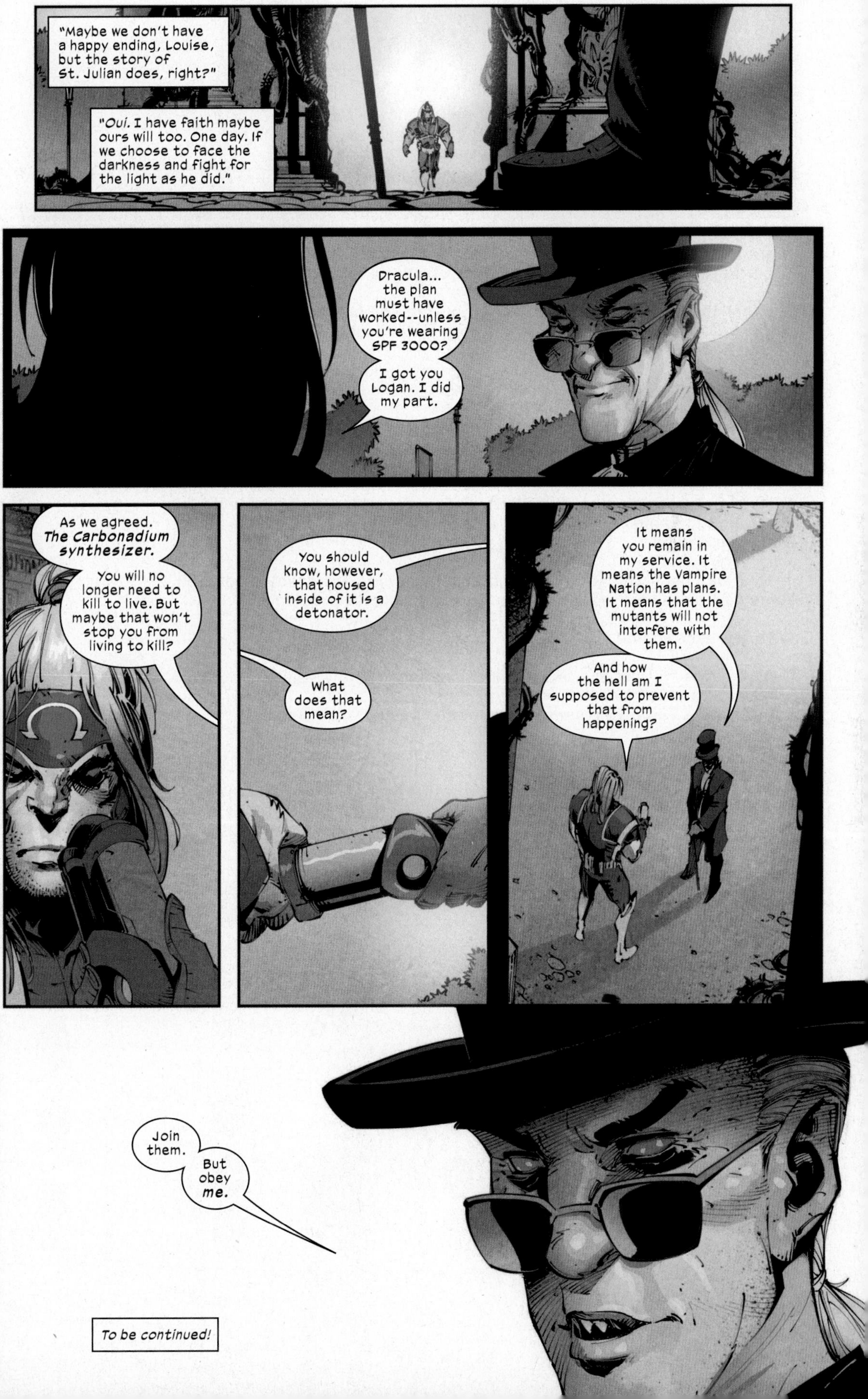
"Maybe we don't have a happy ending, Louise, but the story of St. Julian does, right?"
"Oui. I have faith maybe ours will too. One day. If we choose to face the darkness and fight for the light as he did."
Dracula... the plan must have worked--unless you're wearing SPF 3000?
I got you Logan. I did my part.
As we agreed. The Carbonadium synthesizer.
You will no longer need to kill to live. But maybe that won't stop you from living to kill?
You should know, however, that housed inside of it is a detonator.
What does that mean?
It means you remain in my service. It means the Vampire Nation has plans. It means that the mutants will not interfere with them.
And how the hell am I supposed to prevent that from happening?
Join them.
But obey me.
To be continued!

BLOODWORK

There are four groups of blood (A, B, AB, O) and each of these can be either RhD positive or RhD negative, making for a total of eight types.

But further classification is based on antibodies and antigens (such as carbohydrates and proteins), making for a known total of 36 systems and 346 antigens.

And then the math is further complicated by Wolverine.

Not all blood is alike, but that is especially true of what runs beneath his skin.

It is not merely resistant, but altogether impervious to infection, malignancy, autoimmune disorders. It is infinitely compatible with all other blood families and has been shown to have a brief, curative effect when transfused.

In this way, it bears some resemblance to blood infected (or cursed, some say) by the bite of a vampire. This is his closest cousin.

With few exceptions.

1) His body is not just the factory for his blood, it is the vault -- and once it leaves him, its powers are soon suppressed and its compatibility deteriorates. Whereas a vampire's blood is malignant, virulent.

2) His blood does not deteriorate when exposed to ultraviolet light.

You could say their blood belongs to the same group, but a different type. One positive, the other negative.

Instead of A or B or AB or O, one might call it E -- the endless.

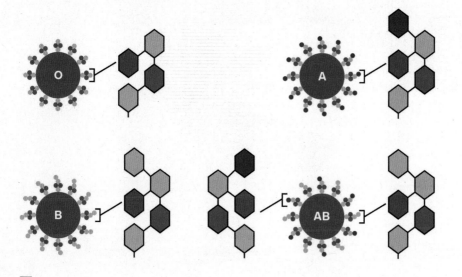

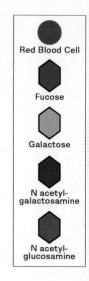

Red Blood Cell

Fucose

Galactose

N acetyl-
galactosamine

N acetyl-
glucosamine

[dawn_of_x]

[kra_]
[koa_]

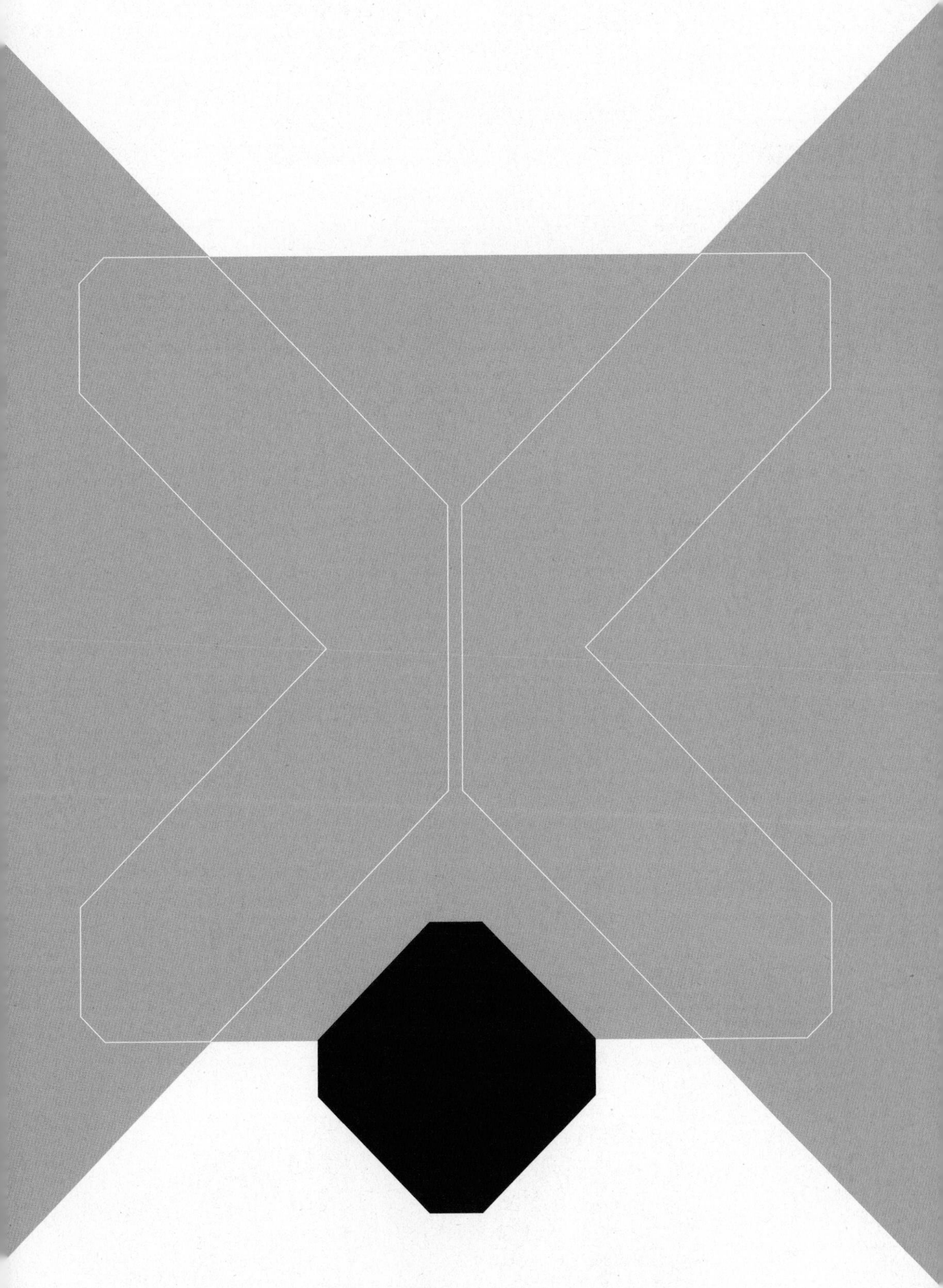

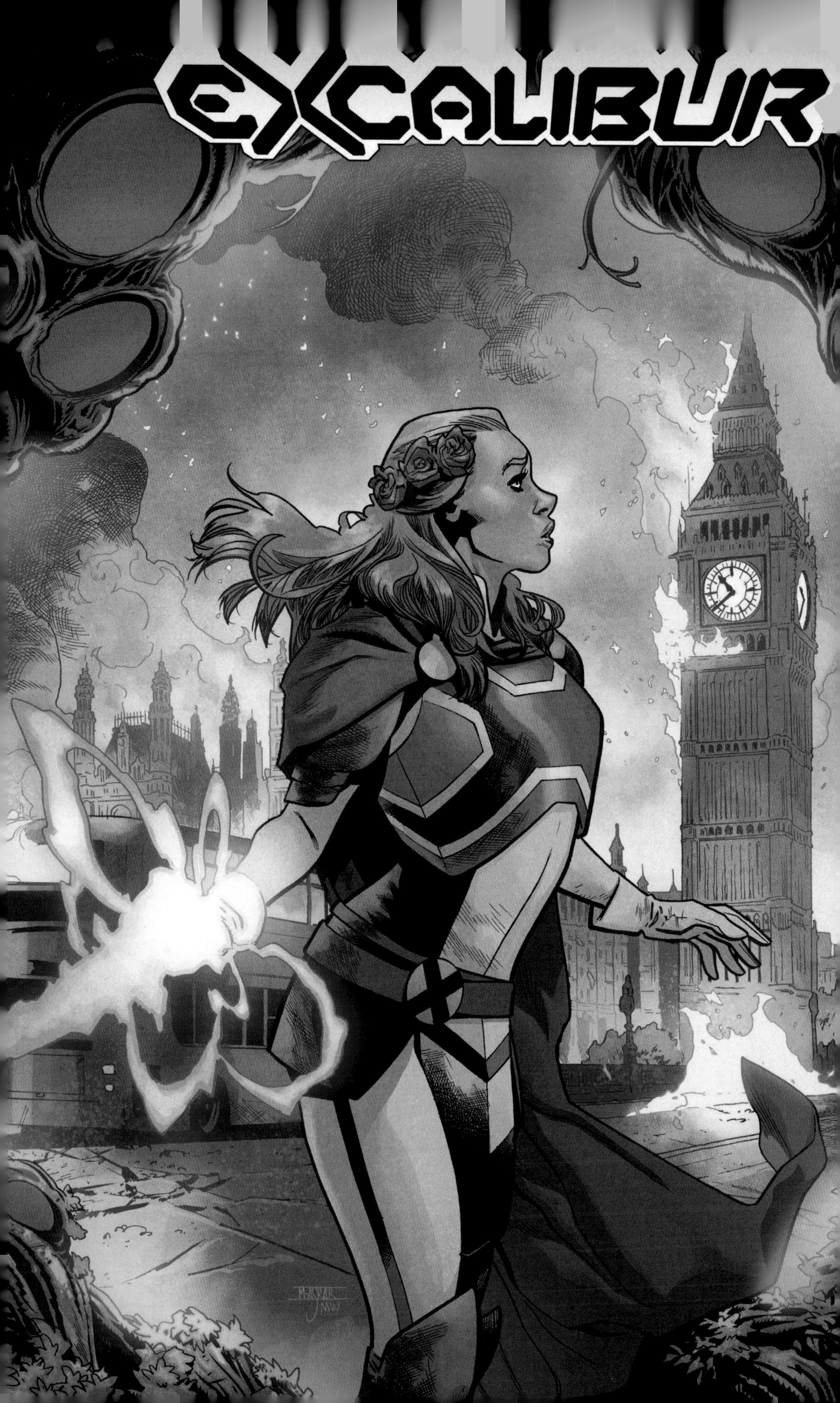
EXCALIBUR

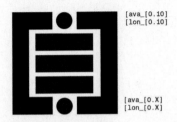

[ava_[0.10]
[lon_[0.10]

[ava_[0.X]
[lon_[0.X]

REALITY

EXCALIBUR seeks unimpeded passage into Otherworld -- but their quest to plant a Krakoan gate has drawn the ire of dangerous enemies, whose first attack badly wounded Shogo.

But what can they expect when their very existence represents an affront to the Omniversal Majestrix, Opal Luna Saturnyne?!

Gambit

Rogue

Rictor

Jubilee

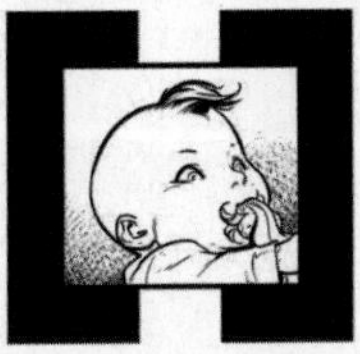

Shogo

Captain
Britain

Jamie
Braddock

[ava_[0.10]...]
[lon_[0.10]...]

[OMNI..versal.]

[00_so_below_X]
[00_as_above_X]

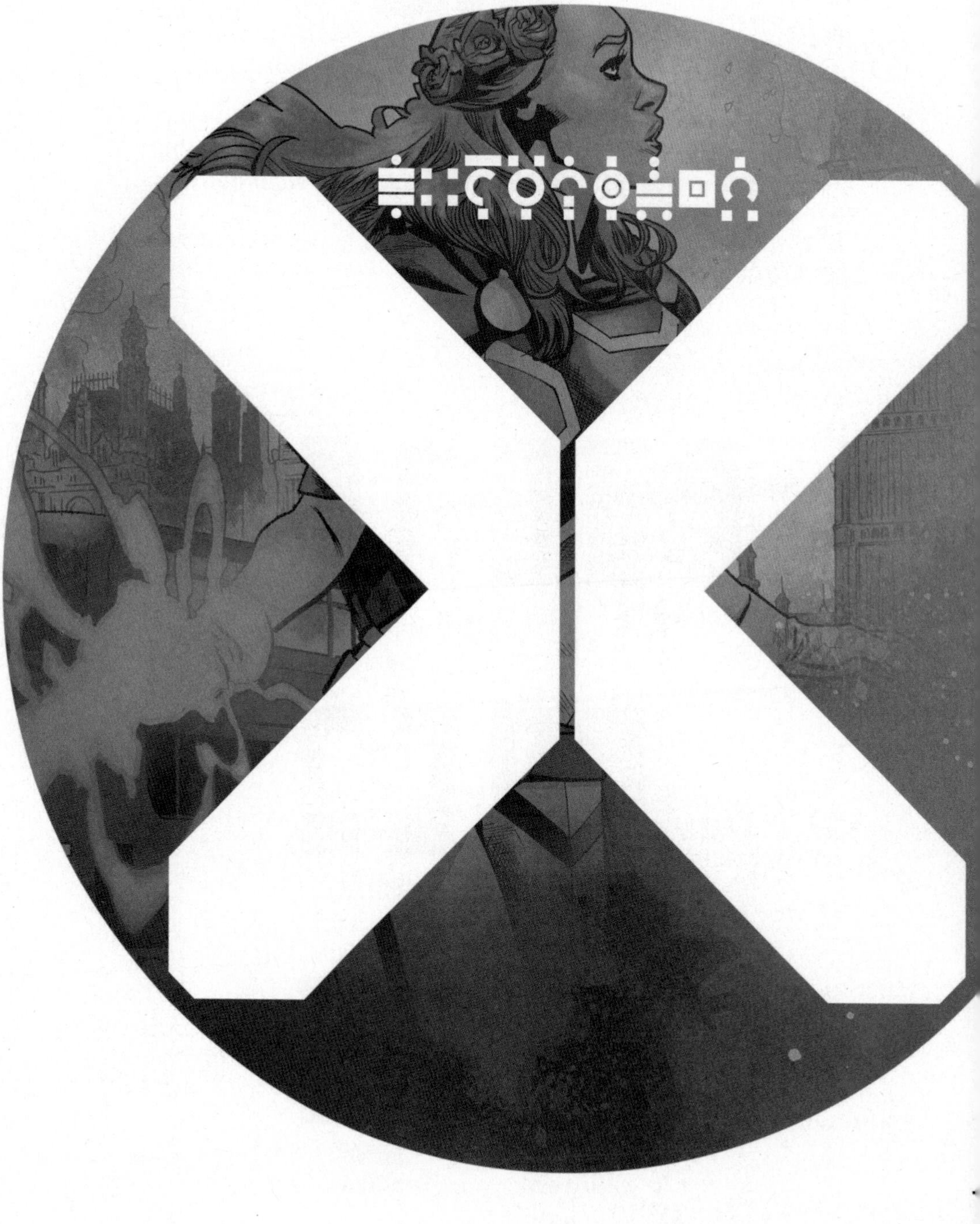

TINI HOWARD.....................................[WRITER]
MARCUS TO......................................[ARTIST]
ERICK ARCINIEGA..........................[COLOR ARTIST]
VC's CORY PETIT.............................[LETTERER]
TOM MULLER.....................................[DESIGN]

MAHMUD ASRAR & MATTHEW WILSON...........[COVER ARTISTS]

NICK RUSSELL...............................[PRODUCTION]

JONATHAN HICKMAN...........................[HEAD OF X]
ANNALISE BISSA.....................[ASSISTANT EDITOR]
JORDAN D. WHITE...............................[EDITOR]
C.B. CEBULSKI........................[EDITOR IN CHIEF]

[10] EXCALIBUR

[ISSUE TEN].....VERSE X: A CROOKED WORLD

[00_so_below_X]
[X‾ɘʌoqɒ‾ƨɒ‾00]

[00_00....00]
[00_00....10]

[00_____the]
[00_realm___]

[00_____of_]

[00_change__]

LONDON: PREPARE FOR WAR

RECENT INTELLIGENCE SUGGESTS THE ISLAND-NATION OF KRAKOA MOVES TOWARD AGGRESSIVE ACTION. REPORTS SUGGEST RECENT ATTACKS CAN BE SOURCED TO MUTANT-SPECIFIC VEGETATION.

Intelligence suggests burning of mutant vegetation until authorities can be present.

Protect and survive!

SEE A MUTANT?
TELL A HUMAN

FOR QUEEN AND COUNTRY

THE HUMAN RACE IS IN PERIL

DEFEND IT WITH ALL YOUR MIGHT

-- *Minister of Information, Reuben Brousseau*

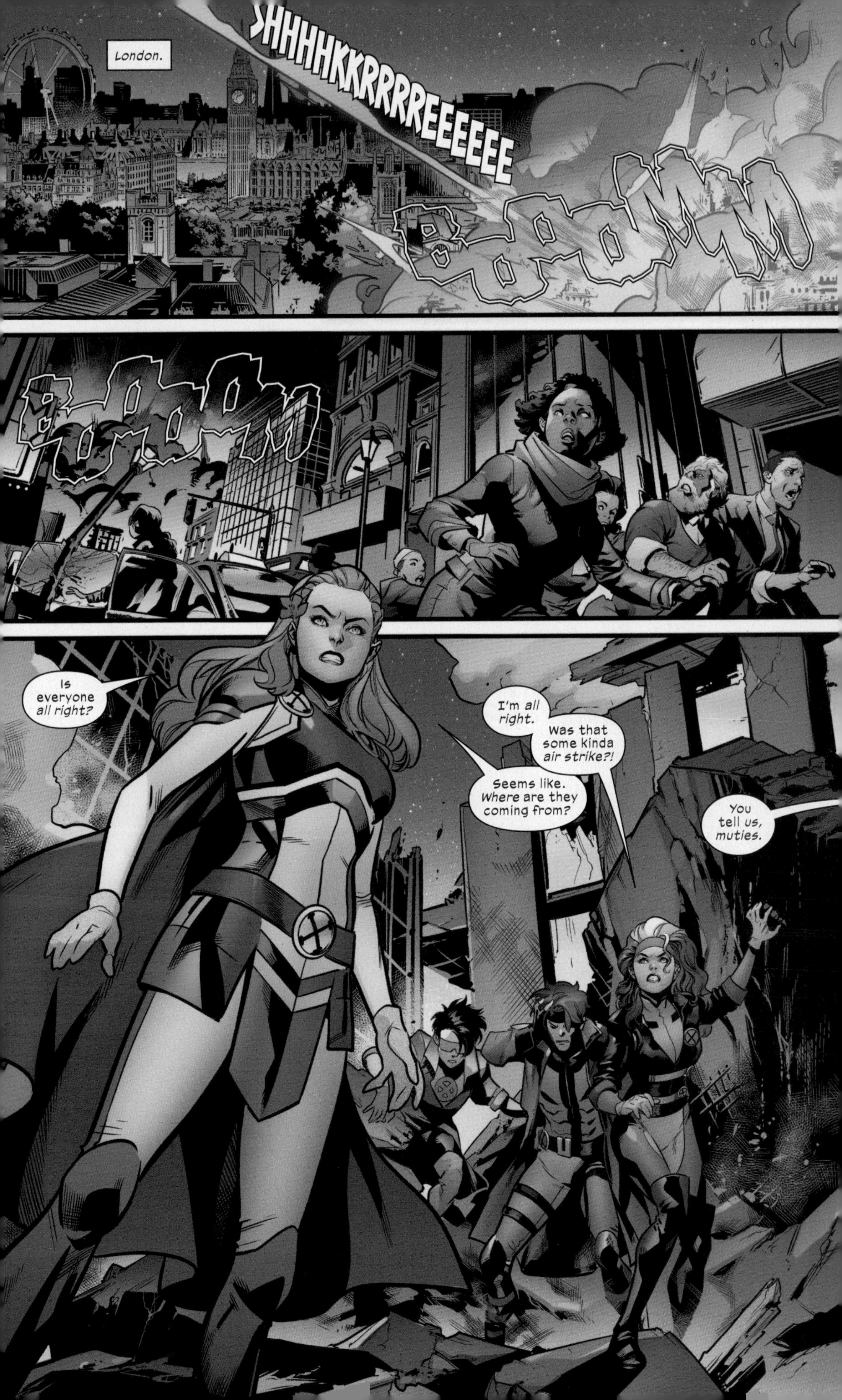

London.
SHHHHKKRRRRREEEEEE
BOOOMM
BOOOM
Is everyone all right?
I'm all right.
Was that some kinda air strike?!
Seems like. Where are they coming from?
You tell us, muties.

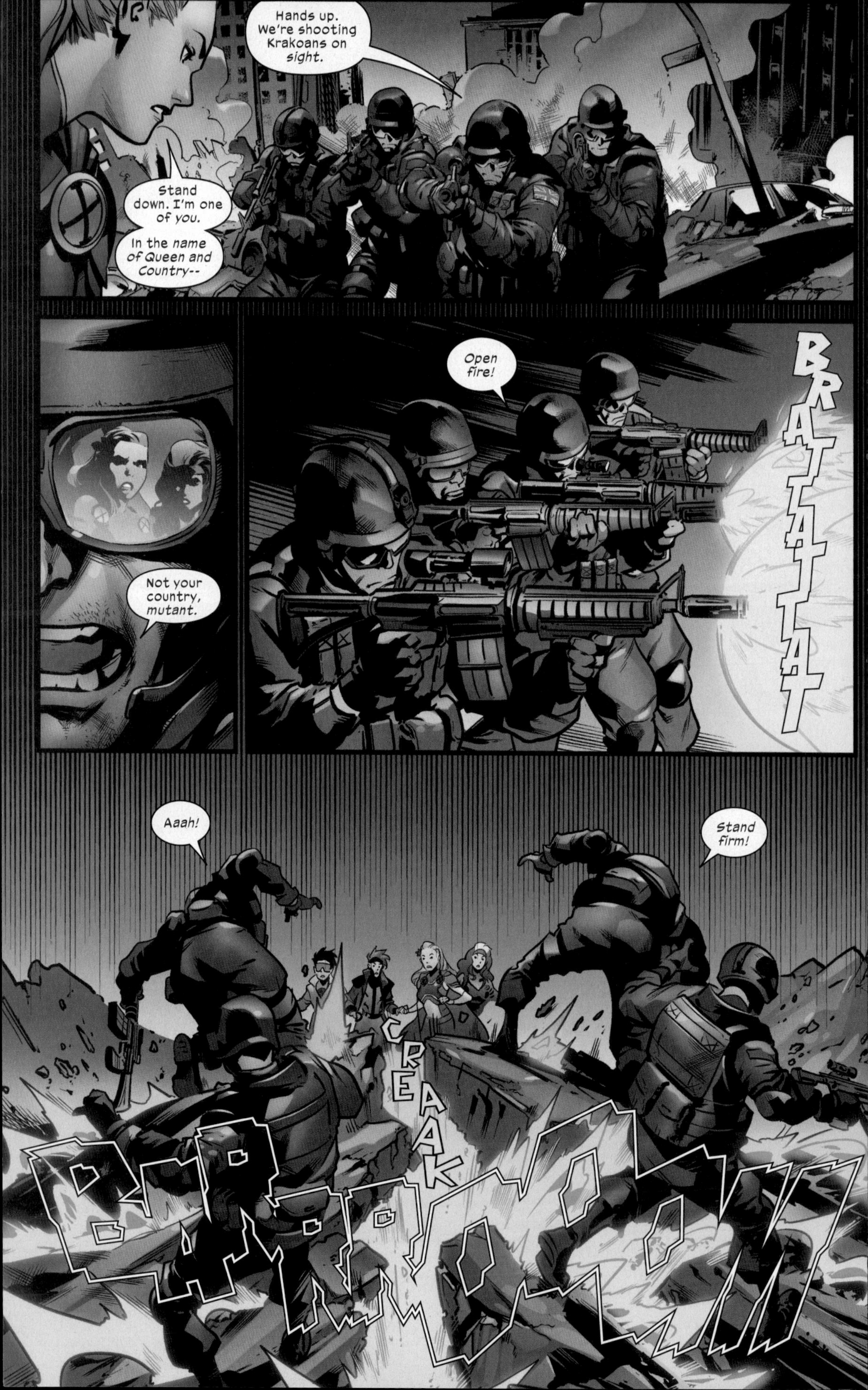
Hands up. We're shooting Krakoans on sight.
Stand down. I'm one of you.
In the name of Queen and Country--
Not your country, mutant.
Open fire!
BRATATATAT
Aaah!
Stand firm!
CREAK
BRAROOOM

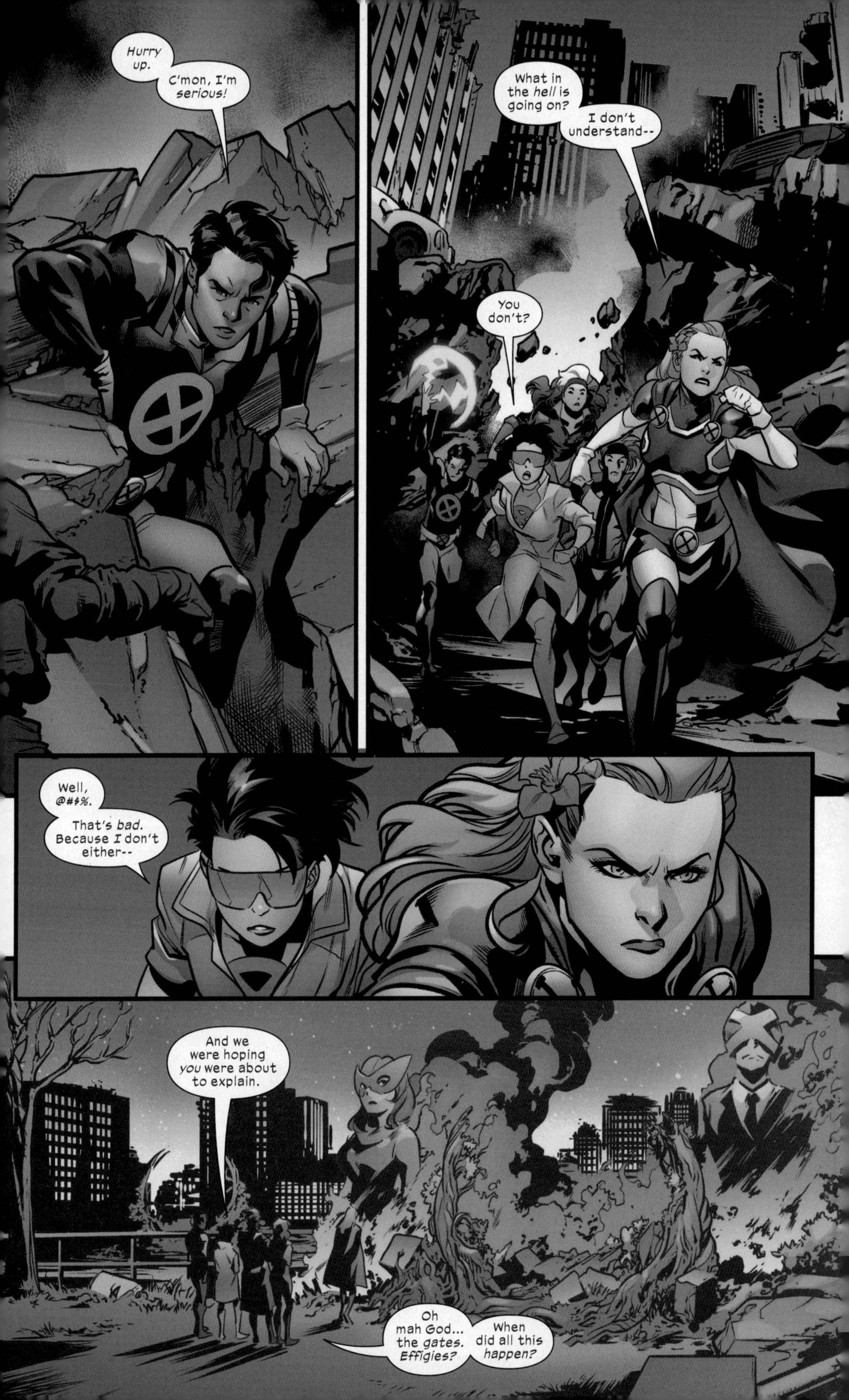
Hurry up.
C'mon, I'm serious!
What in the hell is going on?
I don't understand--
You don't?
Well, @#$%.
That's bad. Because I don't either--
And we were hoping you were about to explain.
Oh mah God... the gates. Effigies?
When did all this happen?

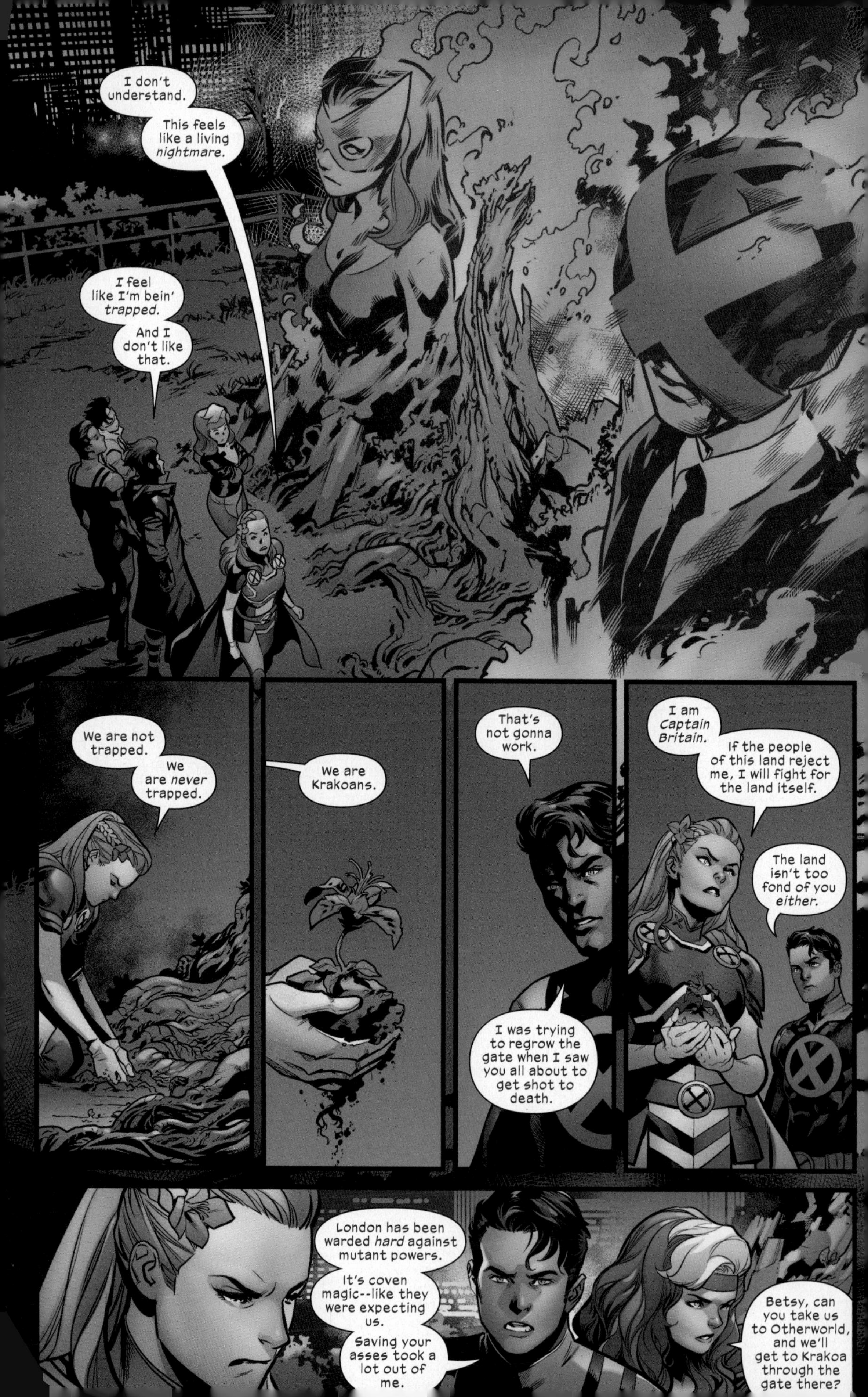
I don't understand.
This feels like a living *nightmare.*
I feel like I'm bein' *trapped.*
And I don't like that.
We are not trapped.
We are *never* trapped.
We are Krakoans.
That's not gonna work.
I was trying to regrow the gate when I saw you all about to get shot to death.
I am *Captain Britain.*
If the people of this land reject me, I will fight for the land itself.
The land isn't too fond of you *either.*
London has been warded *hard* against mutant powers.
It's coven magic--like they were expecting us.
Saving your asses took a lot out of me.
Betsy, can you take us to Otherworld, and we'll get to Krakoa through the gate there?

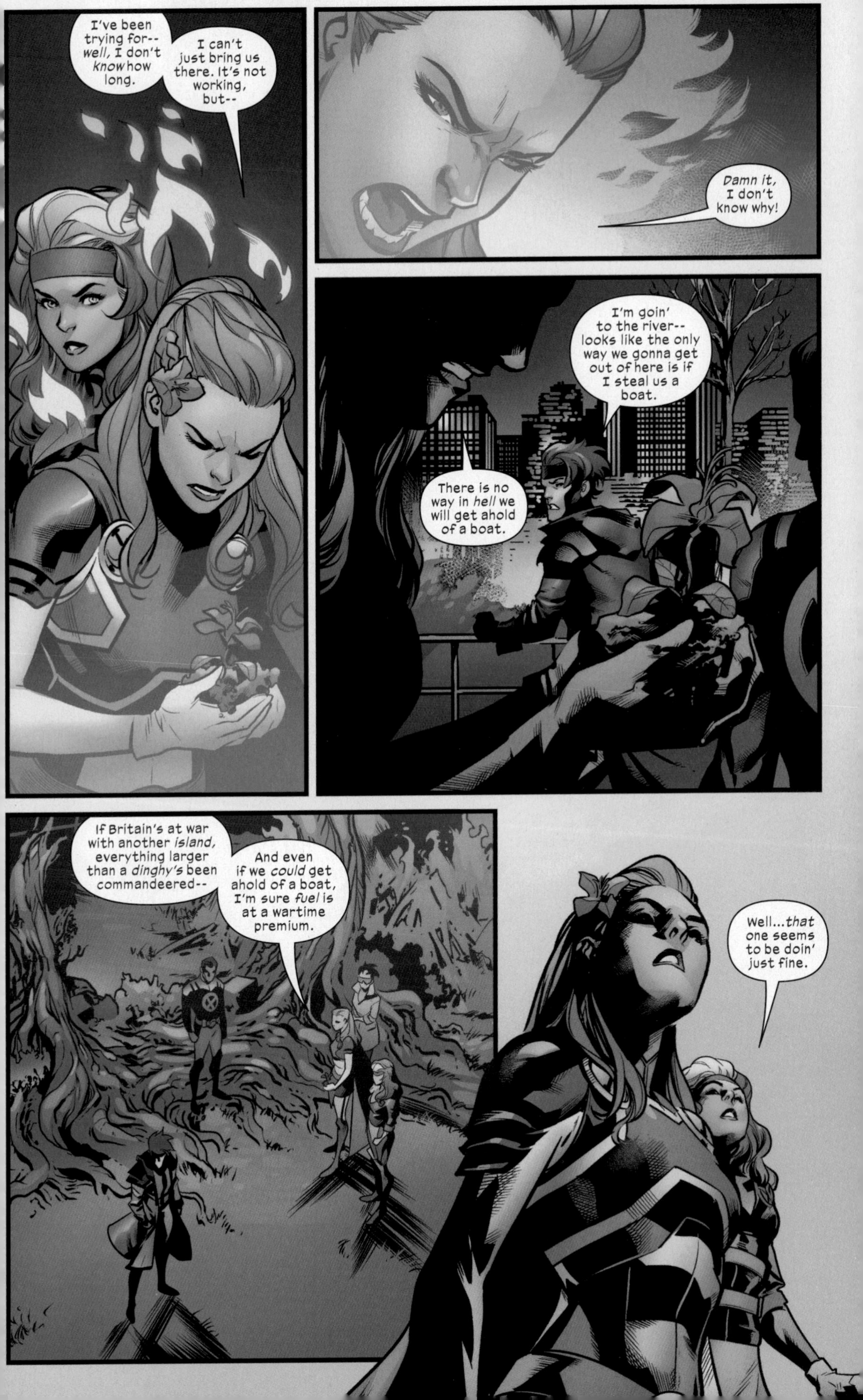

I've been trying for-- *well*, I don't *know* how long.
I can't just bring us there. It's not working, but--
Damn it, I don't know why!
I'm goin' to the river-- looks like the only way we gonna get out of here is if I steal us a boat.
There is no way in *hell* we will get ahold of a boat.
If Britain's at war with another *island*, everything larger than a *dinghy's* been commandeered--
And even if we *could* get ahold of a boat, I'm sure *fuel* is at a wartime premium.
Well...*that* one seems to be doin' just fine.

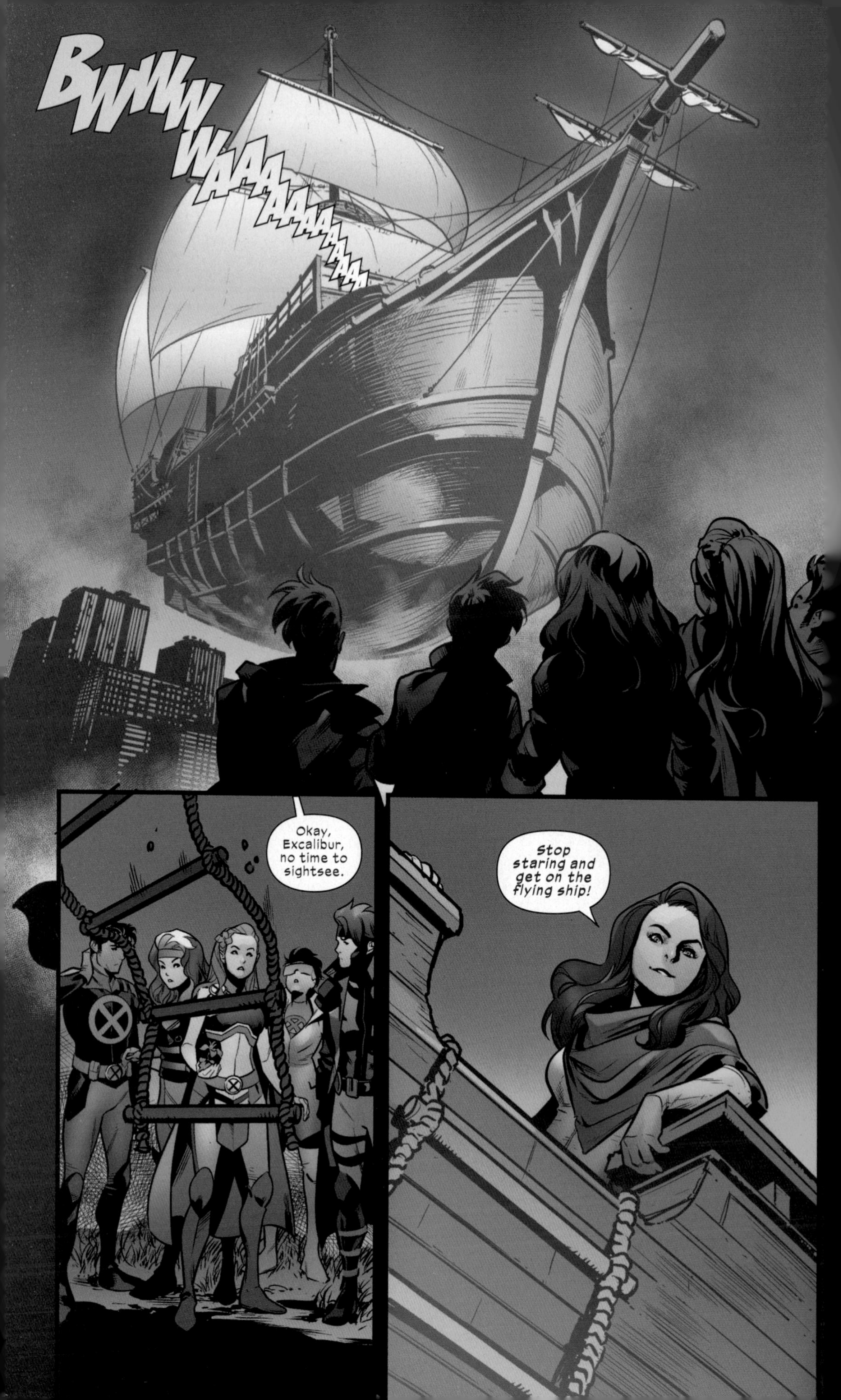
BWWWWAAAAAAAAAA
Okay, Excalibur, no time to sightsee.
Stop staring and get on the flying ship!

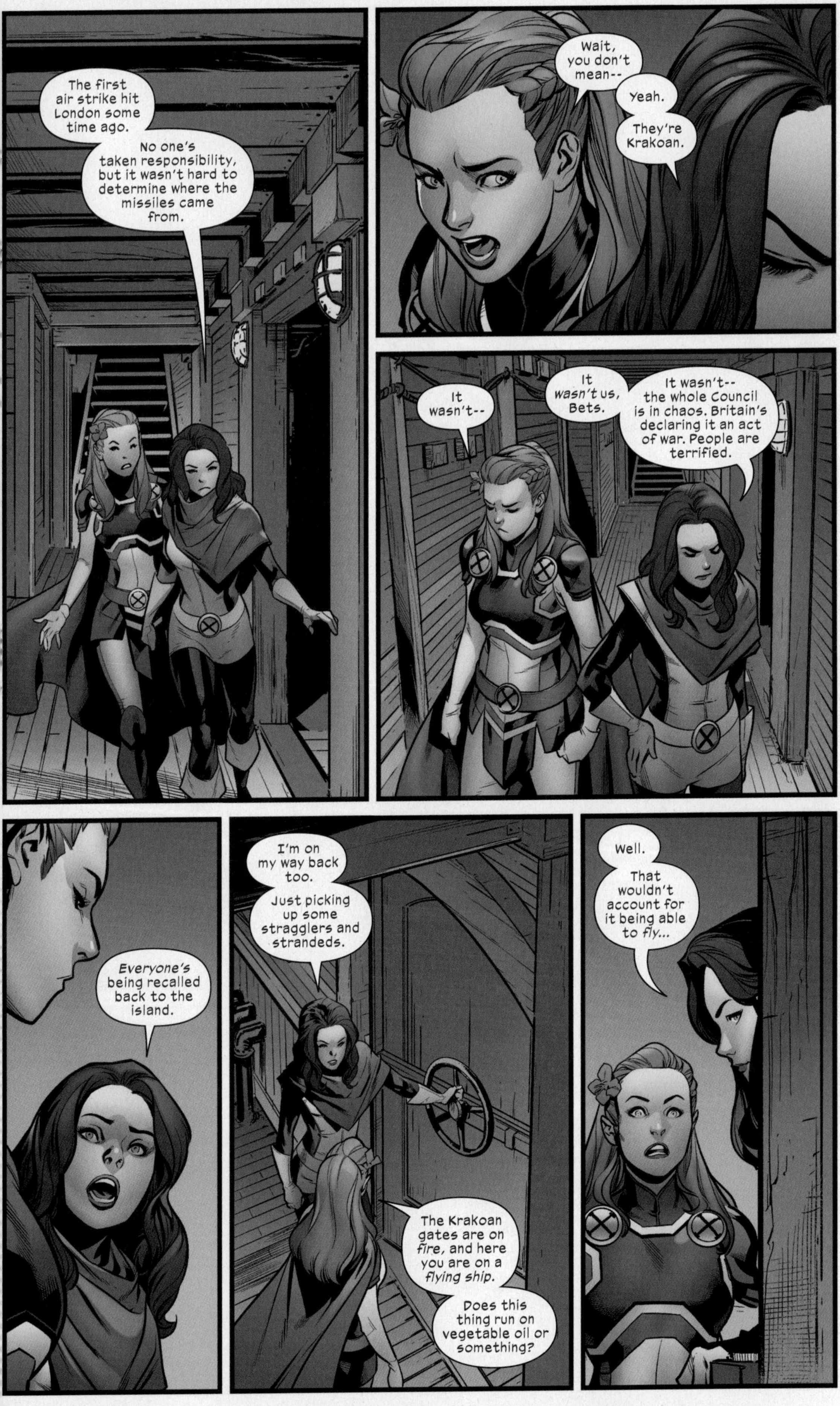
The first air strike hit London some time ago.
No one's taken responsibility, but it wasn't hard to determine where the missiles came from.
Wait, you don't mean--
Yeah.
They're Krakoan.
It wasn't--
It *wasn't* us, Bets.
It wasn't-- the whole Council is in chaos. Britain's declaring it an act of war. People are terrified.
Everyone's being recalled back to the island.
I'm on my way back too.
Just picking up some stragglers and strandeds.
The Krakoan gates are on *fire,* and here you are on a *flying ship.*
Does this thing run on vegetable oil or something?
Well.
That wouldn't account for it being able to *fly...*

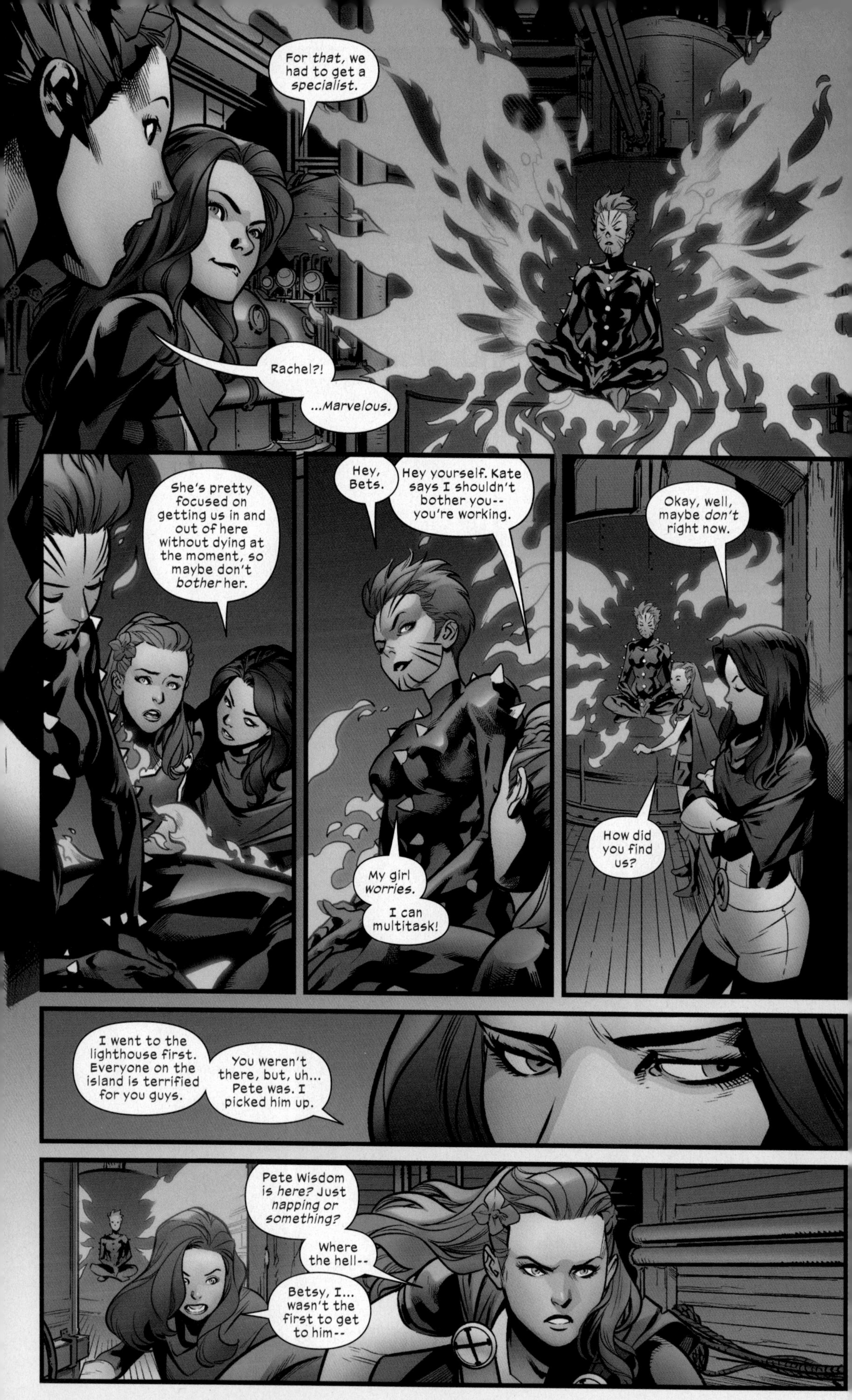
For that, we had to get a specialist.
Rachel?!
...Marvelous.
She's pretty focused on getting us in and out of here without dying at the moment, so maybe don't bother her.
Hey, Bets.
Hey yourself. Kate says I shouldn't bother you-- you're working.
My girl worries.
I can multitask!
Okay, well, maybe don't right now.
How did you find us?
I went to the lighthouse first. Everyone on the island is terrified for you guys.
You weren't there, but, uh... Pete was. I picked him up.
Pete Wisdom is here? Just napping or something?
Where the hell--
Betsy, I... wasn't the first to get to him--

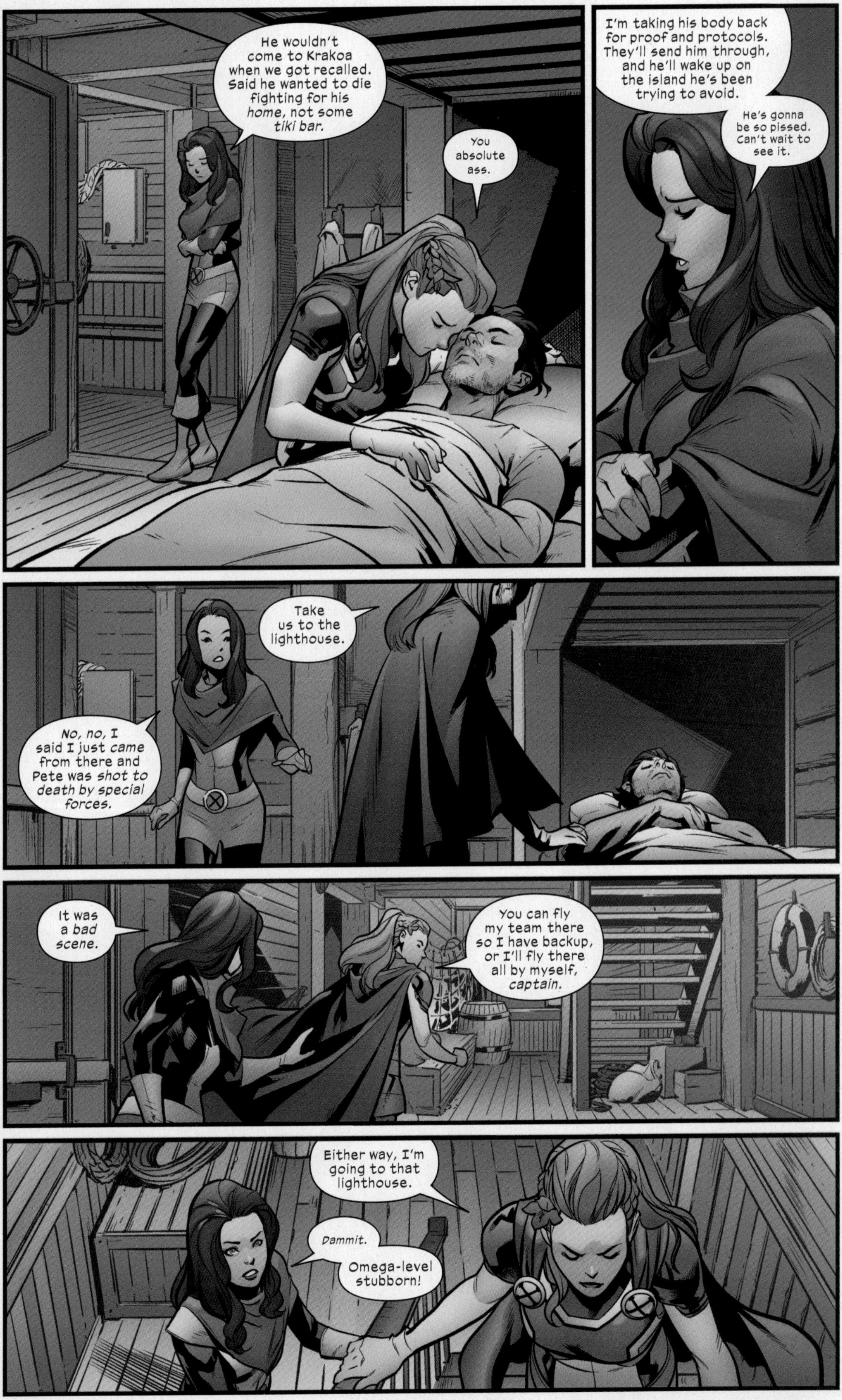

He wouldn't come to Krakoa when we got recalled. Said he wanted to die fighting for his *home*, not some *tiki bar*.
You absolute ass.
I'm taking his body back for proof and protocols. They'll send him through, and he'll wake up on the island he's been trying to avoid.
He's gonna be so pissed. Can't wait to see it.
Take us to the lighthouse.
No, no, I said I just came from there and Pete was shot to death by special forces.
It was a *bad* scene.
You can fly my team there so I have backup, or I'll fly there all by myself, *captain*.
Either way, I'm going to that lighthouse.
Dammit.
Omega-level stubborn!

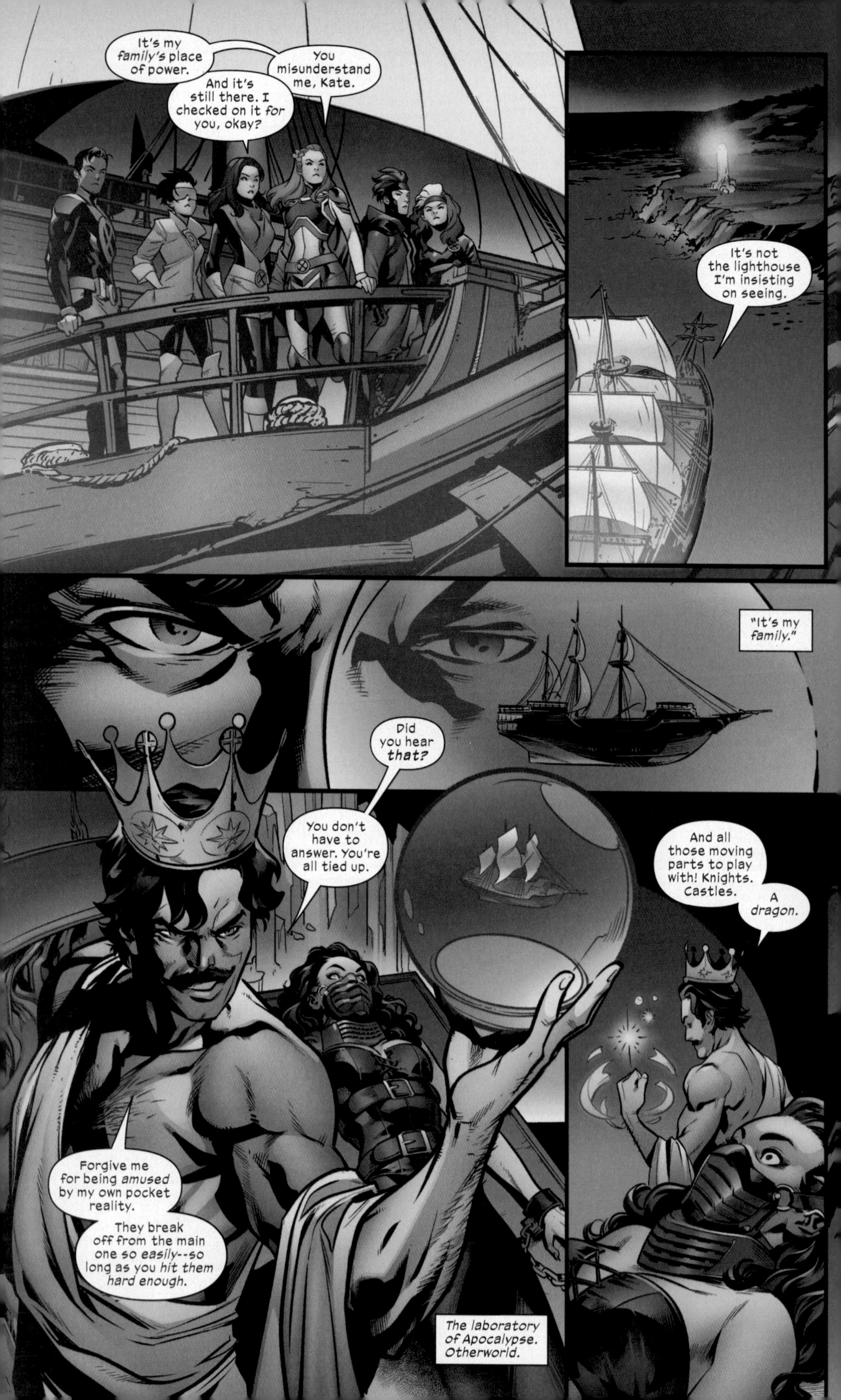
It's my *family's* place of power.
And it's still there. I checked on it *for* you, okay?
You misunderstand me, Kate.
It's not the lighthouse I'm insisting on seeing.
"It's my *family*."
Did you hear *that?*
You don't have to answer. You're all tied up.
Forgive me for being *amused* by my own pocket reality.
They break off from the main one so *easily*--so long as you *hit them hard enough*.
The laboratory of Apocalypse. Otherworld.
And all those moving parts to play with! Knights. Castles.
A *dragon*.

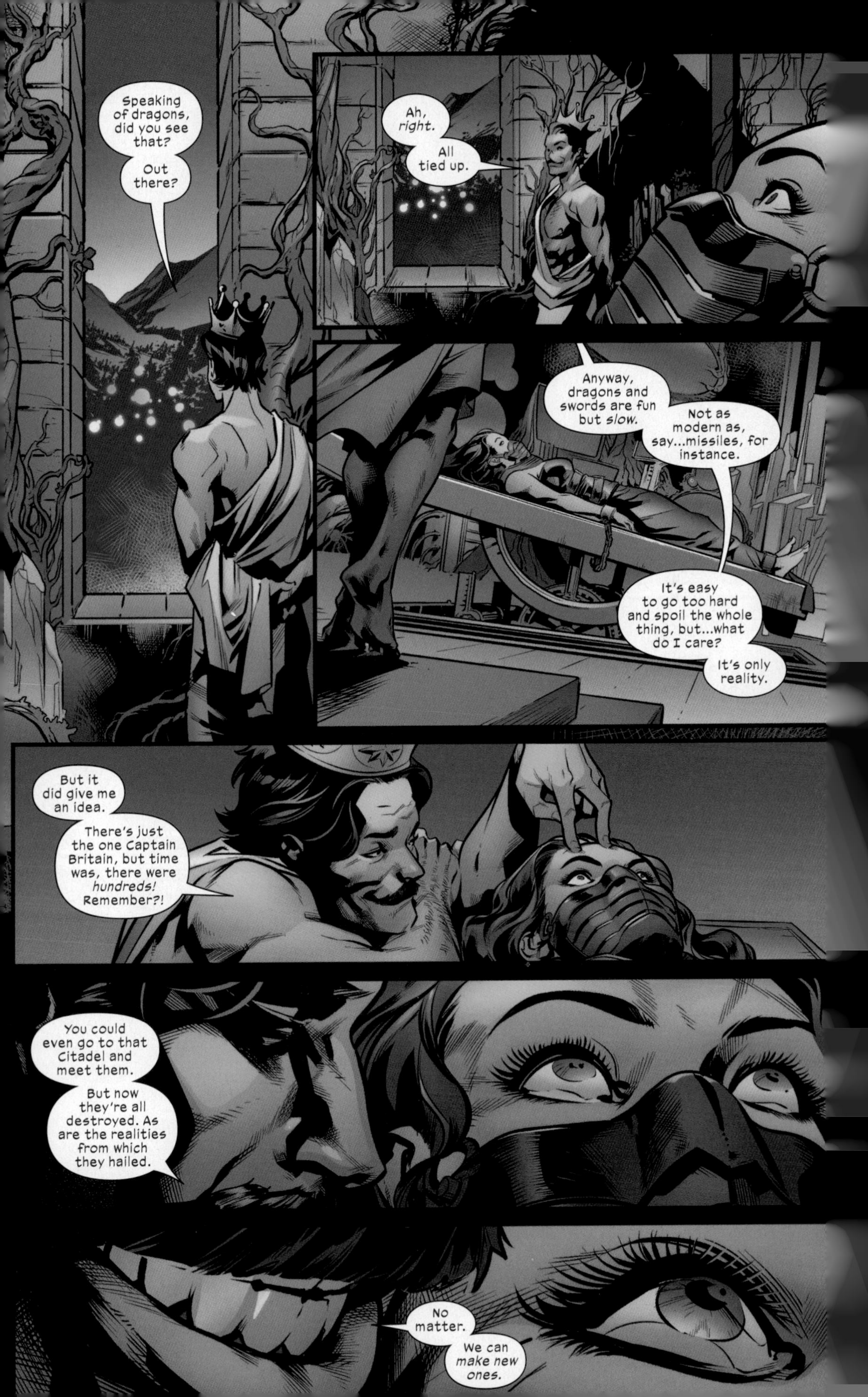
Speaking of dragons, did you see that?
Out there?
Ah, *right.*
All tied up.
Anyway, dragons and swords are fun but *slow.*
Not as modern as, say...missiles, for instance.
It's easy to go too hard and spoil the whole thing, but...what do I care?
It's only reality.
But it did give me an idea.
There's just the one Captain Britain, but time was, there were *hundreds!* Remember?!
You could even go to that Citadel and meet them.
But now they're all destroyed. As are the realities from which they hailed.
No matter.
We can *make new ones.*

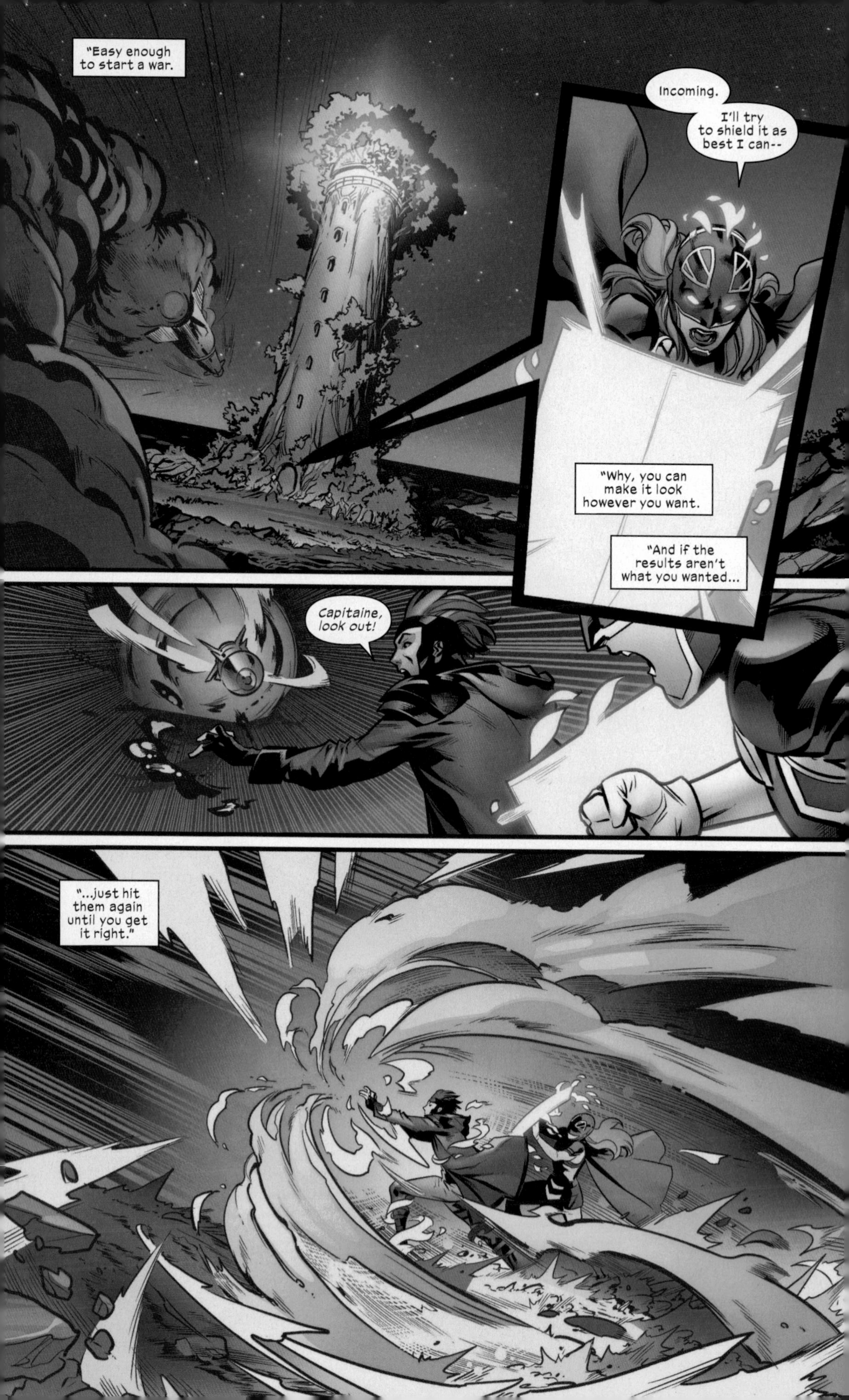
"Easy enough
to start a war.
Incoming.
I'll try
to shield it as
best I can--
"Why, you can
make it look
however you want.
"And if the
results aren't
what you wanted...
Capitaine,
look out!
"...just hit
them again
until you get
it right."

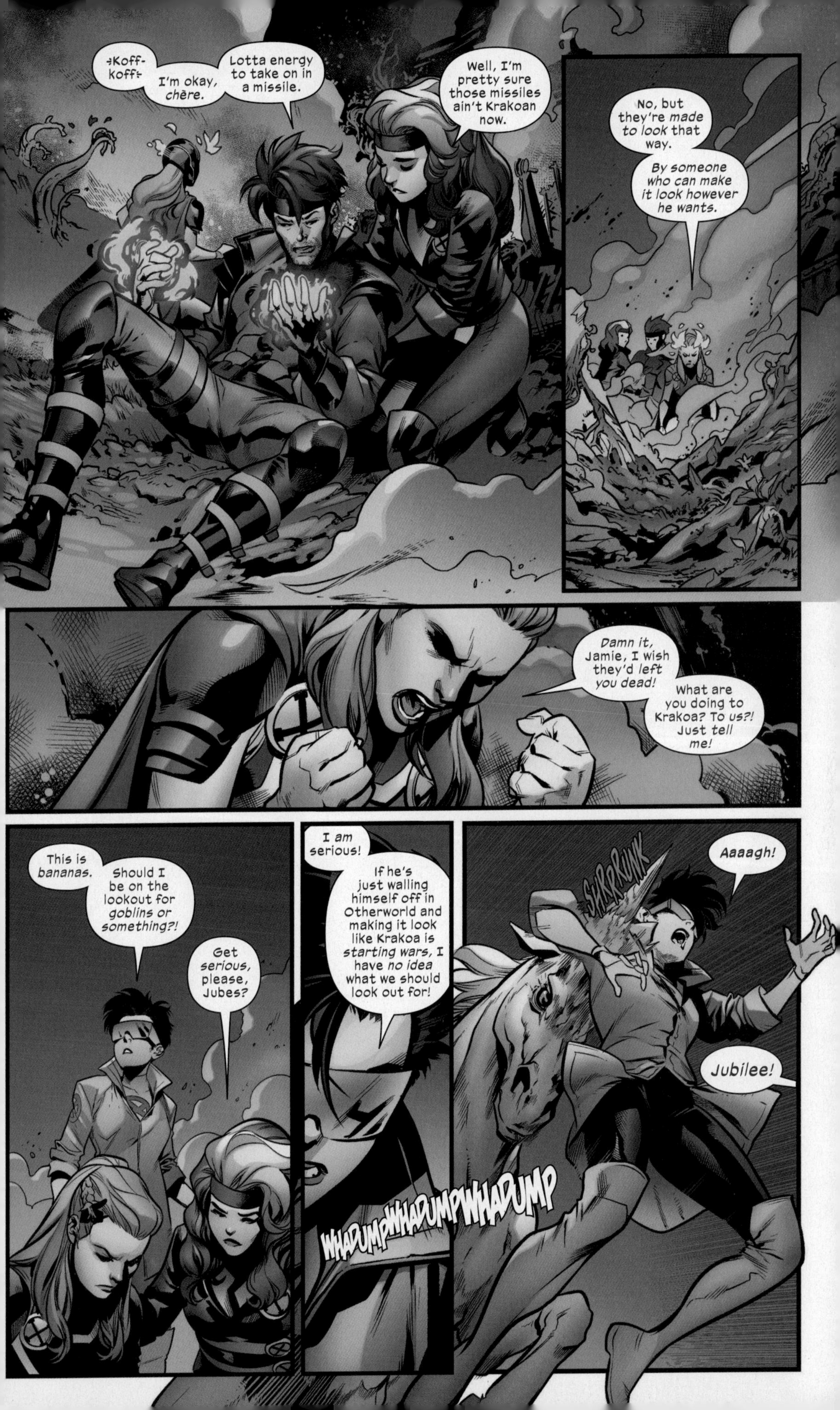
-Koff-
koff-
I'm okay, *chère.*
Lotta energy to take on in a missile.
Well, I'm pretty sure those missiles ain't Krakoan now.
No, but they're *made* to *look* that way.
By someone who can make it look however he wants.
Damn it, Jamie, I wish they'd *left* you *dead!*
What are you doing to Krakoa? To *us?!* Just *tell* me!
This is *bananas.*
Should I be on the lookout for *goblins* or *something?!*
Get *serious,* please, Jubes?
I am *serious!*
If he's just walling himself off in Otherworld and making it look like Krakoa is *starting wars,* I have *no idea* what we should look out for!
SPLRUNK
Aaaagh!
Jubilee!
WHADUMPWHADUMPWHADUMP

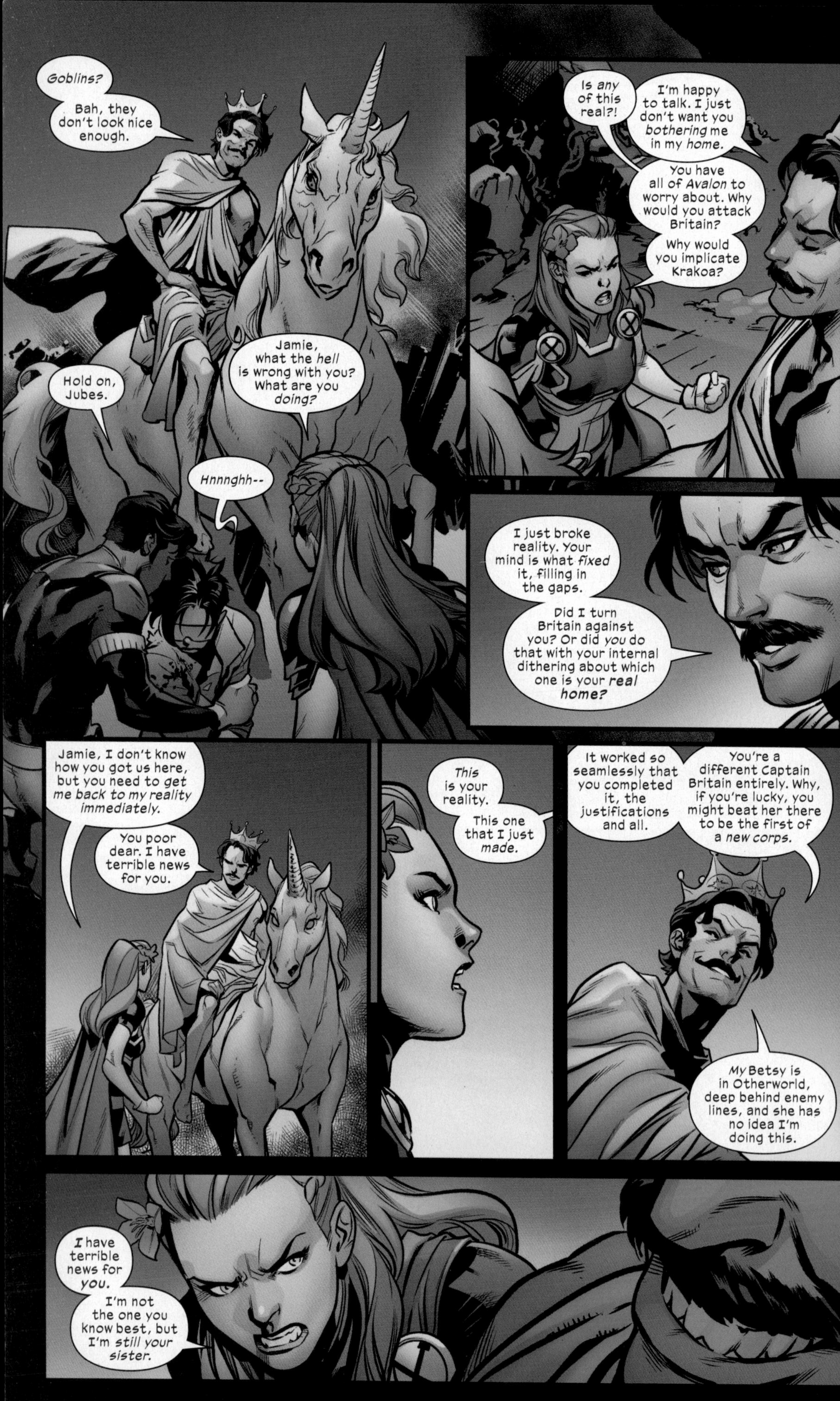

Goblins?
Bah, they don't look nice enough.
Hold on, Jubes.
Jamie, what the hell is wrong with you? What are you doing?
Hnnnghh--
Is any of this real?!
I'm happy to talk. I just don't want you bothering me in my home.
You have all of Avalon to worry about. Why would you attack Britain?
Why would you implicate Krakoa?
I just broke reality. Your mind is what fixed it, filling in the gaps.
Did I turn Britain against you? Or did you do that with your internal dithering about which one is your real home?
Jamie, I don't know how you got us here, but you need to get me back to my reality immediately.
You poor dear. I have terrible news for you.
This is your reality.
This one that I just made.
It worked so seamlessly that you completed it, the justifications and all.
You're a different Captain Britain entirely. Why, if you're lucky, you might beat her there to be the first of a new corps.
My Betsy is in Otherworld, deep behind enemy lines, and she has no idea I'm doing this.
I have terrible news for you.
I'm not the one you know best, but I'm still your sister.

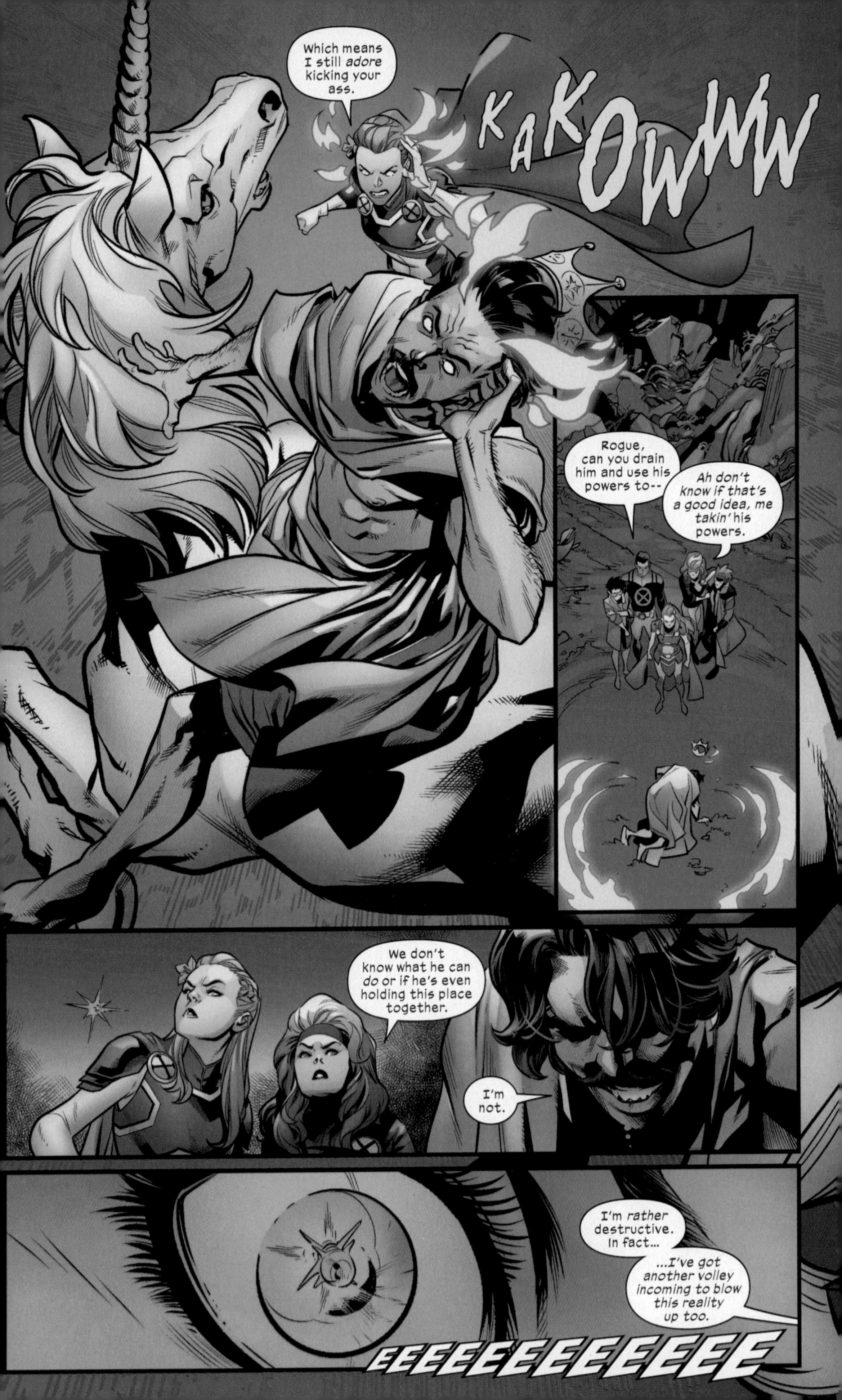
Which means I still *adore* kicking your ass.
KAKOWMW
Rogue, can you drain him and use his powers to--
Ah don't know if that's a good idea, me takin' his powers.
We don't know what he can *do* or if he's even holding this place together.
I'm not.
I'm *rather* destructive. In fact...
...I've got another volley incoming to blow this reality up too.
EEEEEEEEEEEEE

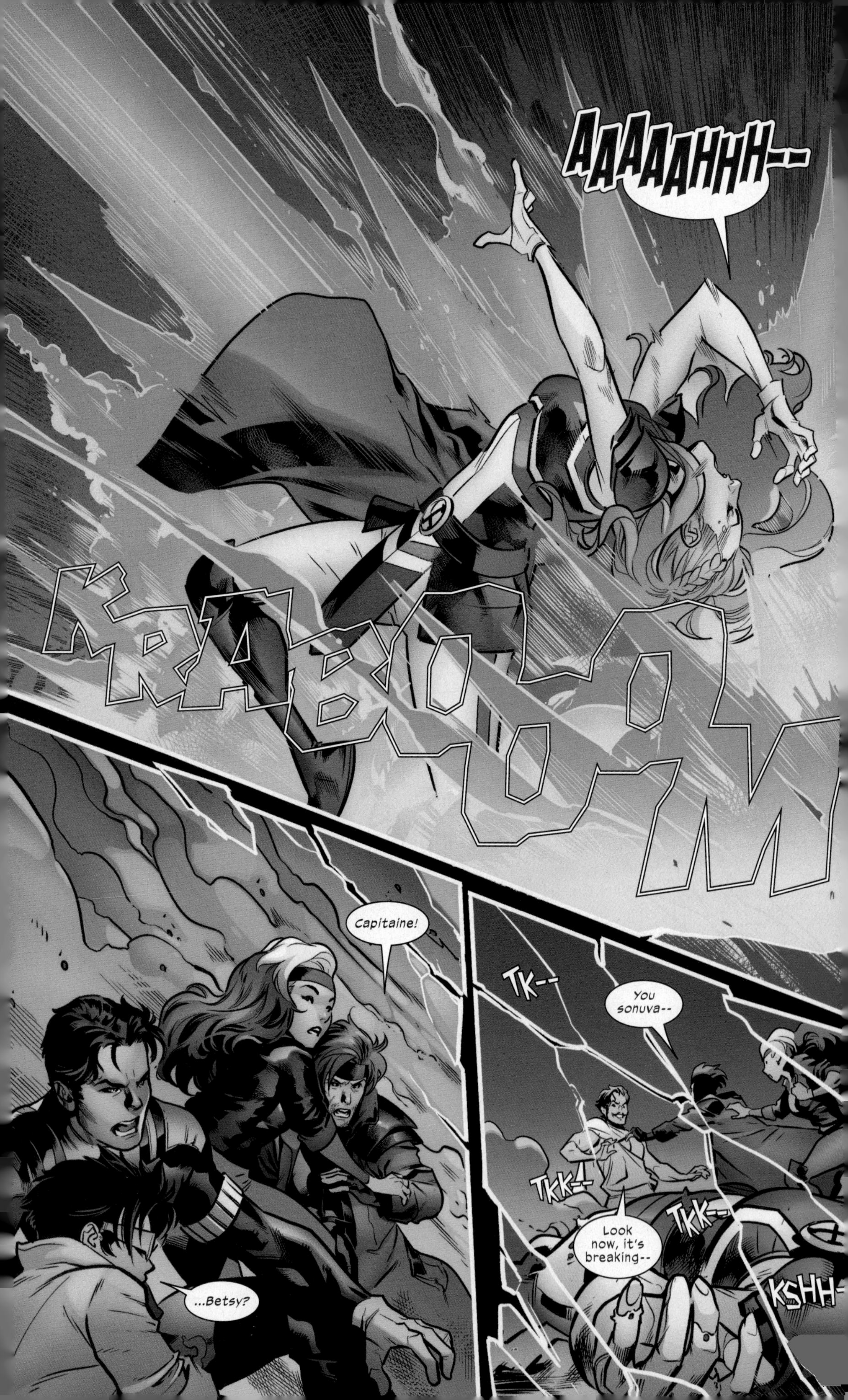
AAAAAHHH--
KRABOOOOM
Capitaine!
...Betsy?
TK--
You sonuva--
TKK--
Look now, it's breaking--
TKK--
KSHH-

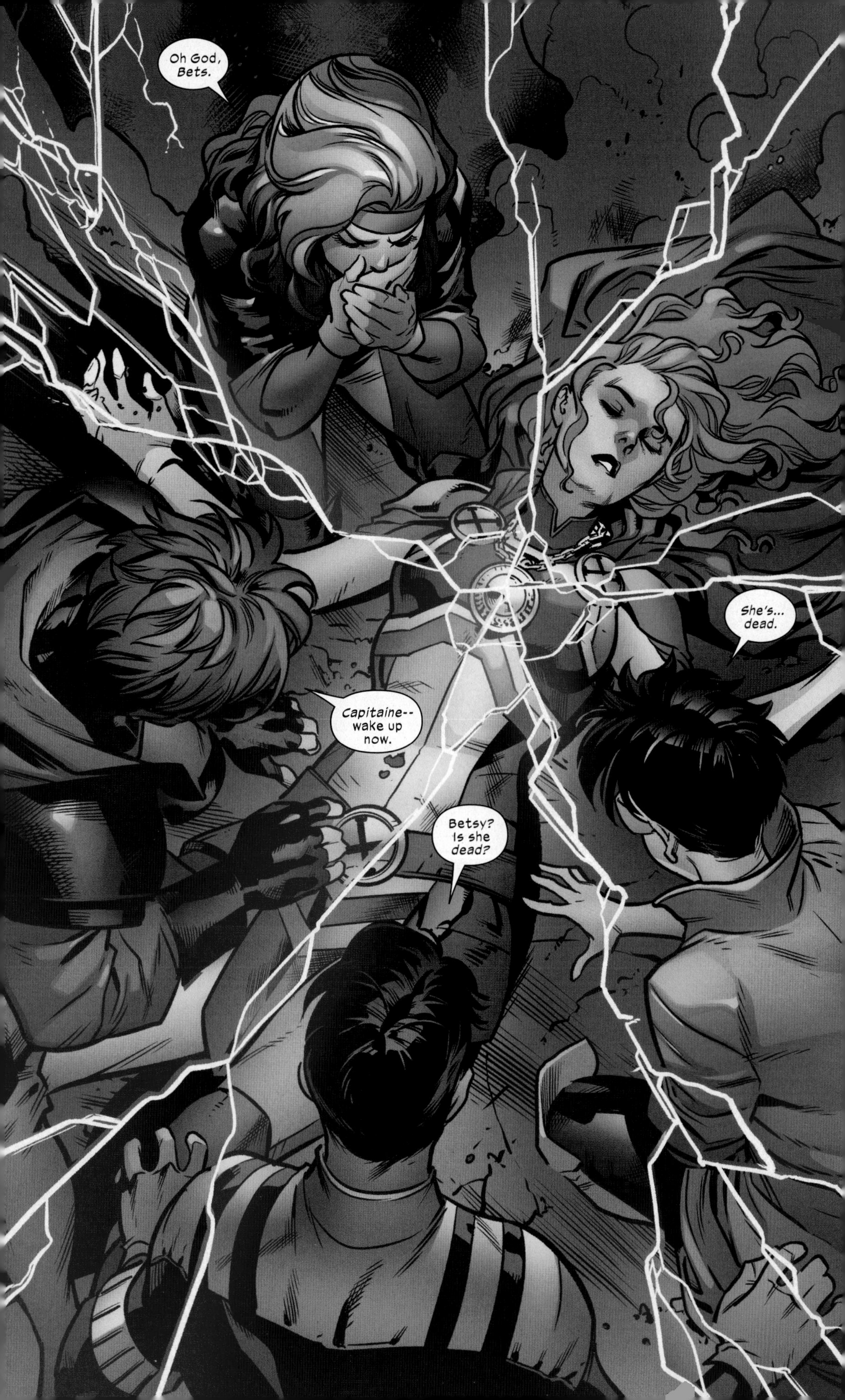
Oh God, Bets.
She's... dead.
Capitaine-- wake up now.
Betsy? Is she dead?

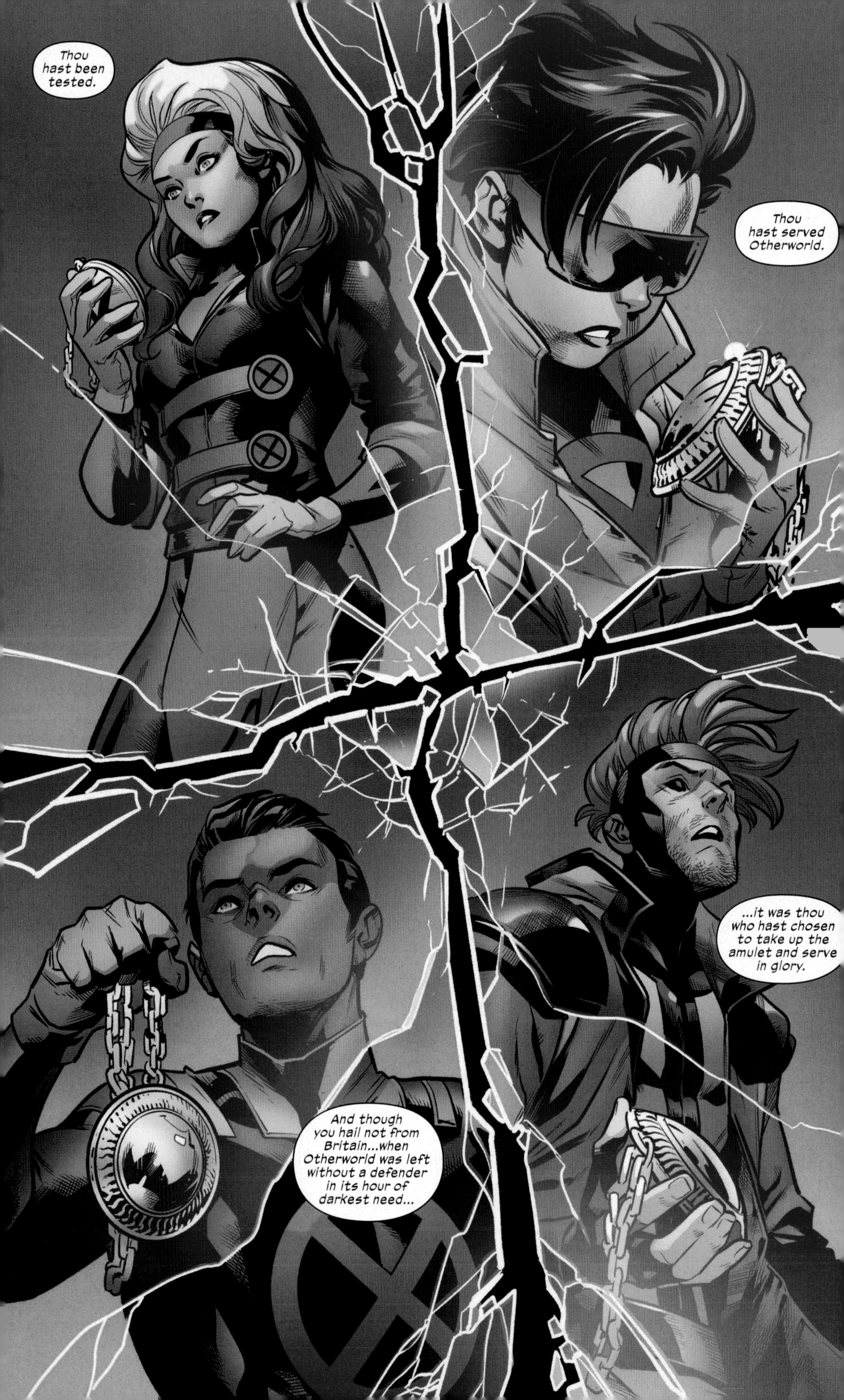
Thou hast been tested.
Thou hast served Otherworld.
And though you hail not from Britain...when Otherworld was left without a defender in its hour of darkest need...
...it was thou who hast chosen to take up the amulet and serve in glory.

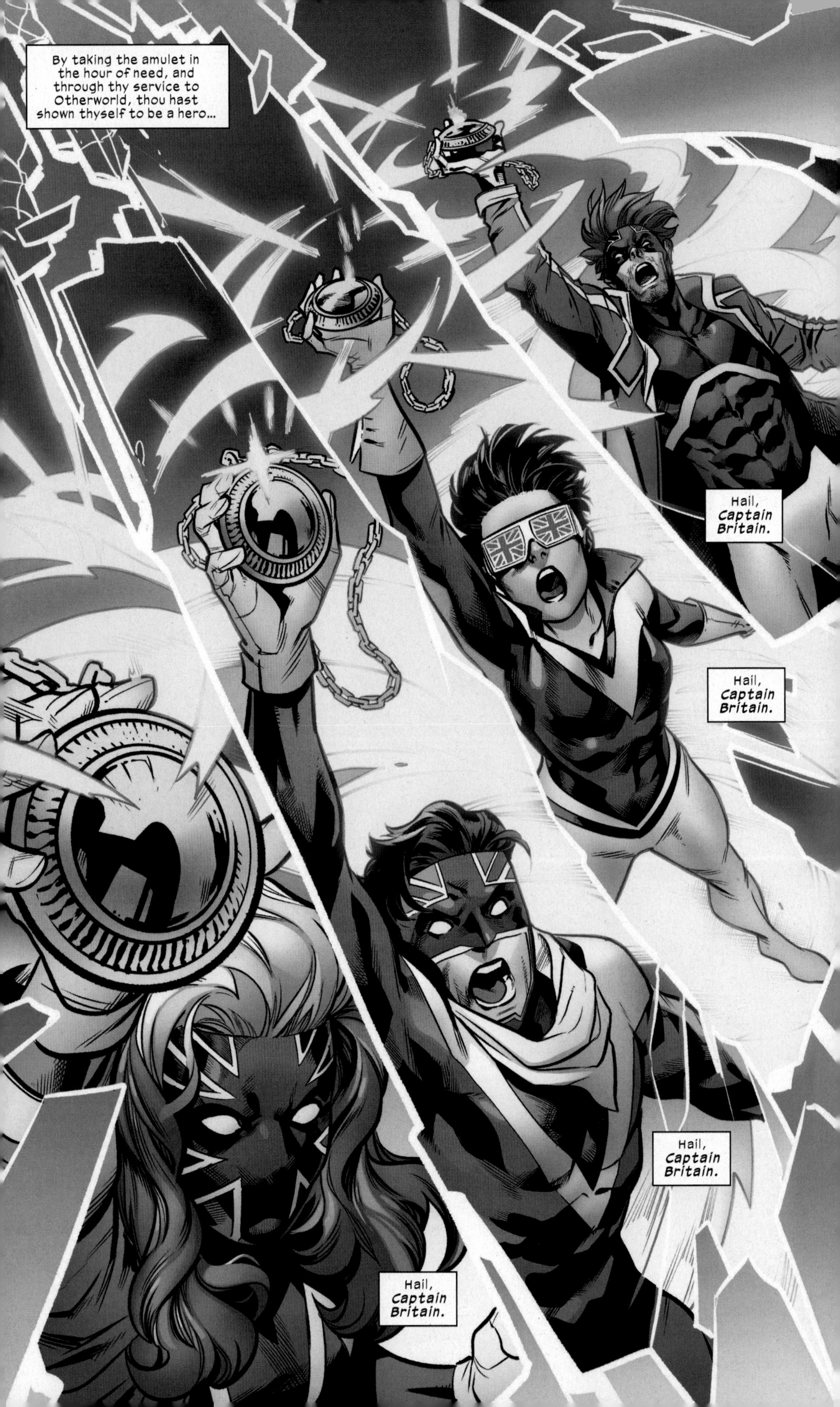
By taking the amulet in the hour of need, and through thy service to Otherworld, thou hast shown thyself to be a hero...
Hail, *Captain Britain.*
Hail, *Captain Britain.*
Hail, *Captain Britain.*
Hail, *Captain Britain.*

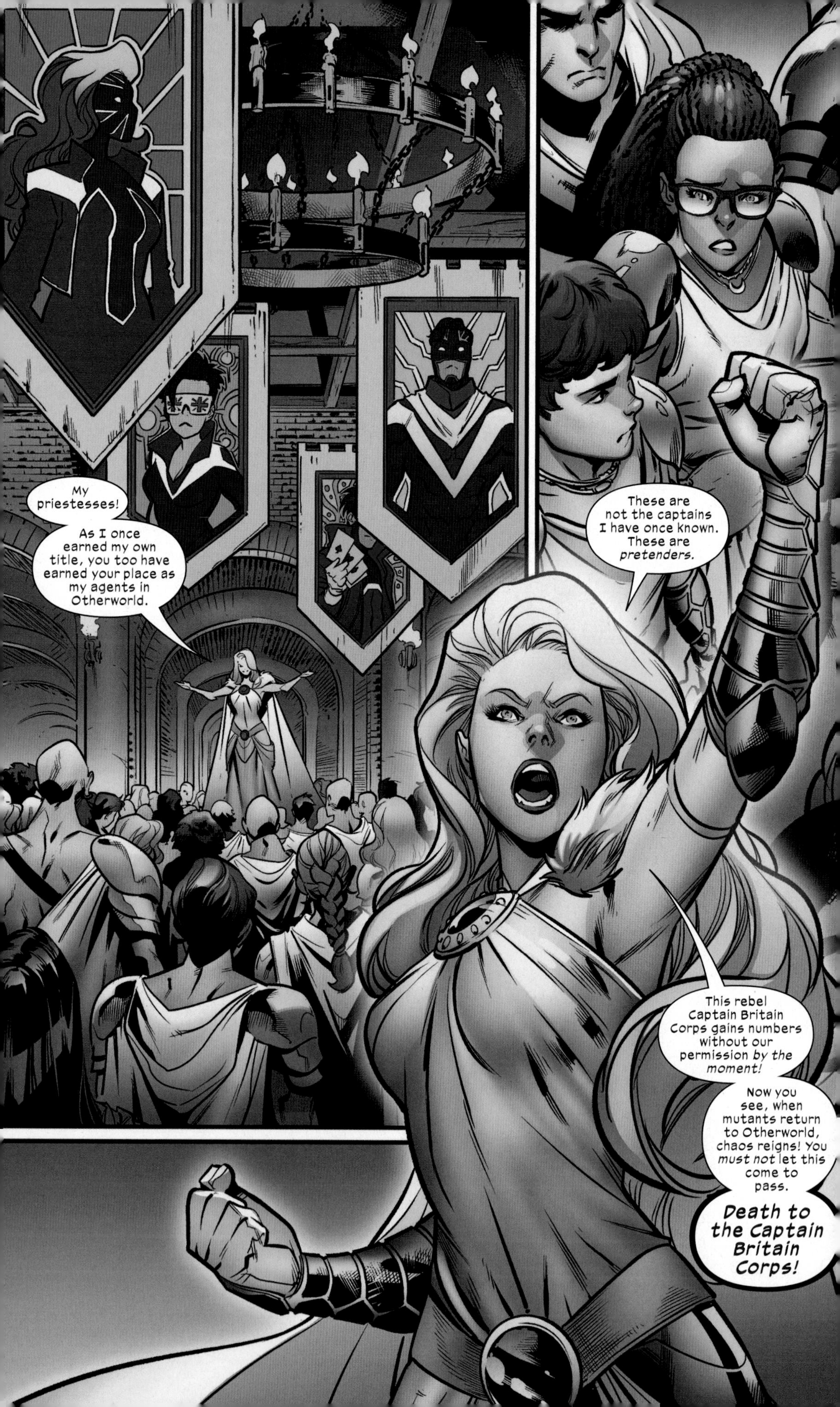

My priestesses!
As I once earned my own title, you too have earned your place as my agents in Otherworld.
These are not the captains I have once known. These are *pretenders.*
This rebel Captain Britain Corps gains numbers without our permission *by the moment!*
Now you see, when mutants return to Otherworld, chaos reigns! You *must not* let this come to pass.
Death to the Captain Britain Corps!

INCURSION

Omega-level reality-warping mutant King Jamie Braddock of Avalon commits a series of attacks on the very fabric of reality. Each one causes a fracture, including a ripple effect that causes reality to 'backfill' with memories and justifications of its own existence. The incursion goes largely unnoticed by the denizens of the home reality.

Traditionally, the accolade of Captain Britain has been chosen by a direct offer from Otherworld leadership to a member of the Braddock family or, rarely, another who would take their place.

King Jamie's method is quite unprecedented.

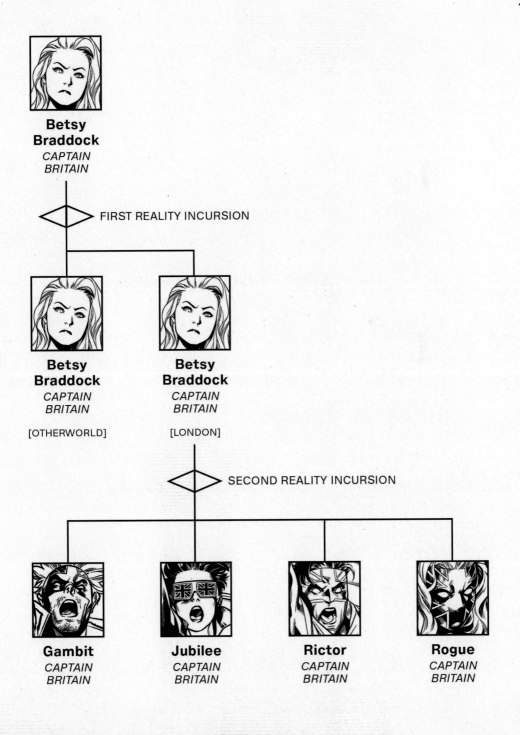

Betsy Braddock
CAPTAIN BRITAIN

◇ FIRST REALITY INCURSION

Betsy Braddock
CAPTAIN BRITAIN

[OTHERWORLD]

Betsy Braddock
CAPTAIN BRITAIN

[LONDON]

◇ SECOND REALITY INCURSION

Gambit
CAPTAIN BRITAIN

Jubilee
CAPTAIN BRITAIN

Rictor
CAPTAIN BRITAIN

Rogue
CAPTAIN BRITAIN

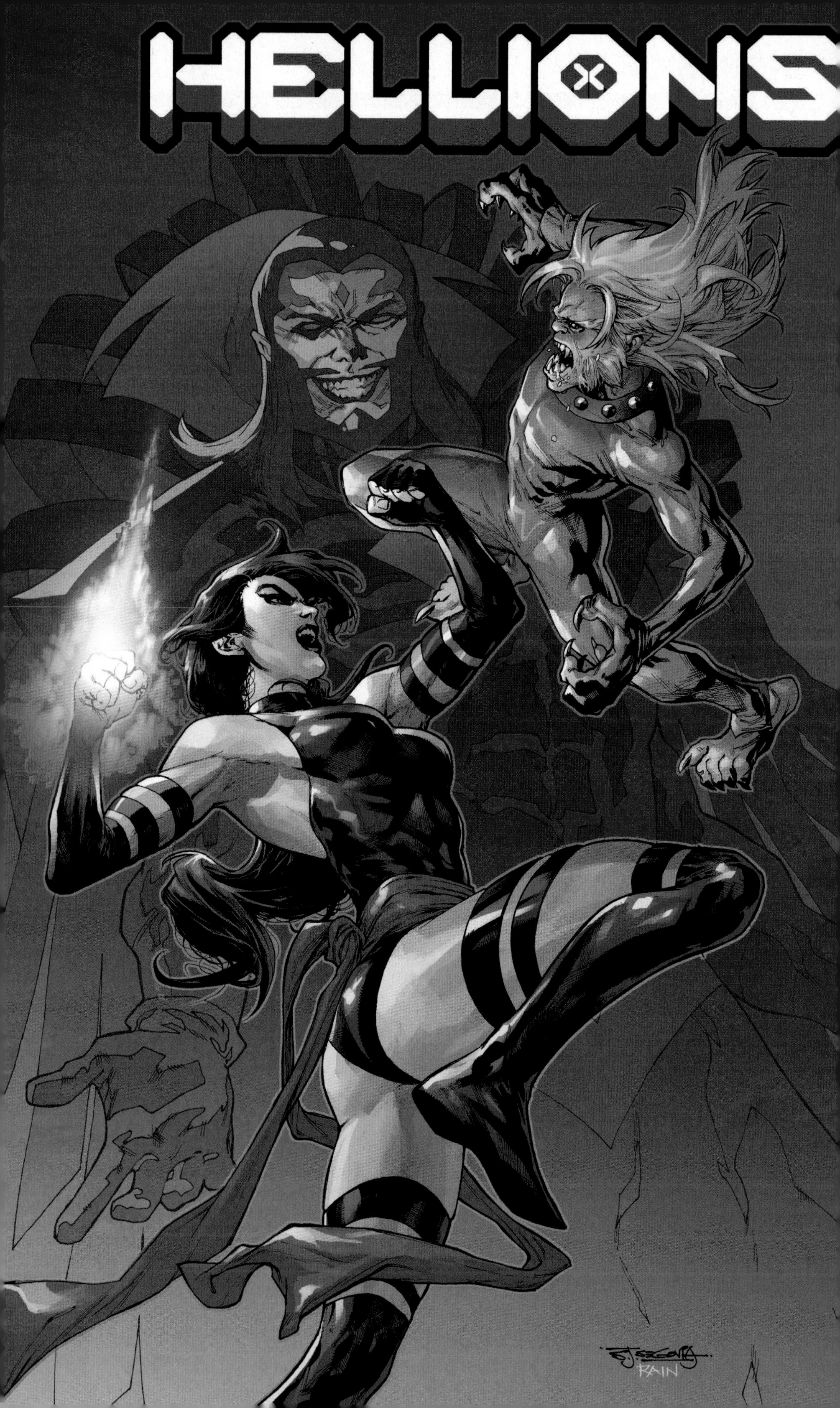
HELLIONS
RAIN

[hell_[0.2]
[ions_[0.2]

Those whose violence you do not understand have often seen horrors you cannot imagine.

-NIGHTCRAWLER

[hell_[0.X]
[ions_[0.X]

[hell_[0.2].....]
[ions_[0.2].....]

[Hellions_alpha.]

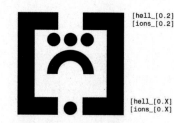

[hell_[0.2]
[ions_[0.2]

[hell_[0.X]
[ions_[0.X]

IDLE HANDS

The island-nation of Krakoa offers a fresh start for all mutants. No matter who they are...no matter what they've done...no matter if they have no intention of ever changing.

But Mister Sinister has a plan for those mutants (including the theoretically reformed Havok and reluctant team watchdog Psylocke): channel their destructive energy into productivity! And now the HELLIONS are on their way to destroy Sinister's defunct cloning lab in the basement of the orphanage where Havok grew up.

Man, could this day get more depressing?

Havok

Orphan-Maker

Nanny

Wild Child

Empath

Greycrow

Psylocke

Madelyne
Pryor

[hell_[0.2]...]
[ions_[0.2]...]

[.wreaking....]

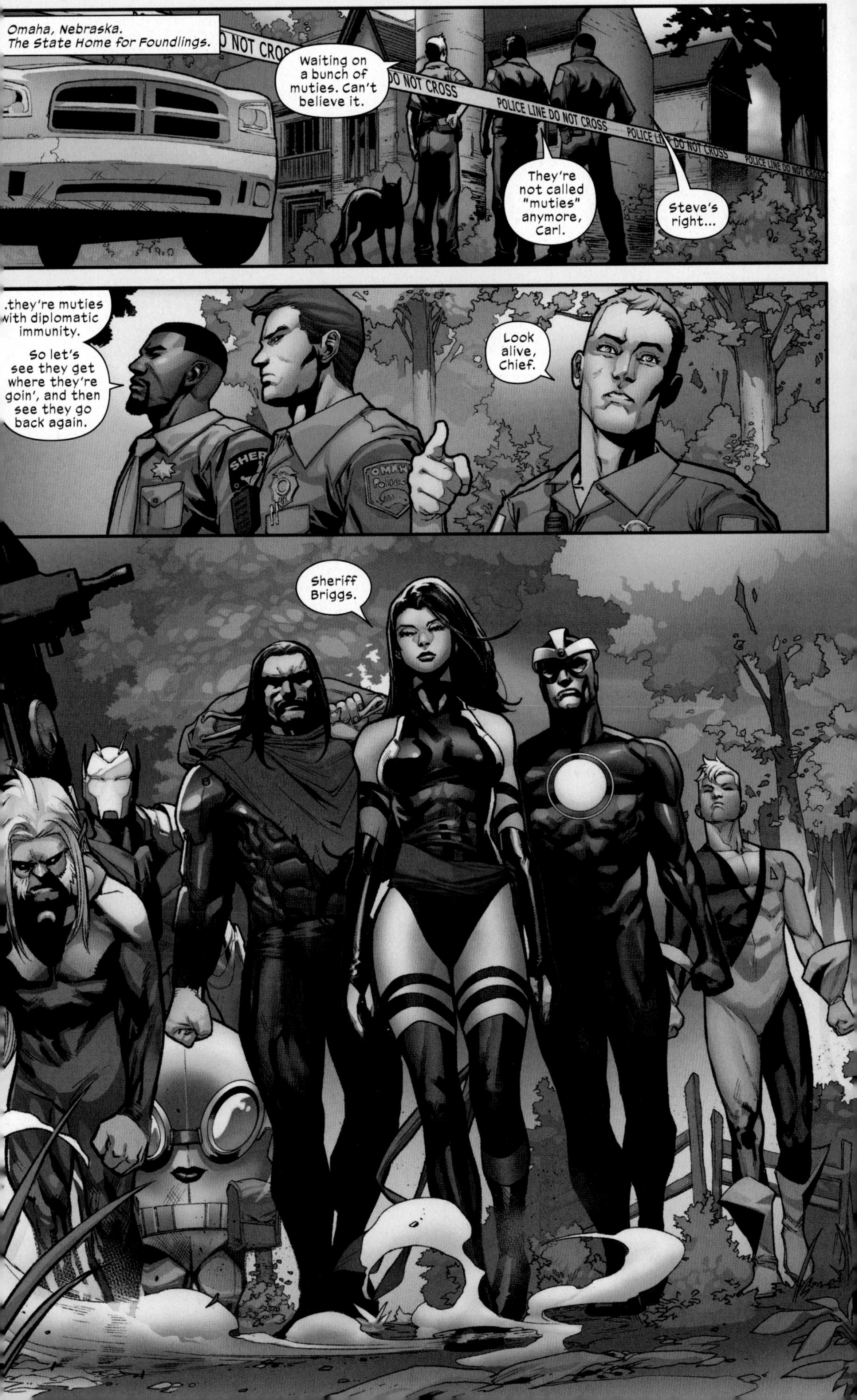
Omaha, Nebraska.
The State Home for Foundlings.
Waiting on a bunch of muties. Can't believe it.
DO NOT CROSS
POLICE LINE DO NOT CROSS
They're not called "muties" anymore, Carl.
Steve's right...
...they're muties with diplomatic immunity.
So let's see they get where they're goin', and then see they go back again.
Look alive, Chief.
Sheriff Briggs.

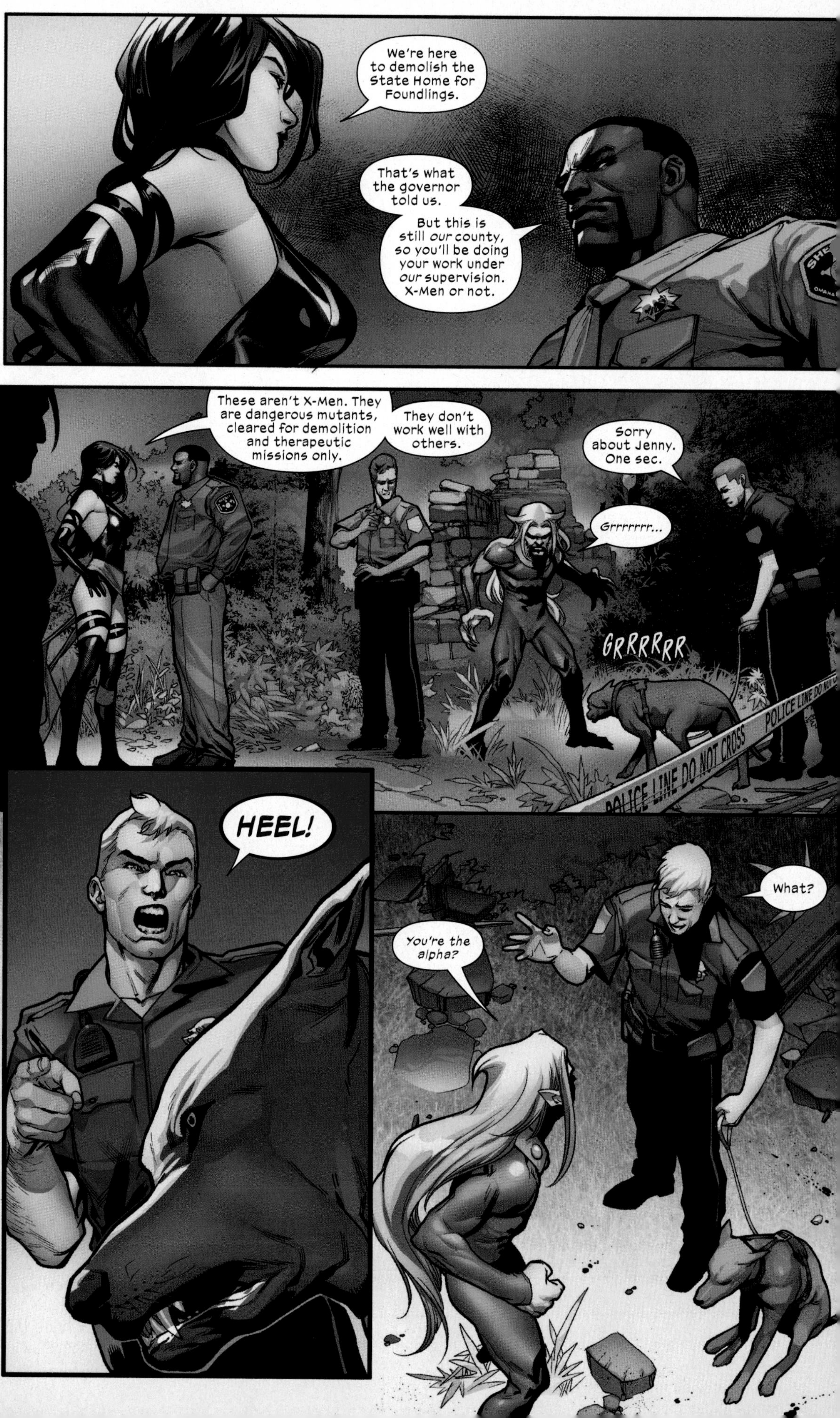
We're here to demolish the State Home for Foundlings.
That's what the governor told us.
But this is still *our* county, so you'll be doing your work under *our* supervision. X-Men or not.
These aren't X-Men. They are dangerous mutants, cleared for demolition and therapeutic missions only.
They don't work well with others.
Sorry about Jenny. One sec.
Grrrrrrr...
GRRRRRR
POLICE LINE DO NOT CROSS
HEEL!
What?
You're the alpha?

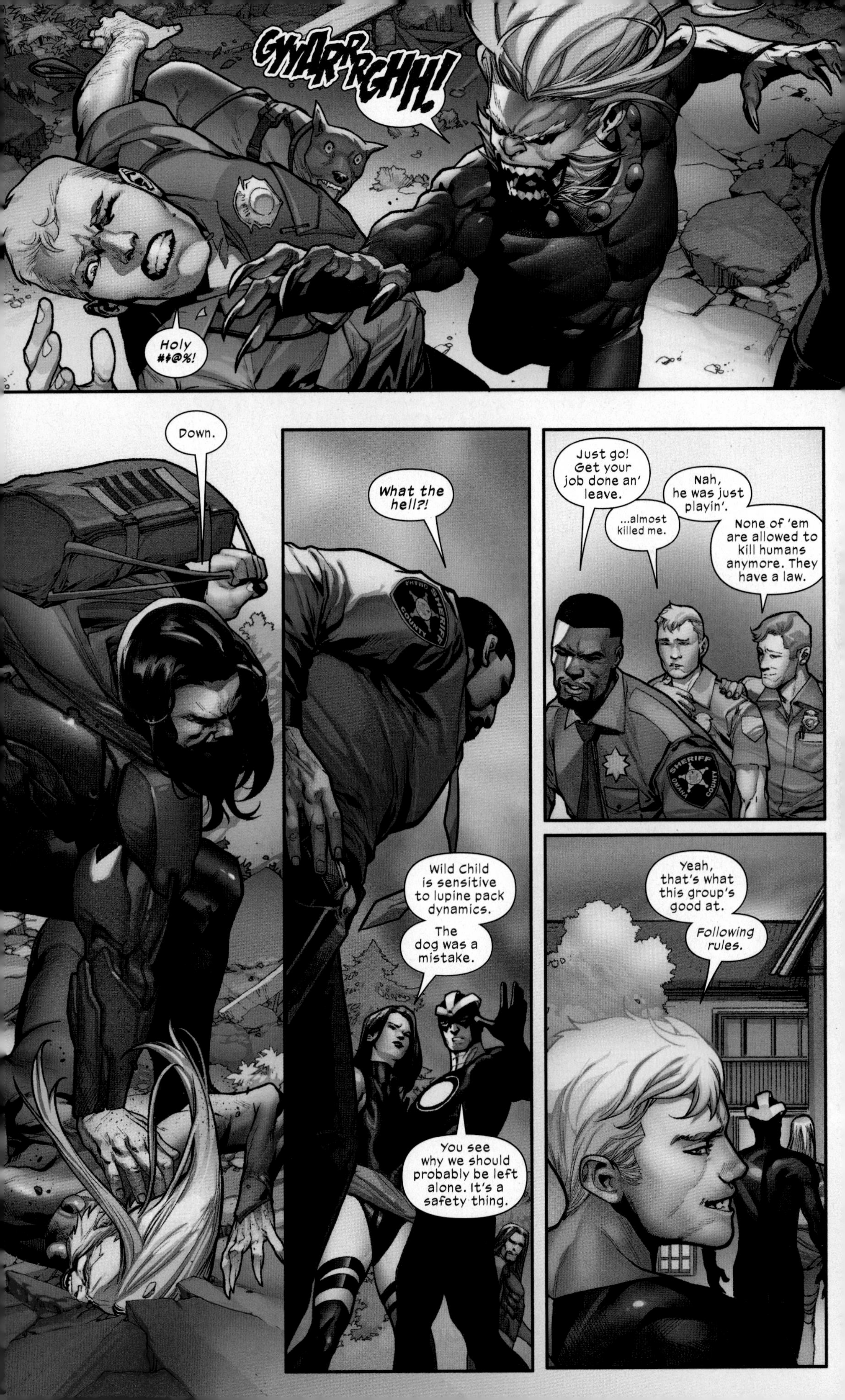
GYYARRRGHH!
Holy #$@%!
Down.
What the hell?!
Wild Child is sensitive to lupine pack dynamics.
The dog was a mistake.
You see why we should probably be left alone. It's a safety thing.
Just go! Get your job done an' leave.
...almost killed me.
Nah, he was just playin'.
None of 'em are allowed to kill humans anymore. They have a law.
Yeah, that's what this group's good at.
Following rules.

[00_bad___X]
[00_news__X]

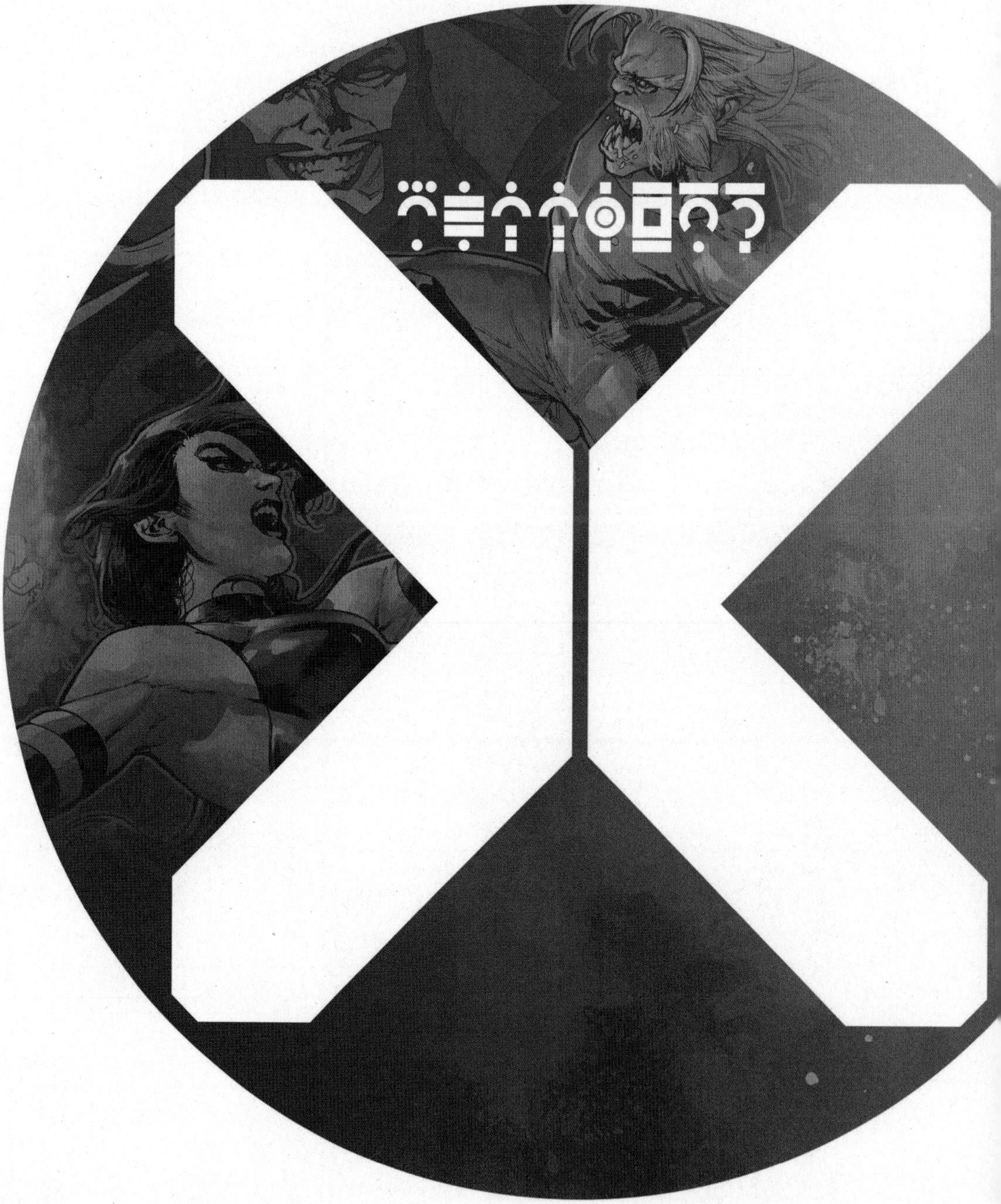

ZEB WELLS..[WRITER]
STEPHEN SEGOVIA................................[ARTIST]
DAVID CURIEL.............................[COLOR ARTIST]
VC's CORY PETIT..............................[LETTERER]
TOM MULLER....................................[DESIGN]

STEPHEN SEGOVIA & RAIN BEREDO...........[COVER ARTISTS]

BUTCH GUICE & RACHELLE ROSENBERG.......................
..................................[VARIANT COVER ARTISTS]

NICK RUSSELL..............................[PRODUCTION]

JONATHAN HICKMAN...........................[HEAD OF X]
ANNALISE BISSA.......................[ASSISTANT EDITOR]
JORDAN D. WHITE..............................[EDITOR]
C.B. CEBULSKI........................[EDITOR IN CHIEF]

[02]HELLIONS

[ISSUE TWO].....................BLOOD WORK

[00_hell__X]
[00__ions_X]

[00_00...0.]
[00_00...2.]

[00_best___]
[00___of___]

[00__the___]

[00_worst_X]

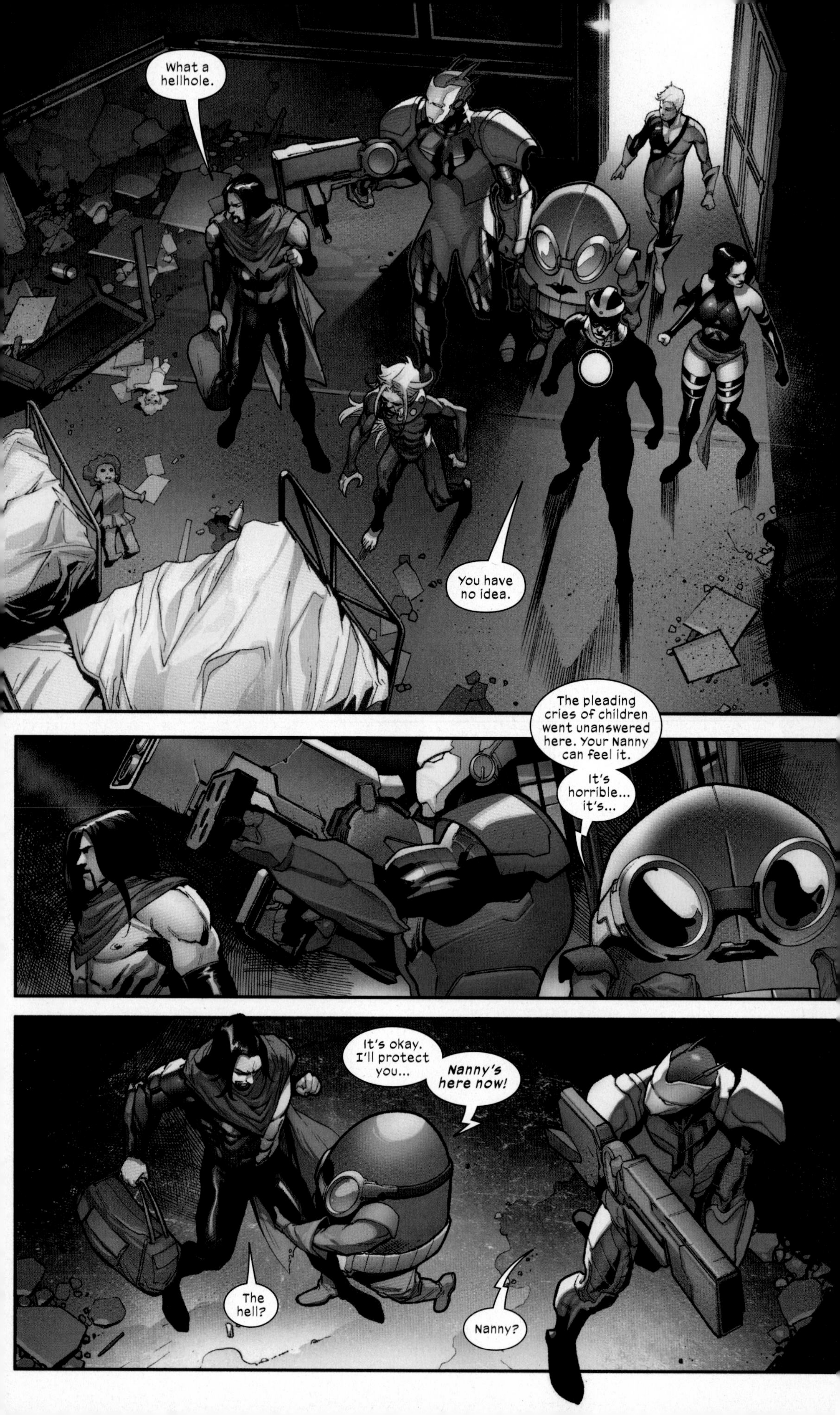
What a hellhole.
You have no idea.
The pleading cries of children went unanswered here. Your Nanny can feel it.
It's horrible... it's...
It's okay. I'll protect you...
Nanny's here now!
The hell?
Nanny?

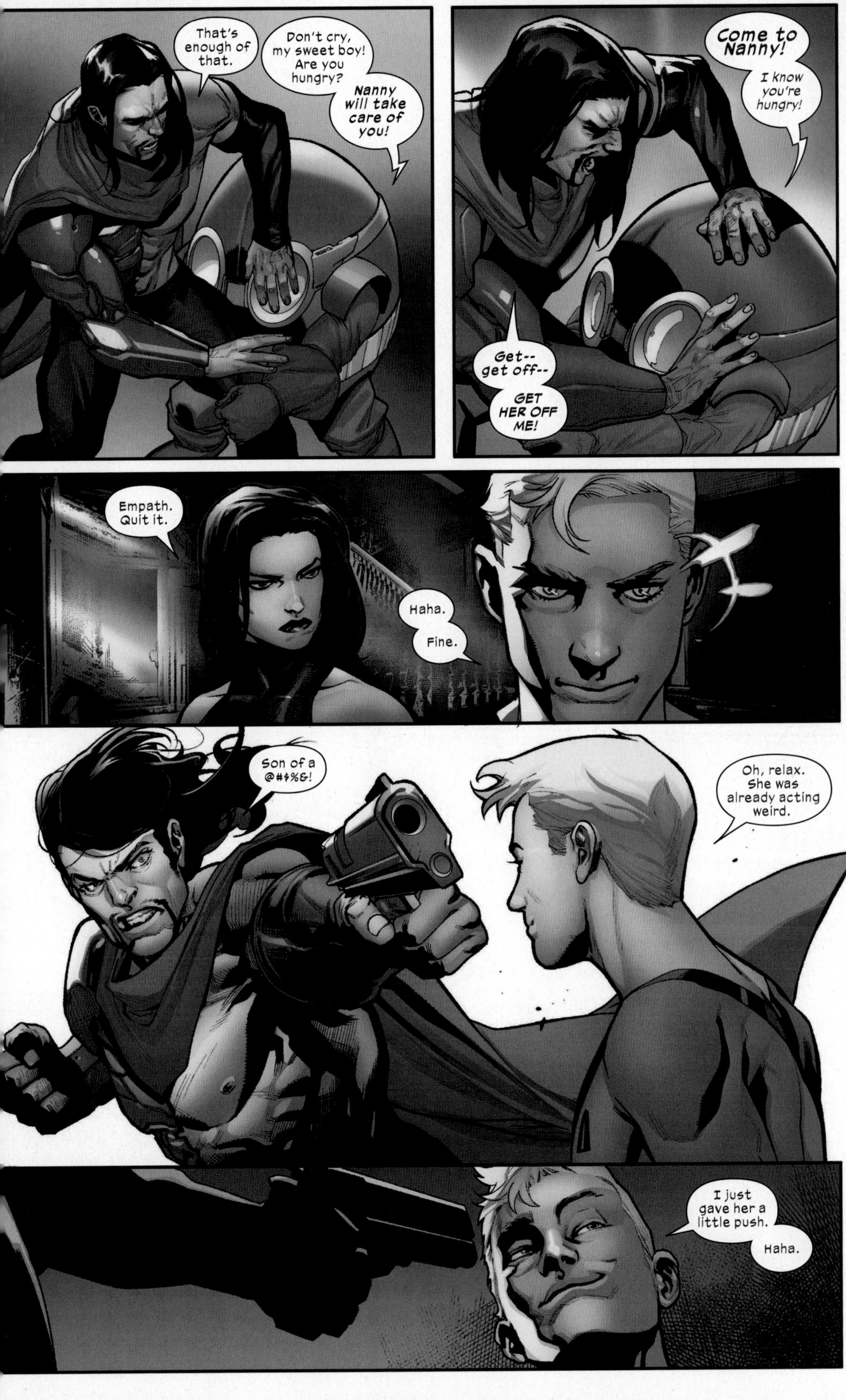
That's enough of that.
Don't cry, my sweet boy! Are you hungry?
Nanny will take care of you!
Come to Nanny!
I know you're hungry!
Get-- get off--
GET HER OFF ME!
Empath. Quit it.
Haha.
Fine.
Son of a @#$%&!
Oh, relax. She was already acting weird.
I just gave her a little push.
Haha.

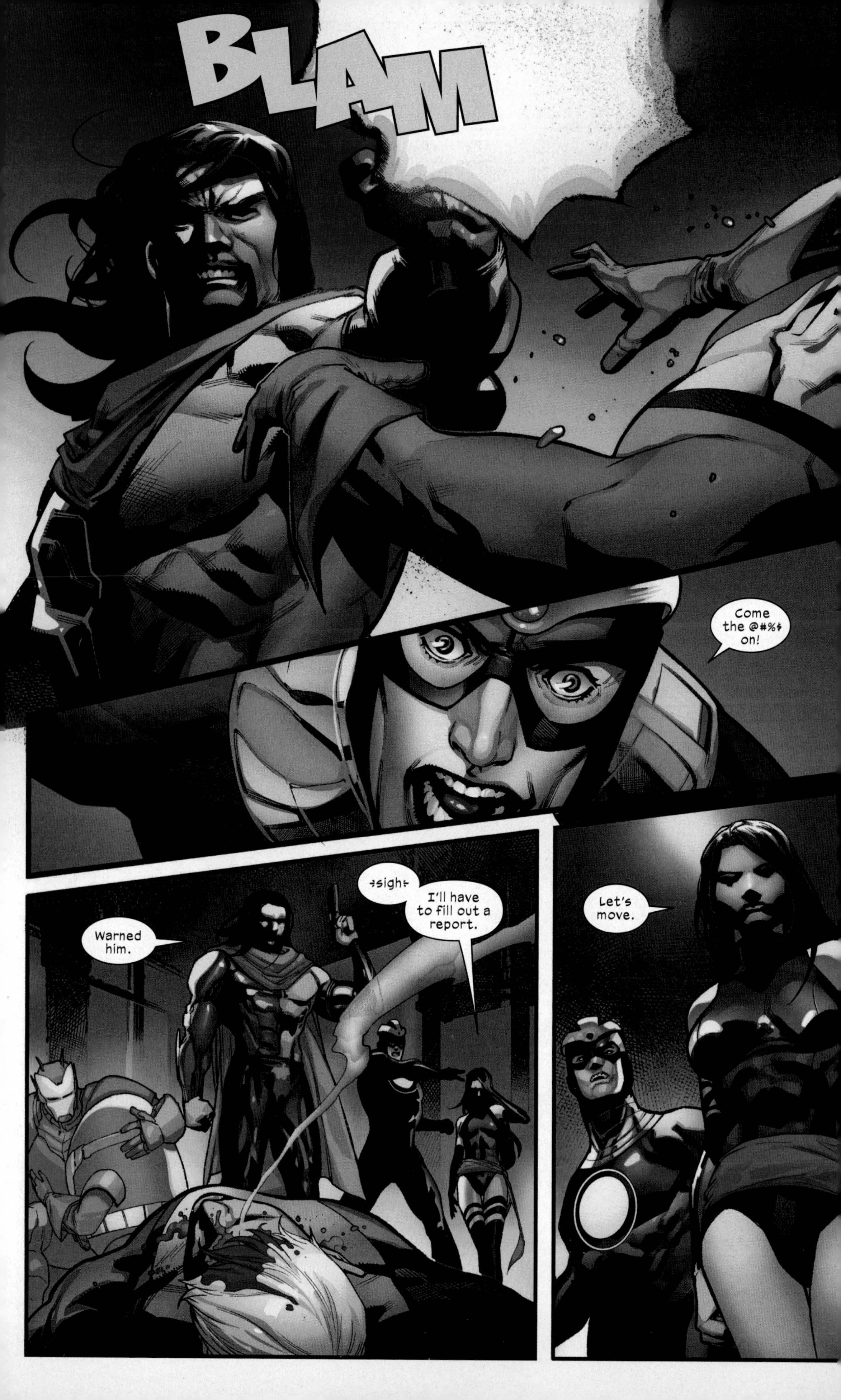
BLAM
Come the @#%$ on!
Warned him.
-sigh-
I'll have to fill out a report.
Let's move.

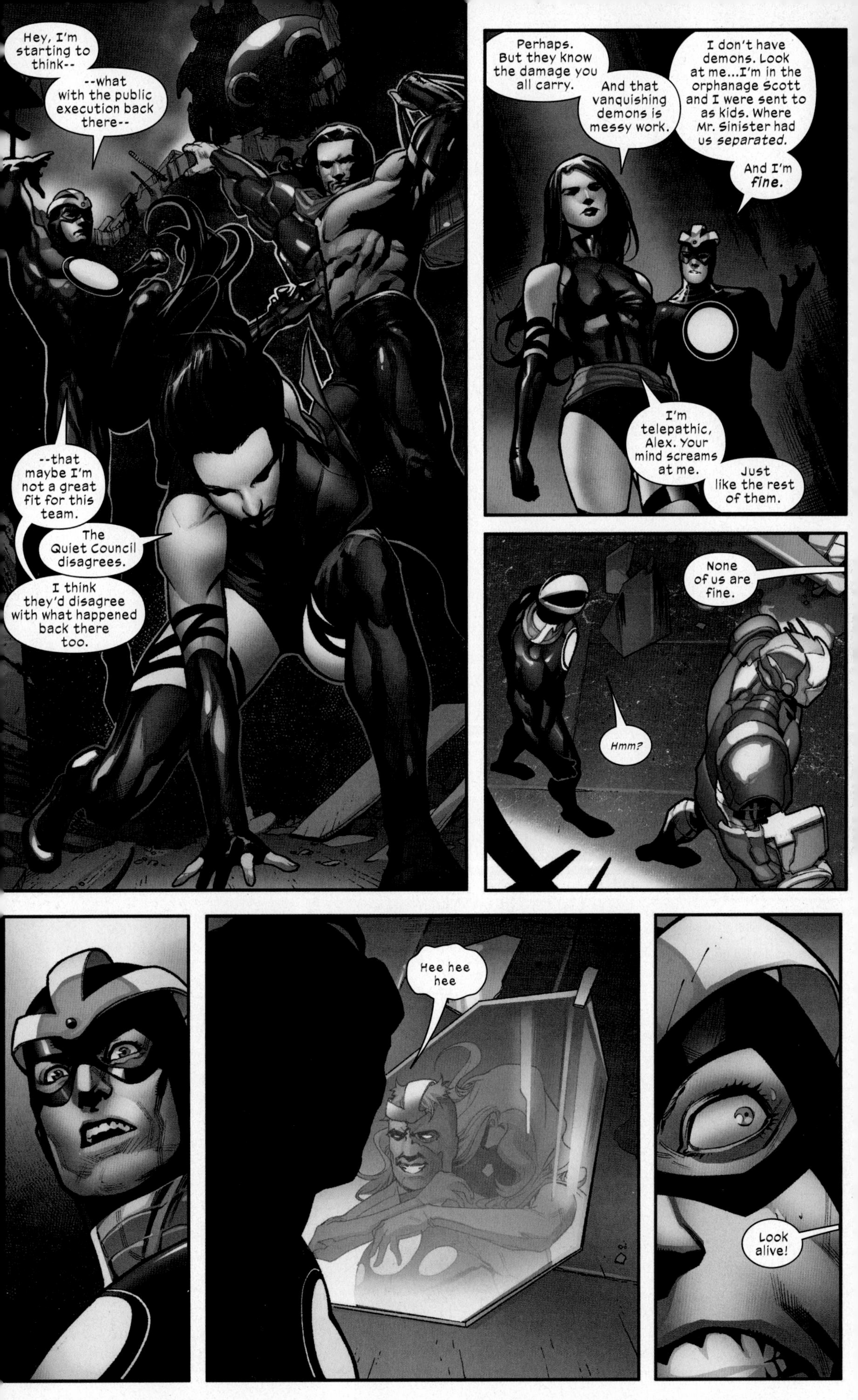
Hey, I'm starting to think--
--what with the public execution back there--
--that maybe I'm not a great fit for this team.
The Quiet Council disagrees.
I think they'd disagree with what happened back there too.
Perhaps. But they know the damage you all carry.
And that vanquishing demons is messy work.
I don't have demons. Look at me...I'm in the orphanage Scott and I were sent to as kids. Where Mr. Sinister had us *separated.*
And I'm *fine.*
I'm telepathic, Alex. Your mind screams at me.
Just like the rest of them.
None of us are fine.
Hmm?
Hee hee hee
Look alive!

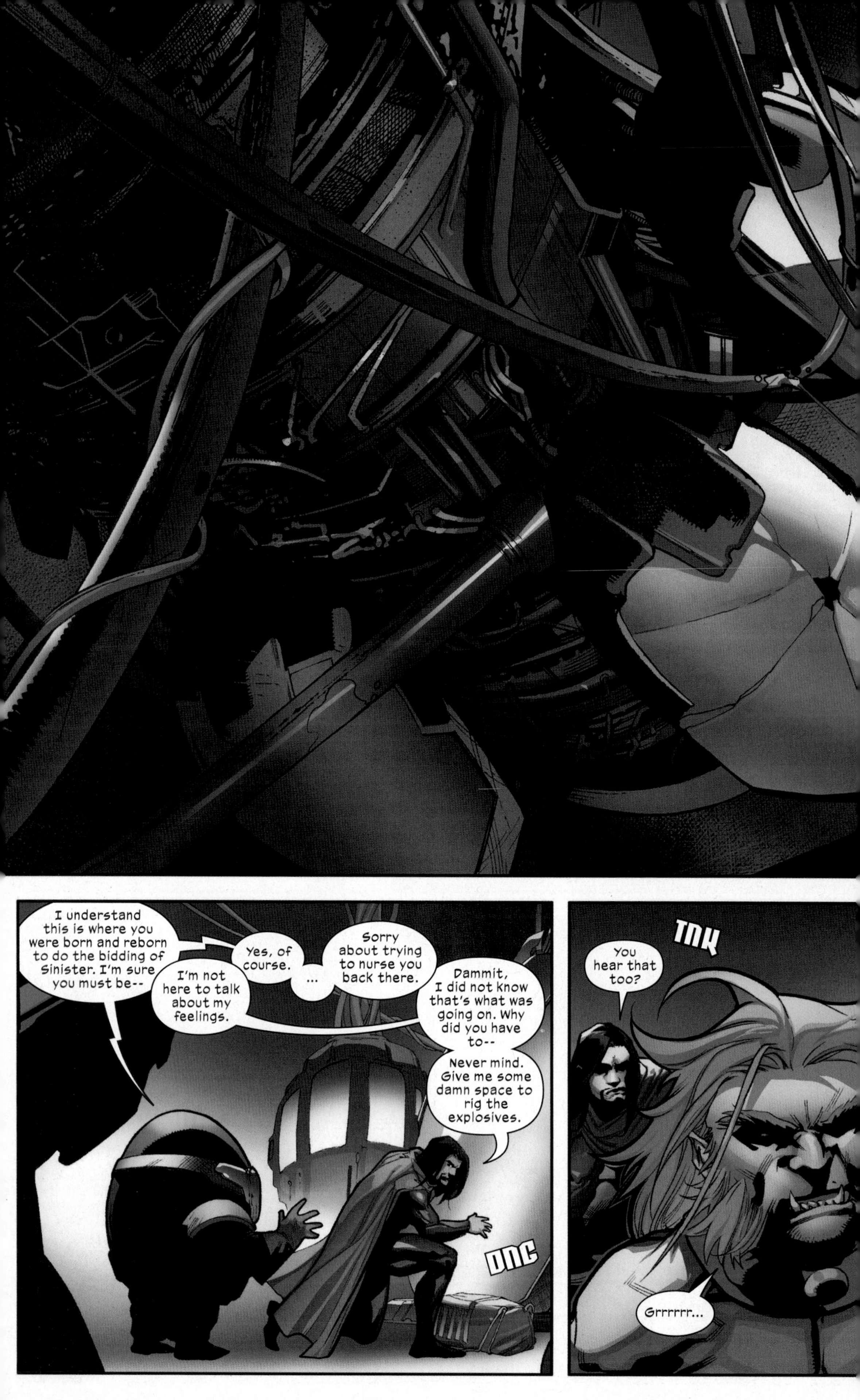
I understand this is where you were born and reborn to do the bidding of Sinister. I'm sure you must be--
I'm not here to talk about my feelings.
Yes, of course.
...
Sorry about trying to nurse you back there.
Dammit, I did not know that's what was going on. Why did you have to--
Never mind. Give me some damn space to rig the explosives.
DNC
TNK
You hear that too?
Grrrrrr...

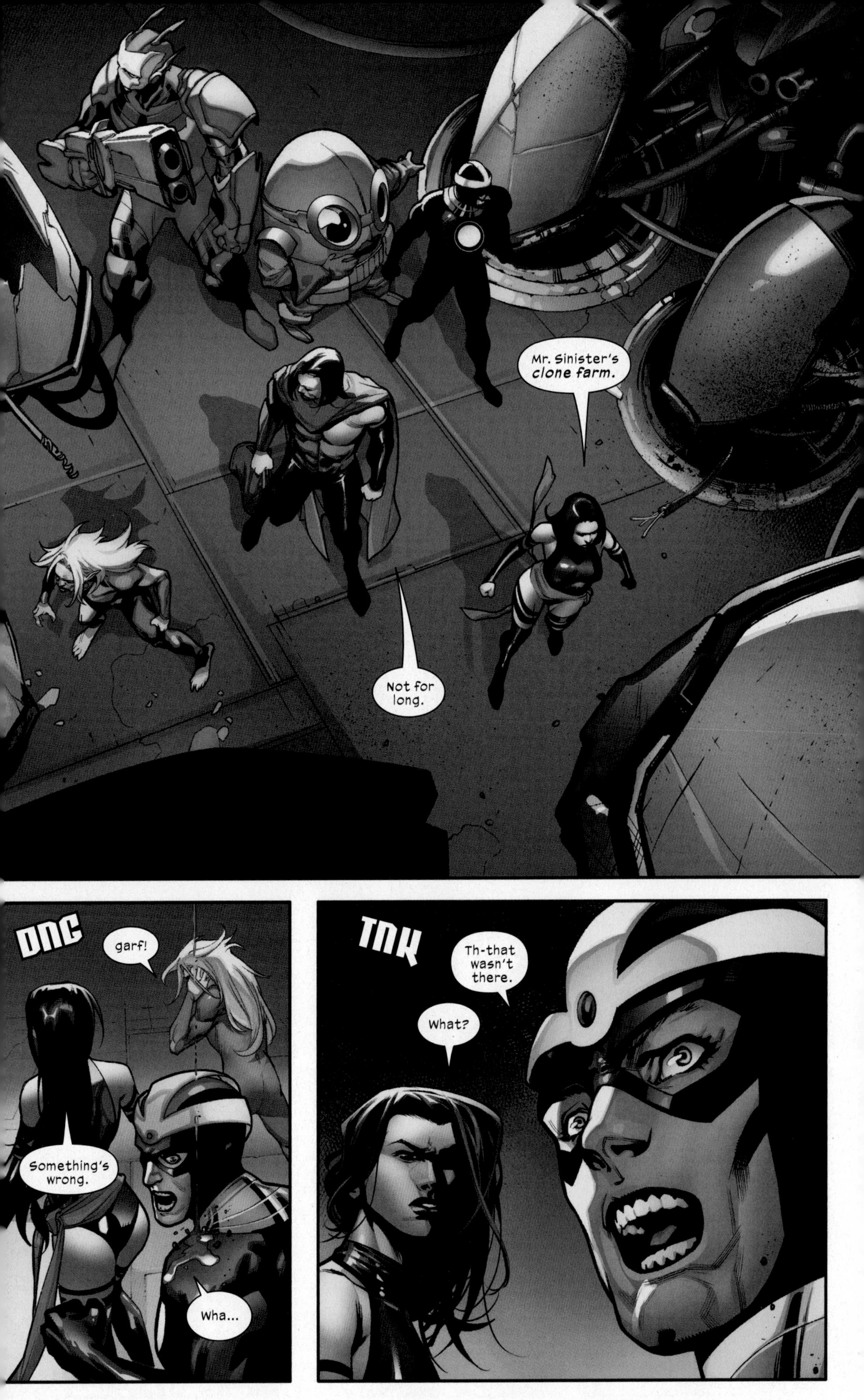
Mr. Sinister's clone farm.
Not for long.
DNG
garf!
Something's wrong.
Wha...
TNK
Th-that wasn't there.
What?

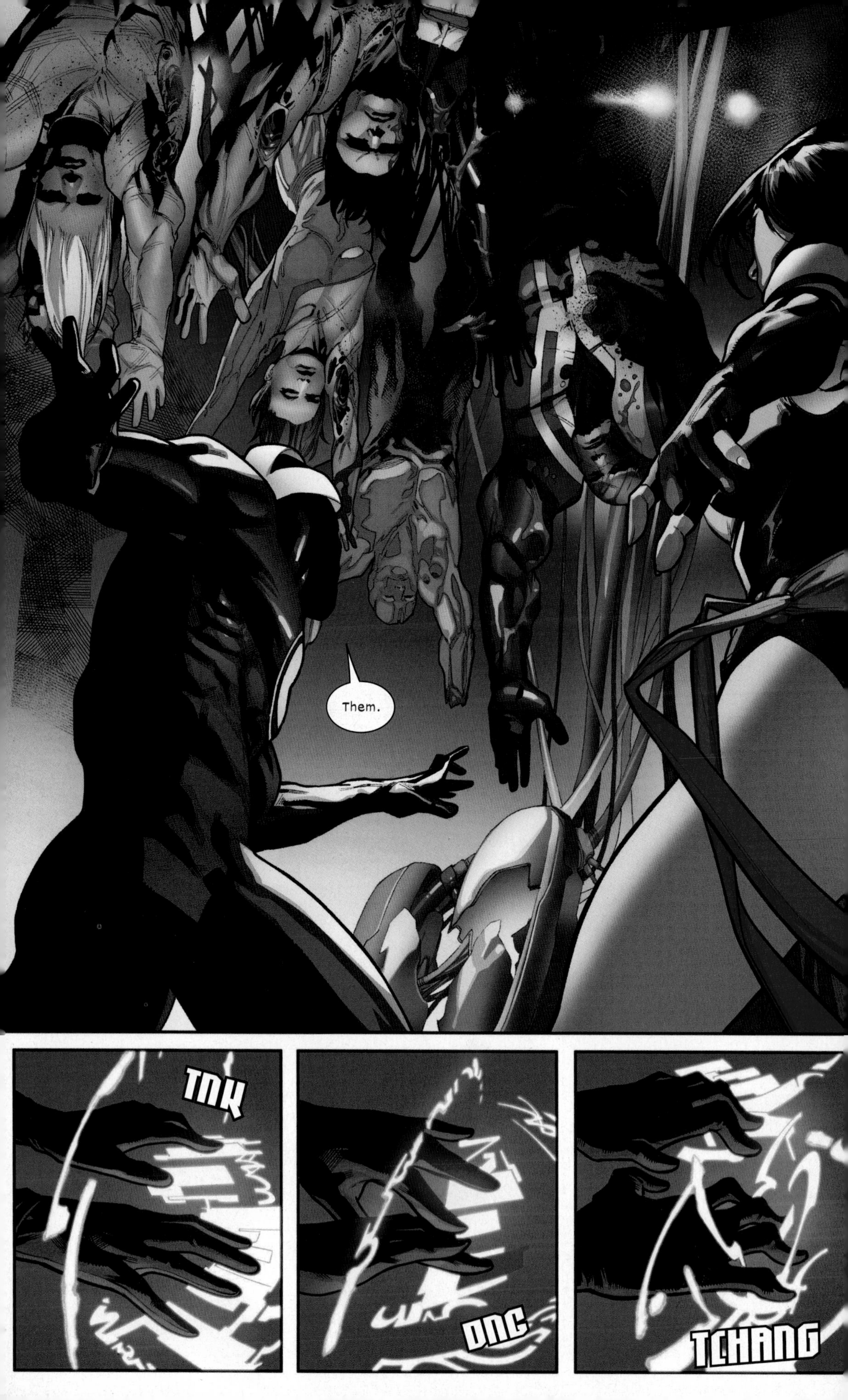
Them.
TNK
DNG
TCHANG

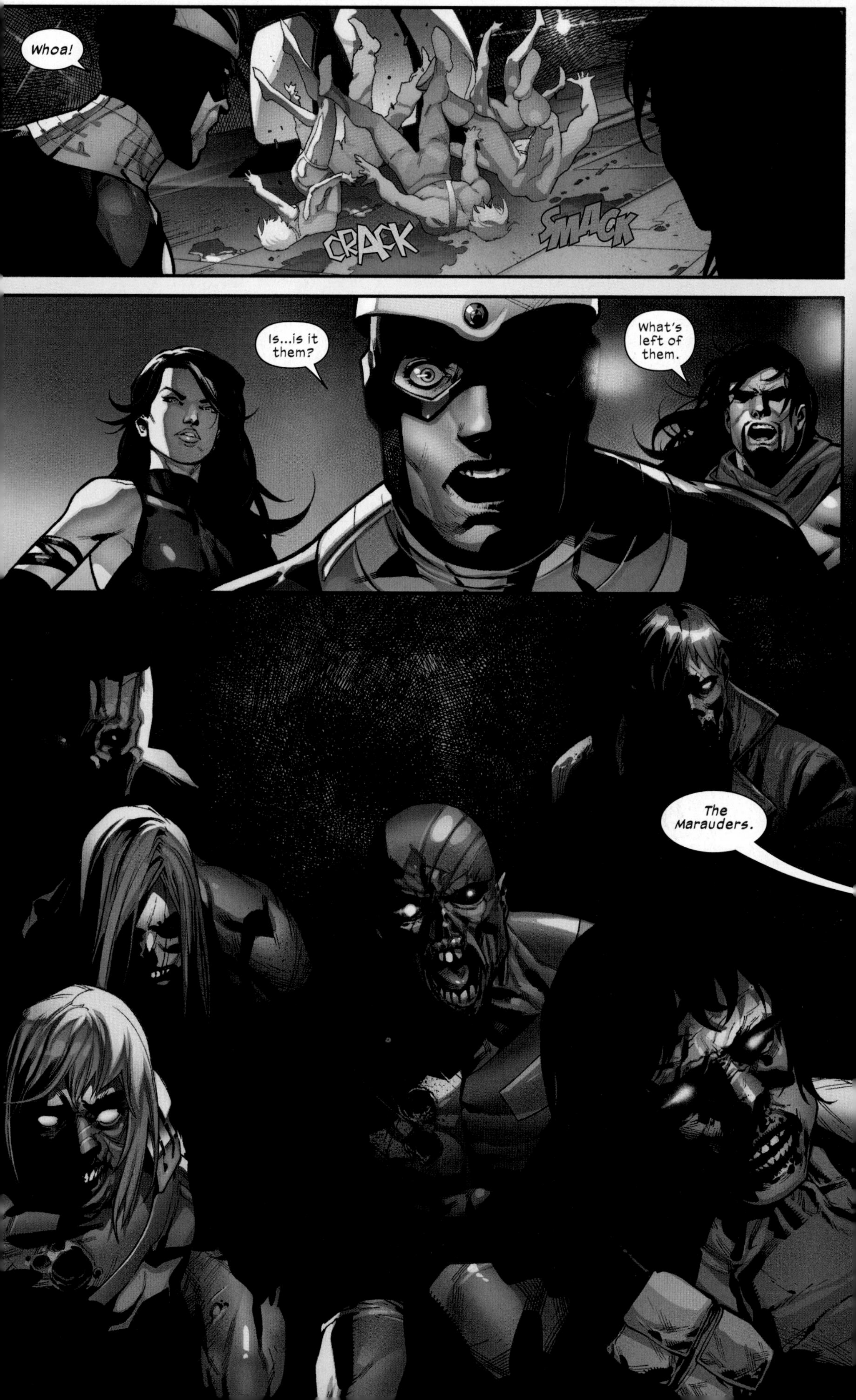
Whoa!
CRACK
SMACK
Is...is it them?
What's left of them.
The Marauders.

THE CONUNDRUM OF
MR. SINISTER'S (LEGACY) MARAUDERS

John Greycrow paid me a visit asking after his former teammates again. I can only call his demeanor "stoic desperation," which would have been amusing if not for the high caliber weapon he assembled and disassembled compulsively as we talked. I'm truly saddened that whatever trauma he's endured compels him to hide his completely natural concern for his comrades. I'll order a temporal psi-topsy from Emma to get to the bottom of that, but to the subject at hand:

Bringing the legacy Marauders to Krakoa is not as simple as it seems. At least not as simple as Mr. Greycrow appears (despite his best efforts) to hope. Mr. Sinister was resurrecting clones of his mutant assassins back when Krakoa was just a murderous island we didn't know how to explain to our friends. To call his resurrection protocols lax does not adequately sum up how antithetical his procedures were to current Krakoan best practices. All that is to say the current iteration of the Marauders are clones of clones of clones, most likely suffering from generation loss and genetic corruption (some, no doubt, intentional.) Are these current Marauders the most natural versions of themselves? If not, don't they deserve to be?

I won't try to force a decision (not a priority, I understand,) but for now we should apply some political pressure towards Sinister dismantling his clone farm. Once we know we're dealing with the last of the line, we can assess the Marauders' genetic integrity and discern if the whole lot of them aren't better left for The Five to sort out.

I don't want to sound like Kurt, but I'd be excited to see what could be made of these mutants if they were resurrected with a little love.

—

ARCLIGHT: Manual techtonic disruption.

RIPTIDE: Hyper rotation. Uber-keratin pentaquill excretion.

HARPOON: Bio-energetic, bio-luminous projectiles.

BLOCKBUSTER: Strong guy.

PRISM: Energy absorption/refraction. Biotransparency.

SCRAMBLER: Electro/Bioelectrosystemic disruption.

—

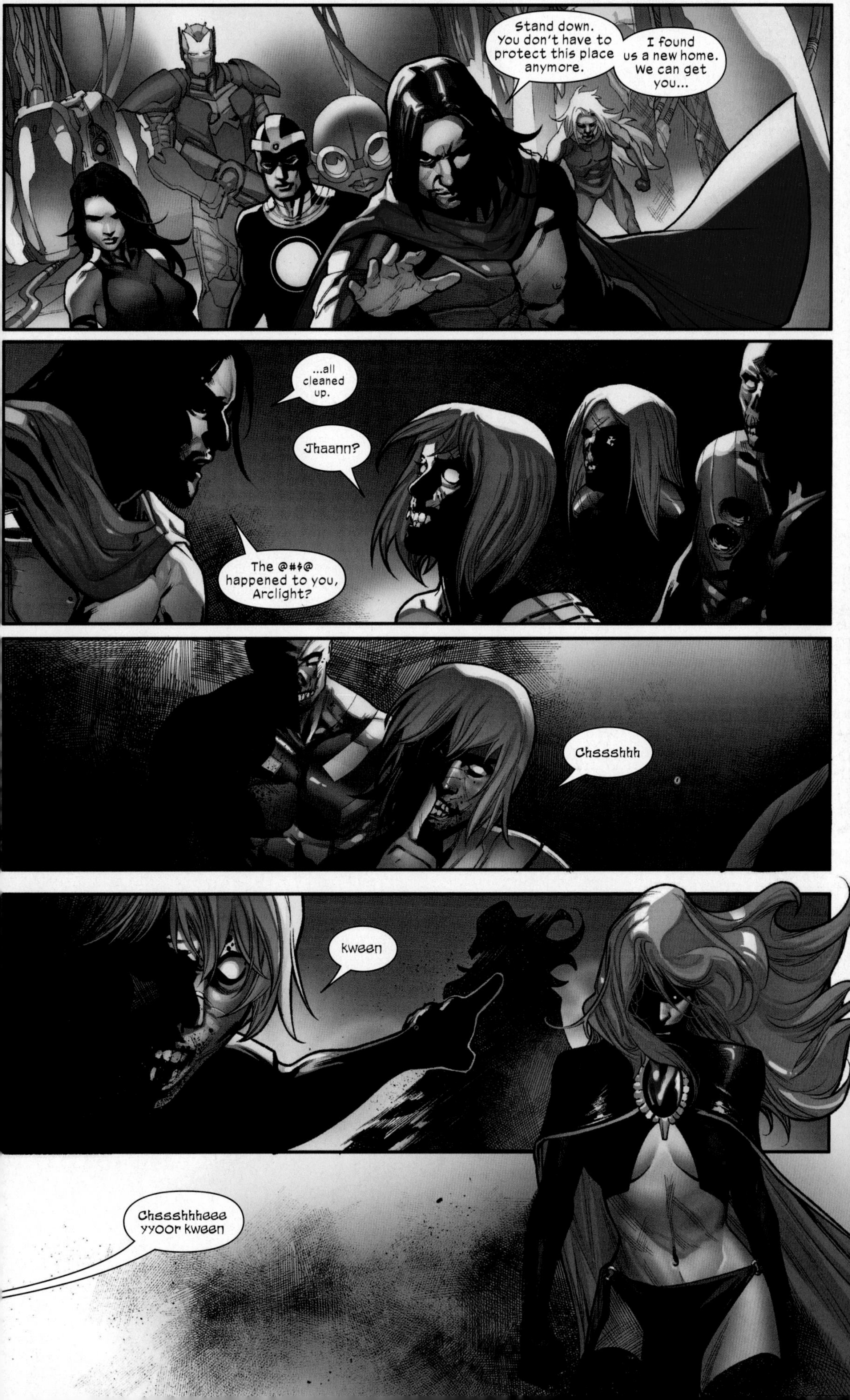
Stand down. You don't have to protect this place anymore.
I found us a new home. We can get you...
...all cleaned up.
Jhaann?
The @#$@ happened to you, Arclight?
Chssshhh
kween
Chssshhheee yyoor kween

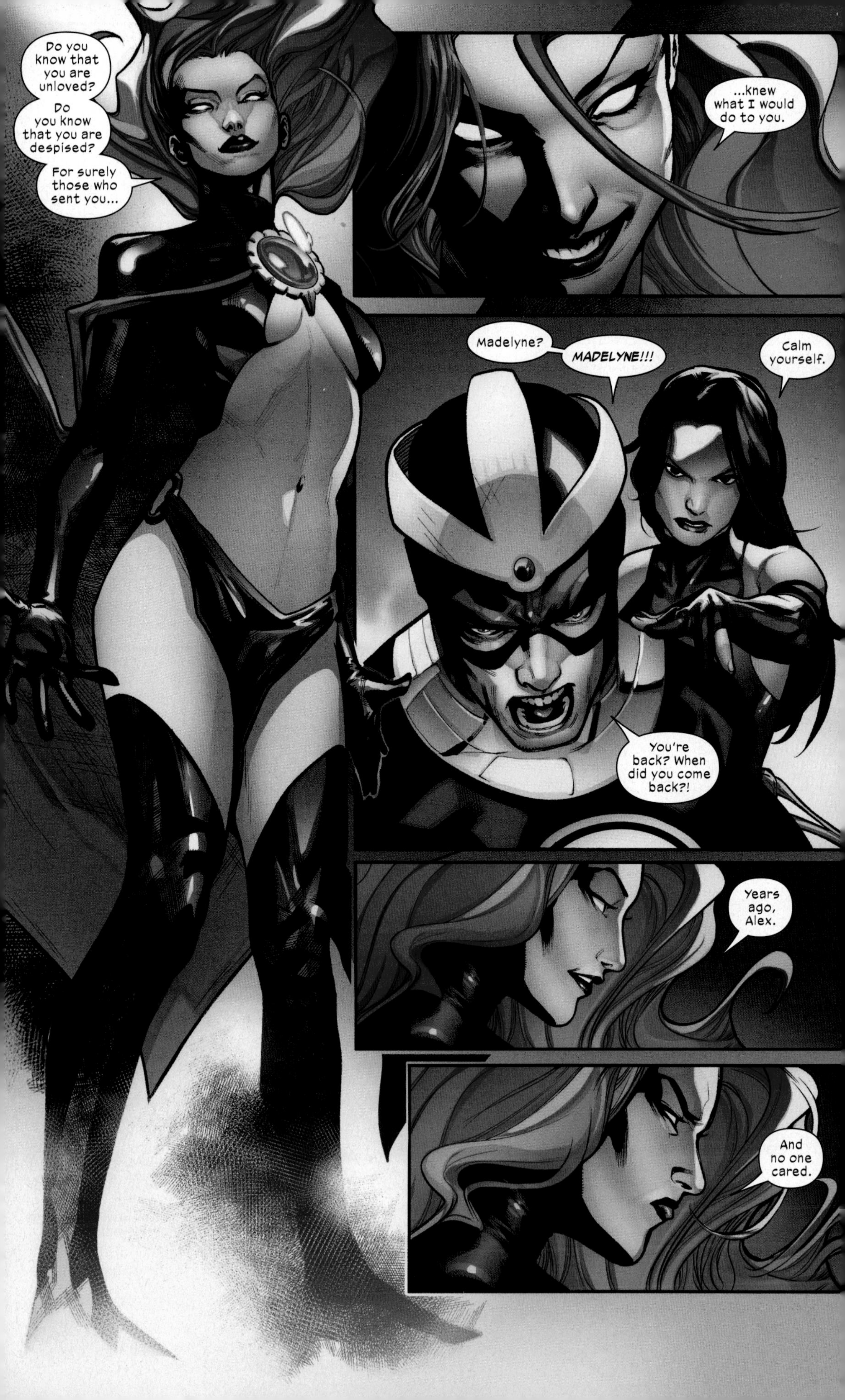
Do you know that you are unloved?
Do you know that you are despised?
For surely those who sent you...
...knew what I would do to you.
Madelyne?
MADELYNE!!!
Calm yourself.
You're back? When did you come back?!
Years ago, Alex.
And no one cared.

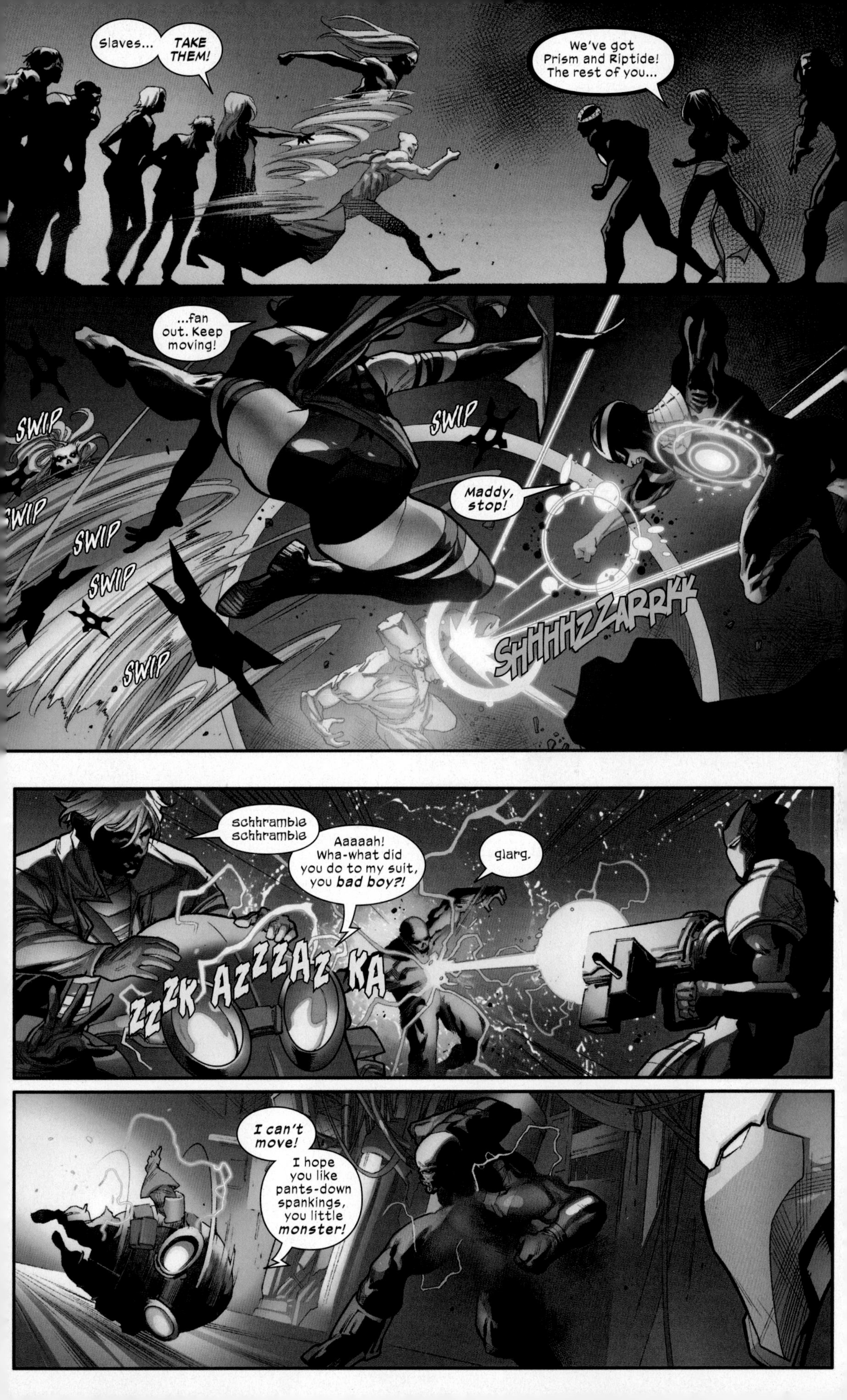
Slaves... TAKE THEM!
We've got Prism and Riptide! The rest of you...
...fan out. Keep moving!
SWIP
SWIP
SWIP
SWIP
SWIP
SWIP
Maddy, stop!
SHHHZZARRK
schhramble schhramble
Aaaaah! Wha-what did you do to my suit, you bad boy?!
glarg.
ZZZK AZZZAZ KA
I can't move!
I hope you like pants-down spankings, you little monster!

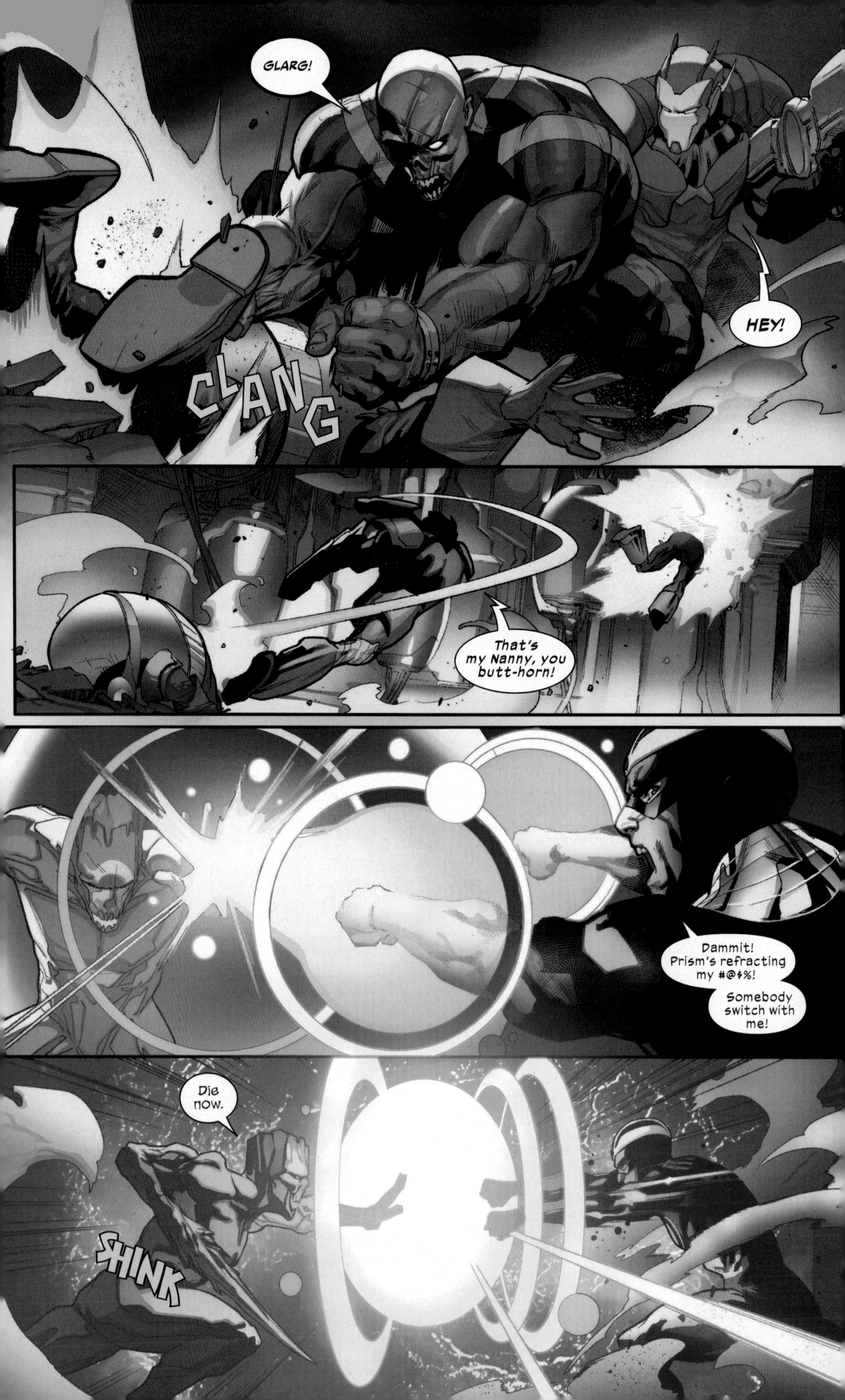
GLARG!
HEY!
CLANG
That's my Nanny, you butt-horn!
Dammit! Prism's refracting my #@$%!
Somebody switch with me!
Die now.
SHINK

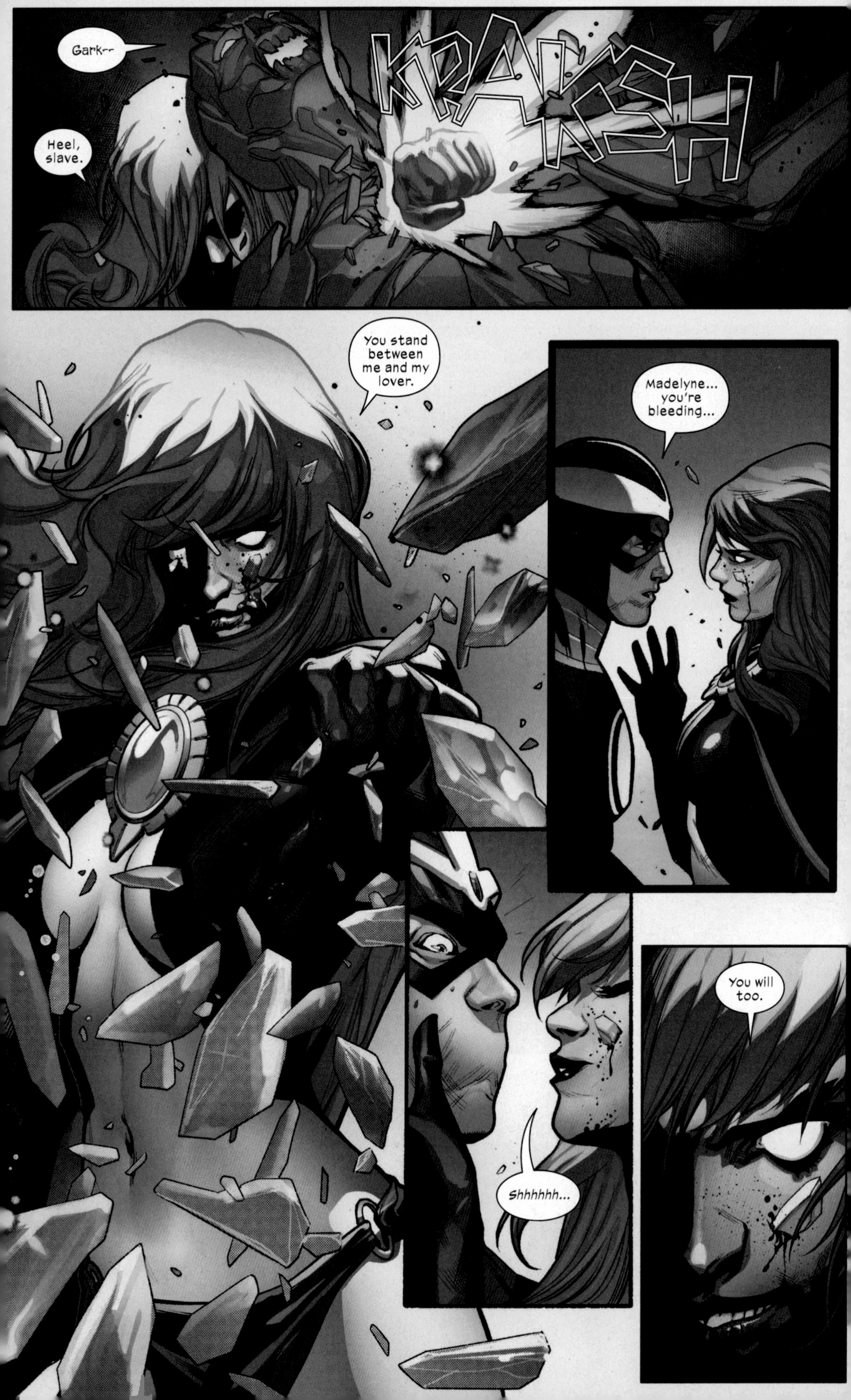

Gark--
Heel, slave.
KRAKSH KSH
You stand between me and my lover.
Madelyne... you're bleeding...
Shhhhhh...
You will too.

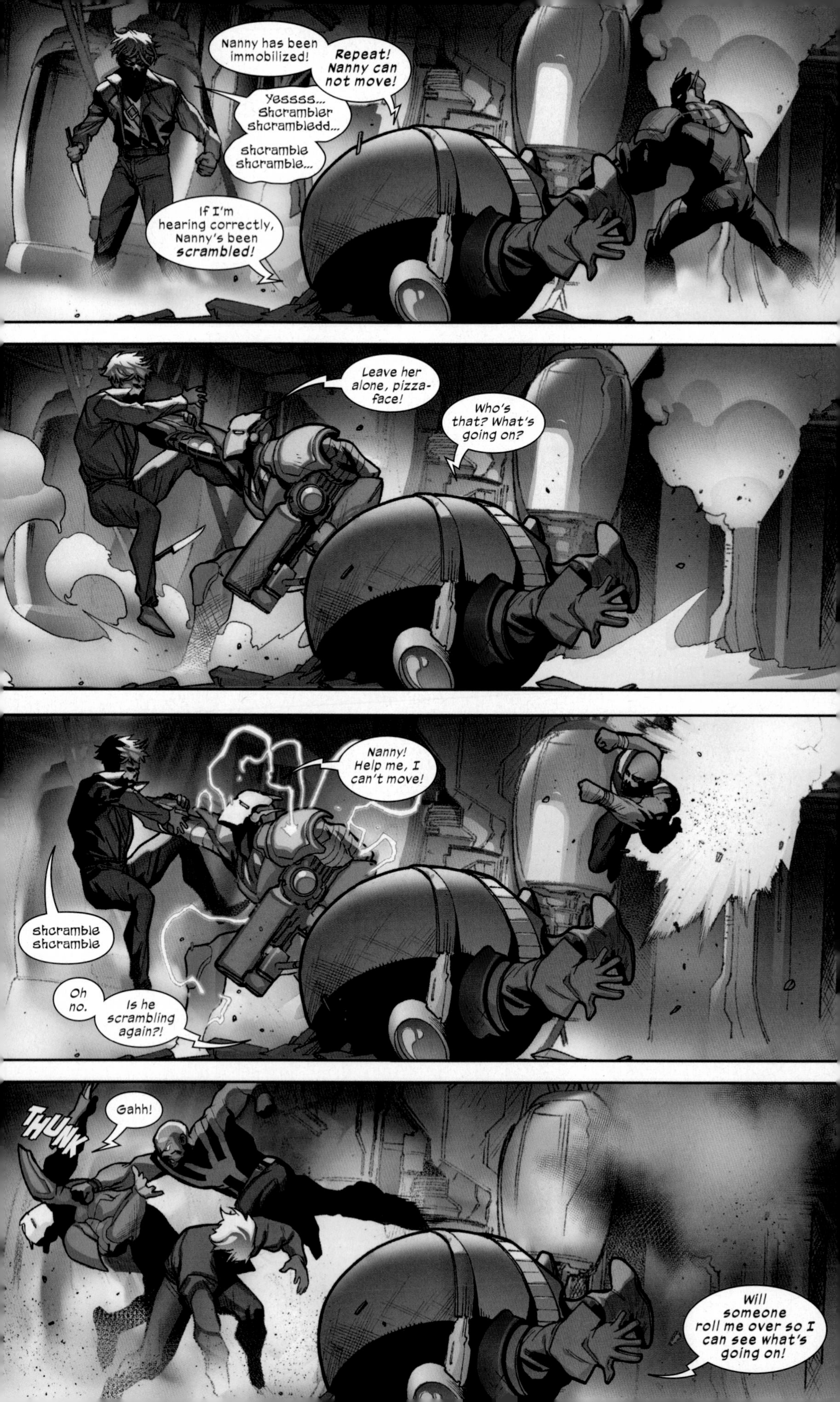

Nanny has been immobilized!
Repeat! Nanny can not move!
Yessss... Shcrambler shcrambledd...
shcramble shcramble...
If I'm hearing correctly, Nanny's been scrambled!
Leave her alone, pizza-face!
Who's that? What's going on?
Nanny! Help me, I can't move!
shcramble shcramble
Oh no.
Is he scrambling again?!
THUNK
Gahh!
Will someone roll me over so I can see what's going on!

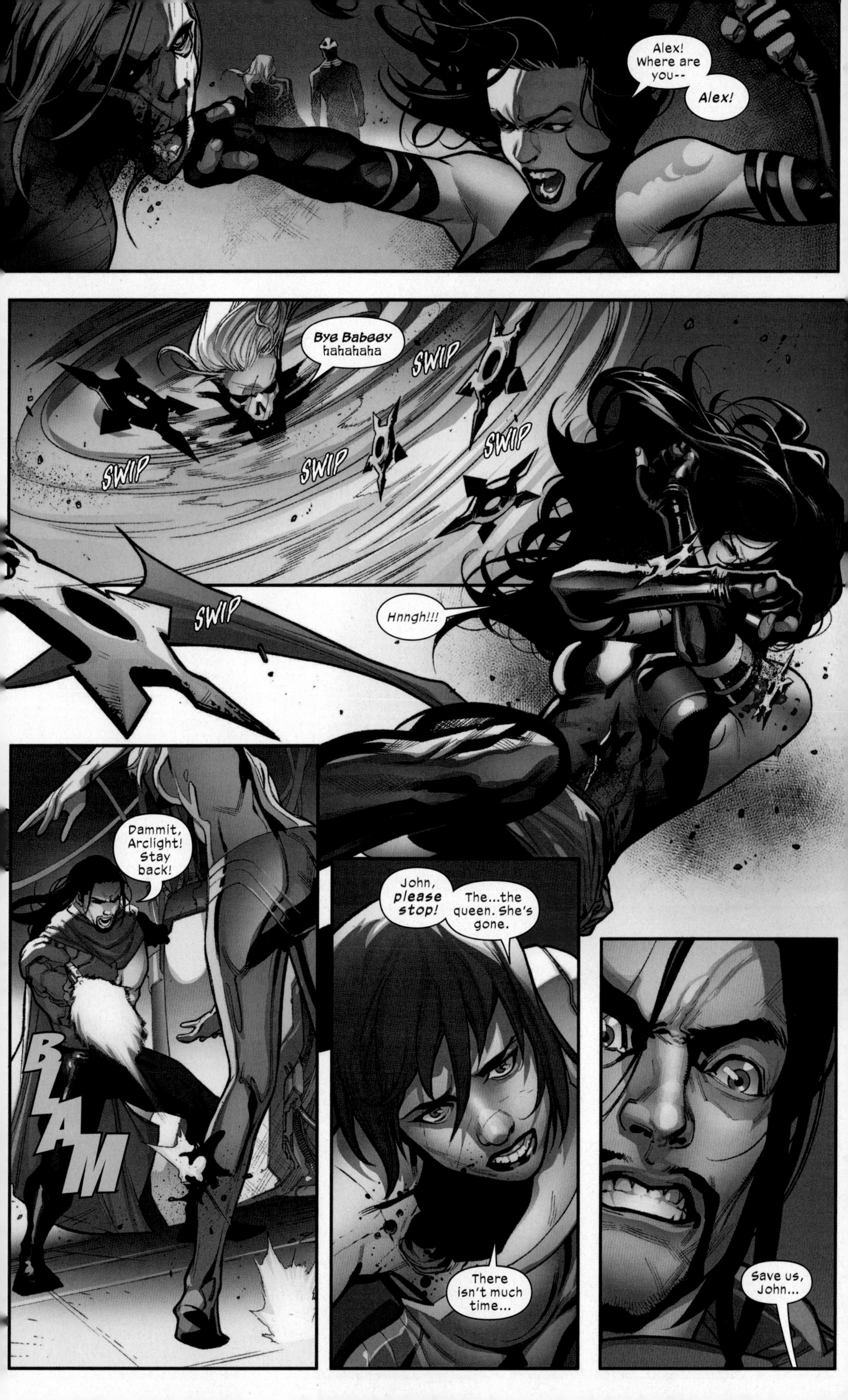

Alex! Where are you--
Alex!
Bye Babeey hahahaha
SWIP
SWIP
SWIP
SWIP
SWIP
Hnngh!!!
Dammit, Arclight! Stay back!
BLAM
John, **please stop!**
The...the queen. She's gone.
There isn't much time...
Save us, John...

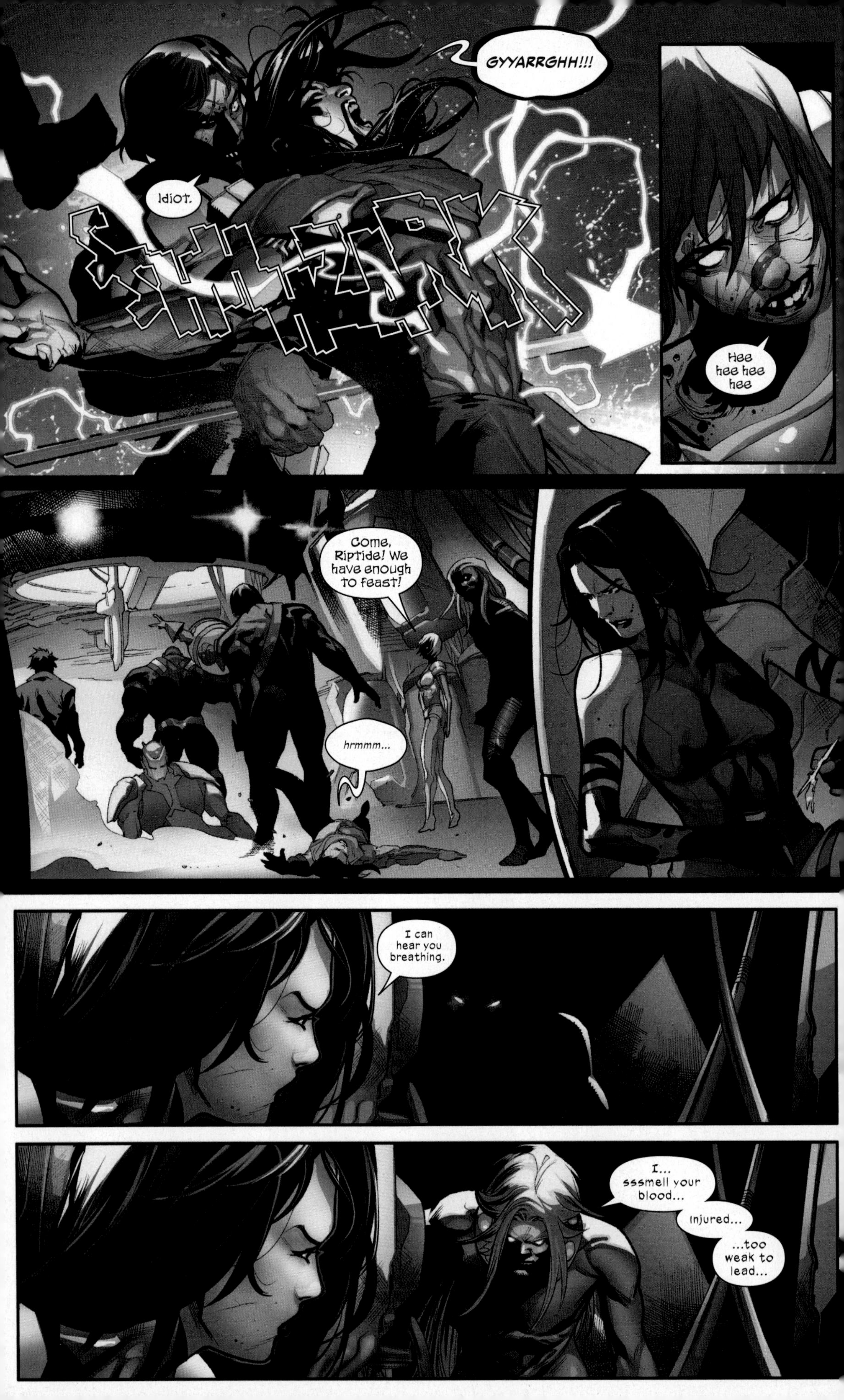
GYYARRGHH!!!
Idiot.
Hee hee hee hee
Come, Riptide! We have enough to feast!
hrmmm...
I can hear you breathing.
I... sssmell your blood...
Injured...
...too weak to lead...

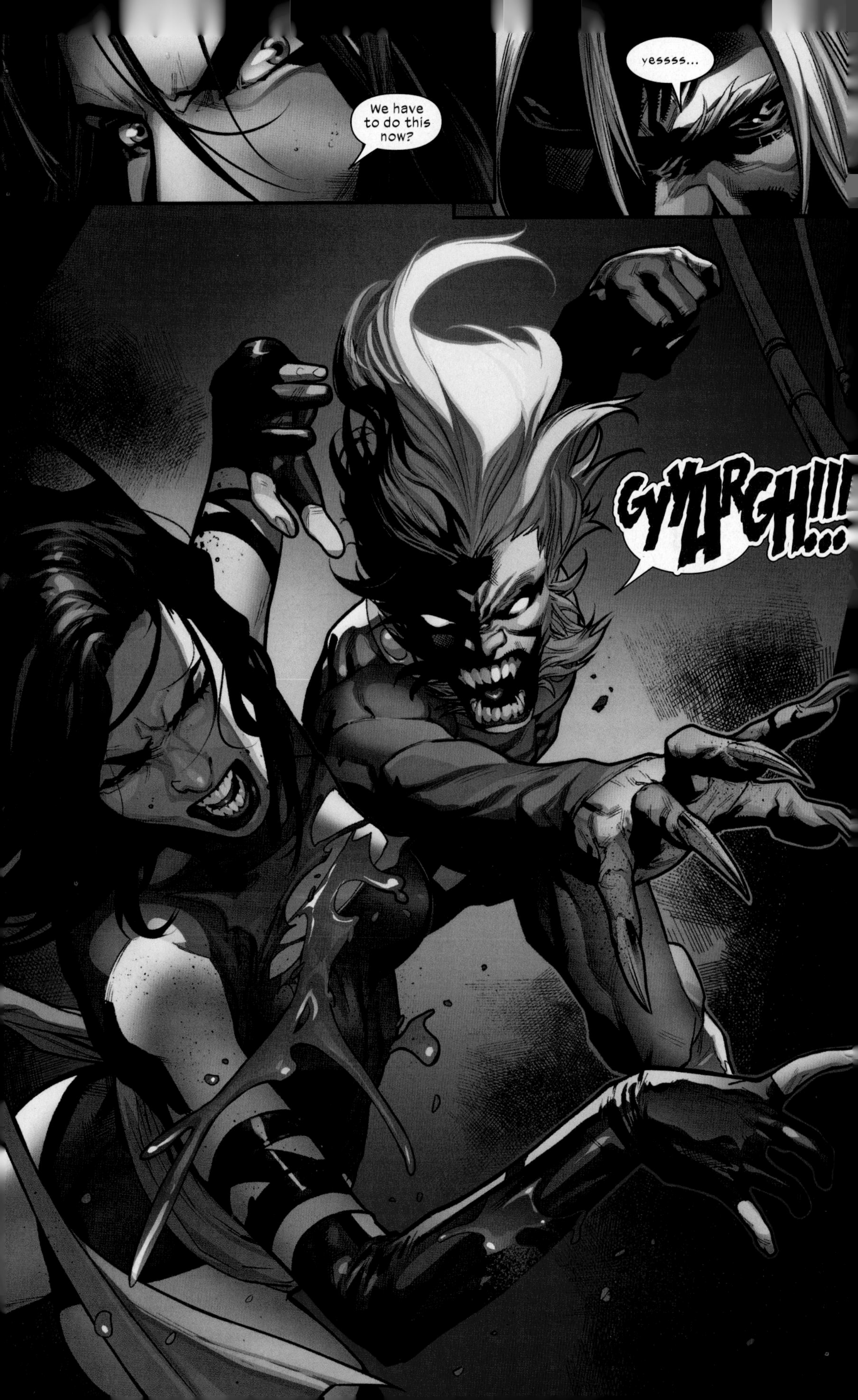
We have to do this now?
yessss...
GYAARGH!!!...

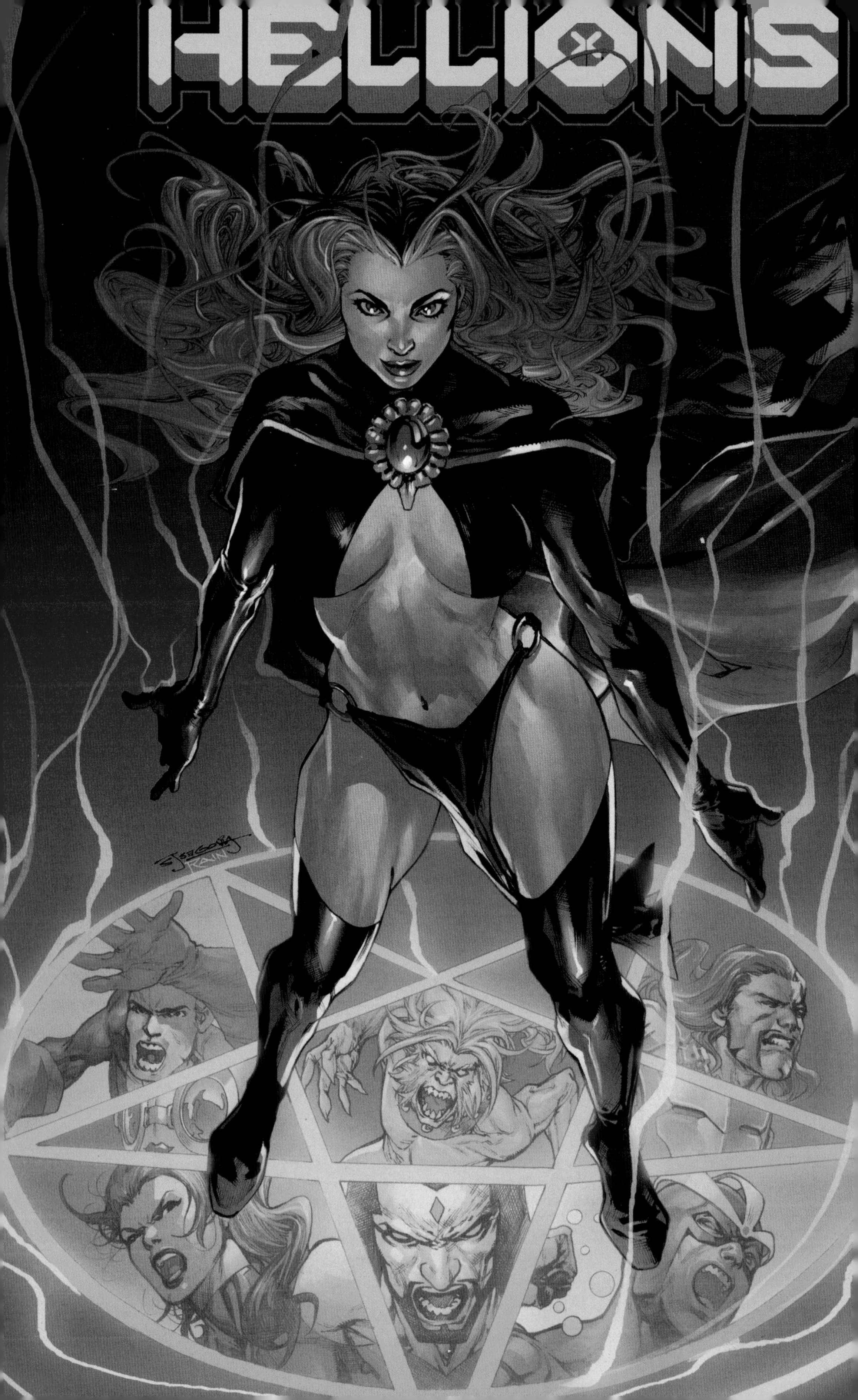
HELLIONS

[hell_[0.3]
[ions_[0.3]

I do wonder which binds us more...
Xavier's ideals or the trauma of being
mutant. The dream or the pain.

-NIGHTCRAWLER

[hell_[0.X]
[ions_[0.X]

[hell_[0.3].....]
[ions_[0.3].....]

[Hellions_alpha.]

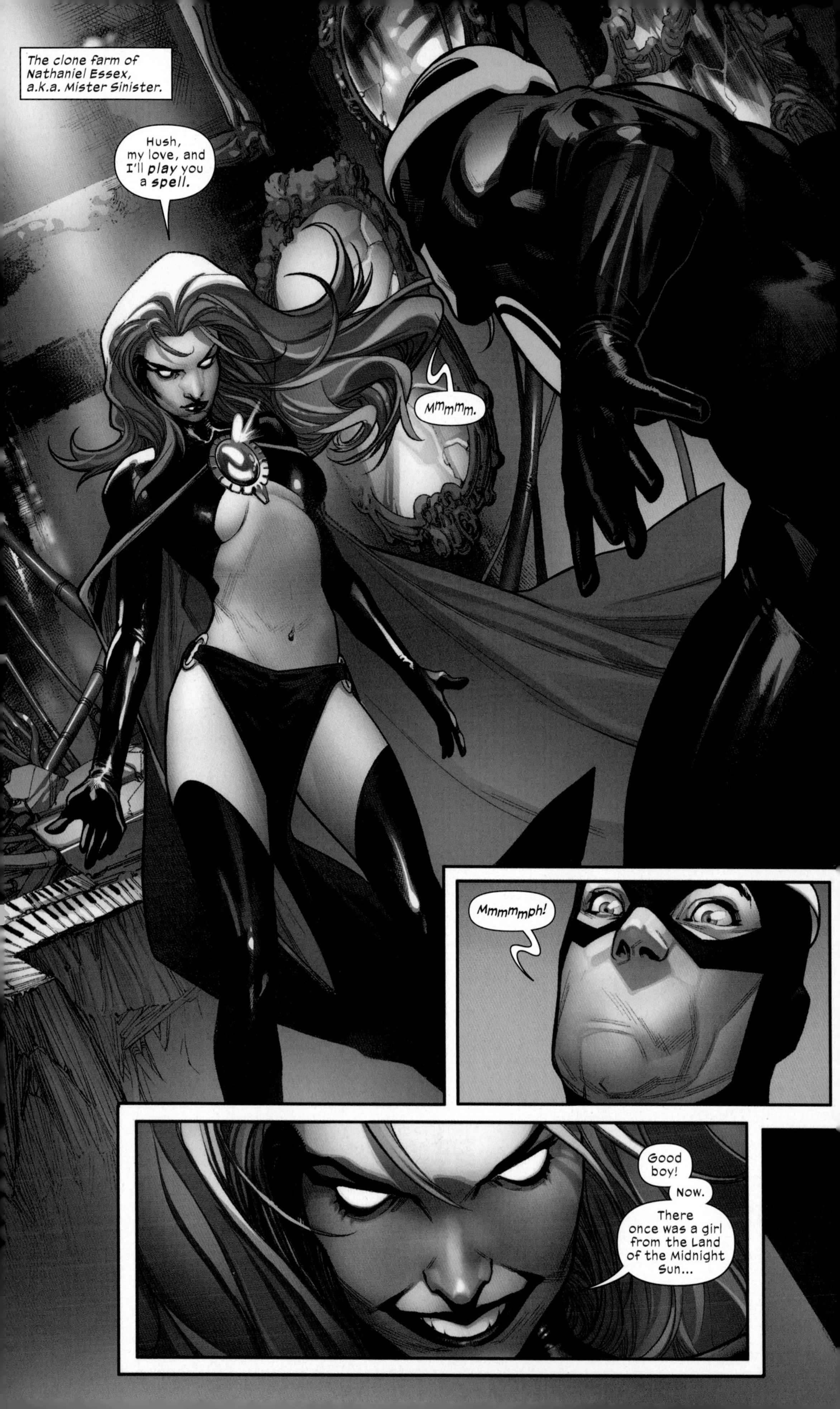
The clone farm of Nathaniel Essex, a.k.a. Mister Sinister.
Hush, my love, and I'll *play* you a *spell.*
Mmmmm.
Mmmmmph!
Good boy!
Now.
There once was a girl from the Land of the Midnight Sun...

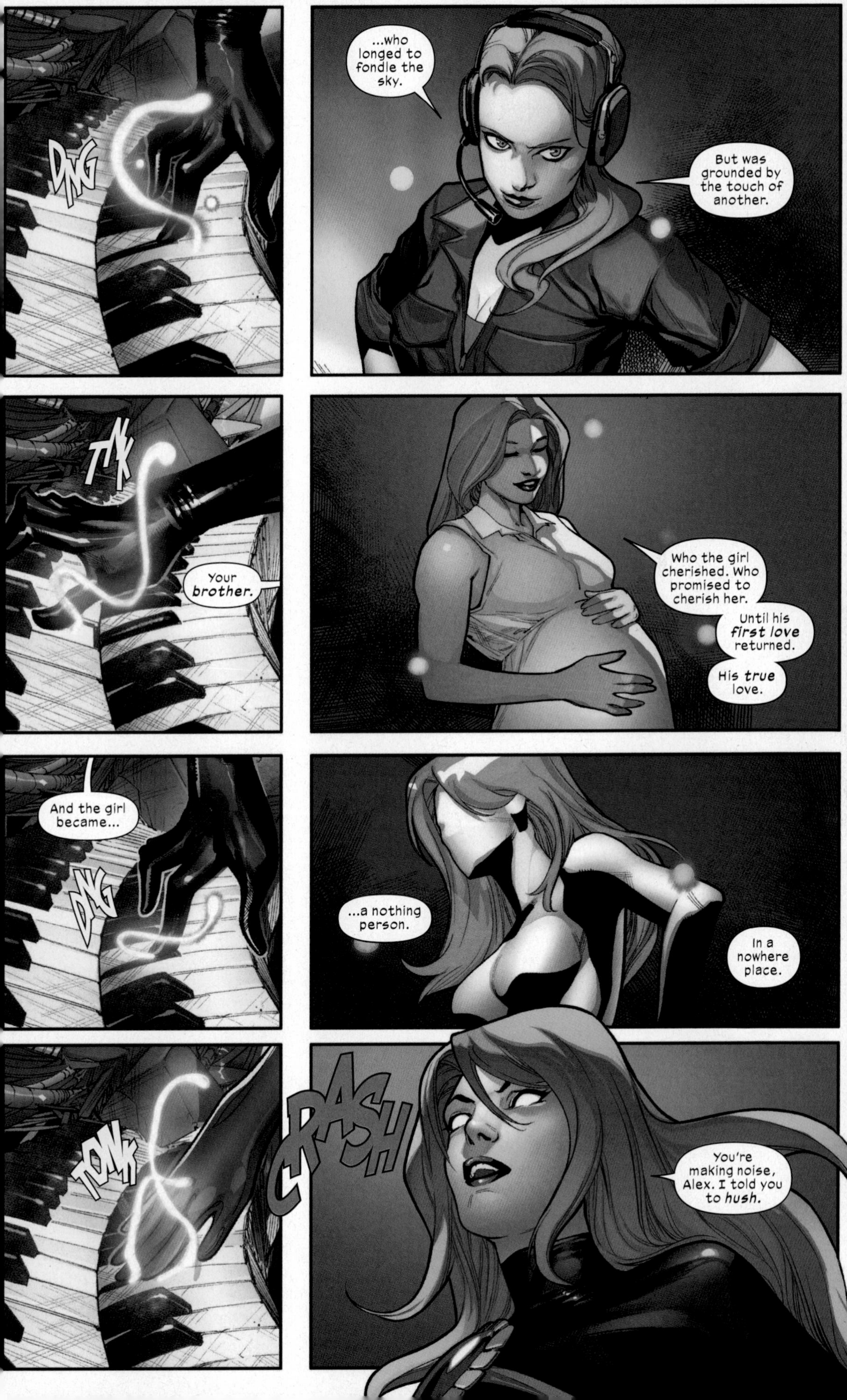

DNG
...who longed to fondle the sky.
But was grounded by the touch of another.
TINK
Your *brother.*
Who the girl cherished. Who promised to cherish her.
Until his *first love* returned.
His *true* love.
And the girl became...
DNG
...a nothing person.
In a nowhere place.
TONK
CRASH
You're making noise, Alex. I told you to *hush.*

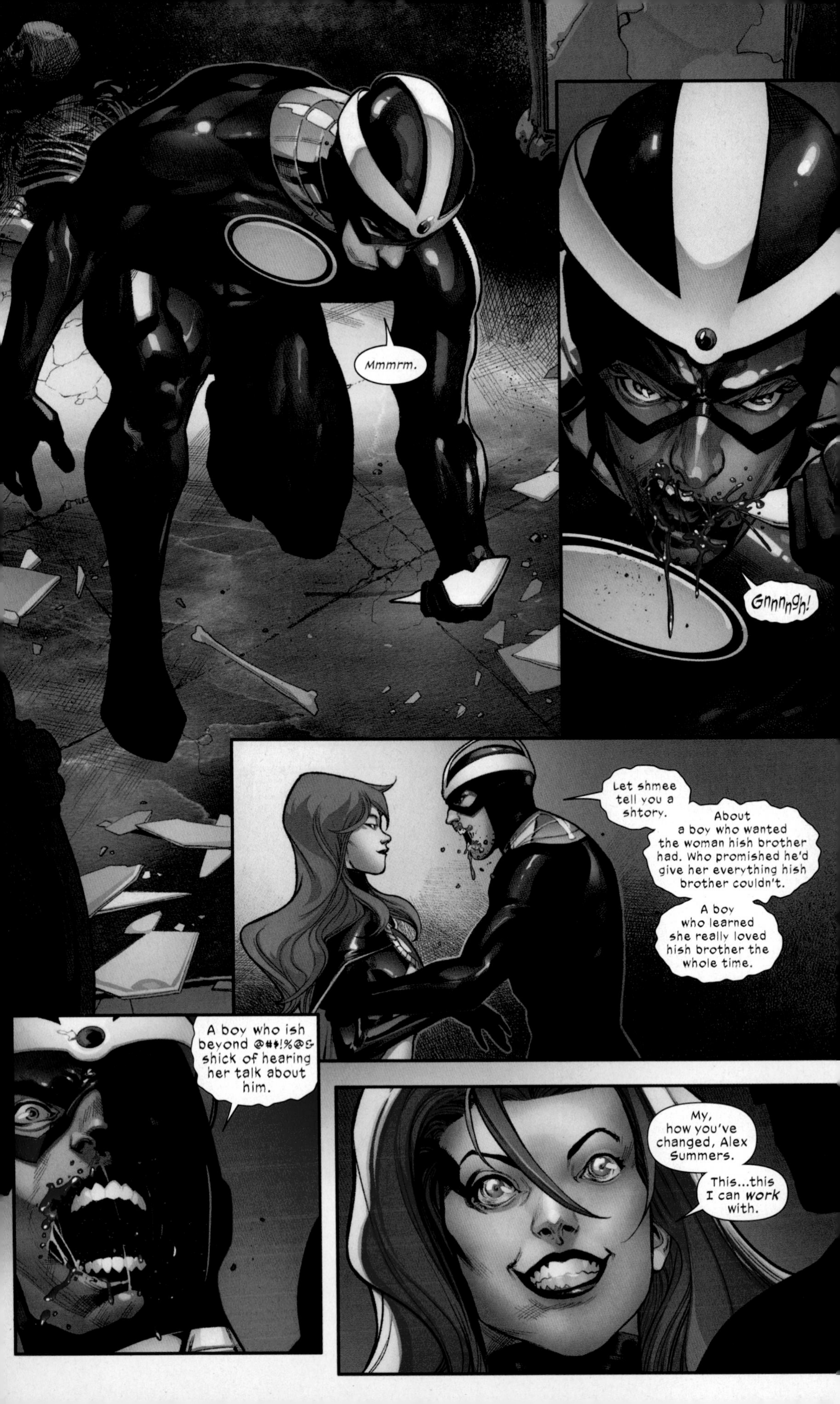
Mmmrm.
Gnnnngh!
Let shmee tell you a shtory.
About a boy who wanted the woman hish brother had. Who promised he'd give her everything hish brother couldn't.
A boy who learned she really loved hish brother the whole time.
A boy who ish beyond @#$!%@& shick of hearing her talk about him.
My, how you've changed, Alex Summers.
This...this I can *work* with.

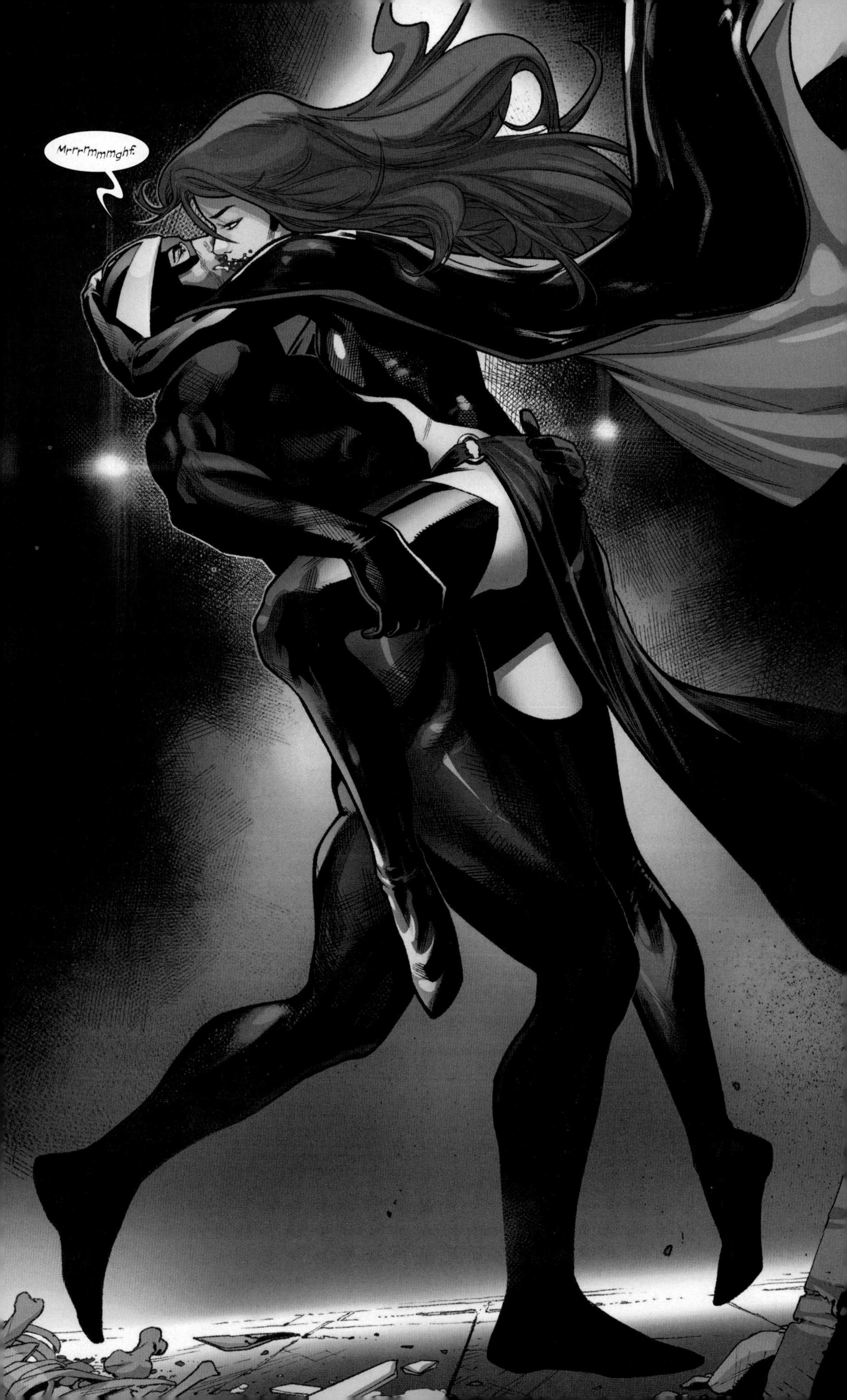
Mrrrrmmmghf.

[00_bad___X]
[00_news__X]

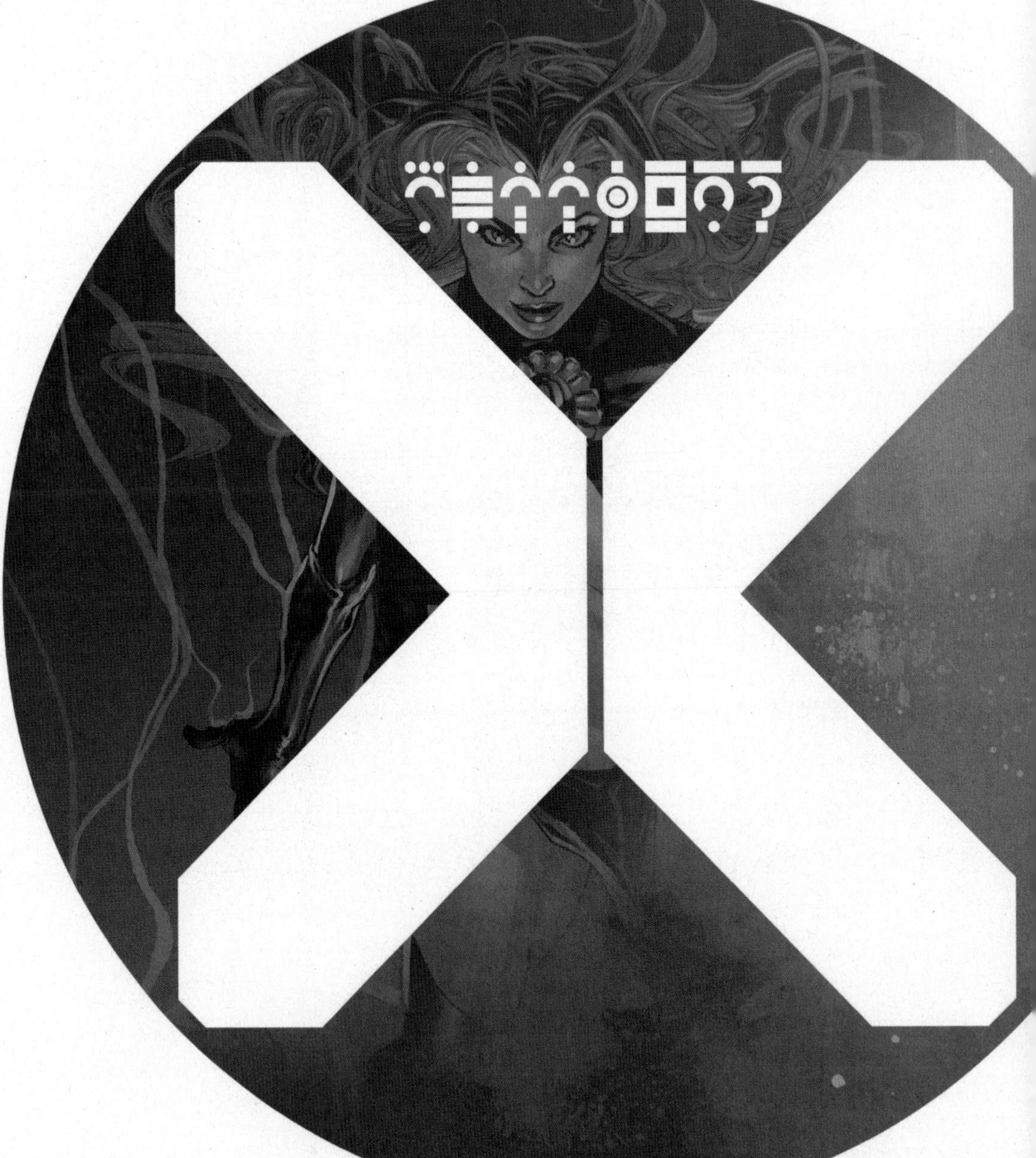

ZEB WELLS..[WRITER]
STEPHEN SEGOVIA.................................[ARTIST]
DAVID CURIEL..............................[COLOR ARTIST]
VC's ARIANA MAHER...........................[LETTERER]
TOM MULLER....................................[DESIGN]

STEPHEN SEGOVIA & RAIN BEREDO...........[COVER ARTISTS]

VALERIO GIANGIORDANO & ROMULO FAJARDO JR. ....
...............................[VARIANT COVER ARTISTS]

TOM MULLER................[DESIGN VARIANT COVER ARTIST]

ANTHONY GAMBINO............................[PRODUCTION]

JONATHAN HICKMAN............................[HEAD OF X]
ANNALISE BISSA & LAUREN AMARO.......[ASSISTANT EDITORS]
JORDAN D. WHITE & MARK BASSO..................[EDITORS]
C.B. CEBULSKI........................[EDITOR IN CHIEF]

[03]HELLIONS

[ISSUE THREE]...............NOTHING PEOPLE

[00_hell__X]
[00__ions_X]

[00_00...0.]
[00_00...3.]

[00_best___]
[00__of___]

[00__the___]

[00_worst_X]

[hell_[0.3]
[ions_[0.3]

[hell_[0.X]
[ions_[0.X]

NO LOVE LOST

Krakoa offers a fresh start for all mutants...no matter their sordid past. Mister Sinister has taken command of a team of disreputable mutants (including the allegedly reformed Havok and reluctant team watchdog Psylocke) as the new HELLIONS to destroy his defunct cloning lab and prove themselves productive members of society.

But when Madelyne Pryor, Jean Grey's clone and Cyclops' and Havok's ex-lover, unleashes imperfect clones of the Legacy Marauders and Wild Child begins attacking his teammates—it'll be all the Hellions can do to survive the experience!

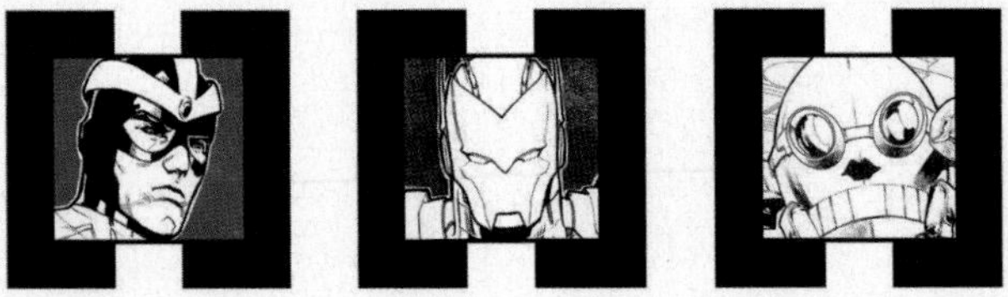

Havok　Orphan-Maker　Nanny

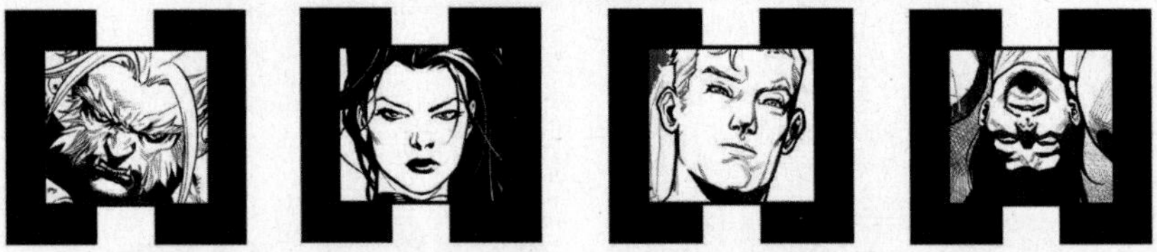

Wild Child　Psylocke　Empath　Greycrow

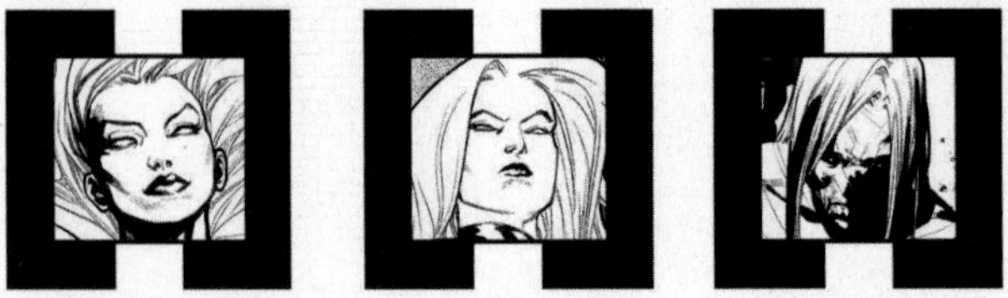

Madelyne Pryor　Arclight　Riptide

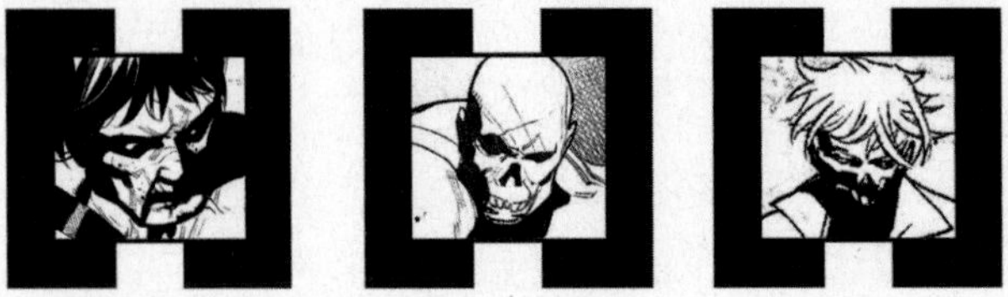

Harpoon　Blockbuster　Scrambler

[hell_[0.3]...]
[ions_[0.3]...]

[.wreaking....]

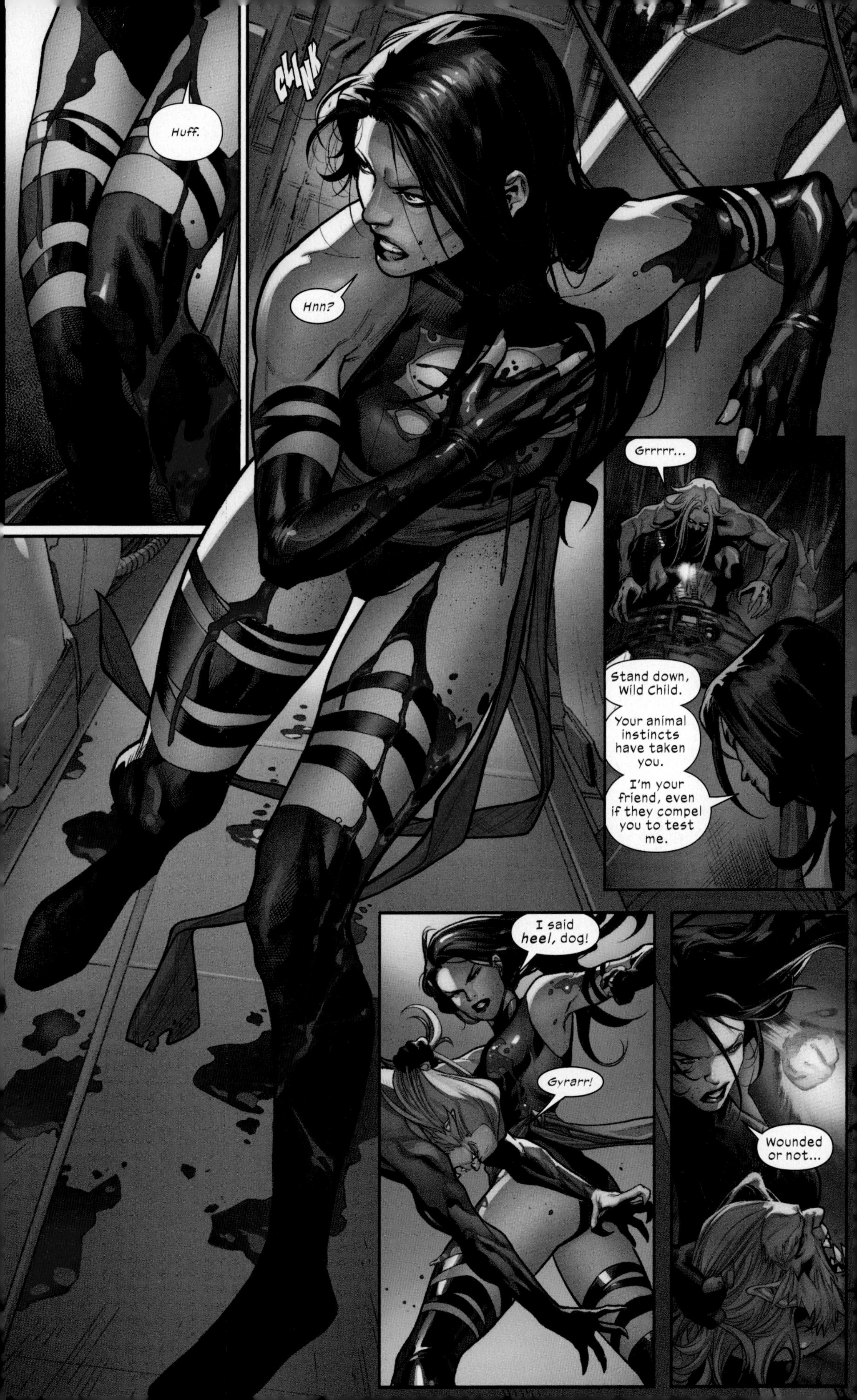
Huff.
CLINK
Hnn?
Grrrrr...
Stand down, Wild Child.
Your animal instincts have taken you.
I'm your friend, even if they compel you to test me.
I said *heel*, dog!
Gyrarr!
Wounded or not...

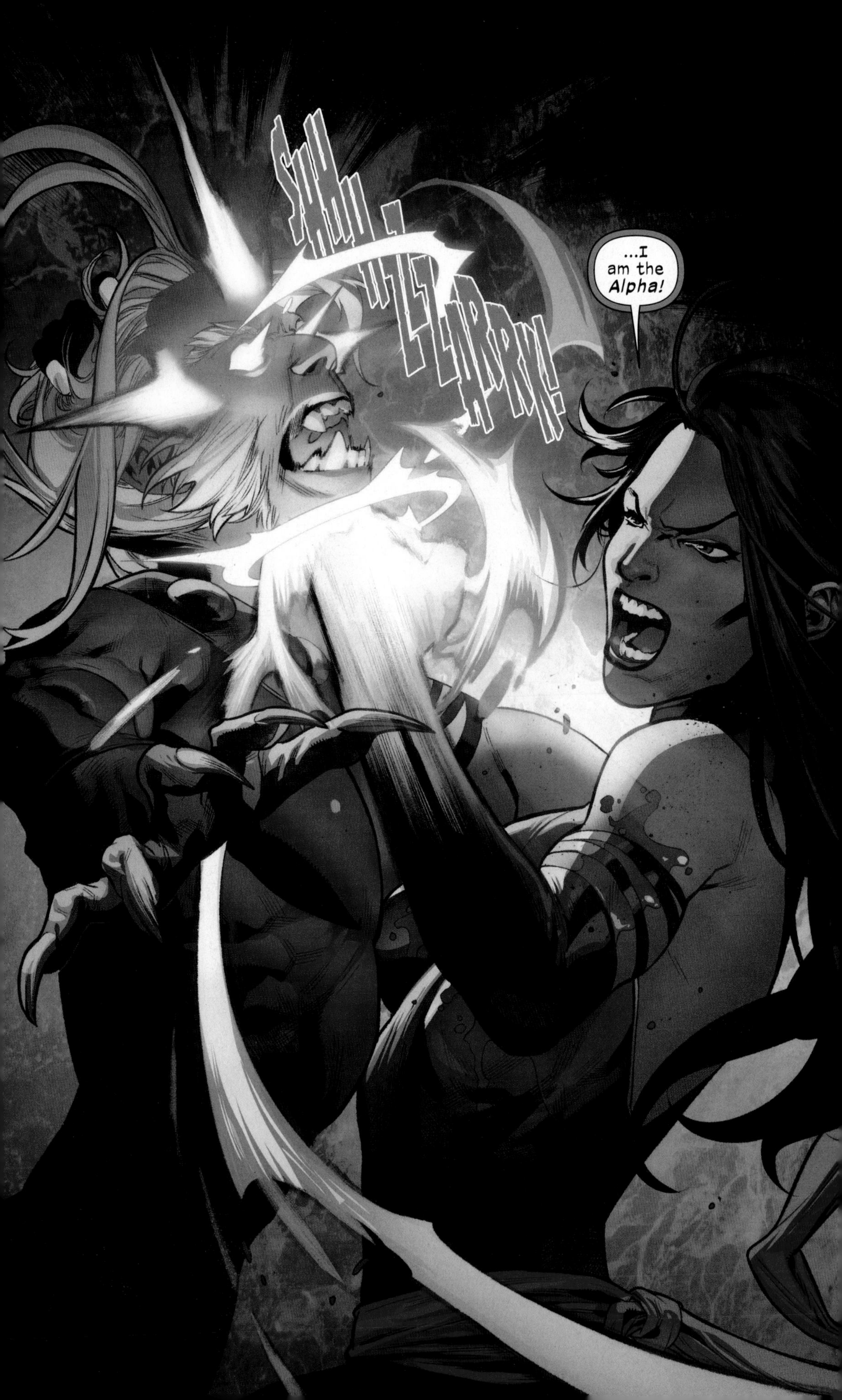
SHHU-LLLARRRK!
...I am the Alpha!

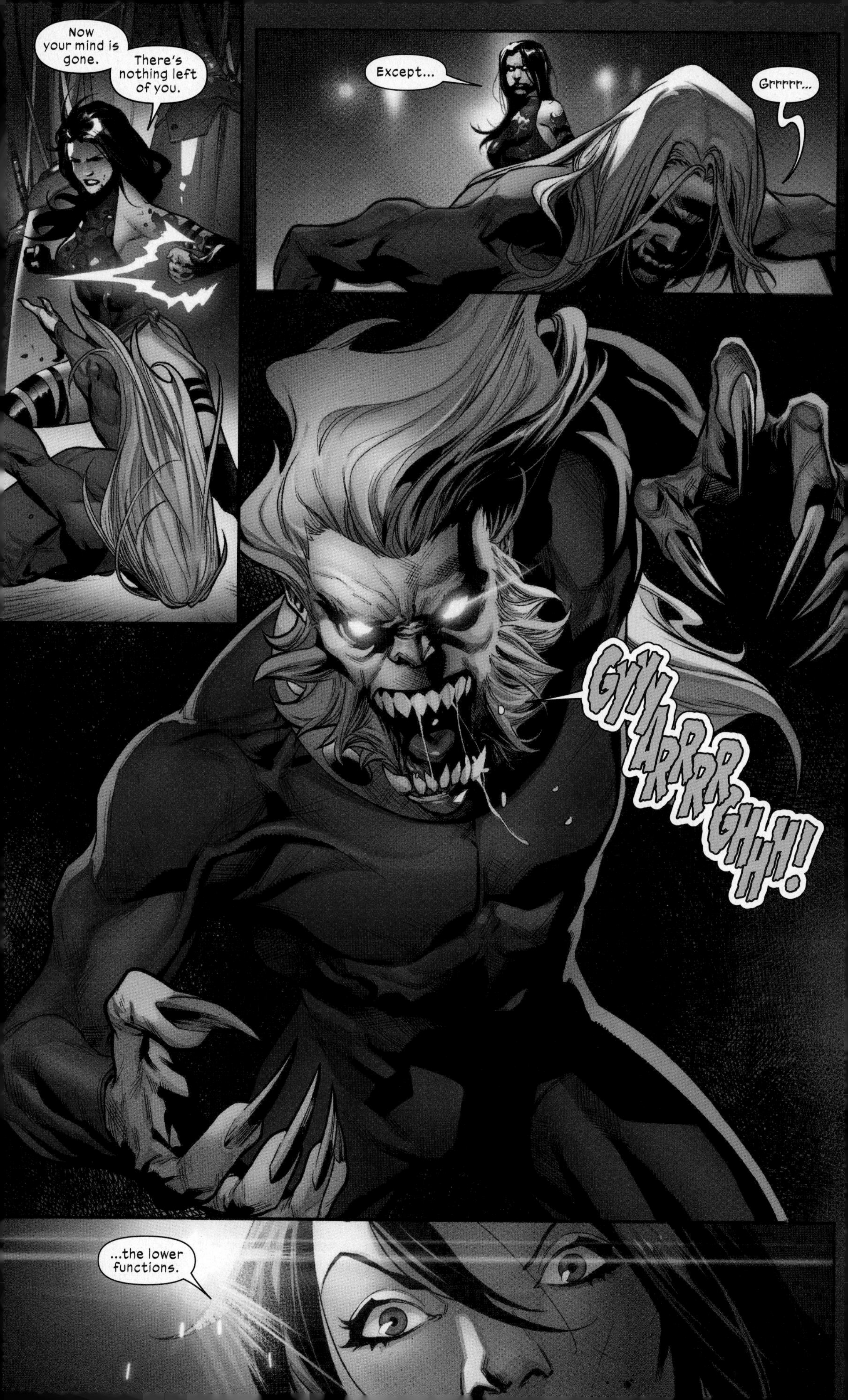
Now your mind is gone.
There's nothing left of you.
Except...
Grrrrr...
GYYAARRRRGHHH!
...the lower functions.

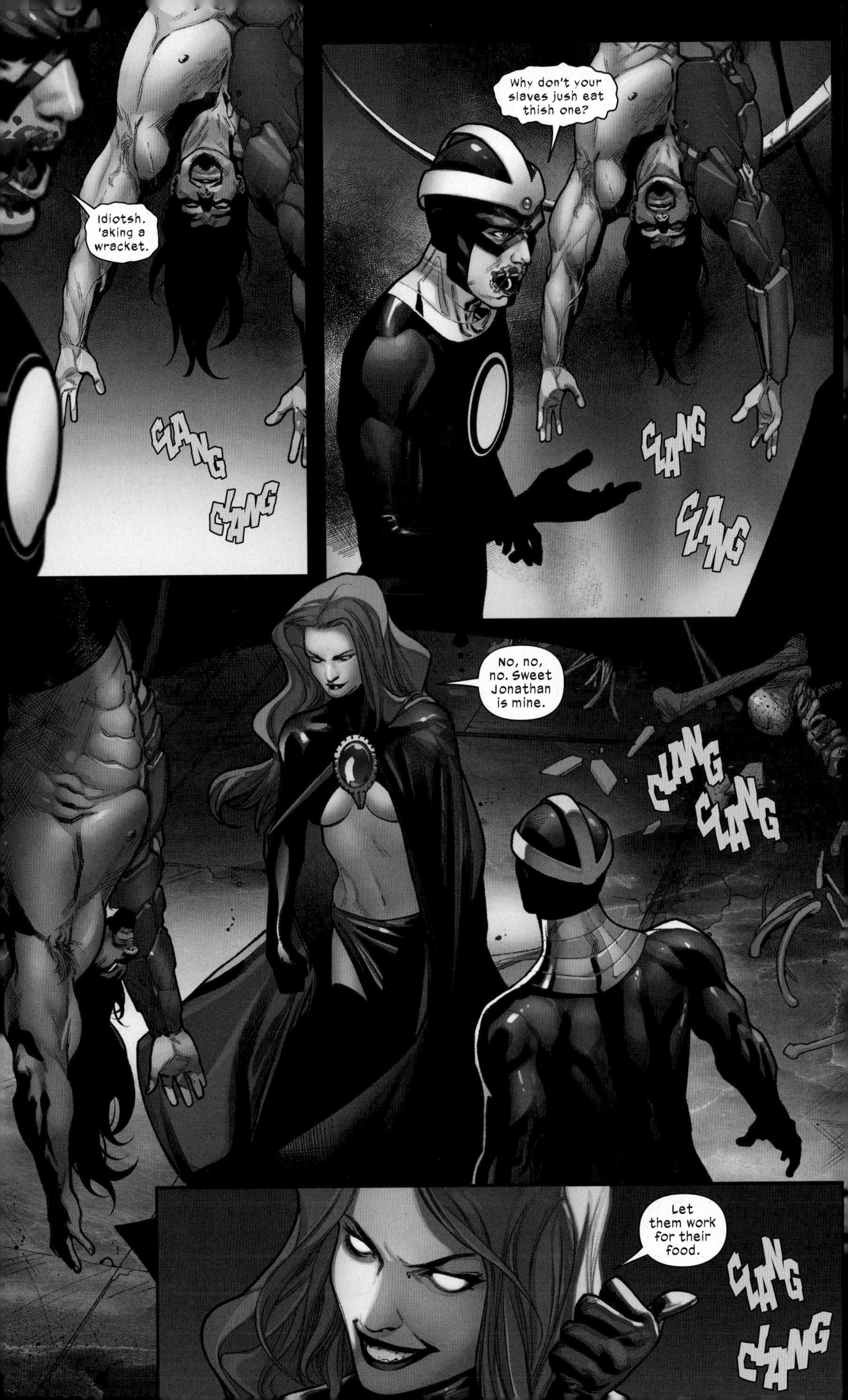
Idiotsh. 'aking a wracket.
CLANG
CLANG
Why don't your slaves jush eat thish one?
CLANG
CLANG
No, no, no. Sweet Jonathan is mine.
CLANG
CLANG
Let them work for their food.
CLANG
CLANG

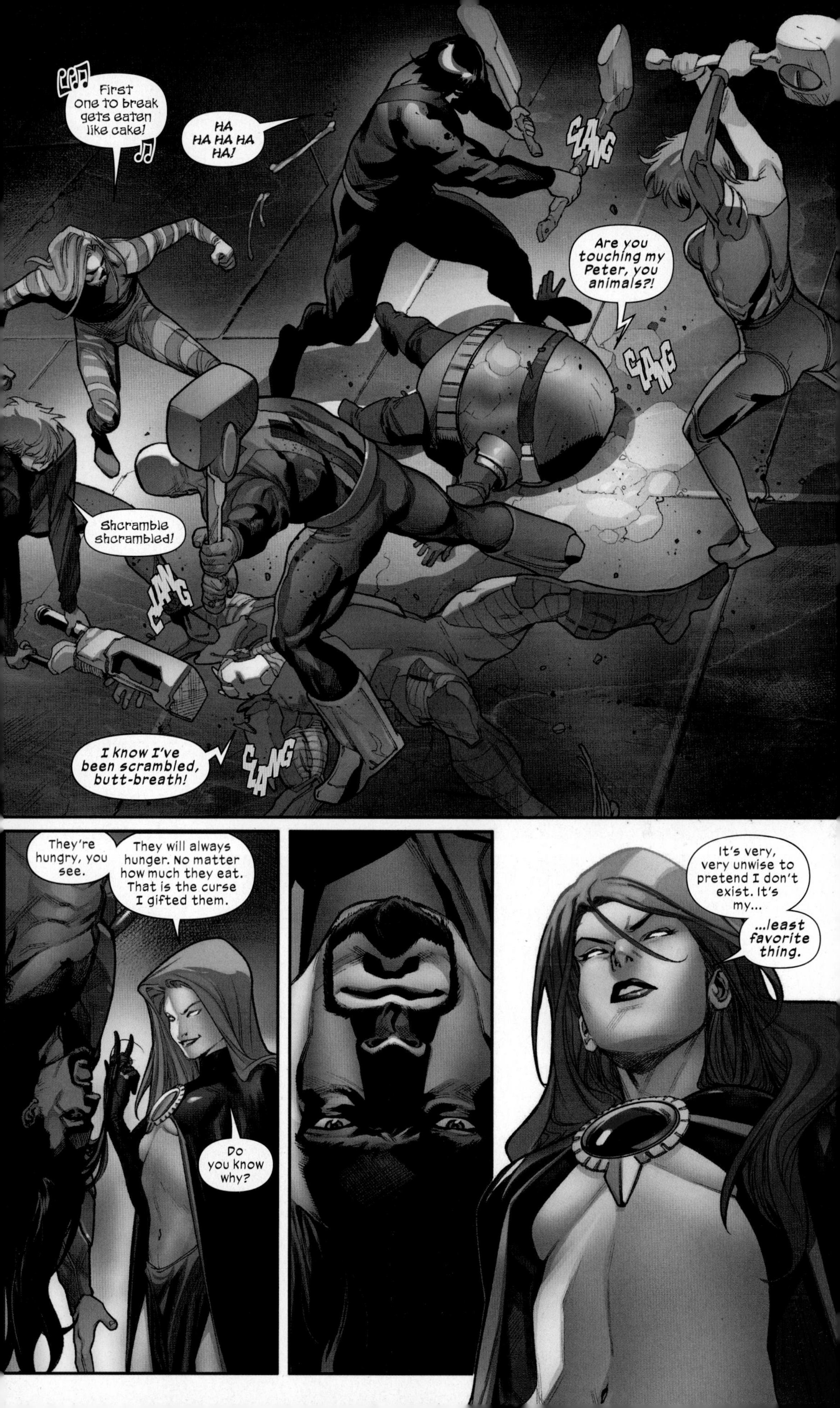
First one to break gets eaten like cake!
HA HA HA HA HA!
CLANG
Are you touching my Peter, you animals?!
CLANG
Shcramble shcrambled!
CLANG
I know I've been scrambled, butt-breath!
CLANG
They're hungry, you see.
They will always hunger. No matter how much they eat. That is the curse I gifted them.
Do you know why?
It's very, very unwise to pretend I don't exist. It's my...
...least favorite thing.

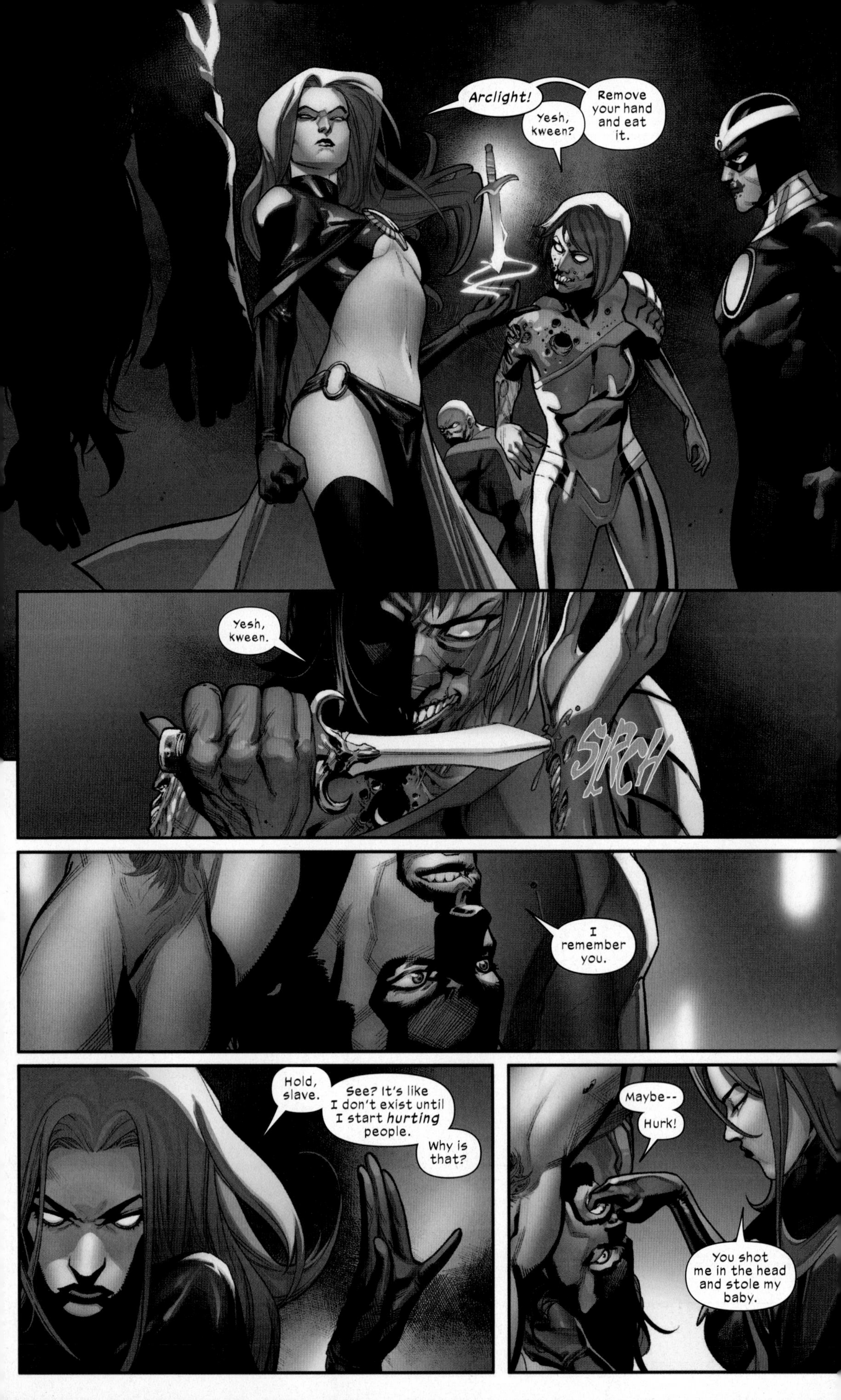
Arclight!
Yesh, kween?
Remove your hand and eat it.
Yesh, kween.
SLRCH
I remember you.
Hold, slave.
See? It's like I don't exist until I start *hurting* people.
Why is that?
Maybe--
Hurk!
You shot me in the head and stole my baby.

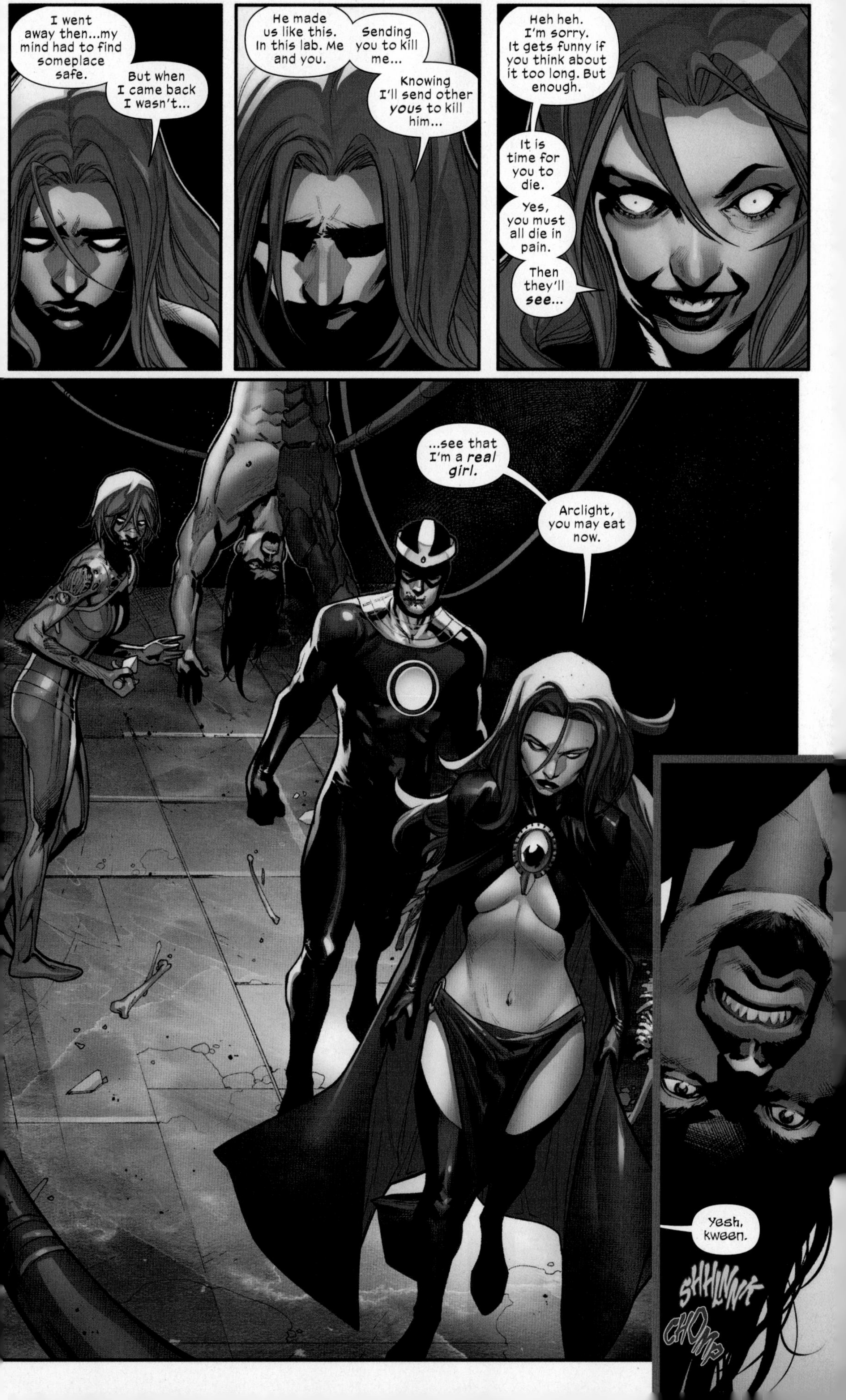
I went away then...my mind had to find someplace safe.
But when I came back I wasn't...
He made us like this. In this lab. Me and you.
Sending you to kill me...
Knowing I'll send other *yous* to kill him...
Heh heh. I'm sorry. It gets funny if you think about it too long. But enough.
It is time for you to die.
Yes, you must all die in pain.
Then they'll *see*...
...see that I'm a *real girl.*
Arclight, you may eat now.
Yesh, kween.
SHHLNNK
CHOMP

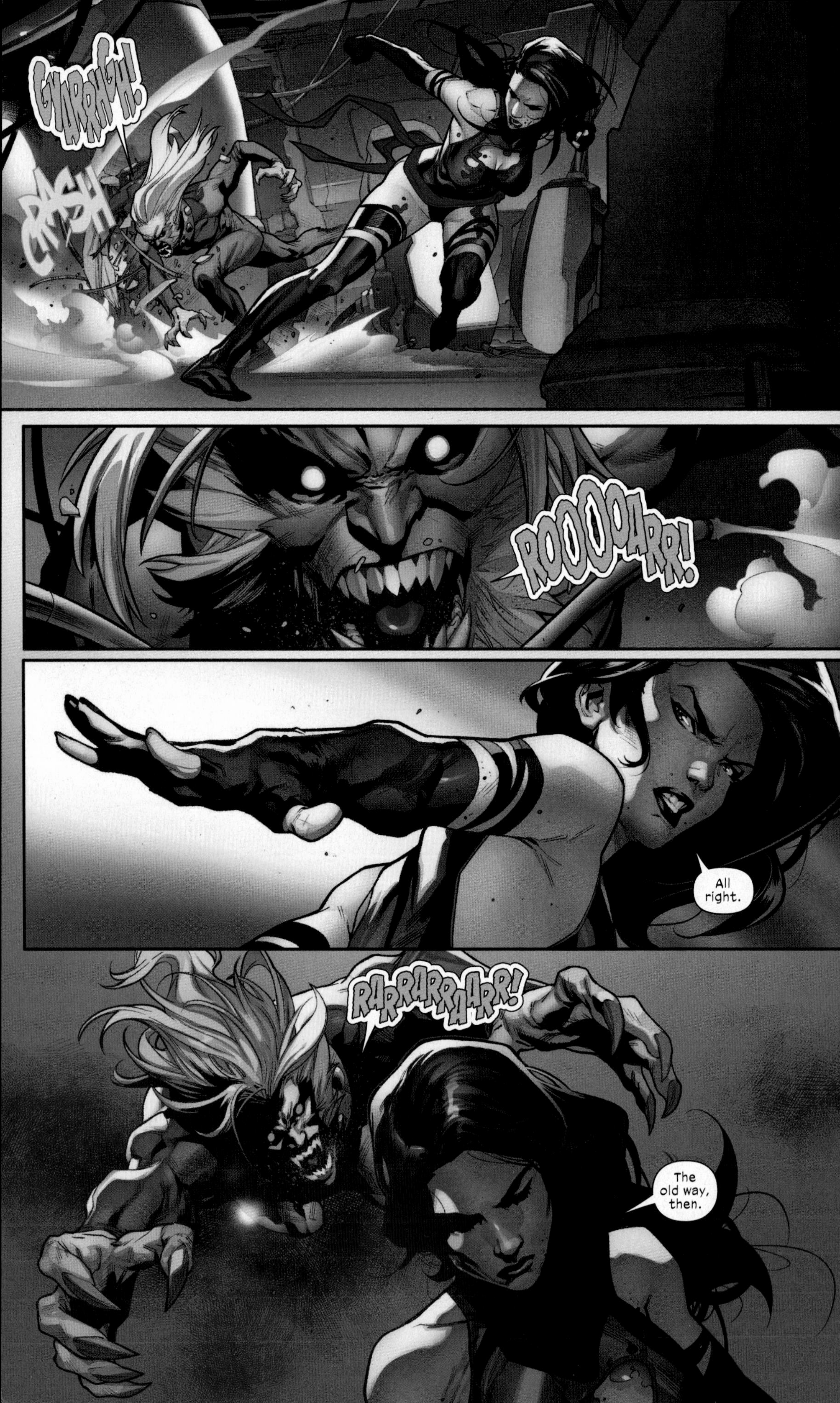
GYARRAGH!
CRASH
ROOOOARR!
All right.
RARRARRAARR!
The old way, then.

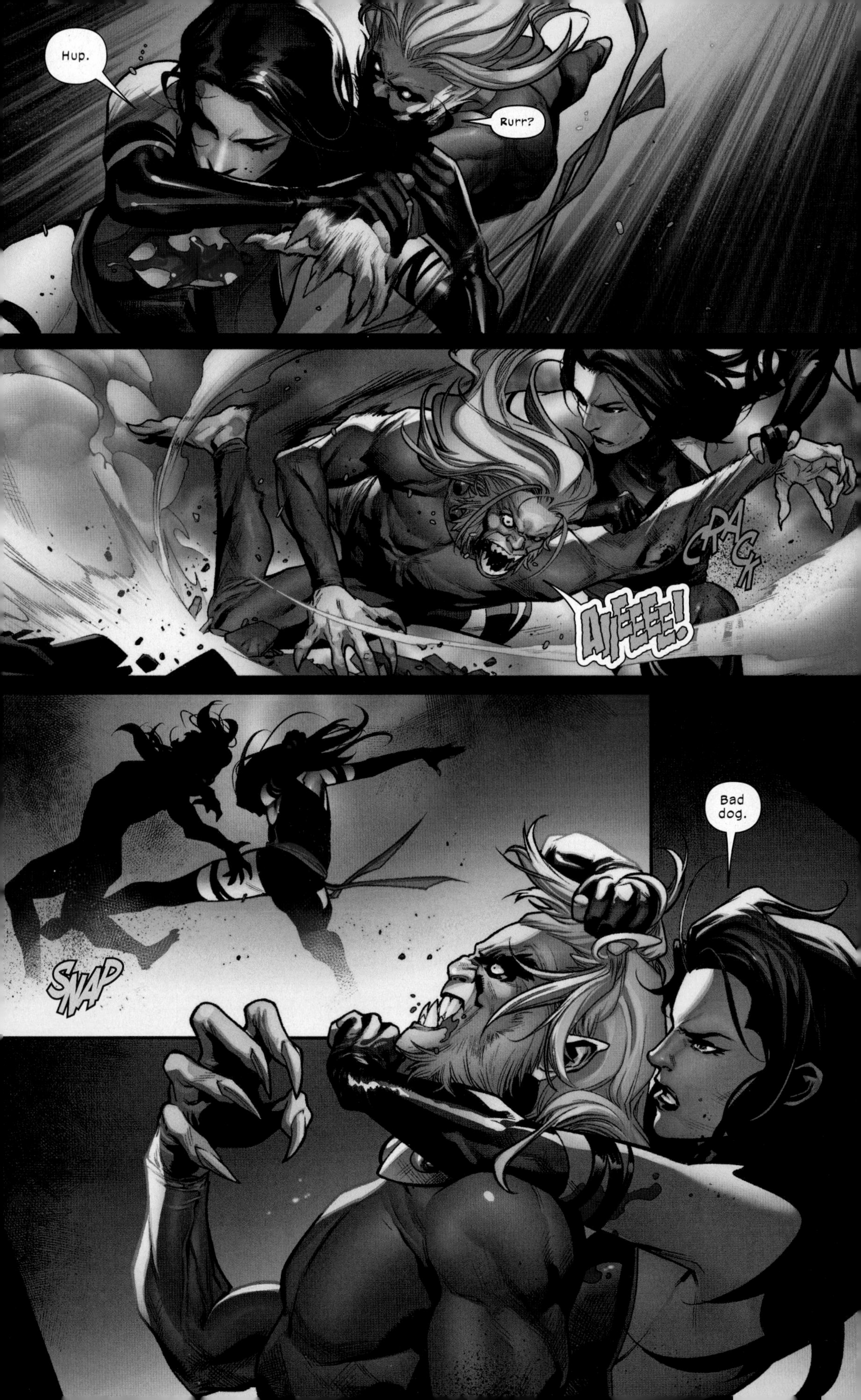
Hup.
Rurr?
CRACK
AIIEEEE!
SNAP
Bad dog.

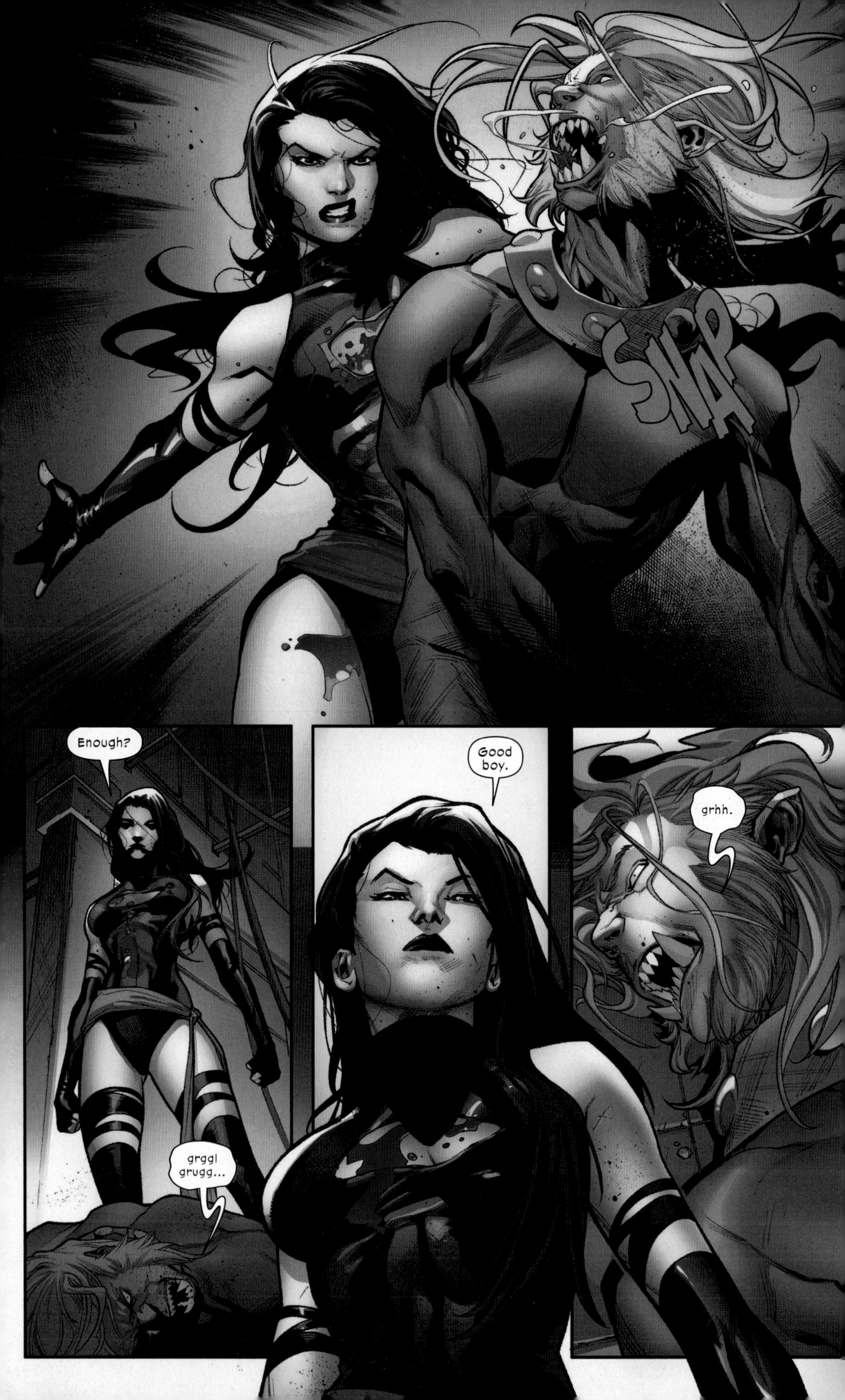
SNAP
Enough?
grggl grugg...
Good boy.
grhh.

THAT TIME WE GAVE A TEAM TO A HAND ASSASSIN

Apologies for the dramatic title. But I think it wise, as with all of Mr. Sinister's "Hellions," to examine Psylocke's membership on the team with clear eyes. Scott thinks adding her as a mediating force is a stroke of genius, but Sinister's mawkish protestations to the idea were stunningly transparent. Good luck feigning surprise when it's revealed *it was his plan all along.*

So yes, Sinister has a measure of control over Psylocke, or plans to. But what concerns me, and what Sinister almost certainly underestimates (not that I don't have the *utmost* faith in his faculties), is the bond between warriors at war. Sinister is ostensibly the leader of this ragtag group, but after a few missions whom will they want to follow? The flamboyant clown pulling their strings for his amusement, or the dyed-in-the-wool assassin who's bled for them in battle? We all showed Professor Xavier due reverence in our younger days, but when the big robots with laser-palms came, it was Scott we followed.

All I'm asking is that we keep a watchful eye as Psylocke's influence over her compatriots grows. We must remind ourselves that she is not Betsy. There is much we don't know. And what we do, while not cause for alarm, is certainly reason for caution. Yes, I'm talking about how *she was raised from youth by a mystical ninja murder cult.*

There is no world where Psylocke has found herself under Sinister's thumb unless it serves her in some way. I'm sure she knows a puppet's strings also bind the puppeteer. As Sinister discovers this, will I want to point and laugh? Of course. I'm only mutant. But not if Krakoa burns behind my back.

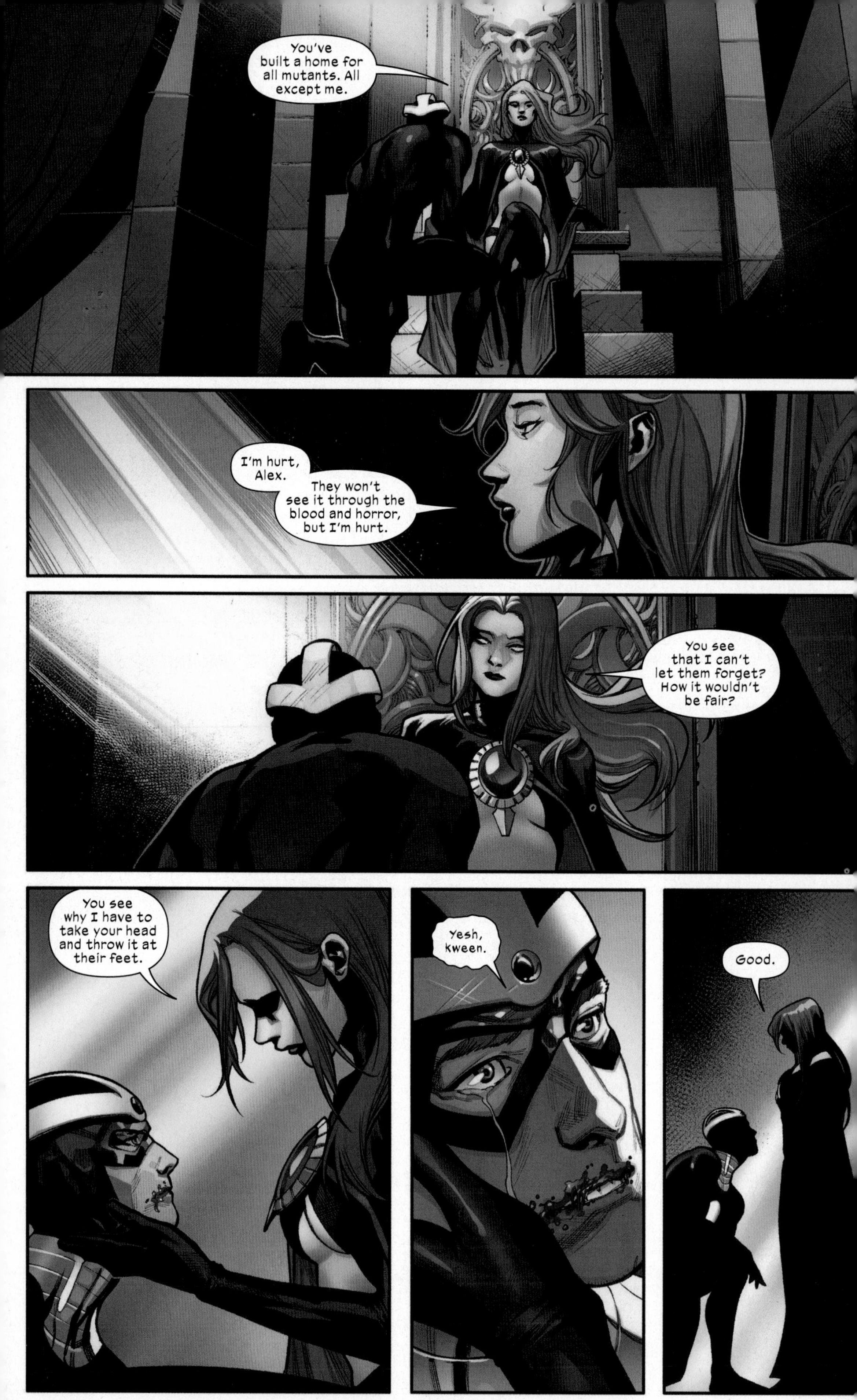
You've built a home for all mutants. All except me.
I'm hurt, Alex.
They won't see it through the blood and horror, but I'm hurt.
You see that I can't let them forget? How it wouldn't be fair?
You see why I have to take your head and throw it at their feet.
Yesh, kween.
Good.

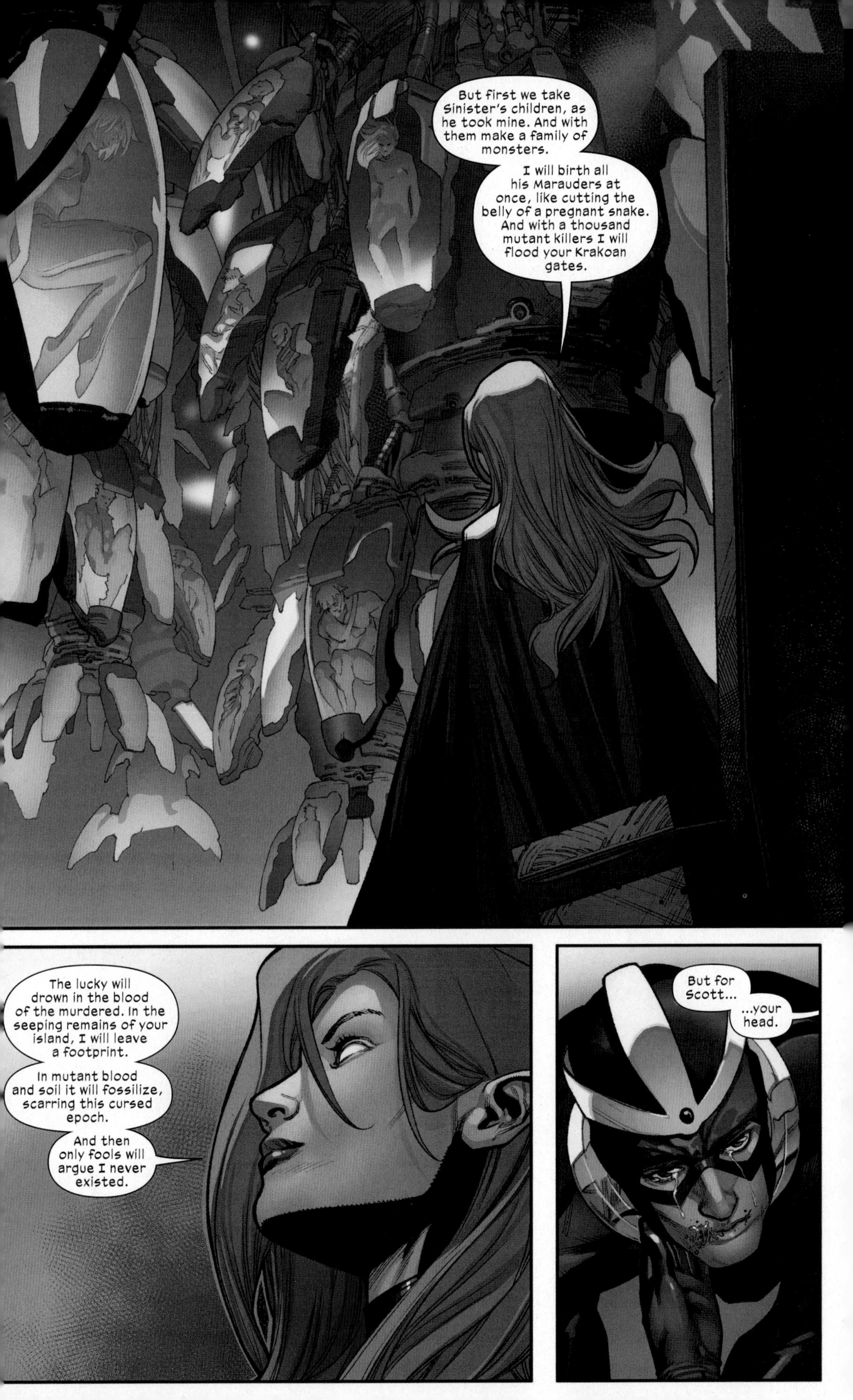
But first we take Sinister's children, as he took mine. And with them make a family of monsters.
I will birth all his Marauders at once, like cutting the belly of a pregnant snake. And with a thousand mutant killers I will flood your Krakoan gates.
The lucky will drown in the blood of the murdered. In the seeping remains of your island, I will leave a footprint.
In mutant blood and soil it will fossilize, scarring this cursed epoch.
And then only fools will argue I never existed.
But for Scott...
...your head.

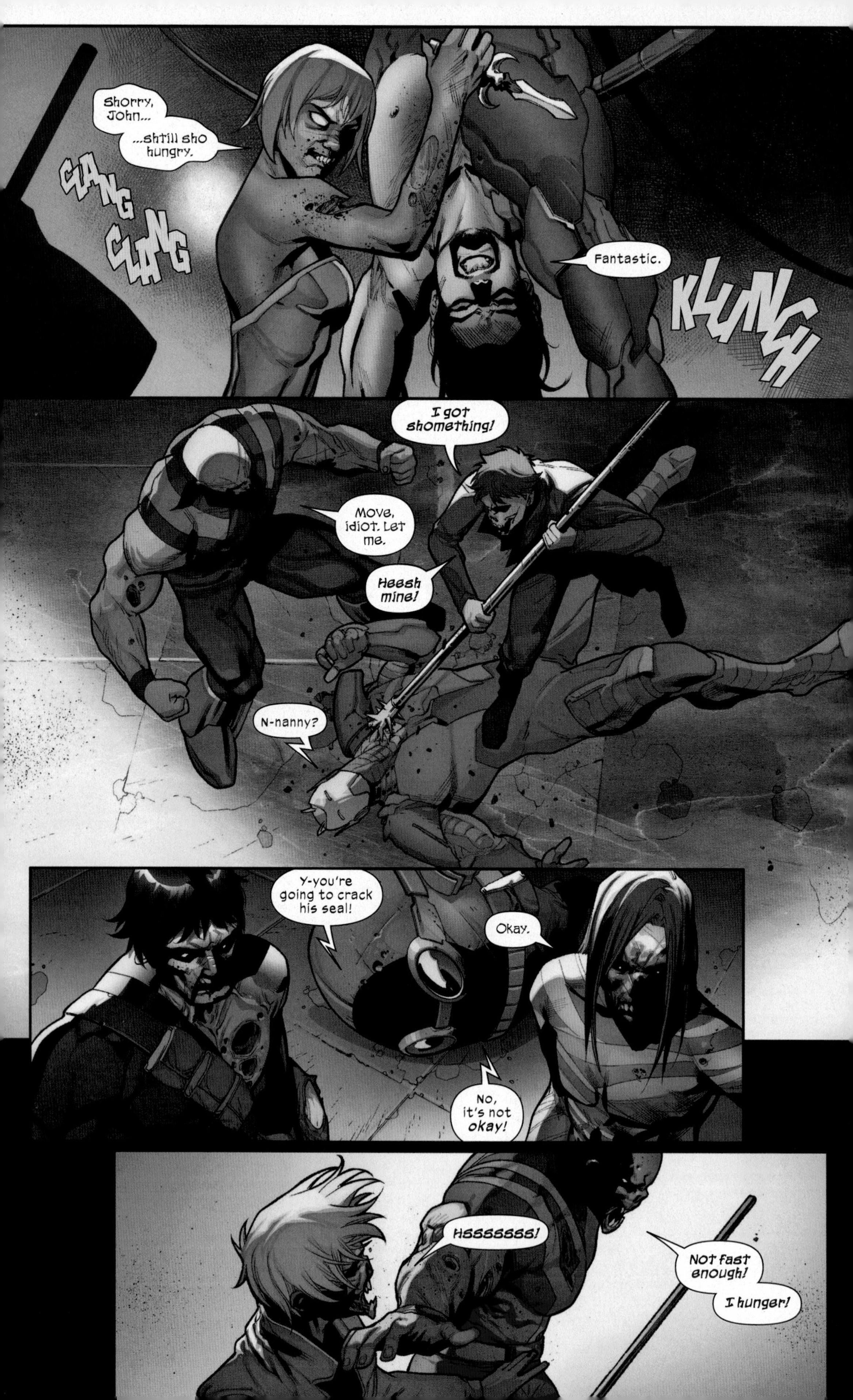
Shorry, John...
...shtill sho hungry.
CLANG CLANG
Fantastic.
KLUNCH
I got shomething!
Move, idiot. Let me.
Heesh mine!
N-nanny?
Y-you're going to crack his seal!
Okay.
No, it's not okay!
Hssssssss!
Not fast enough!
I hunger!

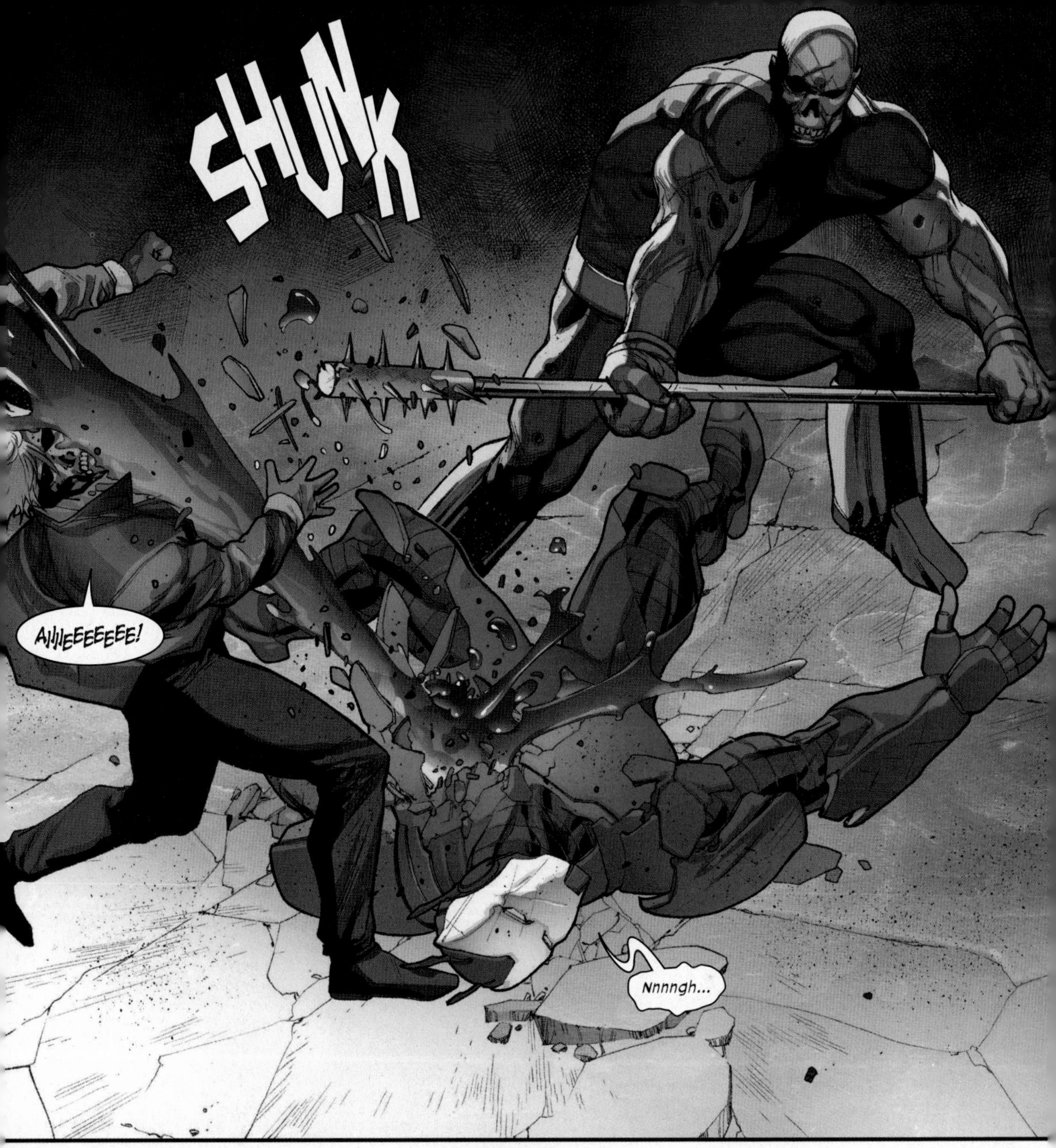
SHUNK
AIIIEEEEEEEE!
Nnnngh...

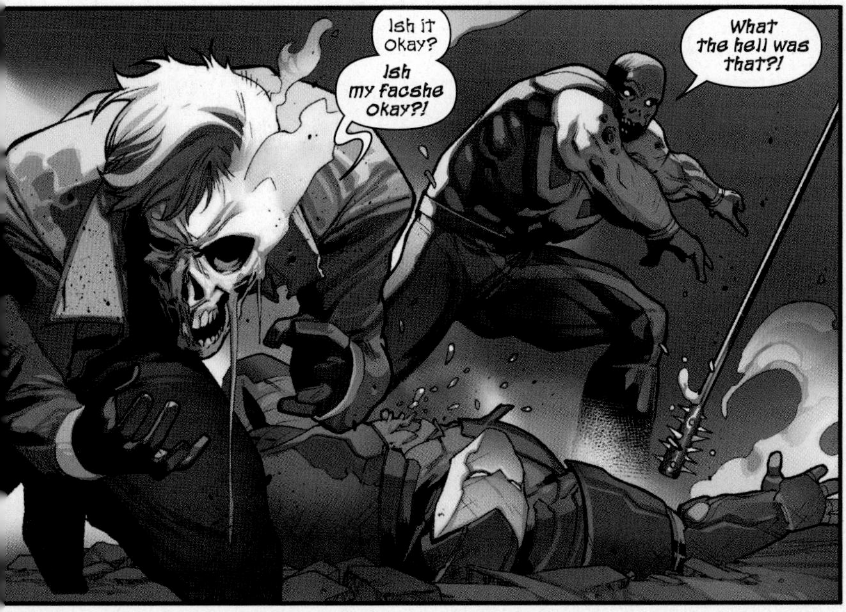
Ish it okay?
Ish my facshe okay?!
What the hell was that?!

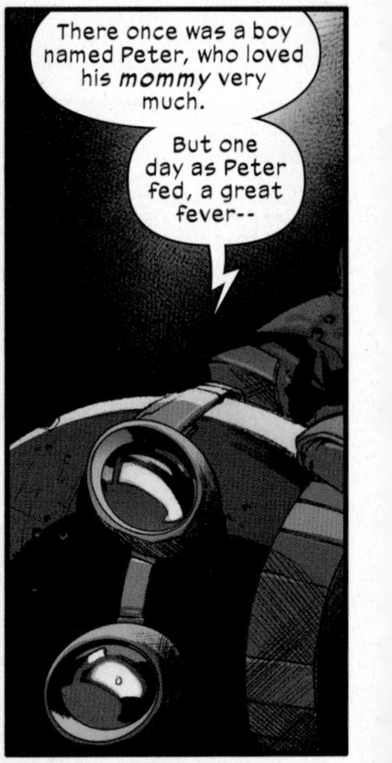
There once was a boy named Peter, who loved his mommy very much.
But one day as Peter fed, a great fever--

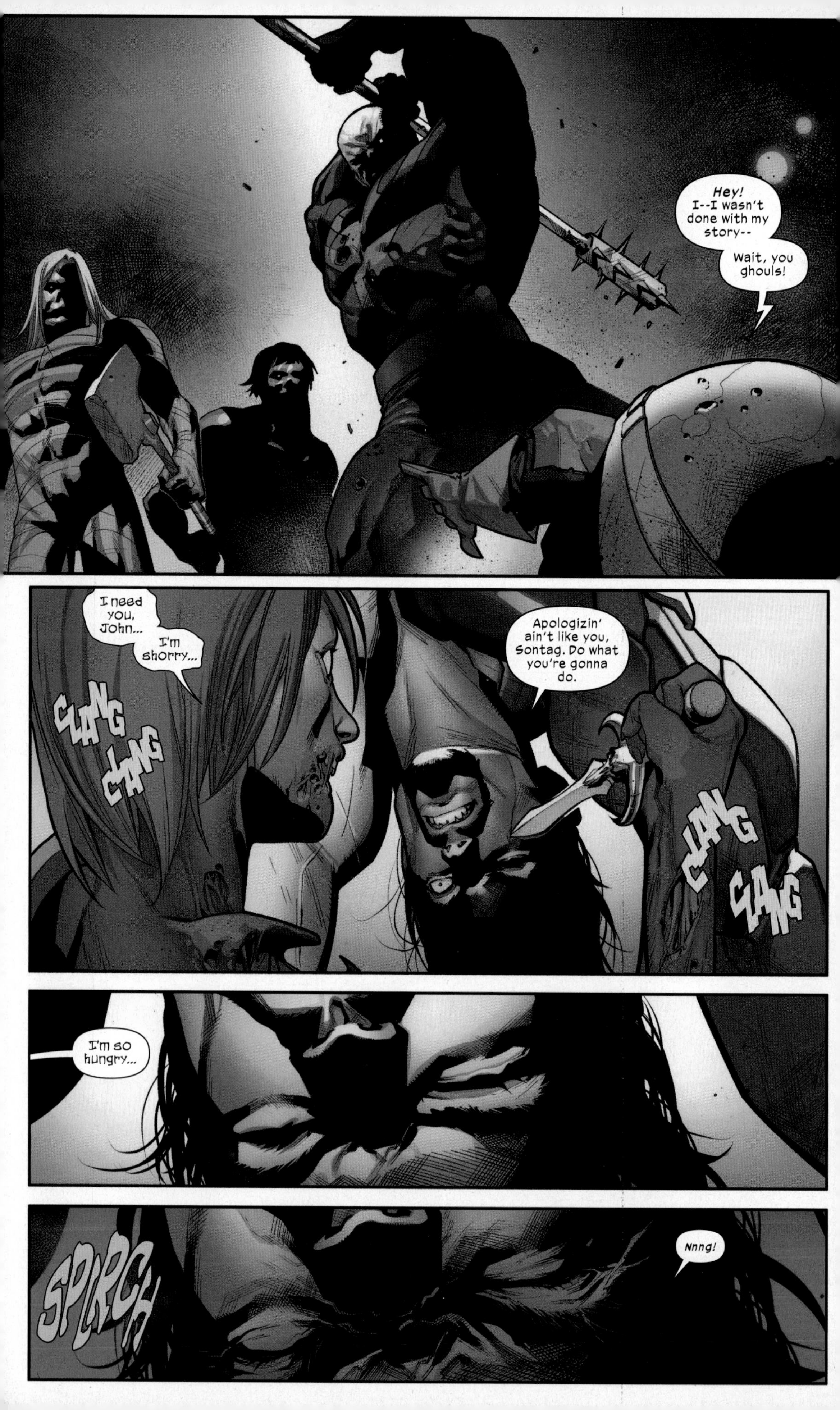
Hey!
I--I wasn't done with my story--
Wait, you ghouls!
I need you, John...
I'm shorry...
CLANG CLANG
Apologizin' ain't like you, Sontag. Do what you're gonna do.
CLANG CLANG
I'm so hungry...
SPLRCH
Nnng!

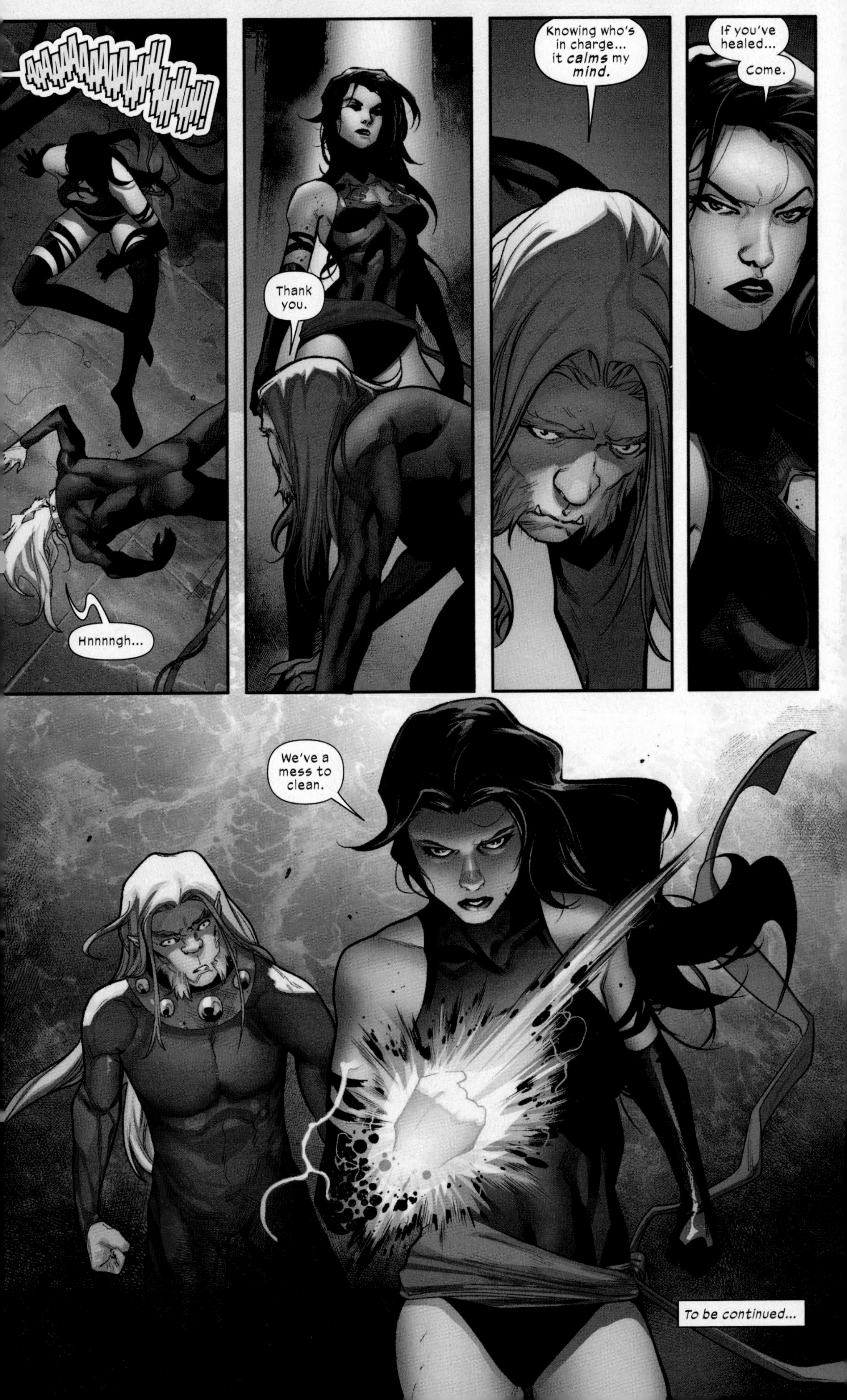
Hnnnngh...
Thank you.
Knowing who's in charge... it *calms* my *mind.*
If you've healed...
Come.
We've a mess to clean.
To be continued...

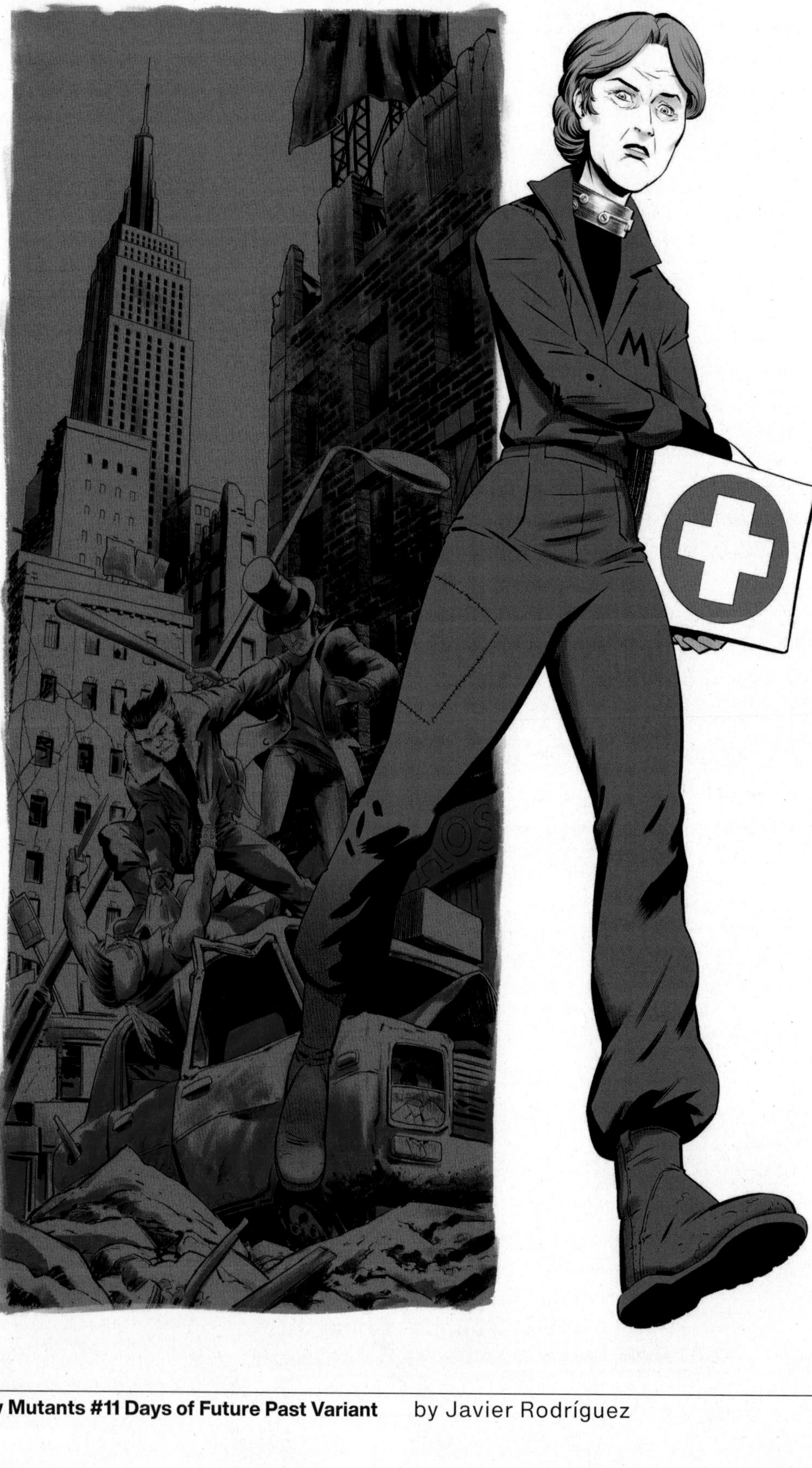
M

New Mutants #11 Days of Future Past Variant by Javier Rodríguez

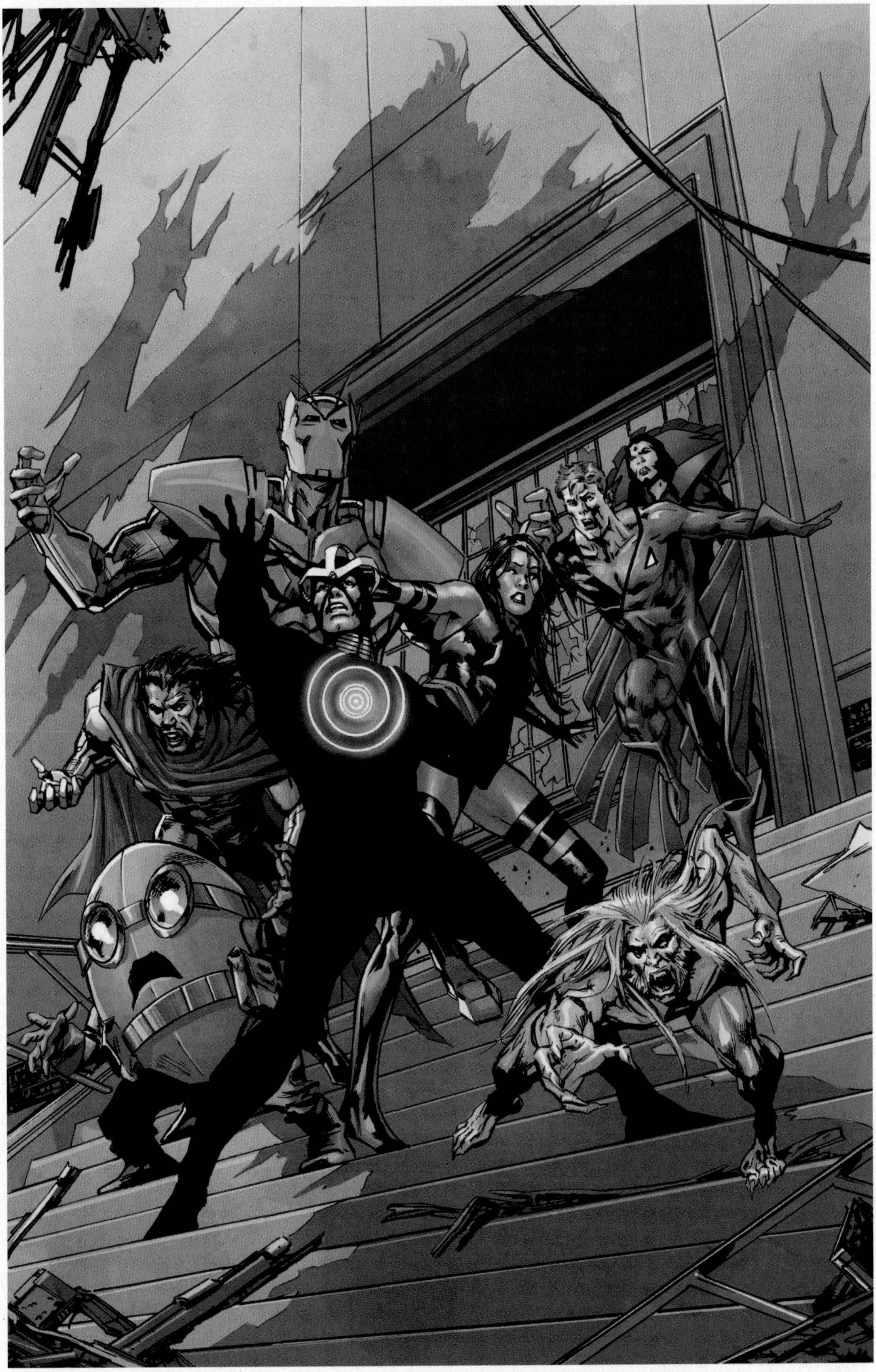

Hellions #2 Variant by Butch Guice & Rachelle Rosenberg

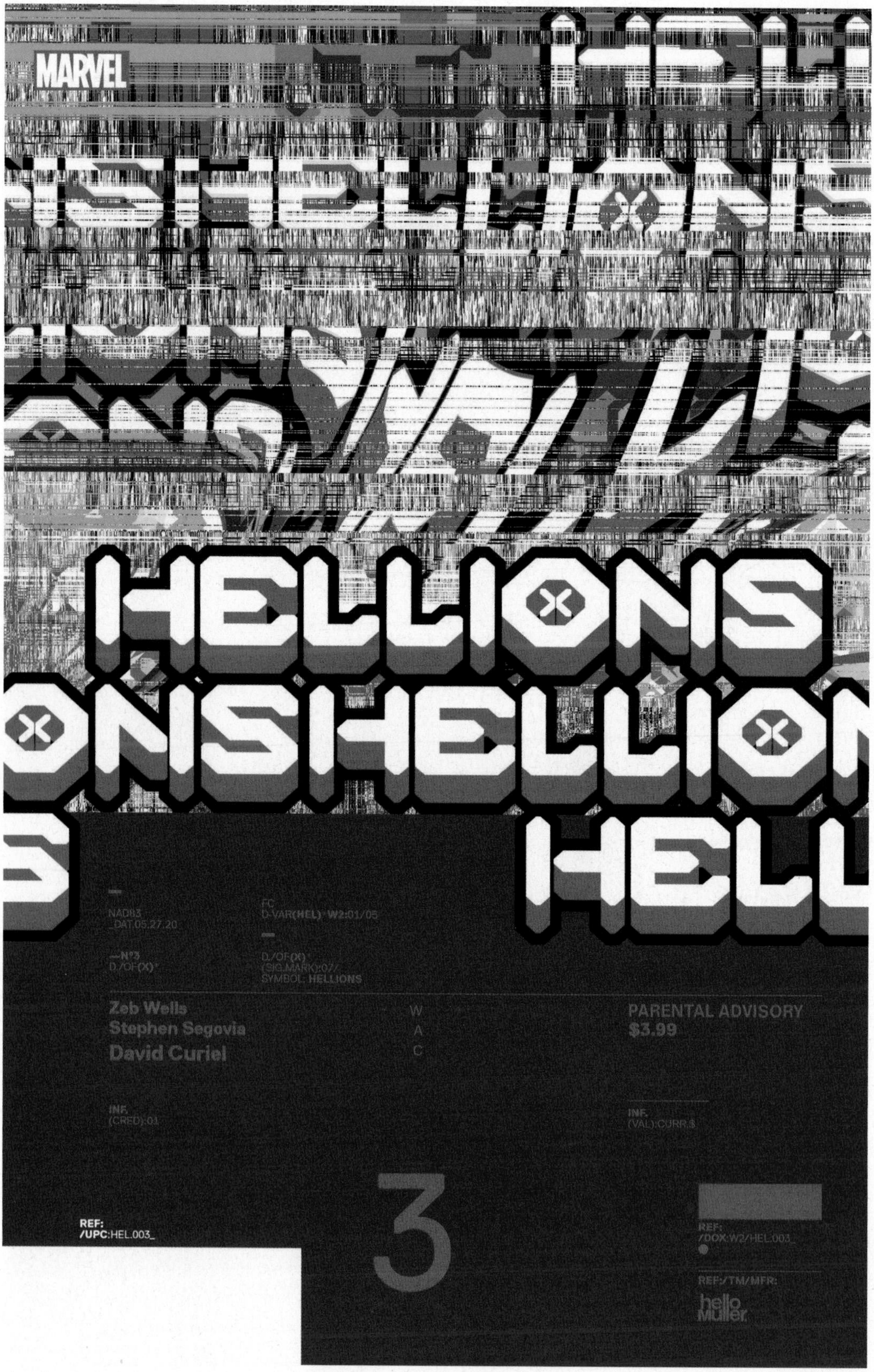
MARVEL
HELLIONS
HELLIONS
NAD83
_DAT.05.27.20
—N°3
D./OF(X)°
FC
D-VAR(HEL)° W2:01/05
D./OF(X)°
(SIG.MARK):07/
SYMBOL: HELLIONS
Zeb Wells
Stephen Segovia
David Curiel
W
A
C
PARENTAL ADVISORY
$3.99
INF.
(CRED):01
INF.
(VAL):CURR.$
3
REF:
/UPC:HEL.003_
REF:
/DOX:W2/HEL.003_
REF:/TM/MFR:
hello
Muller.

Hellions #3 Design Variant by Tom Muller

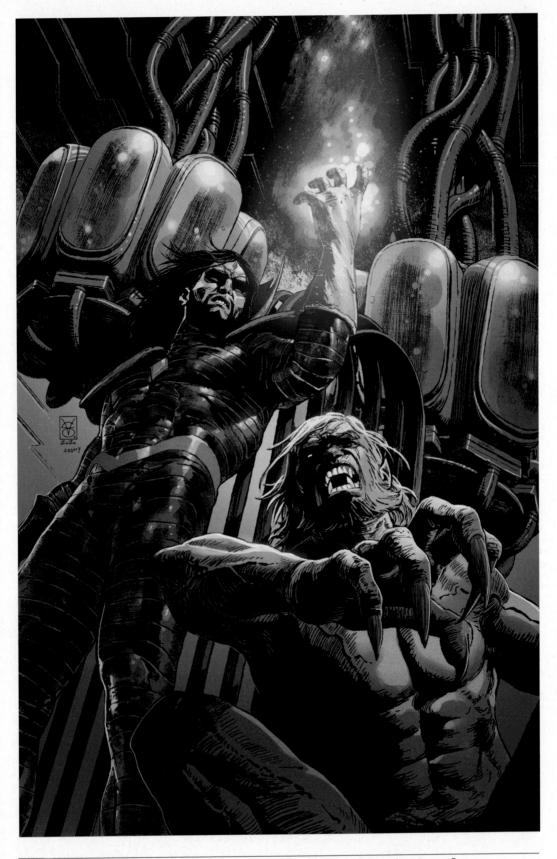

Hellions #3 Variant

by Valerio Giangiordano &
Romulo Fajardo Jr.

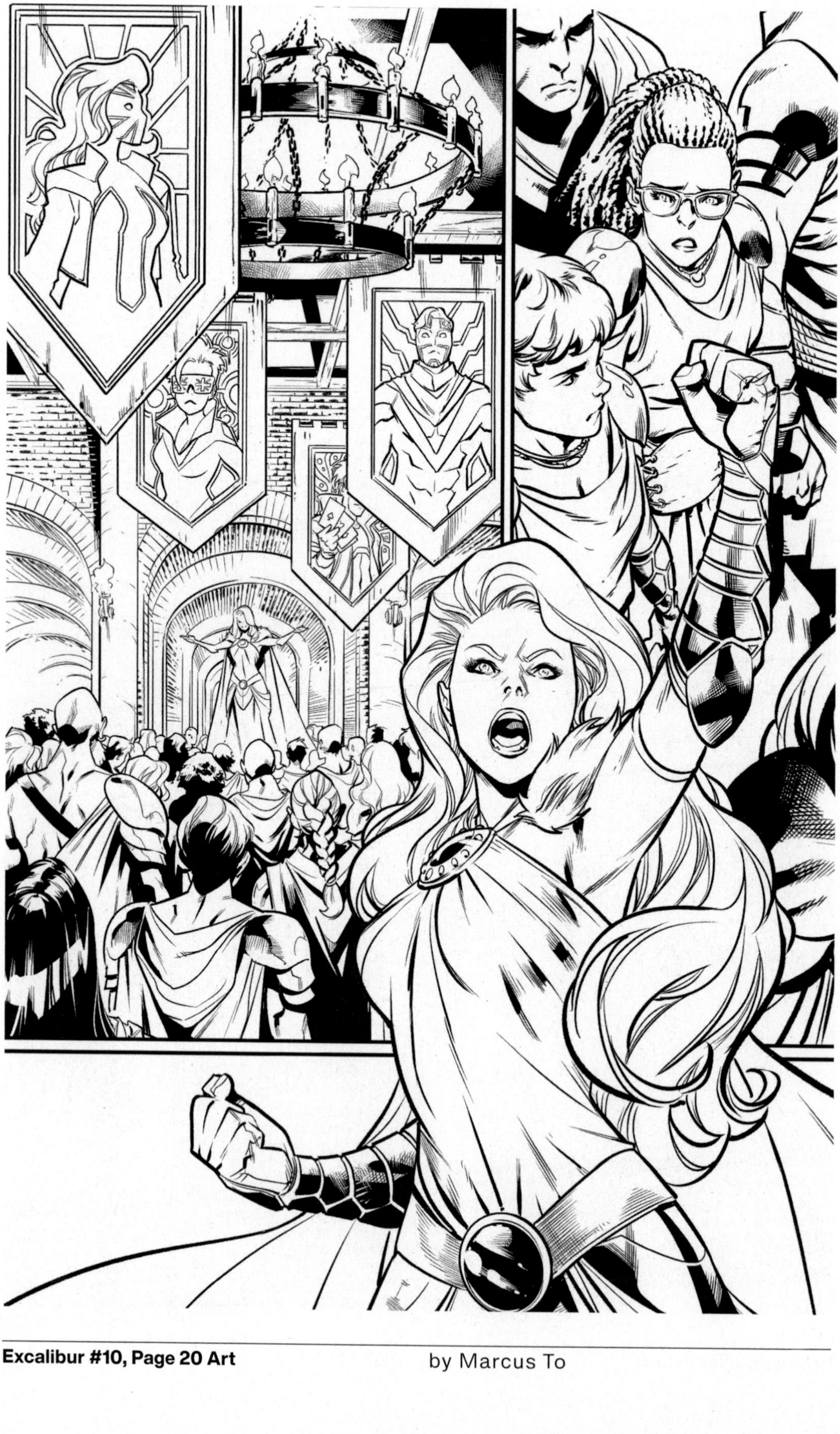

Excalibur #10, Page 20 Art by Marcus To

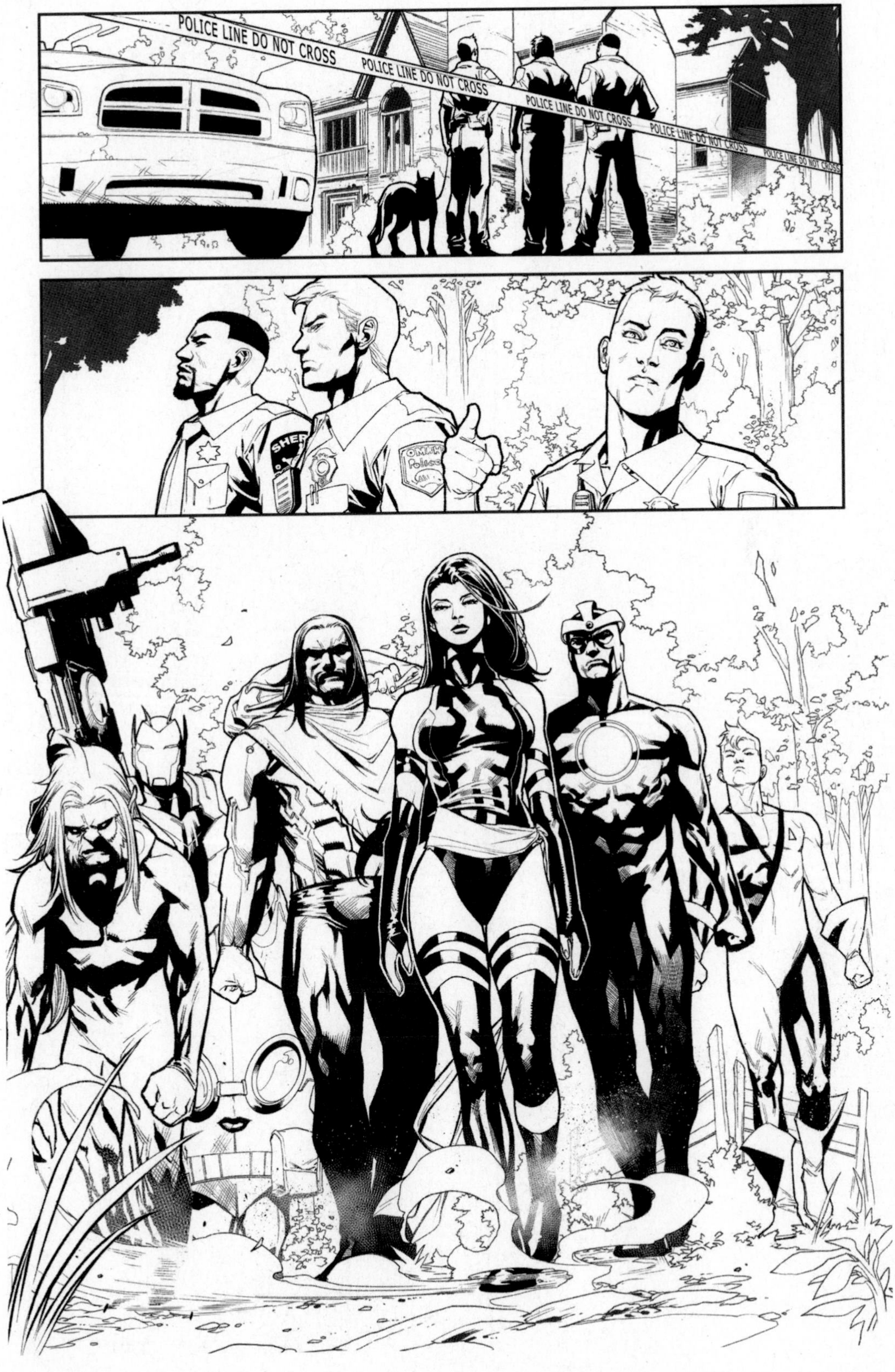
POLICE LINE DO NOT CROSS
POLICE LINE DO NOT CROSS
POLICE LINE DO NOT CROSS
POLICE LINE DO NOT CROSS
POLICE LINE DO NOT CROSS

Hellions #2, Page 1 Art by Stephen Segovia